Zar

TEETH IN SINK, KNICKERS ON LANDING

AUSTIN MACAULEY PUBLISHERS™
LONDON • CAMBRIDGE • NEW YORK • SHARJAH

Copyright © Zara Duvall 2023

The right of Zara Duvall to be identified as author of this work has been asserted by the author in accordance with sections 77 and 78 of the Copyright, Designs and Patents Act 1988.

All rights reserved. No part of this publication may be reproduced, stored in a retrieval system, or transmitted in any form or by any means, electronic, mechanical, photocopying, recording, or otherwise, without the prior permission of the publishers.

Any person who commits any unauthorised act in relation to this publication may be liable to criminal prosecution and civil claims for damages.

All of the events in this memoir are true to the best of the author's memory. The views expressed in this memoir are solely those of the author.

A CIP catalogue record for this title is available from the British Library.

ISBN 9781398488380 (Paperback)
ISBN 9781398488397 (ePub e-book)

www.austinmacauley.com

First Published 2023
Austin Macaulay Publishers Ltd®
1 Canada Square
Canary Wharf
London
E14 5AA

Acknowledgements

To my dearest Ruth, there is not enough praise for your patient loyalty and support and for keeping your promise to try and decipher my terrible scrawl and type thousands of my words written over half a century. Without you my life's work would forever be lost.

To my laughing friend Halina Greer who has taken my words and turned them into these wonderous illustrations.

I have a precious friend Kris McDonald who gives of her help, time and love to keep me going in the old age that I loathe.

Saj Khan who ensures I have the colours I love by gifting me his magnificent paints, his generosity to me is boundless. Thank you, lovely man.

Andy, Melanie and Amber who have shown such love and become my much-needed little family.

I need not have worried about neighbours. Marc, Charlotte, and Rae Lilleyman are the most divine family I could ever wish for. Kind, considerate, helpful – just wonderful. The total opposite to the vile, racist, nature-hating, vandalising gits on my other side.

I am blessed, so blessed with such quality friends, always there for me with help, hugs and laughter. My darling best friend Annette who makes the world a better place just by being in it. Nicky, Mike, Jane, Becky, Margaret and Tony, David and Julie, Peter, Angie, Jim and last but not least Philip and Sharon – If I've missed you, please forgive me, you know I'm an 80-year-old dingbat!

Love ya xx Zara

PS: Destiny has smiled once more upon me. I took Lola to be groomed and from there a wonderful friendship has evolved. He regales me often with his past adventures and has brought much needed laughter into my silent lonely life. Thanks Neville X.

From wacky 'experiments' like this…to this, if only they could have seen the future

Those Magnificent Men in Their Flying Machines

My one and only book is dedicated with pride and love to the memory of my brother, John, a magnificent heroic jet fighter pilot who, after compulsory retirement, lost his will to live. And so, with courage, he chose his own destiny. Forever flying with the angels, now without his beloved metal birds, sweet dreams brother of mine. 1930 – 1976.

Balls of Steel Johnny

Flying a missile loaded jet in the vast stratosphere, searching for hostile invaders from our world or theirs. Him being so very willing and able to bring them down, before they inflicted pain and destruction on this little island we love to call home.

Table of Contents

Acknowledgements 3
Half a Moustache 11
My Mother 14
It was 1942 and I'd Arrived (Worst Luck) 21
Clip Clop 31
Rag Tripe 34
The Grinning Custard 38
Feather Duster 41
The Diamond Trees 44
The Living Scarf 45
The Sewing Moths 48
Where Are You, You Little Bugger 54
Honky Tonk Mama 58
Sugar 62
14 August 1960 65
Aunty's House 74
Back Home, Yet I'd Miss Aunty's House 81
E.C.T. Tell Them to Shove It! 84
2oz of Corned Beef 91
Depression Slays Heroes 94
Funny Overalls 100
Together Again 104
The Dropped Fork 108
The Letter That Was Never Sent 111
Ted 1947-1977 113
Lee – My dearest dear 119
An Unlikely Friendship 123
The Missing Link 129

Sophie, Our Beginning	132
Vincent's Invisible Violin	135
Spike	137
The Poltergeist Part One	140
Poltergeist Part Two	141
Poltergeist Part Three	143
Yabba	146
Needing Carlos' Help Yet again	151
Ruby Ruby	154
£2,000 worth of Follicle	157
Lost Property	160
Approximately 19 Foot of "Mean as Hell" Muscle	163
The Slowest Chamois in the World	173
Smiles	176
Do Pigs Graze?	185
Socks	189
Tutu	190
Froth	194
Barbados, Here He Comes	199
Blood in the Sand	204
The Cunning Art of Make-Up	209
Avon, or Was It?	211
Beryl's Bordello	214
Ebony	216
Lilly	218
Lilly and the Duck	222
Sweet Lilly – Taken Too Soon	225
If It Should Be	230
Chain of Events	232
Trust	235
The Tragic True Cost of Pate Foie Gras	240

Retribution Soup	242
Darling Jacky	244
Cudgels and Bacon Butties	248
Eyelashes	252
Hens	255
Rickshaw	257
I'm a Twat!	259
Argyll Socks and Sequined Waistcoats	261
Trill	265
Gone with the Wind	267
Maasai	269
Bipolar, the Ruination of My Life	271
The Blue Rinsed Viper	278
See Me Bear	279
Our Devotion	282
Caroline, My Friend	285
Eddie	294
Dear Caroline	298
July 2012	299
I'm Now 70 and I Bloody Hate It!	302
Ziggy Doo Dah	305
The Last Leaf	307
The Ambulance Driver from Hell	310
You Want a Conservatory Darlin'? No Problem That Will be 50 Times!	314
Boom!	321
I Died	330
My Angel	332
3 October 2020: The Present Day	335
Mid-October 2020	338
Yet Another Will That Saddens Me to Make	340
Pandemic Lockdown	342

New Year's Eve 2021 346
All My Nightmares! 323
Eight Weeks of Torment 351
The Old Bamboo Chair Rocks No More 355

Half a Moustache

If only she had known that her days were numbered (three to be precise) she'd have fulfilled a long-held ambition and killed the bugger. From what my own mum told me of her, she was a miniature ball of fire, feisty, hardworking, courageous and downright bloody gorgeous.

She was shoved into a marriage with a much older man whose first love was the beer down his throat, this only involved her when its influence affected his fist or nether regions, either way, it hurt her.

Edith Mary used to make ends meet by pushing a hand cart down to Brady's salerooms. There she would buy anything cheap that she could refurbish once she had pushed the loaded cart back home. On these outings, my mother would be strapped on top, and she could remember from a very early age this being so. It had to be at an early age as her mother (whose damaged heart finally gave out on her) died in her nine-year-old daughter's arms one winter's night. My tiny mum ran to the pub to fetch her father, he brought with him Uncle Harry who never left who then had it made, the swine.

All of my adult life, I knew my mother hated her father with a vengeance and one day when in my teens, she told me why! As a young girl, she had always known violence in the home, but one Sunday was very, very bad, and she always believed it was that event that led to her mother's death from a heart attack, just three days later.

My gran was making custard to go with her delicious apple crumble, cheap and cheerful, it had to be, as money was short 'cos of his boozing. He staggered in from the pub, plonked himself in his leather chair by the fire and promptly fell asleep. My tiny gran had been working at restoring furniture to get it sold fast, as the rent man would knock for his money, come Tuesday night.

Everything was ready for when her Lord and Master awoke, demanding his meal, on the table at exactly 6 pm. Then, he would gobble it down, belch a few times, let it line his stomach in readiness for the night's session down at the pub, then bring all her food back up again on his way home, bastard!

This grandfather of mine had a pointed moustache that was kept that way with the aid of black wax; it was his habit to twirl the sod, wiping the remaining on Gran's pristine tablecloth, which drove Gran nuts. In a moment of insanity, she cut off one side of it whilst he snored, threw it into the fire's flames and wondered if she could replicate (in paint) the wondrous blue flame created by the wax. Then, the monster awoke and went for the compulsory twiddle: 'What the fuck.'. He looked at the empty space on his top lip in the mantle mirror and with clenched fists chased my gran around the kitchen. God alone knows why, but she set about him with handfuls of thick custard, not only did he get the yellow offering, but she also covered the gas light fittings on the walls (these were long before electric ones were invented – these would be for posh people – not the poor!) The open fire cooking range got its fair share also, and her poor little nine-year old daughter, who in much later years was to become my mother. The gran, who I would have loved to have been hugged by, died a very sad, young death long before I was born.

Now just a couple of days before, on 18 January 1920 was my mum's 9th birthday. To her delight, her mummy bought her a longed-for puppy; he insisted it be tied up in the yard. It started to bark and yelp at all the shouting and did not be quiet when ordered to by that drunken bastard. Then, he did the most despicable thing, in front of his wife and child he kicked Judy, the puppy, to death. Stomping on its little body until it could shriek in agony no more. Ordering my gran to clean that mess up, he went off to the pub yet again. At 9.30 pm, he staggered back with a new puppy in his arms his pissed mind thinking this was atonement – never!

Gran found out where he'd got it from and with teary kisses gave it back to the woman, telling her to never supply another one, cos he would probably kick that to death also.

Days later the gran I'm sure I would have loved, if only given the chance, died. A little frail nine-year-old girl stood in the pouring rain clutching the goodbye daffodil at the side of the gaping hole that was her beloved mother's eternity.

Uncle Harry who supported my grandfather in his grieved state by pouring yet more ale down his disgusting throat took full advantage of his snoring state and promptly started to rape my nine-year-old mother. This continued for many a year, nothing was done to help this torn in mind and body child. At twelve, she was sent to work in a factory some two miles away. Off she would clump in her too-small tatty clogs that deformed her size 3 feet for all of her life. The threadbare shawl took away none of the freezing cold, poor little bugger. What a tragic start to life.

Not long after, how she must have rejoiced when Harry was knocked down and killed by a heavy carthorse when he stumbled down drunk beneath its thundering hooves, salvation. Good riddance.

Anyway, at the age of twenty, she met my dad, a good decent hardworking man, who treated her well. Thank God for that, she really deserved it.

Our grandmother Sophia holding our mother in 1910

My Mother

Born on the 18th of January, 1910 to a tiny beautiful Italian lady who had the misfortune to be married to an English nasty drunk. My grandmother was short and far from sweet as she tried valiantly to provide for the baby whose birth had weakened even more her already damaged heart.

Standing just five-foot-one, Grandmother looks sullenly at me from the only tiny photo I have of her. She holds the child, my mother that was nearly the death of her, protective and proud, in black shiny boots, a long black skirt and a pristine white high-necked blouse as was the garb of Victorian ladies.

As I know that Mother was put to work in a mill and at some point, someplace, met my father. They were totally mismatched in both looks and background for he was tall and handsome and came from a good home, his father being a goldsmith. Whilst Mother was short and plain and came from a disastrous poor beginning.

Mother had my elder brother when she was nineteen and me twelve years later.

They had moved from the home they shared with my grandfather and now lived in a five-bedroom detached home in a posher area. Things were looking up for her, but she was already blighted by her past, and I'll make that excuse for her later behaviour that drove my father to despair so many times.

Even though she had only one of each garment (as was the way in those post-war days), she kept herself clean and smart and made sure I always had decent clothes and a full tummy. The poor soul never had any of the appliances today's wives take for granted and would wash everything by hand except the bedding which went to the laundry. (Strange that's exactly how it would be in years to come for me, except I'd have to climb in the bath with the bedding and pummel it clean with my feet.)

I suppose I'd be about fourteen when she told me, she had saved enough to buy herself the new coat she badly needed. We headed off to Manchester and whilst she looked at coats that would last her for many years. I drooled over a coral-coloured swagger coat. The upshot of this scenario is that I got the coat I coveted and my generous mother went without until she could save up yet again. How selfish can a daughter be? To this day, I'm ashamed of my callous greed, yet in the years to come, I made up for that action thousands of times.

I became an expert at sewing and tailored dresses and matching coats for the mother who had made so many sacrifices for me.

At last, she could go to her wardrobe and actually choose what she would wear that day. Numerous cardigans, shoes, underwear, handbags, pieces of jewellery, and even umbrellas were now hers. I believe they made her happy, as I intended. And until the day she died, I made sure my mother was safe and dressed as she had always deserved.

My mother had no social life, and I never knew her to even have a day out, let alone a holiday. Just as I did, she lived in a cold, dark, silent world, and I don't believe she ever knew contentment. Her past had damaged her beyond all repair and yet maybe it made her more accepting of the gentle boredom that was now hers. My father was a nonviolent man who worked long and hard in dreadful pain to support his family. They muddled on in their own peculiar variation of marriage, and it ended on Christmas night when he made her a widow.

Of course, I brought her home to live with me. She clung to my every move and took away what little freedom, I'd come to cherish.

This unhappy situation had to end and with this a priority, I moved heaven and earth to find her a home of gentle peace and contentment. The alternative to this was me throwing myself off Barton Bridge like a demented lemming.

It was a truly beautiful grand house on grounds covered with rose beds and shady trees, with comfy chairs underneath for old people to rest in.

I'd stayed there, unbeknown to Mother whilst I did up the room that was to become her home. Treasured small items from her life were placed amongst beautiful new ones and for once she would live in a place where everything was finished, so unlike life before, for my father used to fill her mind and heart with wonderful ideas about the home he would create. He'd start off with such gusto but very soon the incentive would dwindle, and yet another dream would be discarded. Mother grew used to it over the years, and I witnessed her going from excitement to gross disappointment, many, many times. In the end, she just gave up on her dreams, I believe. Little did she know one day I would fulfil them all.

I placed the door key in her hand and said "welcome home Mum" as she pushed the door open, her excited old face was worth all the money and hard work. I sat her in a Parker Knoll velvet reclining chair, turned on her new TV to Coronation Street, folded back the golden velvet bedspread that matched her curtains and gave her first drink of tea in a China mug in her forever home.

She was so proud to be able to invite visitors into her abode, and she never missed an opportunity to show off her treasures.

Each day she would have a change of clothes from the wardrobe, now packed tight with garments I'd either lovingly made or bought. Really, she was in geriatric heaven, just as I'd promised myself all those years ago when my shame at begging for a coral coat reared its ugly head.

Every month, the committee that ran the home she lived in visited to make sure their stringent rules were abided by. Mother looked forward to these times as she revelled in the glowing admiration of her home.

Over time, I'd purchased her a selection of carved wooden animals; these were displayed on the window ledge. Amongst them, were a pair of rhinos, and I took great delight in mounting them for a shag beside the velvet curtain. Mother would phone up and tell me off, this only made me more determined to let the wooden ones have their pleasures. I'd moved them to a different place and had them copulating on a chest of drawers which had escaped Mother's attention. As usual, the committee came to ooh and ahh at Mother's special room, and it was only when a China teacup hit the carpet that Mother discovered where her animals were. Giving his missus a right sorting was the wooden rhino at the side of a photo Mother was explaining who it portrayed.

Jesus, she went right off on one when she phoned, I laughed until my smalls had to be laundered, and she gave the rhinos to the old girl next door. Shame really, as I thought it spoilt the collection somehow.

I tried valiantly to get another two of her wooden friends to play nicely, but the balance never worked, and as we all know it's all about balance.

But time passed and dementia reared its ugly head. I'd been warned that she would have to be moved to a place where more expert help was on hand. This I dreaded.

Our last visit was a harmonious one, she did not seem as disturbed as usual, but she complained of a strange pain in her temple. I closed the window to stop any draft and stroked her old face whilst she rested it against my shoulder. Together at last, we had gentle peace.

We said our goodbyes! It was the next morning that I learnt she had softly died safe and warm tucked up under her golden velvet bedspread.

It was raining hard as we passed over Barton Bridge in response to Mrs Hughes' (the home's warden) call telling me what I'd prayed to hear. Because if my mother had lived just one more week, I would have had to find her a place of safety. For a while now, dementia had her in its grip, displaying its torment by having her believe there were intruders in her room at night, which she would attack with the metal window pole. The result of these dramas were large gouges of plaster missing from the walls (rather like I made as a child) and a screaming mother. Her agitation would awaken the whole house and yet next morning, Mother knew nothing of her nightmare terrors.

For all of my life, I knew my mother to be extremely disorganised and would put things away safe. So safe in fact that it could take three months to find the sods, in which time my father would be driven to distraction as she tore the house apart in her search. The result of this upbringing is that I'm obsessive about everything being in the place I deem correct for them. So much so I can go to a cupboard, thirty, forty years later to get an item I know for a fact to be there. Now should I have a clear out of items that have sat there for that amount of time and of course never be needed, it's sod's law that in a couple of days I will have found a use for the now disposed of item, and so now what I have stays forever.

I entered Mother's darkened room on my own as I did not want my daughter traumatised by her first sight of a dead body. On pulling back the golden velvet spread that covered Mother's body, I was shocked, to say the least. Not frightened in any way, just shocked. For many years, my mother had worn wigs though she swore this not to be the case. So, if anyone should have the nerve to ask. She denied it, so it took me by surprise to see long white hair spread over her pillow and her sightless eyes staring at me. The knocking on her bedroom door was the undertaker coming to remove her old body. But first, I had to find her wig and teeth as she would have been livid if I'd let her meet her maker without them. And so, the search began whilst the dark-suited gent tapped his foot with impatience whilst his face bore a plastered on sympathetic fake smile.

Under her bed, was her wig which was wrapped in her corsets, I found her top set of teeth in an ornament some ten minutes later, I retrieved her bottom set out of the butter dish. It's not what you want or need, is it? A corpse in the bed awaiting removal and hide and bloody seek for her personal items to ensure dignified internment.

The Undertaker wrote down my instructions and off she went, to have done what must be done. She did not need an autopsy as her doctor had visited only two days before declaring her fit and well. But now bloody dead of a stroke. So, that was the heralding pain I'd tried to soothe away from her old face just a few hours ago.

On viewing her body, the next day, I was far from happy as her favourite colour lilac was not the one of her shroud. It was requested lilac but in reality, it was a strange grey with a hint of mauve, and it needed the creases, left from the packet ironing out.

To top it all, they had given my mother a very unpleasant expression, and it did not go down well with the corpse fiddler when I told him, she looked like a Pike that had just been pulled from the water "change it now and get the creases out of her last garment" I spat at him. He, I suppose was used to tears, not fury at the slipshod job he had dared to do for my mother.

The next day she also travelled over Barton Bridge for her very last visit to me. The wonderful home I'd been so lucky for my old Mum to spend the autumn of her life in I decided should keep all I'd provided for her. What was the point of emptying it out with the aid of a house clearance robber who would insult with peanuts for mother's treasures?

All of my mother's clothes were shared out between delighted old ladies (her underwear and wigs burnt), and I only kept one outfit of hers. The one she wore at her grandson's wedding with such pride. The photo, even then shows her eyes troubled with the dementia that was to come.

I asked that her room be kept in its entirety to give a lovely home to some old dears of the future who had nothing of their own. And to the best of my belief, to this day many an old lady has laid safe and warm under Mum's golden velvet bedspread. Shame the humping rhinos were no more!

For a long time, I'd been asking her to let us bring her to my home to see what I'd achieved, but her answer was always no.

But in death she did come to visit, she lay in my front room wearing her favourite perfume, Charlie Clunes played his piano for her cold delight, a magnificent purple gloxinia plant by her side. She was peaceful, and the fear that dementia had etched on her face was now gone. Her flawless beautiful skin glowed in the soft light as I said all the things that needed to be spoken. And I have to admit the expression she now sported made me giggle. Gone was the newly landed Pike, to be replaced with maniacal laughter, the mouth wide open in mirth and her top denture swinging from her gum.

Grief makes you do stupid things, and I was no exception. On them arriving with her body, I insisted they carry her into my back garden so that she could admire it in death as she never got around to it in life. God alone knows what they must have thought as they hauled her coffin down a narrow entry and had to stand her up to survey the flowers. The memory makes me laugh and squirm with embarrassment at the same time.

On removing the lid when finally in my front room, the excessive motion must have made her wig slip over one eye; this mixed with the laughing gob just doubled me up; poor Mother was a laughing stock in death as she had been, more than once, in life.

But the fiasco of her death was far from over. I'd been told how much it would cost to have her placed with my father in the grave the family had owned for one hundred years.

All hell broke loose when I was informed before she was buried that the cost was almost doubled because she had the temerity to die outside the boundary that the council specified. On this information, I contacted the local rag and told them what a bloody rip-off it was and that I would not release my mother's body for burial until this robbing bylaw was changed.

Furthermore, it had to be changed not only for my mother but for all the other grieving relatives who did not know of this con or had not got the balls to fight it. Well, I bloody did have the necessaries and went into battle as only I can. I pointed out that it was the same grave diggers with the same spades removing the same earth in the same amount of time. Opening a grave already paid for and owned a hundred years ago. Cheeky, greedy, conning sods. I was determined that the uncaring council (who allowed the graveyard to look like an unkempt overgrown tip) would not get away with their actions with me and all who would follow. So, with this in mind and knowing it could last some time whilst the newspaper and public poured scorn on the council, I went and bought a job lot of air fresheners.

That's all you need really, isn't it? A swiftly going off Mother next to your purple velvet suite and every fly in Europe planning to visit.

My Mum was still lying-in-state with me doing all I could to resolve a situation not of my making but one I was insistent I would fix once and for all.

I needed comforting words of love and with this, in mind, I once again tried to phone Baghdad. This time, I got through and with the aid of the international operator was told the bad news that made my world crumble. My beloved man who I'd waited six years for whilst he fought a war that he never believed in had been killed on 1st January. I'd waited for the promised letter that would never be written or read. I told my dead mother of yet another loss and my tears fell on the satin shroud (which when wet) then turned it to a colour I'd requested in the first place.

Another day passed while I cursed the hot weather and used another couple of cans of air freshener. Those buggers at the council had no conception of just who they were dealing with and my determination to alter their robbing bylaw just grew stronger.

I suppose I was fuelled by the injustice of it all and the knowledge I'd never look into the beautiful eyes of the man I loved ever again. Not in this life anyway.

Two weeks passed and at last, I had it in writing the council (as a gesture of goodwill to a grieving daughter you understand) had capitulated and done as I had demanded. Bollocks!

My mother's favourite flowers were the roses my father grew but would never allow them to be picked. But on that day her visit to my home ended forever, I was grateful to say the very least.

She was accompanied in that shiny black car by a heart-shaped wreath covered by Ariana peach roses, picked just for her, from me to my mother.

Now, she has lain for many a year with my father, the man of her dreams.

P.S: But before her demise, many were the plots she hatched. Her jealousy made her do the most mind-blowing acts (mostly towards my long-suffering father) and yet they stayed together all of my father's life. The Sewing Moths will explain more! That episode was still to unfold in the not so far off future.

It was 1942 and I'd Arrived (Worst Luck)

A winter's night; the air raid sirens sent out their death warning as my mother screamed and pushed me into a life I never would want. And her death warning was to the bugger who had swapped a moment's pleasure for this torment – my father – should his determined swimmers ever try to reach their destination again.

The black sky was so clear that November night with stars twinkling – nothing could look more innocent yet menacing: death was on its way in the form of Messerschmitt bombers sent by that lunatic Hitler to wipe out the rail lines taking the guns from the ammunition's factories (where both my father and grandfather toiled each night) to the coast for shipping.

Brave volunteer home guards with ack-ack guns, their beams of light criss-crossing the darkness clung to rooftops and chimney stacks, hoping and praying that when the raid was over, they would still have families and homes to return to. Conscripted young men to bolster the fighting in Europe (that stole the lives of hundreds of thousands of brave men) were of little use against Hitler's hordes. A river of tears shed by mothers, wives and children and for what? The present-day asks! The answer is of course to destroy the appalling aspirations of a jumped-up vile cruel little painter and decorator, Hitler, and life here would have been hell had he won.

But in that agony-filled night for my mother, the bombs fell short of the railway line and instead fell onto the bowling green behind our home, but many other houses did not fare so well, where the sleeping occupants would never again wake up for their morning cup of tea.

And so, the heavily laden trains carrying their cargo of retaliation towards the sea continued, saved by just a few feet of land and a bowling green never again to hear the clunk of wood on wood.

Another long, cold, fearful night was at last over and the courage of the home guard who clung to rooftops and chimney stacks giving their all to try to ensure the safety of this little island they so loved. Bless every one of them.

No one could know as I screamed my way into this life through the tunnel that crushed my tiny skull, fuelling my disgust as I smelt and tasted what was my mother that I was a damaged child, a tiny little girl with an unknown bipolar mind that would tear and torment me, all of my unwanted days. This unseen monster that all too often crept from the shadows of my mind, stealing my laughter to drive away friends with little or no understanding, got rid of lovers that craved my body but ran from my mind. But that was long into my unwanted future, for now, I blinked at lights too bright after my nine months of darkness, clenched, outraged tiny fists even then, railed at the two people who had created me. I was to hate them for it, but God help me, I'd arrived.

The sirens wailed, and so did I, and that wailing (all be it mostly silent) has torn my mind for seventy-eight long years now.

I'm now 18 months old, my brother, being twelve years older, was the one who grabbed me from my cot disturbing my deep slumber. My screams of outrage being drowned out by the wail of the sirens, bombs were on their deathly way and with a howling, angry baby tucked under his arm, he galloped out into the rainy night, the starry sky was crisscrossed with the beams from the AK guns and he plunged me into a cold evil-smelling tin place of a thing, this I was to later learn was the air raid shelter supposed to save lives (even those not wanting to be saved) and then the bomb did fall on the bowling green out the back of our home and in so doing blew out our windows. The sticky tape that crisscrossed the glass to stop it from breaking from a bomb blast – did not and failed miserably.

And so, even now if I am awakened from my mind mending sleep, I find the rapid over beating of a panicked heart unearths the siren's screams and wails. I know not where I am.

Now I'm five years old, we have moved from the house where I was born to a large detached one the façade of which gave an impression of dignity, taste and wealth, the inside was a different matter where no one was ever invited and so was born my loneliness and utter disgust at hypocrisy.

My father was a hard-working, handsome engineer who slaved on a permanent night shift whereas my mother was a plain, boring pigeon of a woman on stick-thin legs but sporting huge breasts, like I say a boring jealous hypocrite who at the time I loved dearly. This one day would change, because of her vile betrayal of me.

The leftover black-out blinds from the war still hung at those windows blacking out sunshine and indeed life, except for the flashes of light around their edges where tiny fingers held my dolly. So, this is how my formative years progressed, creeping around so as not to wake a sleeping father – silently dressing dolly in the half-light, breathing in granddad's vile pipe smoke. At that time of course all of this seemed perfectly normal, as I had nothing to compare it to for I was never taken to visit anyone – nor did anyone come to see us. This made for a solitary, lonely disturbed child who evolved into the woman I became.

But one day, I was made to realise how strange my life was. A little school friend invited me to tea in her house, nowhere near as posh as the one I lived in. This is where I found the difference between a house and a home.

Rosie's mother greeted this strange child warmly for I knew nothing of social graces, so sitting down at the lace-covered table seeing and smelling the wondrous spread that lay before us, I was in child heaven.

But what made my tea time visit so very special was that all of my dormant senses were brought to the fore in that one-hour visit.

This so pretty home had lovely flowery curtains pulled back to let the sunshine dance through the room, I looked for the drab brown that cloaked my house but there was none to be seen (to this very day, some sixty-four years later, I still detest brown) Rosie's mother flitted about, her perfume filling my nostrils and mind and making me decide that on one far off day I would smell lovely just like this lady.

Rosie's daddy came home and was greeted by his pretty, blonde, made-up, perfumed, slim, utterly gorgeous, little wife. And even then, I swore that one day, yes, one day I would be a lady like the one before my greedy eyes; no dowdy pigeon for me, I was going to be a bird of paradise, and I was!

Her parents excused themselves to go and get changed, for this was their night to go ballroom dancing, and so Rosie and I played 'Jack's' as the tiny house did not possess a TV as my house did but it was filled with overbrimming love, laughter, prettiness and such welcome as I had never known. Whose was the richest? That moment I knew.

Eventually, they came downstairs dressed in all their dancing finery, her daddy wore evening dress, but he was not as handsome as my daddy, who would hopefully be asleep in readiness for another night's toil. Now my little friend's mother was a feast for young eyes her tiny body was enhanced with a strapless red evening gown, miniature feet encased in high silver shoes, a matching clutch bag in a bejewelled hand, and earrings sparkled amidst the curls of blonde hair. Dear God, I was smitten. Were there really people that looked and smelt and laughed like this? Yes, there was and one day, one day, I would be like that lady.

Music was put on the record player, Rosie's mother and father melted into each other's arms, and Strauss dictated their gliding steps.

What can I say? I was in heaven and from that day forth, I strove to banish the frumpish identity that should have been my birth right and stepped from the brown, dark, quiet world that was inflicted upon me and sought out what I was to become, beautiful! Thank you, Rosie's mum.

John was my older brother by twelve years, he was a good young man of seventeen, but my father excluded him forever from the house (it was never a home) because of a minor dispute. I never was to find out exactly why but that strict father was to do the same thing to me, many years later – when I also was seventeen, but God help me, I knew why he turned me away. I deserved it. I was five years old when John vanished from my life, leaving me even more lonely and disturbed.

The torture of my damaged mind manifested itself in strange ways. I remember clearly the joy I felt when given a silver ring, nestling at its centre was a glorious opal, its multi colours of beauty filling my childish senses. I stroked its wonder and wore it with pride taking it to the still black blinded windows, finding that precious shaft of sunshine and seeing my special ring in all its colourful glory. But the vile monster my mind held in secret was once again to shroud me in its dark grasp, in so doing it made me take my most precious and only possession from my tiny finger, place it in my mouth and crush all the beauty out of it and then swallow it. Later, when my resident monster had returned to his lair I looked at an empty little finger to discover the beauty once held safely there was no more.

I recalled through the mists of recent memory the destructive, vile action my monster had made me commit, and I was truly heartbroken. The crunching of the glass textured opal, the easy way the silver bent between my teeth, the swallow that stole forever my pride and joy I recall so well over sixty years later. Sad tormented little girl, how I weep for how wonderful it would have been to be born undamaged.

My father was a man so clever he could turn his hand to almost any task – the problem being he never finished any one of them, and the house was filled with the disappointing evidence of jobs long since abandoned. The day came when he decided to decorate my room. Little did he know that I had already made a valiant attempt at this myself. Every weekend we had quality street chocolates, the wrappers of this I turned into butterflies (hundreds of the buggers) and fixed them all over the walls and the ceiling which I reached by climbing onto the moveable chest of drawers.

My mother had noticed that the fingertips on my right hand were bleeding and sore and had been for a long time. I never gave a reason for this but my father's wish to completely re-vamp my room would soon enough provide the answer to the quandary.

On entering my room, he looked with amused pleasure at the cocoon he had entered, hundreds of pretty butterflies, "Oh! Bless this child!" He started to remove them in readiness before removing wallpaper probably fifty years old. Said butterfly fluttered to his feet, in so doing revealing a gouged out frilly hole passing deeply into the plaster, the answer to the question of his child's torn up fingers was before him. The only way to try to relieve my mental torment was to create this mayhem. He removed a few more of my colourful little friends only to discover the same unwanted damage. Slowly, he turned to look at all of them then he did something that I recall with much laughter, though at the time I panicked at his wrath, even though I'd never been smacked! He climbed up on my single bed and trampolined many times and with each jump, he pulled off a butterfly exposing the hole beneath it, out of breath he climbed down from the bed, looked at the child that I was before him, shook his head in despair, picked up his ladder and after saying "Fuck it" my dad buggered off.

Now, my tender young ears had never been exposed to what I was to later understand as 'bad language' I stored these bad words in my sponge-like mind should I ever have a call to use them. It was not long before an ideal opportunity arose. Trying to cut up a crispy bit of bacon one time, a piece skidded to the floor where it was at once gobbled up by Danny the farting greyhound. This I considered to be on a par with butterflies and gouged out plaster and used the only expression I deemed appropriate "Fuck it," I said and ate my egg instead. Mother and Father looked like they had turned to stone, and it was explained later that only grown-ups were allowed to use that expression, and it was still wrong. This being so many years later, 'Fuck it' has been needed many, many times.

This instance was never mentioned, my fingertips healed up, and my bedroom was still undecorated when I left that house forever at the tender age of seventeen, seven years later.

I was never told off as a child or indeed smacked, as I recall my parents had an unusual way of getting their message of displeasure across to me in a way I would never, ever forget. An eye for an eye was quite obviously the family motto.

John, my big brother had long been pushed out into a hostile world, but this young man would not only fend for himself admirably but would become one of the greatest test jet pilots this country ever produced. My pride in him has no bounds!

On visiting many countries, he bought me gifts to gladden my childish heart. These he would get to me via an old aunt who my mother would visit once in a while. One of these flying expeditions found him in Switzerland from where he bought me two music boxes. One being of rosewood, the other round green pearlised metal, the lid filled with dried wildflowers, what bliss, the tinkling tunes were not loud enough to awaken my sleeping father, and their beauty was clear at the blinds sunny edge.

There was another smaller kitchen in this large old house that still had the bell, pushed to summon maids now long gone. In this small room was a butler's stone sink that all manner of things were piled in including a clock. In my dark, quiet, boredom I turned on the tap to see indeed if water was still to run. OH God it did and in so doing wetting all the contents and probably spoiling the clock. This must have been discovered by my parents not long after, as one day I went to the bathroom. I remember it being icy cold, in fact that what appeared to be lace curtains was ice (on the inside of the windows) So, there I sat shivering on the loo, my little legs dangling, my panties around my ankles. All is quiet as usual as my father must get his sleep for another night of toil is about to begin. I look to my side and let out a howl of despair, please God I've not woken Daddy. My wondrous treasured music boxes, which brought me such joy, were submerged in water in the bath, I managed to get them out and eventually dry them, but I never heard the tunes I loved ever again.

An eye for an eye, oh! Yes, I learnt my lesson, but would it not have been kinder to smack my bottom, than to destroy my tinkling joy? I believe so!

Once again home from school, Mother stands at the electric cooker with Father's bottom dentures hovering above the heat. The poor man had had to have his fabulous natural teeth removed after getting Pyria (then an untreatable gum disease) that would in time make your teeth fall out anyway. So, before they did, he had a perfect replica made in plastic. These he placed in a pot of diluted domestic bleach before going to bed.

Once more the 'Don't say a word' finger was raised and off I popped to watch *Muffin the Mule* on TV (I believe you can be prosecuted for violating a mule in that way these days!)

Father raises from bed dreading another night shift, as all this time the leg ulcers were still giving him hell. Mother is trying to turn a piece of plaice in the pan but is shaking so much that she turns it into mush. Father rinses off his gobblers and tries to place them in his mouth. Dear God almighty what was wrong with them? Their distorted shape refused to sit against his gums, and he had no option but to spit them out and what did she say? "I told you that putting them in bleach would ruin them" So his pearly whites went the same way as the suits she was soon to knacker, the poor bastard now had bald gums and no decent threads in the future. Like I said I'd have killed the witch.

This was the time of smog; wet fog so thick you could not see anything before you. But still, father got ready for the night shift, tired, so ill, so pissed off.

Now, not only did father have those vile ulcers he also gasped for breath when an asthma attack came. And, to add insult to injury, he was the valiant owner of a bunch of piles that would not have looked out of place in a greengrocer's window. Apparently, his bunch of grapes were of legend, (though of course I never saw them,) I just knew he walked differently from time to time, I suppose the throbbing sods were activated then and doing their very worst.

This smoggy night for a man with so many afflictions was horrendous, but he had a mortgage to pay, a family to keep (because at that time he had forbidden my mother to work, believing it was his job to provide), and this he did to the very best of his ability.

"Oh! Stanley, it's such a terrible night out, let me make you a nice cup of hot cocoa before you set off" she was suspicious because he was allowing an extra hour of travelling time, what or who was he doing with that hour out of her sights?

Chocolate in hand he gulps it down remarking how rich it tasted 'a new kind' she told him. 'Oh, dear God', it was a new kind, being a whole block of chocolate laxative that had gone into making this warming wonder.

Now, the poor sod was caught short with the incredible squits, and his refined dignity was called into question at work. He had an arse like a baboon for weeks as he shat himself senseless thus making his legendary piles drop to the point that another couple of inches, and they could have been tucked into his sock tops. Of course, he knew what the witch had done because she did not have the sense to burn the empty packet, instead it went into the bin where he found it. Even when faced with such damning evidence, the crazy bugger stood her ground and blamed it on a dodgy pie from the work's canteen. How the hell did this man keep his hands off her throat?

The lonely disturbed years dragged by, with lots of times me being the messenger between the two of them after yet another of their domestics "You go and tell your father" So, and so and "You go and tell your mother" These awful times could last for a couple of months or more, me being a nonunderstanding pawn in the battle. I remember walking up the road with my mother (aged five) my father was coming towards us and even then, they ignored each other, and I was so upset that my daddy never said "hello love" But eventually this sorry state of affairs was overtaken by primal lust, and they would rut for a whole weekend behind the locked bedroom door. I hated, hated, hated these interludes as I was not allowed to make my own breakfast, so this cold, hungry child went unfed, and with distaste I breathed in Grandad's vile pipe smoke as he sat in his brown leather chair. Dementia making him oblivious to the needs of a small child, and the fact he'd wet himself yet again, so I sat on the stairs hugging my dolly in the freezing half-light listening to the grunts of copulation knowing not what they meant, but they frightened me as I thought my mother was being hurt. My emotions are once again those of a tiny soul, and I feel sickened.

But just once in a while laughter lit up that house and blew away any lingering animosity and gave me the story I'll tell you now.

I've always loved animals and as a small child, I craved a doggy to love and care for. This was refused for many a year, but a few years hence I was allowed one. Danny would come into our lives, but in the meantime what I did get was a stag. Well not really, I got just its head.

This magnificent beast had been shot by some bad bugger and was turned into a trophy coat rack after its magnificent antlered head had been removed from an unwanted body. I suppose some landed gentry, some hooray Henry on a weekend's fun (a shoot) thought himself a big man to have brought to its dying knees a creature of such stature and majesty (I hate these braying, killing bastards – the men, not the stags), and this antlered wonder adorned the hall of the magnificent manor house that was auctioning off all its contents.

My father had seen this event in the evening news and off we trot hand in hand to catch a couple of buses to God knows where, just the two of us, mother stayed at home for whatever reason, maybe they were mid spat.

After what seemed like hours, we finally reached my father's goal and with eyes filling with wonder I spotted Rudolph.

Christ, I fell in love with the beast of the Glens, the fact that his sightless eyes were glass, and his antlers had a seven-foot span only made me desire him more. God bless that man, my father, that sunny day he bought his nutty child her heart's desire, I don't remember if he bought anything else I was too busy stroking my pet on the buses home. That must have been some sight on looking back – a very posh looking gent who never went anywhere without a trilby hat or a Panama (which he sported that day because it was summer). His sartorial elegance could never be brought into question and that makes it all the sadder that my mother had mutilated his Saville row suits (he really would have looked the kangaroo's conkers in that get up), but she was having none of that.

Many apologies were said to other passengers as my daddy manoeuvred the deadly tips of Rudolf's antlers getting off the bus, at the same time holding my tiny hand, to save me from falling. After a twenty-minute walk we were home, after bearing the brunt of the local naughty boys who informed my father in laughing shouts that it was 'Too early for fucking Christmas' Father would not dignify this verbal onslaught from the riff-raff and strode on regardless – stag's head underarm, a child in grasp. Nice one!

So, my pet was placed on the hall wall too high up for me to stroke unless I quietly dragged a chair underneath it, and this I did almost daily.

For once my mother and father were laughing and much later, I was to find out just why. Dad had a wicked sense of humour that Mother did her best to understand. I'm glad to say that I have carried on his sense of fun and have used it to delight anyone who has bothered to listen to me.

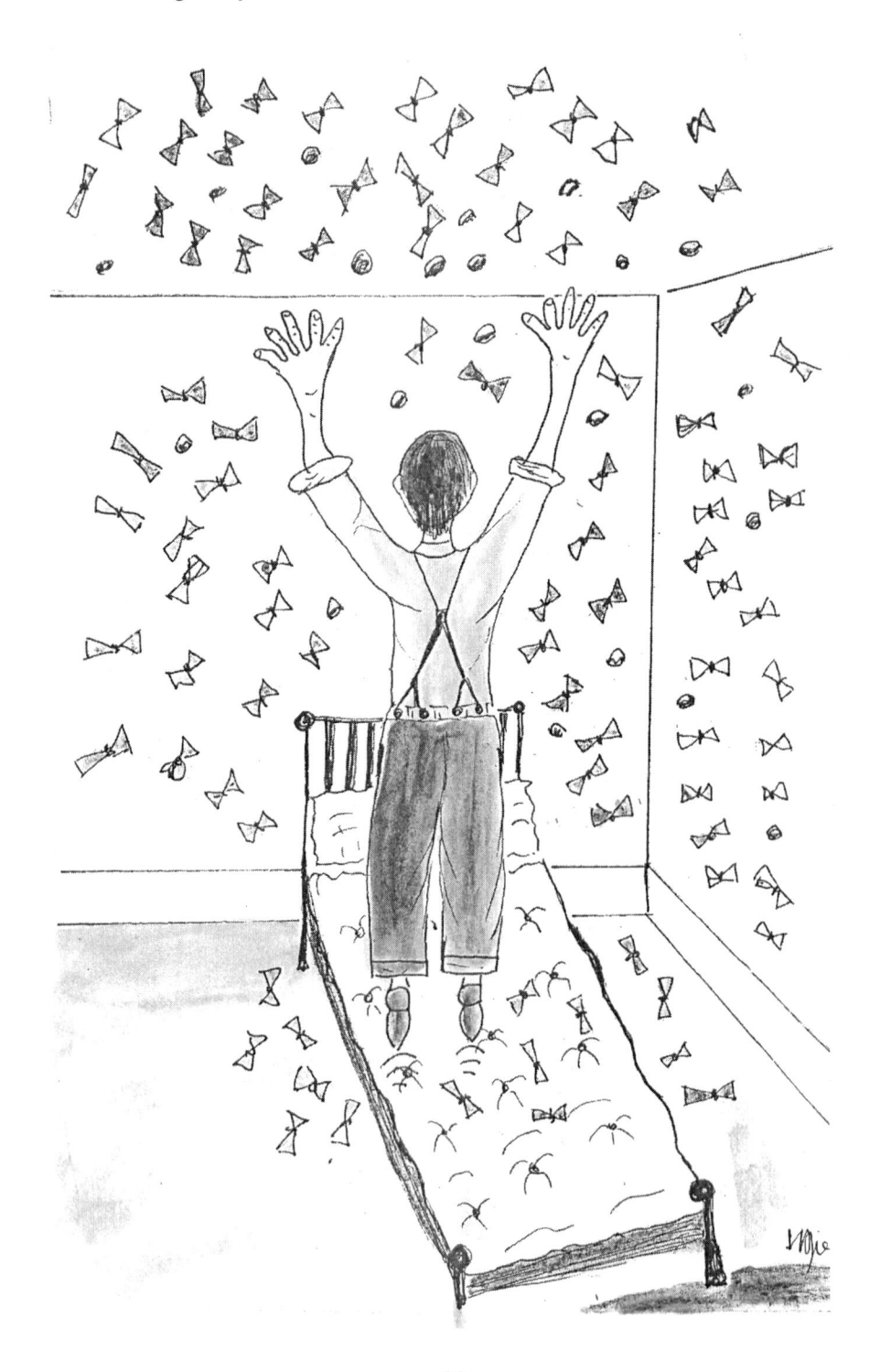

Clip Clop

It was not long before I found out the cause of my parent's merriment. Daddy brought home some coconut shells and set about teaching his puzzled little girl how to make the clip-clopping sound of a horse's hooves. He was most impressed by my progress even though the sound drove my mother bloody frantic.

Now, it was a Saturday ritual (when they were on speaking terms) to have Rose's chocolates and listen to boogie-woogie music on the bur walnut radiogram, and I loved it as the house came alive with that infectious music, instead of the deadly silence needed for Father to get his sleep before another painful gruelling night shift at the engineering factory.

Now, next door on the other side of a ten-foot wall that divided the properties lived two puffs (who pretended to be brothers as it was illegal for two chaps to love each other in those hypocritical cruel days) these two sweet men lived a quiet life and doted on the numerous cats that all had the names of flowers, regardless of their gender. And at twilight each day, the two of them would stand on the steps with a roll call and feline creatures of all shapes, colours and sizes hurried through the weeded garden, flinging themselves off gutters, and shinning down the branches of the fruit trees in our orchard. "Petunia, Marigold, Lily, Daisy and Rosie" the calls went on and on until their dads were satisfied they were all accounted for, and I once counted sixteen.

So, my clip-clopping was up to Daddy's exacting standards and as Winifred Atwell bashed the keys, Rose's chocolates were passed around and it was just coming up to twilight. Quite late really as in those far off days, there were double summer times, which meant that the clocks were altered by two hours instead of only one hour of these years.

Father got my best friend Rudolf down from the hall wall, and I watched in concern as he shoved a brush stale up inside my dead pet's neck. As told to, I followed him into our courtyard clutching my coconut shells.

Father stood by the ten-foot wall with my stag's seven-foot-wide antlered head at the ready. I was primed (sat on the doorsteps) with my coconut shells, and the roll call began. "Petunia, Rosie, Daisy" the cats are on the move, then suddenly the earth-shattering screams of two puffs broke the evening silence. For my daft Daddy had hoisted the stags head above the ten-foot wall, and with my clip-clopping hooves made it walk the whole twenty-foot length of it, antlers tapping the wall top and the dying rays of the evening sun glinting on glass eyes that could never see. The screams continued long after their back door was slammed shut, and those cats that were not fast enough to enter before Rudolf did his thing were locked out, poor hungry little buggers, no doubt to be fed when Rudolf had buggered off.

Father slid down the wall clutching my Rudolf with tears of mirth falling aplenty; I had another chocolate whilst Winifred the queen of boogie-woogie continued to entertain me. What a fabulous Saturday!

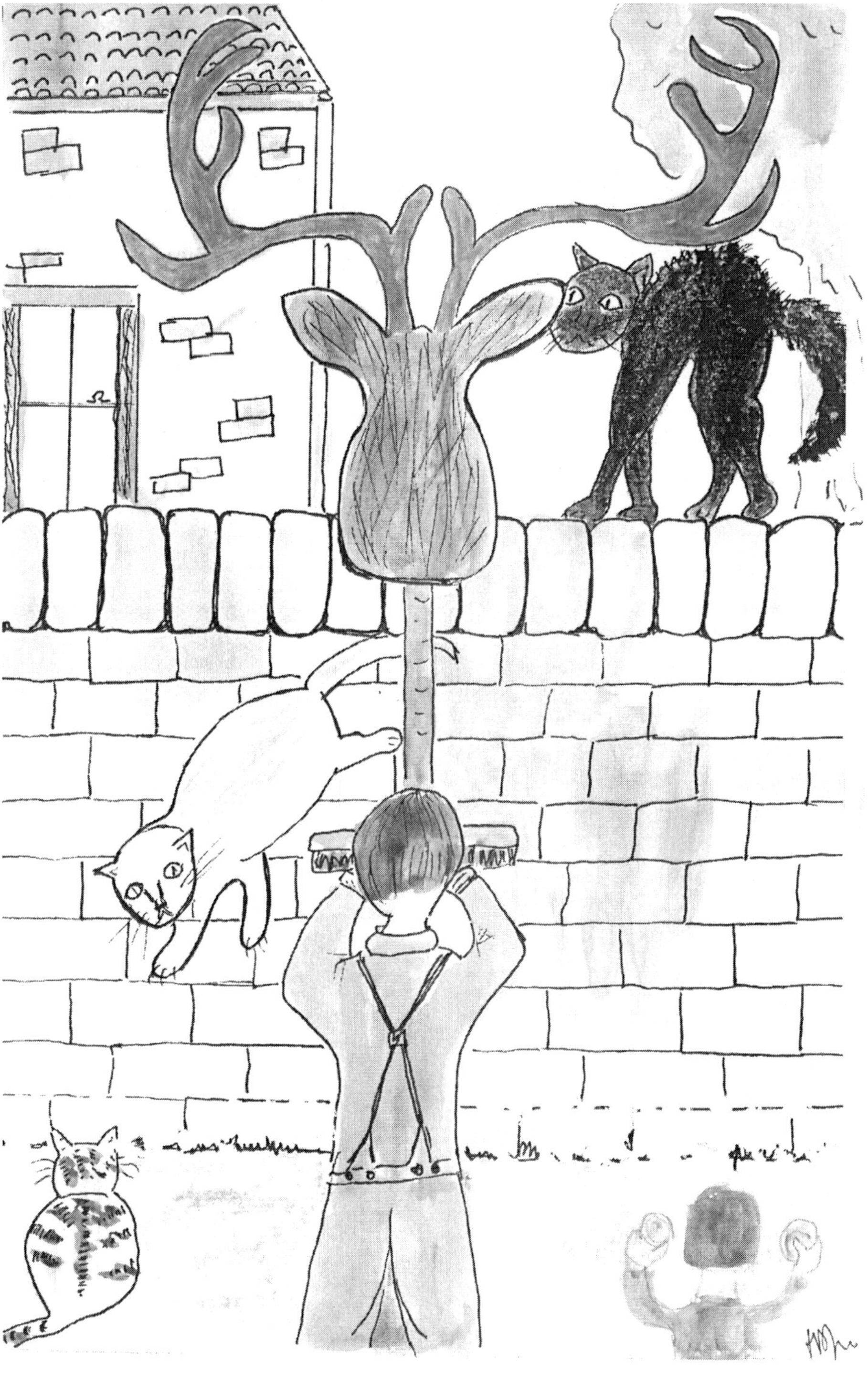

Rag Tripe

Christ, that dog could fart. A small squeak would be the only warning that the sulphurous odour was on its way once more, just time enough to grab a lung full of unpolluted air and drag one's polo neck over one's nose. There we would sit like some strange yash-macked tribe, eyes bulging yearning to inhale, but we dared not until we had no option. Danny the Greyhound would leer with satisfaction as yet again he had asserted his presence, 'Yes' that was some pungent git.

We lived not far from the racetrack that dad had rescued him from. Apparently, his running expertise did not match up to the antics of his overzealous sphincter and the poor brindle lad was to be put down.

It was decided he should feed on rag tripe from the local UCP (United Cattle Products) which he daily devoured with relish. Yes, he was a contented sod, what more could he possibly ask from life? There he laid resplendent on the carpet, full as a gun of his favourite noshes' every whim being catered for by this strange tribe of people, and never again would he have to chase around some stupid track after a bit of fur until his bollocks throbbed.

We had a large fenced off garden to the rear of the house, Danny loved his freedom, and he would roll on his back amongst the knee-high weeds kicking his legs in the air with glee chasing the odd Butterfly and of course, lying in wait for the assortment of cats owned by the two puffs next door, life was so, so good.

Wednesday was the day the bins were emptied, and we failed to notice that some whistling mind-dead plonker had left the side gate open. This fact did not escape Danny's attention, and he promptly legged it. Calling his name and banging all hell out of his food bowl with a spoon brought no response. "Never Mind," Mum said. "The greedy sod will come home when he's hungry." But why bother to come home for food when you know your own way to the UCP?

Poor mother, she was oblivious to the fact her street cred was about to be shagged up forever. It was only the frantic hammering on our posh front door that heralded the trauma she would never really recover from. And, years later her eyes would go glassy at the mere mention of Danny's name even though he was long gone. She was one of those women who cared greatly about how the world perceived her and with this in mind, she shoved on the compulsory purple feathered hat before she responded to the pounding of the door.

Opened it was, and there stood the toothless assistant of the UCP her gums all a quiver with agitation, steam was rising out of the collar of her stained white overall, her white trilby hat askew on her head. This was not a happy bunny. To mother's mortification, the woman proceeded to explain that "Your bloody big git of a dog is lying amongst the pies and tripe in my shop window, and he won't come out."

I really thought mother would expire on the spot, but she had to rally herself as by this time the said assistant was hysterical on our front doorstep, and neighbours were coming from behind lace curtains to find out why. With as much dignity as Mother could muster, she straightened her feathered hat, locked the door and stomped off grasping my hand with the toothless wonder in close pursuit.

The memory of what we saw as we turned the corner lives on, clear as if it were yesterday. A motley collection of amused spectators was gathered outside the tripe shop window, little kids chewing blackjack sweets howled with laughter, dear god this was better than being taken to the zoo. To my great dismay, many of my school chums were amongst the tittering throng and believe me for years after I was never able to forget that fateful day.

Fumbling for her keys (with greasy suspect fingers) the white-coated distraught poor bugger pushed her way through what was now a crowd, and we were all relieved to find ourselves on the inside of that peeling paint shop door. Now there is a mess, then there is a bigger mess, then there is the downright mayhem created by that brindled bugger. This boy of ours did not give a stuff as he lay full length in the window, strands of half-eaten tripe hanging from his jowls, his tail shattering the cold battered cod as he wagged it wildly at the delighted boys knocking on the window at him, 'yes', all his Christmas's had come at once, he was in heaven and was not about to have it stolen from him. No amount of shoving and coaxing by all three of us had any effect on him whatsoever, and I was instructed to climb into the window with him with what proved to be a failed attempt to shove out the grinning sod, this I did and promptly slid on my bum, aided by a steak and kidney pudding, do you know, if some enterprising soul had been prepared they could have sold tickets for that hilarious cabaret, unfurled so unexpectedly before their amused eyes that Wednesday afternoon.

Eventually, Danny did eat his fill and became a little bored with the silly sods laughing at him and when he felt he had made his point, he sauntered nonchalantly down from the mayhem he had created, farted loudly and headed for home.

To add insult to injury, Mother was strapped with a bill she found difficult to pay, but pay she did and not only with money. Wherever she went for years after people would bring up the subject of Danny's excursion to the tripe shop, she'd straighten her purple feathered hat and pretend it had happened to someone else.

It was only a matter of weeks after this fiasco that Danny disappeared forever, I never did find out where, but it was once again a Wednesday, so maybe the bin men had left the gate open again, but somehow, I doubt it.

I think it is more likely that a needle and a vet were involved, but oh, I did miss him!

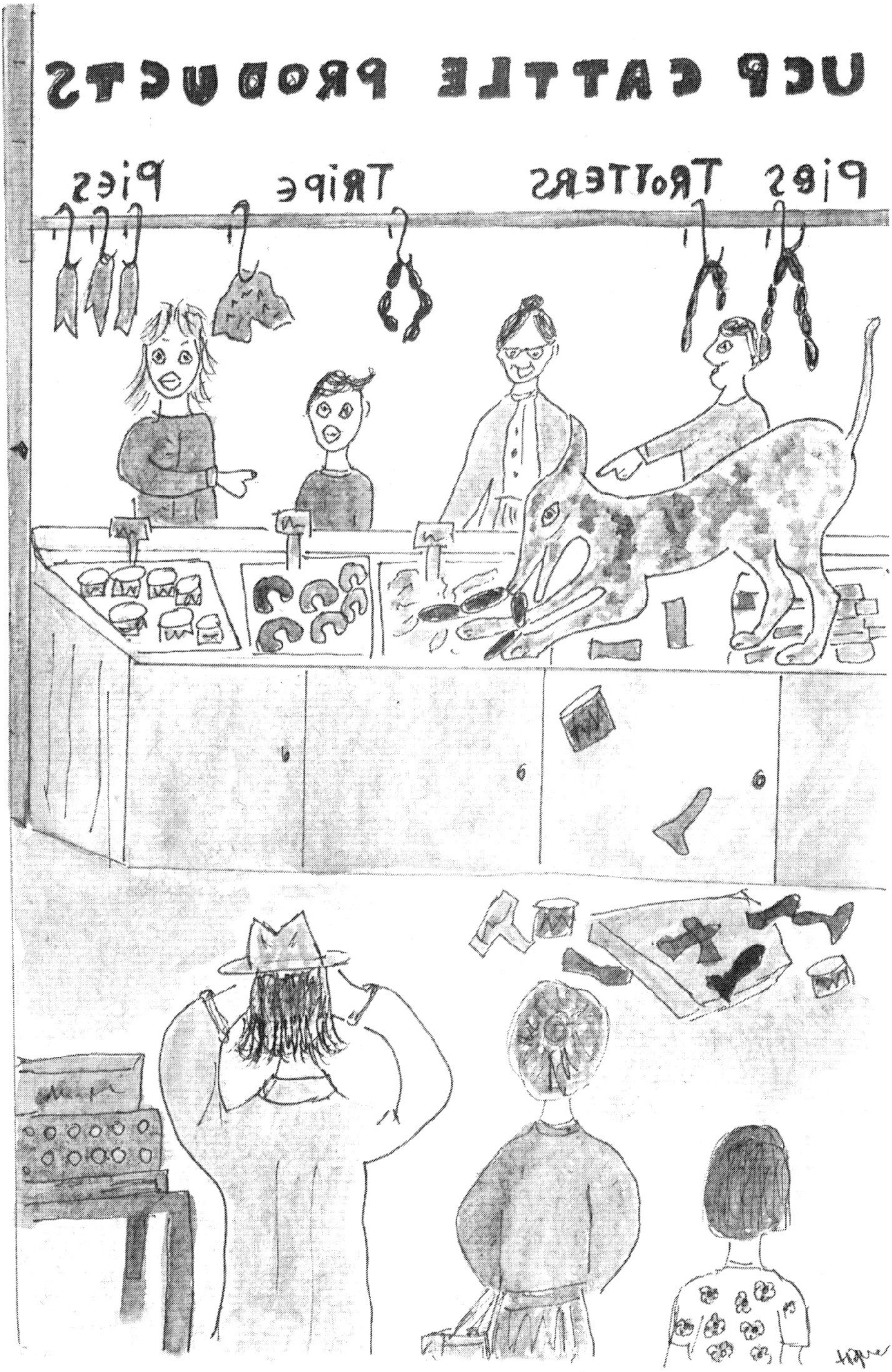
UCP CATTLE PRODUCTS
PIGS TROTTERS
TRIPE
PIES

The Grinning Custard

Poor Mother's street cred had been knackered for a long time, and now she slipped surreptitiously in and out of shops trying but failing miserably to be invisible. It was a rare foray from behind her posh front door that some leering wag would fail to mention Danny the farting tripe stealing brindled git that had been Mother's status downfall in the closeted gossiping village of 1954.

But the sniggers finally did cease, and she felt revived enough to go and work in the local confectioners. Boy…This was a happy time for me as at the end of each day she was allowed to bring home the leftovers. I swear to this day that being permitted to eat simultaneously a cream cake in both hands set me up on the road to ruin and shagged up forever my dream of a sylphlike figure. Blast those women!

Now, the baker toiled from 1 am in raging heat at the back of the shop never failing to please his customers who queued two-deep for his unending array of luscious cakes, bread and pies. Did this man ever sleep?

His speciality was baked Custard Tarts with melt in the mouth very deep, large pastry cases brimming with their secret recipe custard content and forgetting not the liberal sprinkling of Nutmeg… They were to die for, and he was justly proud of them.

He struggled down the steps with a huge tray of these delights, twenty-four in all from the oven…the motion of the journey from bake house to shop made the hot custard crack on the surface…but that mattered not, for soon they would all be sold to his salivating customers.

Safe on the shop counter they lay cooling whilst mother and the other assistant Freda had a breather between customers.

The Baker happened to be very antismoking, (unusual for those Post War years,) and so Freda found herself relegated to the backyard to drag the last puff of smoke from the woodbines she lived for.

Mother, alone in the shop waited for Freda's return and could not fail to notice that the Nutmegs steam arising from the custards was making her nose itchy. Suddenly, she had to steady herself against the counter's edge as the greatest sneeze of all time shook her ample body.

Reeking of woodbine Freda returned to find Mama ashen-faced and her mouth contorted in a rather strange fashion. Her intriguing behaviour was compounded by the fact that she was frantically poking the steaming custards with a skewer.

"Two Custards dear? Yes, they've just been made and they're bloody lovely." The gregarious Freda told the chap offering the half-crown, for the custard, pork pie and small loaf he held out his hand for a three penny bit change. Mother was still poking the confections and by now whatever the malaise was that so suddenly gripped her my God it had affected her speech also.

Fascinated by all this Freda kept an eye on Mum as custard after custard was sold "Bloody hell" she must have something really bad, not only did it make her eyes bulge, but it made her mouth go all frilly too. *"Best be careful I don't catch it"* were her compassionate thoughts as she gave Mum as wide a berth as possible under the constraints of behind that counter.

No one was to know that all hell was about to break loose as the trilby-ed gent was so disgusted that his brown brogued feet barely touched the wet paving stones. But he was on a mission – he'd tell the dirty sods.

He catapulted into the delicious aroma-ed shop, smacking the door back so hard it ricocheted on its hinges, and to Mother's dismay was to mutter the words that would end her days selling custards. As he slapped down the plate with mushed up remains of a once glorious treat, he screeched the immortal words "What the Hell is this?" Mother knew, for had she not been poking around in custard the last two hours, trying to find the plastic sods! Now, grinning for the entire world to see nestling on their bed of crumbs and sweetness were mother's gobblers. With as much dignity as anyone could muster (who had poppy eyes and frilly lips) Mother scooped up the offending gobblers took them into the shop back, rinsed the sods off and came out sheepishly. Lips frilly no more.

Profuse apologies would not suffice the nauseated trilby-ed one and under threat from a visit from the Public Health Inspector a rather less than happy baker promised him free goodies for six long expensive months.

Mam did not come home in her overall that night, it stayed in the shop where it belonged along with all the other goodies; I would never feast on again.

Once more her street cred was knackered, poor posh old Mum.

Feather Duster

Danny had vanished from our lives after his expensive escapade in the tripe shop. I never did find out what happened to the boy, but I suspect a needle could have been involved.

My passion for a canine companion in that dark quiet house and being unable to cuddle one made me a sad child.

Now, I went to school with a girl whose neighbour just so wanted someone to walk her terrier SPOT (who in much later years my Ziggy would resemble) and after knocking on her door, I was given the job and a three-penny bit. This lovely lady told me where the key was hidden and each day after school, I'd let myself in and walk Spot around the block.

On this particular day, it started raining very heavily, and the dog and I sheltered under an overhanging garden tree. Very shortly a man I recognised sheltered with his old dog and started to talk to me. I knew his face and his dog as he used to stand outside the schoolyard railings watching the children play.

At the age I am now, I would be instantly alerted to the fact he was a kiddy-fiddler; but then I had such sweet innocence. Then, he lunged at me clasping putrid wet lips on mine whilst his hand snaked up my school skirt, but gut instinct told me this was wrong. I pushed him away and ran around the corner to tell my mum. She did something never before known: she woke my father long before the time for his night shift at the engineering factory.

He came silently downstairs and asked me so gently to explain what had happened. I now knew it was serious as why was my daddy out of bed at 4 pm instead of 6 pm? I told him that the man lived directly opposite the school gates and that he was always watching the children.

Without another word, my dad strode out into the rain, dapper in his Crombie overcoat and trilby hat. Apparently, he knocked at the door of the perv's house, then knocked him down when he answered and when he was sprawled on his front step tied his ankles together with his own tie. In a vice-like grip, he dragged the sod on his back in the pouring rain up many a street and deposited him at the feet of the desk sergeant in the tiny police sub-station.

With the words "do something with this dirty bastard because he's touched my child" he gave the police his name and address and strode home. He waited for their enquiries. Twenty minutes later (how times have changed), I was sitting on the stairs whilst a policewoman asked me to show her what happened, with the aid of a boy and girl doll. What the hell was that thing stuck out between the boy doll's legs?

This done, I had my tea, and daddy went to slave for another 12 long night hours. That man was known to the police for 'child porn', etc, and it was not long before his house was up for sale, and I never saw him again.

So, my walks with Spot ended, and I still craved a dog of my own. Christmas morning came and a box covered in blankets was placed in my arms. What could this be, because the box was moving? Then, joy upon joy a little face peeped out and Jake, a Staffy puppy, was all mine.

He grew into a faithful, good-natured, strong dog, and I loved him dearly. Instead of tripe, my father decided he needed horse meat to reach his full-strength potential. Now, this particular day must have been a school holiday because my father took me to get Jake's food. Holding my hand, my father had to almost drag me into what appeared to be the bowels of hell. Millions of bluebottle flies buzzed in the gut-wrenching air, and bones of horses crawling with maggots awaited transport to the glue factory. Heart-breaking, all those old injured horses stood shackled waiting for death in the slaughter yard. The look in their eyes said it all: *"am I not worth a better end than* this?" My father bought the fresh meat sliced off the flank of what would have been a magnificent chestnut racehorse.

My heart broke, my stomach emptied, and I cried until my eyes were redraw. Nightmares sent my screams throughout the house, and no one came to comfort me. I never understood or forgave my father for exposing an animal-loving child to such horror. What on earth possessed him that day?

We had an outside toilet as well as the bathroom, and it was in this place that the horseflesh was hung high up on a wall. The place reeked as the meat went blue with rot, and it then turned to slime and dripped onto the floor where maggots devoured it. My mother would retch as she cut a chunk off, rinsed it under the tap and boiled it for Jake. God almighty, what disgusting ways to have.

Come the day at school when I had the most awful tummy cramps. I was 9 years old and knew nothing of the progression of a child to a woman. Then, horror of horrors, I thought I was injured or maybe even dying, worried sick at the sight of blood in my panties; why had I not been prepared for this event? Getting home that day, I went into that outside toilet to try to clean myself up with the newspaper held on a string behind the door. The pain doubled my little body in two, and the flies were drawn to me. The smell made me vomit, and the fear made me shake and cry. To this day periods are remembered with that smell, flies, maggots, rotting bits of horses, is it any wonder I have shall we call them, issues? Welcome to womanhood.

When it was nearing the time when my child was to menstruate, I told her all there was to know and not to be alarmed as it was totally natural and I bought her scented panties and pads, not the torn rags I had to use.

I've digressed again, haven't I? That's Bipolar for you; anyway, Mother used a feather duster to do her chores and would give Jake a quick furtle around the conkers as he passed her. This silly game went on for months and with this daily event fresh in his mind I took him to the park. In those days, there was a cottage with runabout hens, and one had escaped the privet hedge. Jake saw it before I did and stood ramrod still, feet bolted to the grass, tail in the air. *"That's the feathered bastard that's been furtling my bollocks for the last 18 months."* And, with this certainty in mind, he lunged at that poor hen. It was still in his vice-like grip after I had raced home with him, and my father had one hell of a job getting it out of his mouth. "Well, that's Sunday dinner sorted!" he said, as he started to pluck the now-dead hen. Is it any wonder I don't eat meat? But I must admit: the best cleaning device ever is a feather duster.

The Diamond Trees

I believe it was the winter of 1947 that saw the heaviest snowfall for many a year.

A freezing, cold five-year-old peeps from around a wartime blackout blind (the war was long over, and it was daylight outside, but these blinds stayed put for many a year, stealing the sunshine) Deep joy, snow as I had never known it lay thick on the ground, the trees in our back garden's orchard sparkled in the winter sunlight. A fairyland I wanted to play in and explore.

Not being allowed to disturb my parents on this Sunday morn (for the rut was in full swing) bare feet carried me down to the kitchen the freezing stone floor barely registering on tiny feet, blue with the cold. I dragged a chair in order to climb up to get the huge key that would let me escape into that white wonderland. With tiny hands stiff with the cold, I finally managed to turn the lock. The chair scraped back, and I opened the door, only to be faced with a wall of white snow which completely filled the door frame having been there all night, blown by the strong winds.

So, the snowman I so wanted to build would have to stay as flakes, for the time being, I hoped the winter sun would not melt the diamond trees before I could collect some and make a ring, and with a rumbling tummy, I wished my mummy would get up and feed me and a cosy warm fire would be nice too.

Many hours later, a probably satisfied mother made toast for me and my demented granddad; we sat together by a now blazing fire. All was well at last.

And Grandad smoked his pipe!

The Living Scarf

Oh! So excited, I was being taken by my mother to the annual village show, a rare treat for a little kid that always lived in quiet, semi-darkness.

Saturday came on wings of sunshine, mum and I crept around getting quietly ready as usual we did not want to awaken dad, asleep after Friday night's gruelling night shift in the engineering factory.

It was 1948 August to be precise, and who would have thought the summer would turn out to be in such stark contrast to the winter we had just endured – in that cold semi-dark mausoleum that we called home, I remember well wrestling one morning with a huge key that secured our back door and on finally opening it, I was amazed to see a wall of snow far taller than my five-year-old body. Amazement quickly conquered me then I proceeded to transport the lovely white stuff indoors and set about making a life-size snowman sitting in the brown leather armchair that stank of granddad's vile pipe tobacco. I did not feel any chillier as that house was as cold as a witch's left tit anyway, and mum had not made the coal fire yet.

My parents were speaking to each other again after many months of silence, me being their tiny message bearing go-between. Lust had finally overcome pride, and they were on a major rut in the locked bedroom as I sat on the freezing stairs with my Teddy and wondered what strange creature was in there with them, the one that grunted and squealed and later that afternoon I looked for it, once they had decided enough was enough, but of course, I never did find their loud companion!

Rosy-cheeked Mother came to make the fire that should have been keeping me warm for many hours. She said, "Hello" to the back of her father's head sitting in his favourite armchair. *Poor old bastard he's going senile* were her thoughts as she spied at his back, he was wearing his trilby and overcoat beside the spent membered fire grate. Getting no response and secretly hoping the bugger had finally snuffed it, she came in front of him with a mirror to check whether he was still breathing.

Her shrieks of horror brought father downstairs to investigate and with mute dismay, they spied the latest creation of their daughter's bored, stunted little life. Resplendent sat my life-size snowman kitted up nicely in Granddad's clothes taken from the cloakroom under the stairs, it sported a pipe that belched no foul-smelling smoke and had not melted my man one little bit, Granddad was still in bed wrapped up warm, and I told you it was cold in that bloody strange house. So much so that I could draw pictures on the ice on the inside of my bedroom window.

But now I was lovely and warm, excited to proudly wear the crocheted mauve dress my great aunt had laboured with love to create for me. Skipping behind my feather hatted mother the sound of the show greeted my ears, ears that were only used to the constant silence of that cold dark house. 'Yes', I loved every smell, sight and sound. I gazed at canaries singing in show cages bearing blue or red rosettes. Cattle, horses, sheep, cats, dogs, and flowers oh what exciting wonders were before my greedy child's eyes that summer's day in 1948?

Now, each year a different celebrity was given the honour of opening the county show, and this time it was a well-known zoo man from the TV called George Cansdale. Along with the other little kids, I sat crossed-legged on the soft sweet-smelling grass and watched with wide-eyed wonder as a scruffy little lad was handed a bush baby to cuddle. This was great, I wonder if I'll get something to hold, I thought. With theatrical flair, the zoo man reached into his final container and pulled out his pride and joy. What happened next lived on in my horrified memory not even to be erased by the E.C.T. I endured many years later. This long undulating chunk of living malevolence was draped around my neck like a living football scarf. Cruel black eyes stared into mine and petrified I wriggled from underneath its mighty weight and legged it. Mother standing gossiping with another parent failed to notice her galloping offspring shoot, ashen-faced, right past her.

Soon, all the stewards of the ground were looking for me and tannoys announced the loss of a child. Still unfound, my mother had to go home alone to face dad and explain this, her latest cock up. Dreading the consequences she knew so well she fumbled in her copious handbag for her door key. How the hell could she lie her way out of this one? The resulting inquisition and following months of torturous silence were bad enough, but bloody hell she would have to do without a leg over until her naughty bits throbbed with longing.

Sitting waiting on the back doorstep I heard the front gate close then her feet crept over the cobbled side path, God she was getting too bloody close for comfort now, she must be as quiet as possible and let her husband slumber on at least that would delay the fate she so dreaded. But the side gate did creek open, and I don't know if the sound I heard escape from her lips was one of relief or anger. Anyway, she cuffed me smartly around the earholes, then hugged me, then wept and told me not to tell my father.

That afternoon was to set the pattern for a lifetime's fear and revulsion of all reptiles, pity I was going to marry the human equivalent of one some 10 years later, and at a much, much later date actually own one, a monster of nineteen foot and still growing.

The Sewing Moths

She was a rum sod that mother of mine. What she lacked in looks and personality, she more than made up for with devious revenge.

She and my father could not have been more miss matched He was tall, elegant, articulate, funny and clever whilst she pottered around him, this plain, thin-legged, large chested, strange pigeon of a woman.

Dad saw the advert for Saville Row suits advertised in the local rag, apparently, some old boy had died and was so conveniently exactly the same size as him. Off he trots and comes back beaming with his bargain. "Well try them on," said Mum hoping he would look a plonker. But NO! He looked suave and handsome. They fitted a treat, and she was brassed off to some tune.

Sunday mornings in summer he would take me mushroom and blackberry picking on the local golf links, and sometimes he'd carry a spade with him, then I knew he would dig up wild briars from the wood that skirted the mushroom field. We'd get home and mum would set too with the duck eggs and bacon, never since have I tasted mushrooms like them.

"Come in the garden, and I'll show you how it's done" many neighbours jealous of how splendid his standard roses were, wished to know the secret about to be unfurled to me. The wild briar was firmly planted with lots of bone meal from the local slaughter yard. How I hated that vile, death reeking place. What on earth possessed him? To ever take me there. To this day, my fertile mind can still conjure up the stench of rotting flesh and the heart-wrenching sight of petrified horses awaiting their share of death.

Harry Slack was the name of the equine executioner who had no love or respect for the poor souls as they waited in the baking heat, sometimes straining on their restraints if they had the energy to. Not only did the stench of blood but pure fear filled the air. A bluebottle tormented the barely alive poor, poor horses. They all awaited their turn for their pathetic misery to end, but what tore at my young heart was the sight of a starved mare, bones jutting out, trying to feed her tiny foal, from milk long dried out! She let him suckle for comfort and tried to nuzzle him to his feet when he collapsed at the side of her.

I begged and begged my father to let me have both mother and child. "We could get them well Dad, feed them with lots of hay and let them live in one of our sheds safe and warm," and so I went on and on. Of course, the answer had to be a firm NO, but to my desperate caring young mind, I thought he was just being mean. And I despised him for years because of it. Now, of course, I understand the impossibility of my demands, and I'm sure if he could have given them a home, he would have done.

When I was a child in the forties/fifties it was usual to have milk floats, coal waggons and rag and bone carts pulled by horses in various bad conditions. Rag and bone men were known for being cruel to their starved animals, horses were so worn out, their tired heads low down, dejected, frightened and hungry they battled on each and every day in all weathers, unloved and beaten, often with iron bars or staves of wood. Their bodies and heads would give evidence of regular mistreatment, some wounds brand new and bleeding others trying without much success to heal in the infected skin. The loads they had to pull would get heavier and heavier as the day wore on. No water or hay to keep them going in the baking sun or a blanket to shelter them in blizzard snow, but the callous bastard who held the reins, and the most utilised of whips always had an ale at his side. You would see these spindly-legged souls faltering on the cobbled streets without a kind word or anxious look from anyone, except me. My tiny young heart would tear open at the sight of yet another sad tormented creature, and I so wished to help, but how could a tiny child make any difference when no one would listen to her?

Out shopping one day with my mother, I once again saw the dreaded rag and bone cart. Its driver was well known for his ill-treatment of his staggering animal pulling a great weight of scrap metal (also the vile lazy driver), and that's how it was to be until the end of its torturous life. It swayed and fell down on the wet cobbles, legs splayed, and that cruel bastard jumped from the cart, picked up a steel bar and proceeded to beat and kick the old animal to its feet. It could not, would not stand and yet it was still beaten about its tired face and body. No one except me, a tiny girl, tried to stop this example of terrible cruelty, needless to say, my tears of compassion and kicks of hatred to his shins were ignored. Eventually, the ragman had finally decided the animal would be of no use to him anymore and went to find a phone box to call Harry Slacks slaughter yard.

My mother sheltered me under her black umbrella, but I broke away from her grasp and pushed through the gawping crowd to get to the sad sight.

Now I'd got in my little pink raffia bag my Wednesday treat for being a good girl, a rosy red apple (the highlight of my week), and this I offered to Dobbin, for I'd seen my daddy do this to other horses on our walks out together, now this was wartime, and everything was rationed, but my mother exchanged one of her precious food coupons for the apple from the greengrocer to keep her sacred promise to me. Dobbin did not know what to do with it, so I bit a piece off and placed it in his gasping mouth. It seemed to just stay there for ages, unknown, unchewed and then he must have understood, FOOD!! Soon, he was biting pieces of my offered treat, chewing as best he could with that awful spiked bit tearing at his torn mouth. All this time, I stood and stroked his skeletal face and neck, telling him of my childish love and concern for him. I was by now wet through and filthy, much to my mother's disgust. The ragman returned and was the victim of five-year-old revenge and temper shouting "Cruel horrid man" I once again kicked his shins repeatedly to the applause of the amused crowd, and no one attempted to stop me.

Harry Slacks waggon rumbled across the wet cobbles, and I knew my lovely friend and I were soon to be parted. A swift bullet in that old head ended a life that should never have been lived with such cruelty, and the rain washed the blooded cobbles until there was nothing left to be seen of the tragedy that had been.

I often wondered how many years Dobbin had slaved for that excuse of a human being, now at last his torment would finally be over. At last, released from the shafts that still held him, chains were placed around his hooves; he was lifted towards the cloudy sky and unceremoniously thrown into the back of Harry Slacks' truck. I suppose he was to join the other corpses back at the slaughter yard ready to be stripped of their flesh and their hooves that had trudged the cobbles in all weathers to be sent for glue and their blood and bone to make into bone meal to feed the prize roses that my father and other keen gardeners grew.

Seventy-three years have passed since that day, and I now sit in my comfy warm room and watch the torrential rain of February 2020 lash my windows. Tears of a child that now belong to an old lady fall down a creased old face, and the compassion for a beaten old horse still grips my heart just as it did all those years ago.

But I believe that all creatures go to a place of peace when they leave this world, just as you or I do. Maybe, I will find that old horse again in a field of flowers, lying contented, unharmed on sweet grass, but I doubt he would recognise the old lady offering him a rosy apple as the little girl of yesteryear who gave him his one and only apple seventy-three years ago. Or will he?

Yet again I have digressed so back to rose propagation!

His nimble strong fingers would strip off all of the briar's shoots and leaves – all that had to be left was a straight tall standard briar to work on. He'd make an I-shaped cut just slicing the bark then he would fold back the sides and place in a bud from a cultivated bush, fold over the flaps of briar and secure the parcel with raffia. In time, this would create a magnificent specimen and as he would use buds from different coloured parent plants, his creations were unusual, to say the least. A profusion of glorious roses, two or possibly three complementing shades, a joy to behold and one that pissed off the rose growing vicar across the road.

But sometimes Dad would go out without me or Mum. She never knew where… But I did! I followed him once at Mother's insistence to a quiet place by the river where he lit a cigarette and read from his book in the sunshine away from her, before returning many hours later, looking somehow complete.

Suspicious and devious she always was, and she decided those bloody suits were making him look too bloody good. A bit of crafty alteration was called for.

Dad worked permanent nights at the engineering factory and whilst he slumbered during the day, she set about the beautiful garments with gusto. Back they went in that huge carved wardrobe, the wardrobe that held a secret they were never to find out. A secret only I and my teddy knew.

And my mother awaited the tornado she had brought upon herself!

Days later (a Sunday), Dad's up and shaved pomaded to hell (and this was in the days when only puffs smelt like whore's handbags), but he was a real man, and he was about to get dressed up, go out and bloody prove it by having just one pint of bitter before lunch, in the Red Lion pub.

The starched shirt so much a labour of my mother's love was in place, now the subdued paisley tie, of course, knotted to perfection. Diamond ring on pinkie finger and his one pint of bitter beckoned.

Reaching into the dark camphorated depths of the mystical wardrobe, he selected the suit of the day; it was only as he was zipping up the fly that he caught his reflection in the cheval mirror. I can hear the bellow of rage again, so many years later. Christ, mother must have been quaking in her shoes, at the same time as wetting her bloomers.

Dragging up his jacket, he stomped downstairs and stood in front of the guilty party, for once he was bloody speechless, but his face said it all, the veins were standing proud on his throbbing temples as he pointed down to what his senses still could not believe. Christ, he looked funny, but it was more than my life was worth to laugh as Dad in a temper was a case of light the blue touch paper and sod off…Quick! Yet never, ever was he a violent man to us.

Now, I knew why she had sat with needle and thread and sworn me to secrecy. A fine example of what a spiteful woman can do was unfurled before my very young eyes. For even though dad had pulled up his trousers properly, whilst one leg reached the top of his black socked foot, the other showed at least three inches of hairy leg, above the sock top. That crazy bat had taken a good ten inches from just one trouser leg and then God help me sewn back on the sodding turn-up.

He cavorted with rage as the following strangled words escaped my mother's lying lips, "I told you we had moths" galloping upstairs he plundered the mahogany wardrobe for his Saville Row beauties and 'yes' those industrious moths and laboured so hard and altered every bloody pair of trousers. His sartorial knock'em dead days were over.

He wept with frustration at not being able to squeeze the life from her scraggy lying neck.

They did not speak for many months after that but I can remember him putting me on his knee that very afternoon holding me tight and saying "I'm in purgatory pet, I'm in purgatory." Little child that I was I did not know such big words, but I held him tight anyway as his tears of frustration fell on my hair. But I know the meaning of such a grown-up word now, for purgatory is what I've felt for most of my bipolar life.

And when I crept into the magic wardrobe a tormented tiny girl trying to find peace, I also used to whisper to the moths that could sew. Maybe they could teach me! So I taught myself and eventually became an expert at it.

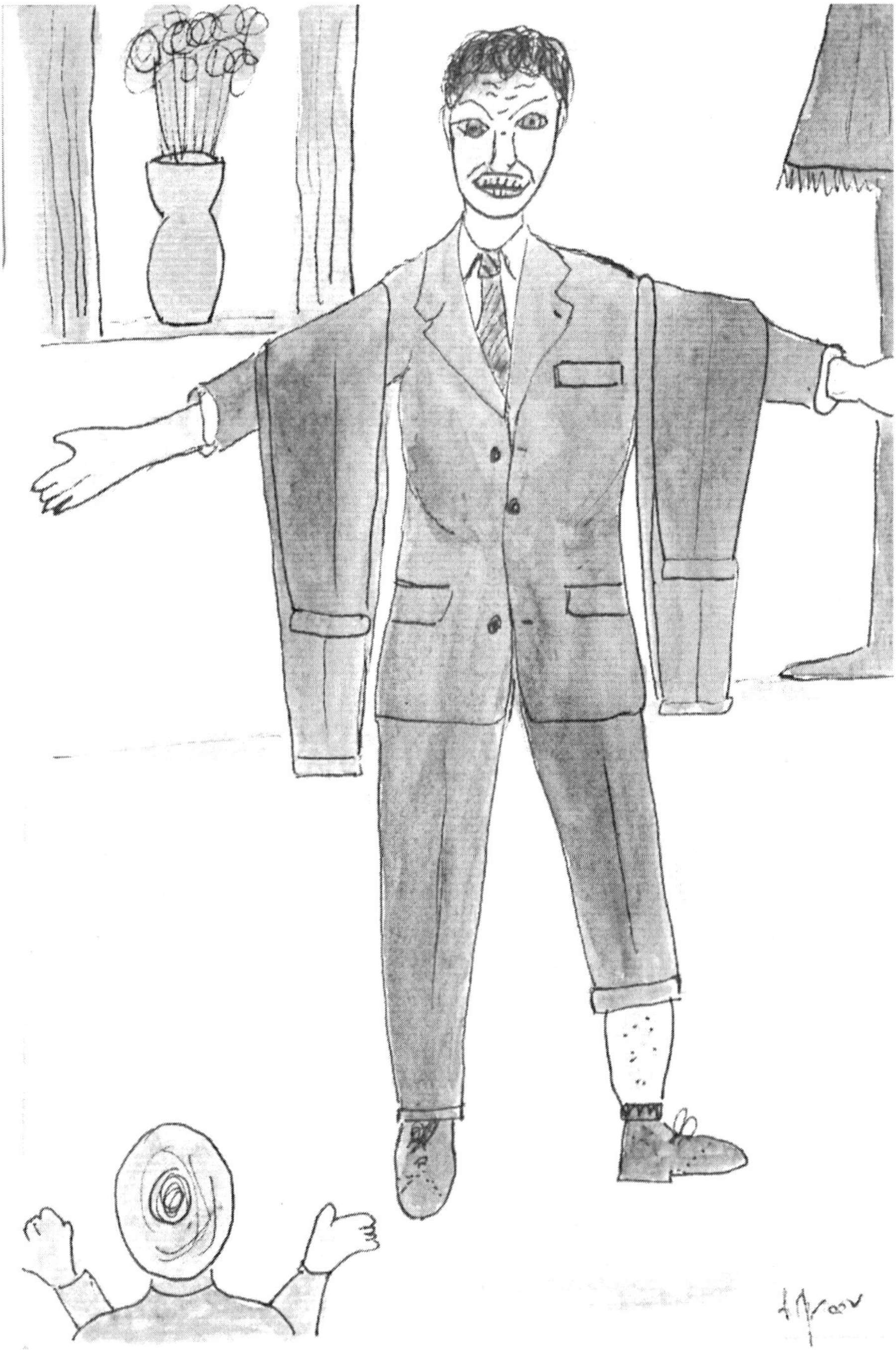

Where Are You, You Little Bugger

I could hear my mother bustling about and calling my name and getting more irate by the minute. Father was out on one of his auction jaunts which always brassed her off, so I used to just vanish, seemingly into thin air.

Many months before I'd been exploring as little bored lonely kids do, and I decided the giant mahogany wardrobe in my parents' room was my next port of call. Climbing in I was almost suffocated by the camphor used in a vain attempt to kill the sewing moths. Oh yes! I'd have a good old route in here, I'd try Mother's only pair of best shoes, why could they not be pretty ones with high heels like my friend's mummy wore? How the hell was I to know at such an innocent age that Rosie's mummy's follow me home and fuck me shoes assisted her earnings in the local box making factory as she sauntered the dark nights' streets a bus ride away from our village, as a lady of the night.

Now, then what's this funny handle in such a strange place for? Let's pull it and see. I can't remember now whether I was afraid or just plain nosey as before my very young eyes the back of the wardrobe slid to one side. It was so dark in that bedroom anyway, as the blackout blinds left over from the war were never removed from the windows and stayed down day and night, summer and winter, don't ask me why. I've told you already it was a dysfunctional family or to put bluntly a collection of bloody dingbats. Scampering out I went to get the torch which was a necessity in the dark silent hell hole I called home. Back in the wardrobe I climbed, the watery beam of light guiding my way and there before me was my dream come true. A secret place where the buggers couldn't reach me, I saw another handle, one pull, and I was trapped behind the sliding door.

When you're a child, (a strange one at that) you don't realise the danger like the mind of a full shilling adult would. Dear God when I think back, I could have died in that tiny hidden room, no one would hear my cries of despair and fear as the walls, ceiling and floor were covered in some strange, thick, nicotine-stained wadding.

With the beam of that cheap torch, I was able to make out a canvass folding bed a kerosene lamp and a large chamber pot and a yellow newspaper dated some fifty years earlier. And there I lay alone on that canvass bed, its metal frame making my thin little back sore, but I did not care as I made lighted pictures on the walls and ceiling with the borrowed torch.

Time without number I used this retreat from the reality I hated and one by one my dollies and teddies made it their home also. I'd hear mother calling my name and getting more and more frustrated, I did not give a sod I'd come out when I was good and ready and not before.

They never did find out about my room and my adult mind has often wondered why it was there. Did it once hold a conscientious objector or was it to conceal an escaped prisoner on the run? It was a very odd, spooky old house, and I never did find out the reason for that secret place; all I know is that it comforted the troubled child I once was.

Many years later, I found the courage to go back. I was trying so desperately to cleanse myself of the recurring dream that haunted my night and made me afraid to sleep. My father's harsh words to his broken child "And who are you?"

The door was opened by yet another new owner, she took pity on the crying young woman who stood on her step and begged to be allowed in. I remember her holding my hand as she showed me around, rightly proud of her improvements to the old house. Yes, she had turned a sanity sapping mausoleum into a home full of colour and laughter, the old building deserved that. And finally, I stood with her in what was once my parents' bedroom, the wars blackout blinds were no more, and sunshine smiled in every corner. The stately wardrobe was gone forever and where my secret haven had been was now a pretty pink ensuite bathroom.

I told her of my tortured past in that house, a tiny lonely little girl who locked herself away in the secret room hugging her teddy, trying not to hear her mother's insistent call.

Bless her, this stranger wept with me as I buried the ghosts of my past. I walked in the sunshine out of the door I'd been banished from many, many years ago. That night I was not afraid to sleep my ghosts had been laid to rest at long last, and I never had that tortured reoccurring dream again. No more would that cold voice say "And who are you?" As with yet more broken bones asking for help that I was never given, I stumbled away in the rain.

I'd had yet another beating from than the man that was supposed to love and cherish me. Nothing could be further from the reality that was my life. From the ages of sixteen to twenty-seven, I endured hell with no one to help or support me because I'd made my bed, hadn't I?

By the time I trudged in the rain to my parents' home, my feet were bleeding as he had thrown me out into the evening storm without shoes or a coat. Eventually, I reached where I'd hoped I'd be helped, even though many years had passed since my father disowned me. And I don't really blame him because like a stupid, hot-headed, arrogant, know-it-all young girl I chose Rasputin AKA my husband instead of the sanctuary offered to me by my parents, me and my baby girl. I left with that man who my father had warned me would "Knock me to the ground and kick me whilst down there." That prophecy was to come true numerous times over the eleven years it took me to escape his torture. My husband took me and our baby to live in a ratty spare room of his father's. His dad was okay with me, but his mother was a vile, chinless, Welsh witch who also made my life hell. I could do nothing right for her and to be honest I did make a lot of mistakes, because what did I know? A sixteen-year-old girl who had never even held a baby until I was presented with one, MINE.

I've digressed again, haven't I?

So, I climbed the three steep steps up to the beautiful leaded glass front door, lifted the heavy knocker and heard it boom in the front hall. No answer, so I went around the back, up to three steps and knocked on the wooden door. The kitchen light went on, the key turned in the lock, the door opened and there he stood, the Daddy I used to adore. He looked down at the blooded wet shivering, broken thing that he knew to be his child and said the words to destroy me "And who are you?" My mother came scurrying to the steps and demanded to know "What do you think you're doing, upsetting your father like this?" The door closed in my face, and, bare-footed, I stumbled the long, painful walk back to where I lived, it could never be called a home.

I was quaking with fear as I slipped in the unlocked door, no light was on, and I suppose he was in bed in yet another drunken stupor. Please, God, he did not wet the bed tonight and I would have to lay there in his foul-smelling urine until he got up and went to work. I did not dare to disturb him or I would end up with yet another good smacking.

"And where the fuck have you been? Out to see your bloody fancy man have ya?" Oh, Jesus, he had been sat in the quiet dark, waiting to pounce on me when I got back. I wet myself with fear, but you could not tell as it just blended with the rain dripping off me. He threw me like a rag doll up and down, bounced me off the walls and did not even stop when the noise made by my screams woke up my children who begged Daddy to stop. Eventually, he did, I cuddled my little ones who'd witnessed domestic violence many times before. The police could or would not do anything as it was deemed 'a domestic' in other words, I was owned by this cruel bastard the same as the table and chairs, and he could do as he wished with me. And, he did for eleven long, long years.

And the nightmares started. I was wet and hurt. I'd hear the boom of the door knocker and my father's words, so indifferent, so cold: "And, who are you?" I'd wake in tears from one nightmare to a living one that was my life. But the visit to my old family home years later, to be told to knock at the door again, and to have that wondrous woman greet me with such kindness as she hugged me and invited me into its pretty warmth, drove away the night terrors and never again did the Daddy I once adored say "And, who are you?"

Honky Tonk Mama

Winifred Atwell's records often played on the radiogram that graced one of our front rooms in our spacious house, this was a marvellous piece of furniture comprising of two parts: a very large speaker of burr walnut, and a smaller matching cabinet that housed the turntable, with the bottom section being a cupboard for the vinyl 78s records.

This boogie-woogie music could only be played at the weekends or on a summer evening when my father had left for work, and I was allowed the treat of staying up later. Him sleeping all day (before yet another night's toil) really put a stop to lots of noisy things I wished to do, wake him I must not as his sleep was precious!

I really, really loved the raucous boogie-woogie type of music even then and if it was played on a Saturday when we had Quality Street chocs, the combination of the two pleasures was absolute bliss to little me.

My mother did not have any skills to speak of, but she could knock up a wonderful Christmas cake, and one would be made each September. She would return to it weekly and tip a couple of spoons full of brandy into skewered holes. Delicious! The best part for me though was the wonderful almond paste, thick on the top. This she made herself from ground almonds, etc., no packet muck for my father.

On my mother's side were relatives who lived in Eyam Derbyshire, a long bus ride from the family home where we lived. This delightful little village was once nearly wiped out by the Black Death, a plague of 1665. (We now have in 2021 COVID-19). And this lovely old cake decorating aunt of my mother was a direct descendant of the Friths of 1665. The Friths were heroes, as they stayed in the village (whilst others fled) to keep people safe. They were left daily food at fences from the surrounding villages, but they did not all survive, but those that did were treasured and respected for their bravery.

My great aunt lived there (who up until this visit I had yet to meet) and had apparently been a Master Confectioner, who excelled at her craft. Now, why had it taken seven years for me to be introduced to this kindly old lady? I'll never know! This was the reason for the snowy journey: to have this sweet old lady ice, to perfection, mother's Christmas cake. This was done and duly brought home when we finally left the village, and it was a masterpiece. Such a shame really to spoil its beauty by cutting into it and tasting Mother's finest Christmas cake.

It had started to snow heavily as the single-decker bus headed into the Peak District and as mother disembarked from the vehicle, she sprained her ankle very badly on the snow concealed pavement's edge. Waiting relative's arms supported her to their little cottage, some distance away twinkling Christmas lights welcomed us through mullioned windows. Safe and warm inside with mugs of hot cocoa defrosting our hands, mother and I relaxed in the welcoming front parlour.

In those days, a front parlour was kept for use only on special occasions, and this must have been deemed one of them. Gracing one corner of the chintzy room stood an upright piano, polished to within an inch of its life the red mahogany reflected the fire's glow. Then, I heard the words I did not fully understand "Give us a tune Eddie." This request was aimed at my mother, why? Straightening the compulsory purple-feathered hat that rarely left her head, mother sat on the pianos stool and on lifting the piano's lid, slid her fingers lovingly over the keys. This was all new to me, and then a wonderful thing happened. This dowdy mother of mine, who I believed (up until this point) could do sod all, made the gleaming instrument come to life. With fingers flying across its keys, she belted out Boogie Woogie just as good as Winifred Atwell played at home. With stomping uninjured foot, she thrashed the pedal, feathered head bobbed to the music; she could play without any sheet music. All the years I'd been alive, that wonderful talent had lay dormant and after that night, I never had the pleasure of listening to her skill on the keyboard again. Indeed, it was never, ever mentioned, I told you it was a strange family.

Whilst we were in Eyam for a few days, Mother's ankle recovered a bit, but the snow fell thick and deep, making the Peak roads impassable, so returning home had to be delayed, and I loved this so rare adventure.

Most homes in those far back days had outside 'privies' (a toilet at the bottom of a cobbled yard). Not a toilet as we know and appreciate today but a hole in the ground surrounded with bottom high bricks and a piece of wood placed on top cut out to allow one's body contents to fall through the hole. These detestable places were blue bottle heaven, and the buzz of them was constant. A nail on the back of the door held cut up pieces of newspaper, with which to clean one's bum. This was farcical really, as the black print was left on bare buttocks, and if you ever got bored with life, and with the help of a mirror, you could read your own arse.

One freezing night, I just had to hurry down the yard to that dreaded place, I'd been given stewed plums, and they had given me the incredible squits. Not wishing to mess my nic nics, I swiftly climbed onto the wooded plank that was too tall for a little lass and in so doing got a bloody great splinter stuck in my bum. I suppose I shouted in pain and whilst reaching for a newspaper square hanging on the bottom half of a stable type door, I saw what was to frighten the life out of me. If I did not have the incredible craps beforehand, the sight before me would certainly have ensured them. A row of eyes reflecting the kerosene lamps flickering light stared at me over a snow-topped dry stone wall. I was far too terrified to leave my wooden perch, and it was only when a moo broke the silence of the night that I realised that neighbouring cows had come to investigate my shout of pain. I scurried back inside the house hoping to hear my mother play again, of course she never did. A mug of cocoa was placed in my hands and when drunk, a gentle hand removed the splinter from my bum. I went to bed cosy in a feathered haven, I'd decided not to try to read my bum as I'd had enough excitement for one night.

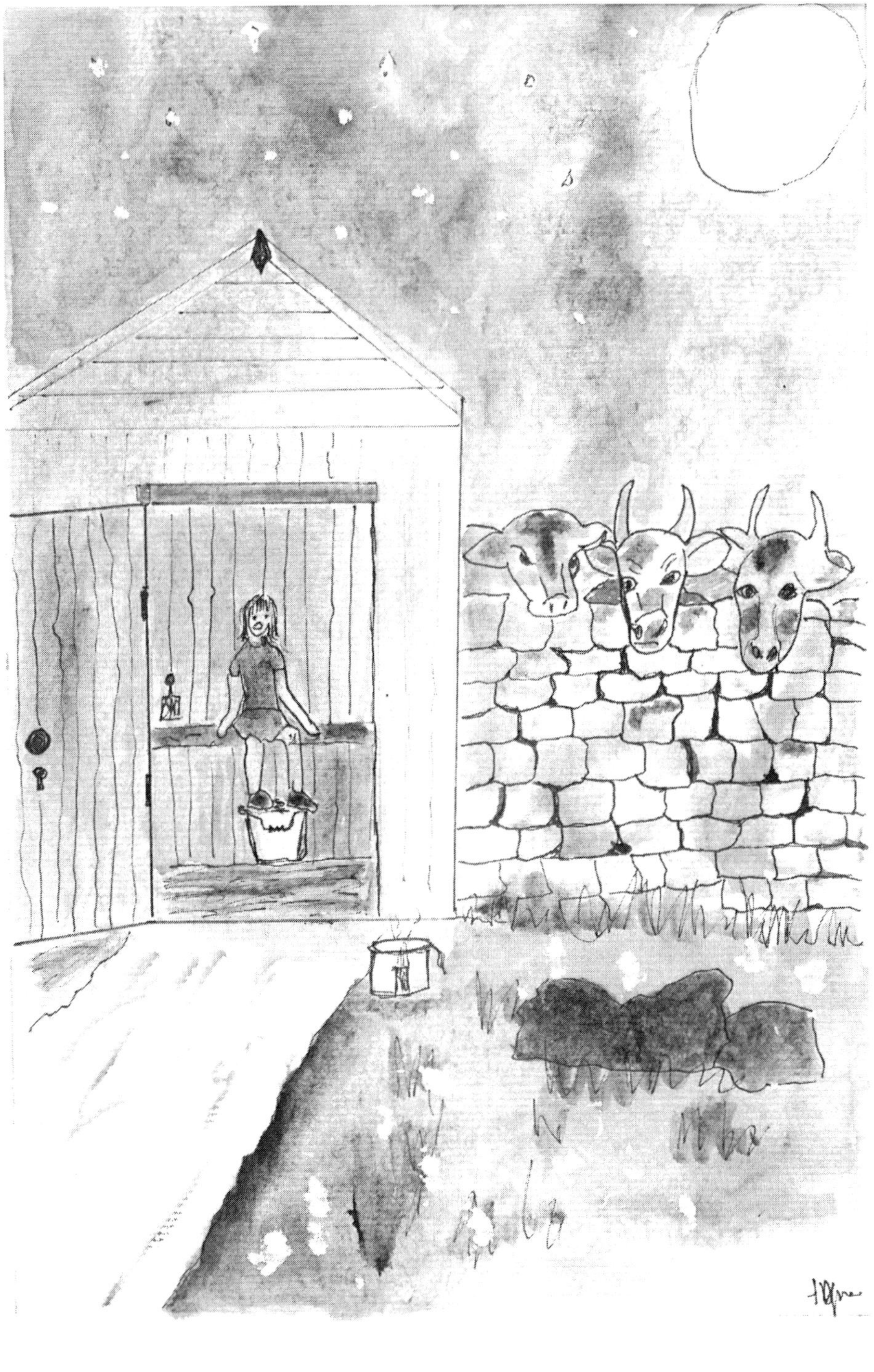

Sugar

Oh! How my daddy must have suffered all those long lonely nights slaving in solitude in a huge room in the engineering factory, standing for twelve-hour shifts on legs that were rotting.

You see my daddy had varicose ulcers on his lower legs and feet so bad that the ankle bone protruded through the rotting flesh. He'd come home in the morning before I left for school, and I'd watch him remove his shoes and socks (that were slippery with matter) and start to unwind the yards of elastocrepe bandages that held the pieces of lint, that in turn held the St James Balm Ointment, that in turn, held my daddy's broken flesh. It would adhere to the lint, and the bone would be sticking out, and my daddy must have been in agony even though he did not let me see. But I knew, little as I was; I recognised torment, but only fully understood the extent of true pain when I was giving birth at nearly seventeen years of age. Silly, stupid girl!

The ointment daddy used was useless, and the ulcers just got worse and worse, until it was discovered that gangrene had set in. I don't know just how long penicillin had been available when daddy's ulcers started to go gangrenous, but it was decided to use this wonder drug, and the outcome was very nearly a dead daddy. Almost at once after administration, my father went into an asthma attack so severe that it brought on a small heart attack, stabilised, at last, my daddy awaited with trepidation the loss of both his legs in three days' time. My mother took me to see him in the Infirmary where he was about to have a double amputation of his legs, below the knee. This would of course alter all of our lives forever as he would be a cripple in a wheelchair, unable to work hard as he'd always done. Work to provide the roof over our heads, work to provide the clothes we wore, work to provide the shoes on our feet, work to provide the food in our tummies. Work, work, work, never-ending work. In excruciating pain.

Bless my daddy, in his hospital bed, afraid of all the tomorrows to come, he told me stories to make me laugh as I was cuddled in his arms as always. It was difficult to listen properly as music blared from a wall-hung tannoy playing the Sabre dance over and over and over, until it drove my poor daddy crazy, to this day I only have to hear this rotten tune and once again I'm little, sitting on his hospital bed, afraid of what was to come. But, unknown to us at that time, destiny was about to be averted.

Soon, it was time to go home as daddy was to have his operation that afternoon, and he must have been petrified at the forever outcome.

Then, an Indian doctor, a rarity in those post-war days, who had never seen my daddy before, stood at the end of his bed reading his notes, then he very politely asked if he could see the infected legs. He examined them for quite some time, bending down to sniff at the infected skin before he said the words that would change my daddy's destiny forever.

"Sir, have you ever tried sugar?" he asked. "You see, in my country, we are not blessed with modern medicine and must rely on tried and trusted natural remedies. If sugar is sprinkled over the open flesh it will draw out all the impurities. Then it will form a crust that can be peeled off, taking the badness with it, and the skin will start to granulate. This has to be repeated times without number over the weeks and months, and soon you will realise that not only are the ulcers getting smaller and less angry and infected, but the pain is much reduced. I suggest dear sir that my method is used before such drastic action as amputation is resorted to." With this, he bade Daddy farewell and was never, ever seen by anyone again. No one seemed to know who this mystery doctor was when my daddy asked about him. Now I ask you, was he real or a figment of my daddy's fevered state of mind? Was he sent to help or was he daddy's Guardian Angel, much the same as I have one some seventy years later?

Daddy hobbled to the ward phone on the wall and sent for a taxi to take him from that Sabre dancing hell hole. My mother and I could not believe it when he entered the dining room where we sat in tears believing that at the precise time my daddy was having his legs chopped off.

So, he did what the Indian doctor said and religiously applied the sugar to his ulcers and sure enough, the outcome was just as promised. And, whilst the new skin bore its story of gross pain from many previous years, it became strong, and the ulcers became a distant memory, Daddy was able to resume his work, so grateful to be pain-free, at long last.

So, over the years whenever I've been told of someone suffering from the same complaint as my brave, hardworking daddy, I tell them of the mystical turbaned Doctor, whose knowledge, compassion and wise words saved my daddy from the life of a cripple. And yes, the remedy worked for the people I told also. So, if you are a sufferer, please try daddy's remedy. It works! Bye, bye.

P.S. Once my daddy was well enough he bought a gift for the wondrous Asian doctor who had saved his legs from mutilation. On enquiring of him at the hospital he was told many times that they had NEVER had an Asian doctor on their staff. He was never found, Daddy brought the gift home with him and we kept it as a memento of just what a guardian angel can do.

14 August 1960

My mind goes back to that blazing hot Saturday afternoon fifty-two years ago. I was all alone as pains tore through my just seventeen-year-old body. My mother was visiting my father in Bagley Sanatorium, where he was waiting to die from gangrene of the lungs. Dear God, he was a skeleton in torment, and yet against all the odds, thanks to me, die at that time he did not.

Needless to say, the thing I was married to was in the pub our house did not have a phone, and I was a terrified child in pain about to have a child.

Picking up the battered brown cardboard suitcase that held a nightie and a couple of terry-towelling nappies, I staggered up the road, it was boiling hot, and the melting road tar made me feel so nauseous.

To this very day, its smell transports me back and once again I'm that young girl alone and wracked with pain. Begging for help that never, ever came. Every few yards, I'd have to sit and rest on a wall and was told many times to bugger off and, after what seemed forever, I reached the bus stop across a busy main road. It must have been apparent to anyone that I was in dire straits and yet no one held out a supporting hand or gave a kind word. Never have I been so alone. In the 1960s, I was considered scum, being a child myself with a huge tummy to carry around. I managed to crawl onto the bus, but the callous conductor swiftly rang the bell throwing me onto my knees on the platform; It hurt, and he did not help me to my feet.

My waters had not broken, but the pains were from hell. Why, oh why had I believed that sod when he'd told me I would not get pregnant? I was a completely innocent and untouched child when he gave me my first experience of sex; it was painful, smelly and vile. Thank God that in later years I was to learn the true beauty of making love.

Finally, I got myself to the maternity hospital and really thought that I would die from the pain. These nursing strangers gave me an enema and horror upon horror stood in the toilet doorway as my bowels exploded. I don't know which was worse, the embarrassment or the pain that would continue for many, many more hours. I tried my best to lie still as instructed as they shaved me, but ended up with a few little cuts. At that stage, little did I know of the big cuts that were to follow and the twenty-odd stitches that would be needed to close them up and repair me. And each time, the doctor put in the anaesthetic, he got a drenched gown. When I asked about this, he laughingly told me I'd just spent three pence. What a nice way of putting the fact I'd wee weed on him. Three times!

And so, Sunday, 14 August 1960 dawned. I'd writhed and whimpered for twenty-two hours. I felt alone and exhausted. Still, no concerned husband with a bunch of flowers had come to see me, you understand, but there again, I didn't expect it.

The tray of instruments clattered, and I felt the skin off my vagina spring apart, my legs were restricted by stirrups and in the throes of pain, I heard a cry that was not mine and I was now a mother. How the hell had a sixteen-year-old child got herself in this situation? I'd never even held a baby, and yet now I was responsible for a tiny life. I'd had no help or guidance, and it would prove to be an uphill struggle against poverty and marital violence for another eleven years of hell!

At this time, I'd not been diagnosed with bipolar disorder; that was to come thirty years later. I believe I also had postnatal depression, but no one talked to me or gave me advice, or held me when I sobbed. I was engulfed in an existence that robbed me of all smiles. Laughter was the sound that other people made. Happiness was a feeling I knew nothing of. My mother's time was taken up trying to heal my father with no time for me, and Auntie was an old lady so could not be of assistance.

My father had managed with my help to sign himself out of the hospital, even though we'd been told he'd never complete the journey home alive yet he *was* home and alive, because of my intervention when I was eight months pregnant.

I'd heaved my baby filled young body onto three buses to get to him in that hospital hell hole (that should in those days never have been given the name hospital) The disapproving stares of the passengers made me blush with embarrassment, and the theatrical whispers left me in no doubt that I was a fucking disgrace and should be ashamed of myself, I was a slut! Yet this innocent child had only known one vile experience and paid the costliest of prices for my future, and eleven years of abuse were on its way.

When I saw my father's condition, I almost collapsed. He lay there hardly making a mound under the green bedspread. He reached out bony fingers to try to hold my hand but could not reach me, as his shoulder was in such pain. After much probing, he told me a male nurse had twisted his skeletal arm up his back, and that this sadist was the scourge of the night shift. Was he indeed!

It just so happened that the sod was on a split shift that blistering hot Wednesday and was finally located by me in the sluice room. He turned around at the slamming of the door behind me, looked at my protruding tummy and with a lascivious sneer said, "And, what can I do for you that hasn't already been done?"

Oh! The dirty swine, not only did he bully and injure men about to die, but I believe he fancied kiddies too. His name badge confirmed I'd got the correct man within my sights, and retribution for my father's torment was about to be his.

Picking up an empty metal bedpan, I swung it at his head, knocking him to the tiled floor. Right, bastard, now it's your turn. So, so many hypodermics were waiting to be discarded into the sharps box and discarded they were, into every area of his writhing body I could deeply plunge them into and leave them there. But his comeuppance was far from over. I counted seven very, very full bedpans awaiting a good sluicing and fourteen urine bottles.

That coward, that excuse for a human being, lay trying to pull out the needles (impossible, as most were in his back and vile, wrinkled arse) whilst I emptied all the filth and urine upon his fat stinking body. Revenge was mine.

I closed the door and just walked away, never knowing or caring what the outcome of my attack would be. This behaviour was alien to me for did I not cower from my violent husband? And I believe it must have been the sight of my emaciated daddy and his abuse at the hands of a fat sadist that triggered such an unknown reaction in me.

It seemed I did not have the courage to protect myself from violence, but let anyone hurt a loved one, and I became a tigress.

What a sight it must have been, a heavily pregnant little girl, half carrying her skeletal father in a hospital gown into a taxi. All hell had broken loose when I'd demanded the nurse phone for a taxi to take my father away from that hell hole to die in his own bed. They tried to restrain not only me but my dad, as he tried to stumble to the waiting vehicle. As we drove away, I held him in my arms and fully expected to be holding a corpse by the six-mile journey's end. Yet against all the odds he survived, flesh filled out over jutting bones because at last he was getting food inside him. The bastards at the hospital would just plonk his putrid food on the locker beside the bed, often out of his reach and when it had not been touched on their return, just bin it. So slowly they were starving my father and others like him to death. SHAME ON THEM!

I knew nothing about sex; this was proved when I became pregnant. In those 60s days it was shameful and against my parent's wishes I married the sod. You see I thought I could change him. Me, a stupid, headstrong young girl of sixteen.

The rainy day arrived, and it was the dowdiest so-called ceremony ever to be witnessed. Instead of a bridal gown and bouquet, I wore a brown dress and coat to conceal my bulging tummy. I looked at my husband to be and bloody loathed him, why did I not just run away?

We went together on the 92 bus to the registrar's office – no fancy cars, no flowers, no guests, no cake, no reception, no photos. Nothing! Just the pair of us in a dismal room saying words I wish I did not have to.

Auntie Eliza and her friend were witnesses and signed for what they saw, forthcoming cruelty and poverty.

Once man and wife, we got on the 92 bus to Manchester, went into Lewis's café and had our wedding breakfast, fish, chips and peas.

We returned to my parents' home, what we had done was never mentioned and from then on hell was mine.

I was a wayward child who should have been taught the true price you pay for a deed that not only hurt but knocked me sick. My parents should have locked me in my room away from his clutches.

My bed was now lied upon, and I paid the price with eleven long, heartbroken years, in that time giving birth to my second child.

Now, I'd had my baby and my father would be in his bed and reach to stroke her tiny cheek, as she grew in strength and so did he, but he was disgusted with the man I had allowed to take my virginity and knew of his continued violence to me but was unable to intervene as he was still far too weak. That evil bastard used to wait until I was breastfeeding my baby, then he would kick my shins and forbid me to cry out.

But my poorly old dad did hear me shout in pain as my husband kicked my shins black and blue, and it broke his heart as through being so ill he could not stop it. What sort of beast does that? Father could not tolerate the situation any longer and told my husband to get out of the house. Of course, that git swore he'd never hurt me again and like a stupid naïve girl I believed him. My father gave me the choice: "Stay here with the baby and your mother and I will help you raise her, or go with that man, and I disown you forever." He told me the man was a monster and that he would "knock me to the ground and kick me whilst I was down." How many times did my father's prophecy come true over the coming years?

So, I packed up my meagre belongings, said goodbye to my parents who wanted me to get away from that man, and went to live with my mother-in-law – a little Welsh bastard.

How I hated living with his parents, sitting alone in the front room whilst he was at the pub, and his parents held some dodgy wife swapping events in the rest of the house.

My mother came to the rescue and gave me the money (£450) as a deposit on the £1,400 house that has been my home since 1962.

Because I was only nineteen when I moved in (heavily pregnant), it was impossible for me to have my name on the house deeds also. So, on paper, that violent, drunken git was the sole owner of the house, which I was forced to accept by his parents.

And years later, aged twenty-seven, a court bylaw allowed my name on the deeds! Whilst his was removed!

I endured many a year there, with much violence and poverty, attempting to end my hopeless life, more than once. (I hear the sound of the train in my memory). Forgive me please, I digress yet again.

Many times, over the past 4 years, I'd wondered and dreamed about the distance of my considered choice. I knew it was very far away and decided to get there by train would be the simplest. I'd been told to expect all things good in this wondrous place, and my excitement knew no bounds.

I'd stepped out of the house in the early hours, intent on my getaway and now here I was so, so close to the station and my salvation. I wore just a little cotton frock I'd made on the sewing machine Auntie had given me 10 years before. Treadling away the 2/6 ($12\frac{1}{2}$) remnant of cloth slipping under my fingers. Many were the nights, I've stayed up to finish a garment for either of my sleeping children and because I was going away, I'd made such a stock of clothes for them. I hope they fit, and they love them.

It looks very steep from up here, and the station lights glint on the muddy incline, throwing into shadow the wild briars that cling so tightly.

I try to ignite the spark of courage that glistens deep inside me, what was once a flame is now barely a flicker. But now I need it so badly.

Almost at once, one of my shoes is sucked off by the glutinous mud and I start to topple, my cheap little homemade frock torn to shreds on the briars. My shoulder hits a felled tree trunk and is torn from its socket. The pain does not matter as I keep on rolling, rolling, down, down. I come to a stop at the bottom of the embankment; my hair is clogged with mud and both shoes are now missing. My dress hangs in tatty shreds, my skin is bleeding and torn – and I don't care, because my destination beckons.

I stumble on bleeding muddy feet over a couple of yards of stone pebbles and at last, I see my salvation. It lies straight and cold, glinting its welcome under the station lights. "Come to me, come to me." My face welcomes its icy hardness and yet I know it will deliver me, as those before me. That's all I need and want: deliverance; peace; nothing.

Long before I hear its roar, I feel the train's momentum under my face. I sigh with relief, not long now. My eyes are closed, and I don't think I can look the metal monster in the face; A rush of wind, and it's gone.

I open my eyes and I'm not pressing my face on the cold metal rail. Now I'm lying on the white pebbles some three feet away. How on earth had this come to be?

Suddenly, I was filled with a calm serenity as I had never known before that the spark within me was returned to flame; that would last my whole lifetime.

I suppose I must have stumbled through the broken fence and over the bridge to find myself at the waiting taxis. I stood trembling against a cab until the driver realised I was there. I remember his words well: "Jesus Christ, girl, what's happened to you?" Did I tell him? I don't really know. I seemed in a dream-like state, not knowing who or what or where? But I must have told him where I lived because he helped me through the back door I believed I'd closed forever, only three hours before.

The bathwater was cold and filthy, my scratches were deep and sore. The dislocated shoulder that had hurt so much was now re-aligned. HOW?

Dawn broke as that tormented young woman hugged a cup of tea and waited for the monster to awaken from yet another drunken sleep. Forever unaware of his nineteen-year-old wife's nightmare journey to, hopefully, oblivion.

Was it really only yesterday the doctor told me that the rape from my husband (in front of my child) had diseased my body? This must have been the final straw that sent me on my journey; the one I never completed: The destination of my soul.

I truly believe that my angel came to my rescue and over the years, I've cursed her for her actions, that dark dreadful night, in keeping me alive. But now, I look back on 60 years since my face rested so gratefully on a metal track, and I know I was saved for a reason. Bless my angel! Because in that half-century I've saved, healed, or buried more creatures than I can ever remember. I'm known as the lady who helps everyone because that night I was helped.

Not long ago, I was reminiscing and showing my animal photos to a friend, and she said the words that make it all worthwhile: "you have no need to worry about dying darling because every animal, bird and human you have helped will stand at the gates of heaven and wait to welcome you home." And many years after that fated night I will have reached, at last, my destination.

Then, Aunty's house became empty (because of her age and dementia), and a new chapter of my life began.

Anyway, I never saw my father alive again, except for once more fourteen years later on; it was a Boxing Day that the police came to tell me I was needed, to identify his body. He'd got up on the night of Christmas to go to the bathroom, came back to the bedside and fell down dead. My mother managed to get him into bed and cuddled a corpse until the morning. Then, she must have got to the street phone and sent for help.

And there, I stood looking at the man who had created me, the man who tried to save me from my worst enemy: myself. Gone was the titian hair, to be replaced with silver curls, curls that now held flecks of ice. I told him I was sorry for the pain and disappointment I had caused him, that all of his warnings had come true many times. I asked for his forgiveness for choosing a monster instead of a decent human being. Did he hear me? Did he forgive me? Who knows!

I brought his widow, my mother, to live with me as I'd long ago divorced that monster who had stolen eleven years of my young life.

She turned my life, my sanity, to turmoil, as she would not let me out of her sight without tears and panic, but I did the best I could for her until her death, in her sleep, which I welcomed.

My mother was petrified of dying (why) so each night I talked to my Guardian Angel and ask her to give my old mum a gentler death than the first twenty years of her tragic life that she endured. My Angel granted my pleas, for mother died without pain, fear or struggle never knowing death was to embrace her. The golden bedspread I made for her was unruffled. Beneath it she lay comfy, but now so cold, her spirit hopefully with my father at last.

I made a time capsule of her life out of a heavy glass Kilner preserving jar. This she had filled many times throughout my childhood with the fruits of our orchard / her pears in brandy were heavenly! In the jar I put a newspaper front page from the day of her birth and also one from her demise. The comparison was vast, and the interim seventy-seven years had not improved the world and how its inhabitants shamefully behaved TRAGIC! I enclosed photos of her family and animals and the funny little story of Danny the farting greyhound that brought shame and notoriety to my purple feather hatted mother in those gossiping days in a small village. It told of Danny's escape from our garden and of him finding his way to the tripe shop (where we bought his food from.) He jumped into the window after clearing the counter and with each wag of his tail (and the delighted crowd egging him on from the pavement), he sent yet another steak pudding or battered fish skidding through the air only to land on the white tiled wall and slide down in bits, whilst the crowd cheered him on. What he did not crush, eat, or wag to death he farted on and had the very best day of all of his life.

It amused me no end at the thought of a hundred years hence when the graves will be reclaimed for newer occupants, that some hairy arsed bloke with a digger (or whatever will be used in those far off times) finds mums time capsule and laughs with his mates and be able to put a face to the name on the gravestone he's just smashed to bits.

I had found her a wonderful home to live in with people of her own generation. Lonely no more, she loved the room I created for her. She did not know that whilst she was housed in an upstairs room, I lived downstairs for three weeks, whilst I created the home of her dreams. It was 7.15 pm on a

Friday, and she was surprised to see me at the door. I took her hand and led her down the majestic mahogany staircase and put a key in her hand. She placed it in the lock and opened her future. At last, what she had always yearned for (a finished pretty home) was hers. With a kiss and a "Welcome home mum," I myself then went home for a deserved rest, after three weeks of making an old lady's dream come true.

The only comfort and love I had throughout that terrible time was the company of darling Sophie, my German shepherd. She was an old lady now and more precious to me than ever. I had bought her to try (without success) to fill the huge gap left in my life and heart when Hamid had to return to the place of his birth: Baghdad. I never saw his beautiful face ever again, and even though Saddam Hussain promised my man's return to England, it never happened.

And so, just as I did, Sophie welcomed into our home on Christmas day the abused tiny body, placed in my hands by a young boy, to try to heal it just as I had done with hundreds of the other pitiful animals.

Once on the mend, little Ziggy and my beautiful Shepherd dog became inseparable and just as she had helped him live, soon it was his turn to help her die. And losing her broke what was left of my heart.

So, for sixteen and a half years Ziggy and I loved and played without Sophie and his devotion to me was more than a reward for when I rescued him on that Christmas day, I nursed back to health his broken little body. A vulnerable, defenceless dog being tortured by the hands of a sadist, just like my poor daddy had been by that fat slug of a so-called nurse. Neither of them was expected to survive, but survive they did, and I believe love and care conquer all.

So, a new chapter of my life was yet to begin, and I decided to start to write again for you dear readers. I had no family who cared for me, and my life passed in solitude, except for my wondrous dog and a few loyal friends, who I bless every day of my life! For they are of such good quality and kindness, in them I want for nothing. The little soul, my Ruth, my beloved friend, came into my life very recently, and it is through her skill and help that you are able to read my thoughts, wishes and dreams in words. She has the patience of a pretty saint as she tries to decipher my appalling writing or get around my curses on the tape machine when I dictate yet another cock up. Bless that girl for being just Ruth.

Aunty's House

My brother had been banished from the house for many years now, and I saw him infrequently as his prestigious flying career took him all over the world. But when stationed in this country, he would return to his town of birth and stay with our Great Aunt in a tiny terraced house that he loved to call home.

How this memory takes me back still further. Each Sunday, John would have to take me to Aunty. Bless the boy, he would put his roller skates behind my pillow, and off we'd go. The coach-built pram would take the corners on two wheels as we sped through the quiet streets, we'd arrive at Aunty's welcoming door, to a day of bliss. This wonderful old lady would enfold us in love and tenderness and fill our tummies with delicious food, let us listen to the old Bakelite radio; such heaven was ours on the Sundays when it was rutting time back at the mausoleum. 'Yes,' mother and father had put their differences behind them once more; this resulted in sex for many, many hours. Of course, I did not understand it then, but my life's experiences have made it all too plain.

So, there I sat in Aunty's kitchen holding the last of my roast lamb. John told me years later that I said my first words, with a banging fist I demanded: "more meat" (and there was created the greedy git I am to this day). But the Sunday feast did not end there! 'Oh no', for Aunty's speciality was now served into pretty dishes, a spoon was put into my fist, and I was transported to food heaven by her slowly cooked rice pudding; nutmeg on the top, the skin sparkling with little globules of butter that decorated the fluffy rice interior; bliss, utter, utter bliss. To this day, I've never been able to recreate Aunty's pud. Maybe the old black range cooker held the secret answers.

And as we sped through the quiet Sunday morning street seventy-seven years ago, a twelve-month-old (of course) undiagnosed bipolar baby girl, strapped into her safe pram, and her already speed fiend big brother; how could we even possibly guess what the future held for us both?

That big brother of mine would become a hero test pilot and live for just forty-six years, and I would always be ill with bipolar the whole of the seventy-eight years I've existed. Surely, it can't be much longer?

And so, the years fled by, and it was I who looked after Aunty when she became the victim of dementia, this being proved to me when I went to visit and help her one evening.

Letting myself into her old, terraced house, I called out her name and was worried when I got no reply. She was not in her bedroom, bathroom, or the small back garden. Then, I heard a rumbling from the cellar, going down to investigate after putting on the light, I found the old lass lying amongst the coals, piles of it covering her legs and lower body. When I asked why she was laying there, her reply hurt, worried and shocked me, for I'd never encountered dementia so far advanced before. "I've come to bed because I was weary," she said, and firmly believed the coal was her eiderdown. It took a lot of cajoling to get her out of her black cosy bed, but eventually, I persuaded her it was now morning and time for her bath.

She sat hunched on the closed toilet seat, whilst I ran the warm bubble bath that would wash away the cellar's filth. Taking off her now black nightie, my heart wept at the skeletal old lady who was my granddad's sister. She had never been married – nor had her sister, who died some years previously, leaving Aunty to a lonely old age as they had always lived together. They had shared this happy little house all of their lives, but soon it would be time for Aunty to live in a place of safety. But that was not quite yet! I lifted her from the grimy water and tried my best to get her into her bed, but she would have none of it and demanded to be taken home. There was nothing else for it I covered her nighty in a warm coat, replaced her slippers with shoes, and took her down the stairs and out into the twilight.

After just a few tottering yards up the road, I turned her around; bringing her back to the front door I'd just slammed shut. "We're home now Aunty" and with these words she happily went in and went to bed safe, cosy and clean. I had to leave her then to walk the two miles home, for probably yet another punching, as the piece of filth I was married to would once again accuse me of going out to meet my imaginary fancy man (I should be so lucky).

Just a few weeks later, Aunty had a fall and had to be hospitalised, and there it was decided that her going home again was not an option, so her last months were spent in St Thomas's Hospital which used to be the dreaded, shameful workhouse. Thank God, she was too far gone to know of her whereabouts as was her brother (my granddad) who died in that still horrid place, many years before. I remember his passing well as I was stood at the side of him as he started singing the words of a little song to his eleven-year-old granddaughter, "Silver threads amongst the gold, darling we are growing old," then he fell back on his pillow and just died.

Just before he died, a toothless smile lit up his old face and with outstretched arms, he greeted the loved one, only he could see, who was to take him to eternal rest. When I had looked at the place that he had been so bewitched with, there was no one there.

My elder brother was flying jets in Greenland teaching American pilots to land jets on ice when my mother informed him of Aunty's hospitalisation, and he suggested I move into her tiny home to get away from my terrible marriage. This I did with my two young children, two pet bunnies and my yellow lab Elsa. We were happy there and no poorer than at the family home where there was never money left over from his drinking for the essentials of life.

One day whilst buying food for my animals, I overheard a conversation between two yobs sitting on scooters outside the pet shop, with the toss of a coin it was decided that the lout with acne would become the proud owner of the foxtail that was joined to the cub in the pet shop window.

I had used all in the way of spare cash but decided the electricity bill could get stuffed for a few weeks longer, for that sweet cub's life was in danger and was therefore my priority.

Just why and how that cub, sat alone waiting for its never to return mummy, I never found out. But now it had a human mum and lots of new friends in the shape of children; bunnies; a dog; and an injured pigeon, not yet ready for release.

Amber was the prettiest tiny boy you could wish to love, and he played like a young kitten with Elsa, chasing a ball and stealing his favourite treat if he got the chance (tinned pears). His love of them was discovered when my son put his dish of pears down whilst he ran to the loo, when he came back again Amber was smacking his tiny lips, and the dish was empty.

I'd taken him to the local animal hospital which treated animals for free if you could not afford a vet. That was most certainly me.

The lady vet said he could not infect my animals, but when Amber became nine months old he would mature — almost overnight — and become most aggressive, the only way around this was to make him live in fear of me, this was to be achieved with me knocking seven bells out of him daily to break his spirit. What a lousy thing to do to my boy. So in my wisdom, I thought plenty of tinned pears would ensure his love for me. Time proved this to be so very wrong.

Now, Aunty never had her chimney swept and used to do what all her neighbours did, fire the sod, which entailed putting blazing pieces of paper up it. This achieved bugger all, and the soot just got thicker with each coal fire lit.

God alone knows how many years of that black stuff was waiting up there for my inquisitive amber boy. Going back into the kitchen where I'd left him playing with his teddy, I must have startled him, and like a bat out of hell he shot up the chimney. The good news was that it was a warm day, so not needing the comfort of the usual coal fire.

Now, he had a brush of his own on his rear end and used it with much success to bring down years of soot. He raced around the ledge inside the chimney and with each circuit, another pile would fall, and soon the kitchen was deep in the stuff. I tried calling him down, but he was having the time of his life and offering his favourite treat of pears up the blackened hole did not entice him back either. By this time, I'd donned a pink plastic mac, which in retrospect was bloody stupid as I was already filthy underneath it.

Thinking about sending for the fire brigade (or maybe more about the firemen!) to rescue my wayward pet, I was still pondering about where was the nearest phone box for my 999 call, when there was a final gust of soot, and a cheeky little face peeped at me around the fire grate edge.

So, there I stood amongst years of soot in a pink plastic mac, holding a squirming (not so amber now) Amber.

After running warm soapy water, I then tried my best to immerse him in it; he was having none of it either. Determined, I set about showing him just who was boss and when I got him out, to my horror I'd half-drowned the poor little sod. He was clean but not so far off dead. Placing his now limp body on the draining board, I proceeded to pump his little tiny chest and give him the kiss of life. After a couple of minutes, he sputtered his return from death's door and was rewarded for just being alive with? You've guessed it! Tinned pears.

Now, the old lady next door used to like to sit in her garden with a cup of coffee on the table next to her, book in hand and rollers in her hair.

It had become my habit to put Amber's harness on and tie it with a long rope to the washing line because there he could prance and play without getting lost. He would swing back and too in the sunshine and took a very adventurous leap and in doing so, he shot over the small dividing fence and landed on the rollered head of the old bird next door. Dear God, she looked just like a geriatric Davy Crochet with Amber's tail hanging down her back. My hysterics did not endear me to her, and I swiftly prized off Amber's claws that were embedded in the pink foam that created her hairdo. She told me in no uncertain terms to get rid of my piece of vermin. I took great exception to this and after apologising for the distress caused by a playing baby animal, I never talked to the sour old git again.

It was not long after this episode (that still makes me laugh half a century later) that my Amber must have reached the dreaded nine months that the vet had warned me about.

Coming down one morning, instead of his usual greeting of rolling on his back for a tummy tickle, he stood with eyes blazing and snarling at the mum who loved him.

Back at the vets I was given tablets to sedate him. These were placed in the treats he would relish at home for the very last time. He enjoyed his pears as he had always done and soon fell into a deep sleep.

The lady who had sold him to me eight and half months ago drove me to an unused stone quarry in Derbyshire, Rabbit droppings beside a stream showed this was a place he could live quite easily, and the vet had assured me he was now nasty enough to do just that. The free nature that had been denied him when his mummy died had come to the fore. Now he was a grown-up boy ready to take on the call of the wild.

I put in different places piles of his food, including of course his favourite, pears, and held and kissed him for the last time whilst he still slept. Finally, he awoke and stumbled a few paces looking behind him as though wondering why I was not chasing him as before. Then, he stood fully recovered on a mound of grass, his glorious coat of amber gleaming in the sunshine; at last, he was where he always should have been. Free and happy he gave me a last glance and sped away. I missed him very much and so did my Elsa. She would search for him often, but of course, he was never to be played with again. My tears of loss finally dried, and I gave my attention to getting well a greyhound that my children had found injured under a hedge.

When I went back with my children and Elsa to the park (where we had picnic teas whilst watching the old chaps play bowls), many were the ones who asked about my gorgeous fox who used to sit and watch the match they played. Everyone seemed to miss his beauty, but soon they would be able to admire and pet the greyhound (as well as golden Elsa) that I was getting well at home in Aunty's little house.

Next door was the end of the terrace where lived old Mr Moss. A sweet little man whose marbles had long since rolled away. I used to pop in and make sure he was ok, taking him in a share of our evening meal when I could afford to.

A snowy New Year's Eve came, and I'd gone to bed at the same time as the children, about 8 pm, but was woken up by the midnight fireworks. Lying in the dark, I was so grateful to be alone and safe and not listening as in years before for the sound of that dreaded key in the lock that would herald another good slapping. I did not feel the shame of wetting myself with fear anymore, I had nothing and yet I had everything, gentle peace in Aunty's house.

I heard the sound of a slamming front door and looking through the window, I saw old Mr Moss trolling off barefooted in the snow, a cap on his head, pyjama hems getting wet and with only a Fair Aisle pullover to cover his frail body, off he went up the street. Now I had a dilemma, dare I leave my sleeping children whilst I went to his rescue? I put aside my fears and went to fetch him home. He had quite an amazing turn of speed for an old chap, but it was easy to find him around street corners by following his bare footprints in the snow.

On reaching him, I asked him where he was going "to buy my rough shag" was the answer. Now, rough shag was the pipe tobacco of his choice and not the warn out old slapper offering trade just a few frozen doorways along the high street.

As I encouraged him home with the promise that he already had some tobacco at home, a cop car pulled up and moved the lady of the night onto pastures new. It slowly pulled up beside the young woman, linking the old boy with nothing left to give. Leaning out of the open window of the car, the incredulous copper enquired, "Is that the best you can do on New Year's Eve love?" We continued arm in arm, Mr Moss and me. I tucked him up safely in his own bed before I went back, cold but happy, to Aunty's house next door, and all was well!

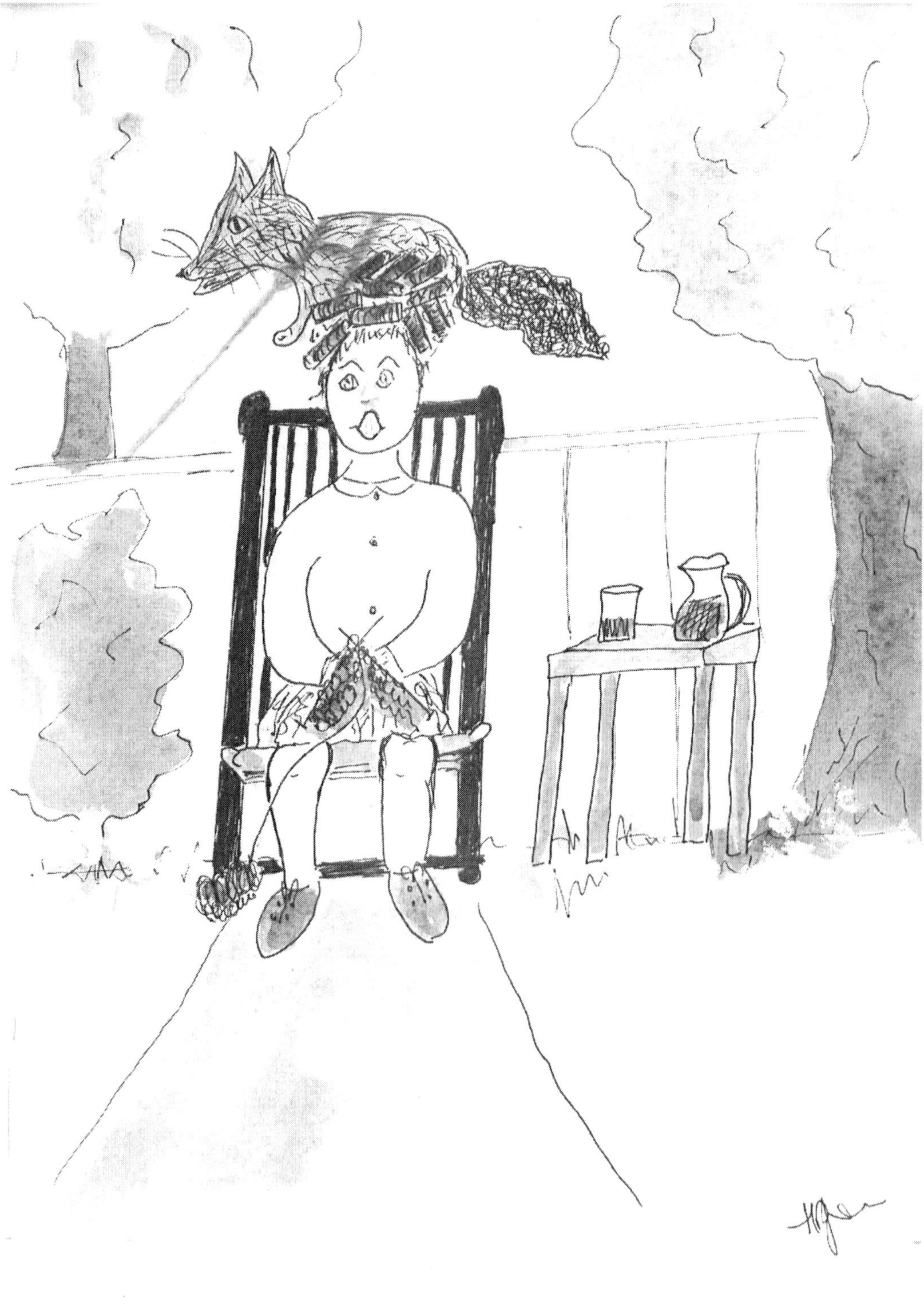

Back Home, Yet I'd Miss Aunty's House

When Aunty had become hospitalised (never to return home), I took my brother's advice and moved into her tiny home. I took both my children and bunnies and golden Elsa my Lab.

I'd walk my children safely the two miles to their usual school, repeating the return journey at home time. I'd have packed up a picnic tea, and we would stroll with Elsa and Amber (my pet fox) to sit on the benches in Alexandra Park to watch the old boys playing bowls. To this day, the sound of wood-on-wood transports me back to freedom and laughter in the sunshine. Heaven!

Even though that man I'd left stalked me (jumping out from behind trees to startle us), I was staunch in my decision to never return 'home' whilst he still lived in it. On wet days, I'd catch the bus with the children, and once he stood up drunk and told all and sundry that I was fucking (in particular) black men in the afternoon. This hurt and embarrassed me as he was the only person I'd known sexually. You could read the passengers' faces (no smoke without fire)

Three years passed quite quickly at Aunty's and that way of life became the norm. Eventually, my divorce was granted, but the judge made many stipulations.

That vile (now ex-husband) of mine had lived in the 'family' home in my absence for three years and in all that time paid nothing! No rates, utilities, or water, running up debts that ran into thousands of pounds and the home I'd fought for three years to return to with my children and animals was about to be repossessed, due to non-payment of the mortgage. Knowing all this, the judge decreed that the house was to be mine, but I had to clear that bastard's debts. How? And more to the point, why?

So, the twenty-eight days he was given to leave what was now my home is up and on the 29th day, I had to have a police escort (because of past violence) to get possession of it. He answered my knocking with a string of threats and abuse but changed his attitude when the police joined me on the step. What we found within was gut-wrenching, cockroaches, fleas and bluebottles had made my home theirs, feeding off the thrown down rotting food and the faeces that he'd defecated onto the lounge carpet. This is probably because the toilet could no longer be used as the water had been turned off because of non-payment and was full to the brim with faeces and maggots. He had obviously had menstruating women in all of the beds, and their blood was mixed with copious amounts of semen and had to be destroyed. He had also put half-eaten fish and chips inside my clean sheets in the airing cupboard and maggots had a home there, also soiled underpants were in the cutlery drawer, the filth broke my heart but not my spirit. There was no glass in the windows; no locks on the doors; he had torn out the bathroom fittings; the evidence of this was the partly burnt remains in the open fire grate. In short, that misogynistic judge had given me a stinking broken shell that a homeless person would turn away from, rather to sleep on a park bench.

The policemen were appalled at what awaited me after a three-year legal battle and set about helping me and my children. They told me to be in that shit hole at 6.30 pm that day (where else would I be?) 6.30 pm came and so did numerous cars, vans, motorbikes and sidecars, people on push bikes, etc... I could not understand just what was happening, and then it all became crystal clear. These wonderful strangers had come to my rescue. An ex-farmer chiselled away the filth and maggots from the toilet (he was used to poo and maggots but usually from four-legged animals) others dragged mattresses downstairs, pulled up defecated on carpets and made a bonfire in the highly weeded back garden. A lovely lady dragged in a mattress telling me, "It wasn't new, but it was clean" as she put it along with bedding for me and my babies. Another stranger put in new glass in the empty window frames where possible and boarded up the remaining ones, whilst yet another stranger put strong locks and bolts on the back and front doors, there was much scrubbing and sweeping up because of no electricity. Every empty beer can, every bit of rotting food, every bit of human waste (sixteen bin bags in all) was disposed of on that night. I could never forget. They had brought groceries and a kettle that could be used when the electricity was back on and when they had finally said their goodbyes and good luck it was 2 am the following morning. They had even left me a transistor radio and by the light of candles, my children and I sat on the mattress on a scrubbed and bleached pristine floor, the candles flickered, music played, and we enjoyed a picnic to end all picnics, provided by the hearts and souls of generous strangers before we cuddled up in each other's arms, afraid of the future.

I thought I would never ever recover from the trauma of what I found that day but with the help and kindness I received it gave me the courage to fight for my children's future in their home. Bit by bit, for many years I paid off that scum's debts and took courses at college to learn how to plaster, decorate and such, to turn my home into what it is today, a wonderful one some fifty years later.

I think back to those scary, hungry, worrying days, weeks, months, and years and wonder how I've survived that night (without the help of those wonderful people I wouldn't have) For I would have taken the lives of all three of us, as I could not see a way out of the destruction of my home and soul that vile man had deliberately orchestrated.

Our Great Aunt Eliza, who was John's saviour. He was the son she was never lucky enough to have.

E.C.T. Tell Them to Shove It!

Should God forbid you ever become poorly as I had in 1975 that E.C.T. is prescribed, unless you wish to experience licenced hell: refuse it at all costs.

Let me take you through this barbaric practice, one that rarely cures the reason you have submitted to its violence in the first place.

You lie on a bed with iron cot sides, these are to stop you from flinging yourself to the floor whilst you convulse. Your arms will flail and thrash with each volt crashing against the iron rails, causing cuts, bruises and sometimes even broken limbs.

The relaxant drug you are given makes you a helpless immobile prisoner, but does not stop you from hearing or feeling!

The electrodes are placed on your temples, and the torment begins. "Another couple of volts I think," the Indian doctor tells a nurse (more interested in her forthcoming holiday in Benidorm than her patient).

Lightning flashes behind closed eyes, your brain feels like it is going to burst from your skull and still the inane chatter goes on, with no regard for you, the poor bastard whose temple flesh is now blistering.

When the relaxant wears off the pain in your skull is beyond description, vomit heaves from your stomach, and your thoughts are like rice pudding; do you get my drift?

If you have a creative analytical mind as I have (albeit a damaged one), this vile treatment will drive you to the depths of despair, as rational thoughts are now impossible. And what is even worse, the reason you're submitted to the barbarism in the first place (to rid forever your troubles) these same troubles are still with you and added to them is the trauma of the consequences of E.C.T. The tragic part is that all that was bad stays, and the nice trivia that makes up life goes walkabout forever.

This was proved to me some three years later when I was walking in a shopping centre. A delicious gentleman walked towards me, arms outstretched, and a smile of 'hello' on his handsome face. He hugged me close and said, "Long time no see." Who the hell was this stranger who had obviously mistaken me for someone he once cared very much about?

I stood in his hug for a while before explaining I did not know who he was (well I did say he was gorgeous). He held me at arms-length and said with not a little disgust, "Oh that's charming, I must have made one hell of a good impression on you, good God girl we almost lived together for six months." With this he took himself away, and I never saw him again. Now, what the hell was his name? Of course, I've never remembered it!

Now, if I had known then of the existence of Carlo Sanchez and his mind healing methods, believe me, those electrodes would never have blistered my temples. This genius man was to be the most important part of my future and the healer of my mind.

Another three years pass, and my memory is still mostly non-existent (except for past trauma that I'd longed to escape)

I was standing in a queue at the greengrocers, waiting to pay for the huge cauliflower I'd chosen from the outside display.

Before me is a small dark-skinned man, and I recognised even the back of his head. He must have been able to pick up the vibes of pure hatred and venom pouring from me and straight into his back. He turned and went a shade paler; dropping his apples he hurries out onto the pavement.

Cruel little bastard, I followed him out, got him in my sights and let fly with my considerable cauliflower. My aim was spot on; I got the uncaring git right at the back of the head. He fell to the ground, immobile just as he had made me three and half years previously.

He lay for some time surrounded by curious passers-by and florets of white. Eventually, he got to his feet and buggered off on unsteady legs. Not one person had helped him up! I am not one for letting things go to waste, so I collected my cauliflower florets and went back to the shop to pay for them, not needing to explain their condition as the greengrocer had stood on the pavement and watched with much amusement the downfall of the arrogant customer he had never liked anyway.

Sunday lunchtime came, and my sister and I tucked into the roast chicken and the cauliflower that had been my revenge.

The E.C.T. was meant to be a cure for my reaction to many years of marital violence whilst my need for revenge had been repressed, and it had manifested itself in me being more than able to handle myself, should anything or anyone threaten me or those that I loved. A feeling of swelling up with strength, of now being invincible, never scared of those who might harm me.

The balls I wish I had had when I was married to that unwashed git now hung heavy and low, bursting with courage. Woe betide anyone who challenged me. But this was getting out of hand, hence my submission to E.C.T. But Carlo Sanchez was to find and expel the dark being whose strength I have unknowingly used, so many times now.

I don't want you to think that I had become a bully; far from it. I just could not bear to witness something vulnerable being at the mercy of a sadist's fists and feet, as I had been.

On a rainy day on this suburban road, the shouts of the rag and bone man drew me to the window. He stands beside an already overladen wooden cart begging for yet more junk. What swayed in the ratty cart's shafts filled me with horror. The poor creature's bones were easily seen from my window, and its tired out old head hung to the ground. As I looked on, the so-called man got a heavy tire iron with which to encourage the knackered horse to move on. I don't know how many times he crunched it onto the poor soul's back before I'd reached him. I'd gone across that busy road without it even registering that my bare feet were now cut, my Kaftan was stuck with pouring rain to my body.

That vile cruel bastard raised the weapon yet again but it never reached its intended target. Already blood dripped from the horse's back and mixed with the running rain into the gutter.

With lightning speed, I wrenched the tyre iron from the bastard and brought it down hard on his sticking out forearm. He screamed with pain at the crunch of a broken bone. Now it was his turn! An eye for an eye, remember my family motto!

He cried out even louder when I tapped his knees with the heavy object and listened with horror as I delivered my future plans for him. With a snarling voice, he was informed that if he did not relinquish the damaged emaciated creature into my safe custody at once, he could put a down payment on a wheelchair of his choice, because I was going to knee cap the fucker.

Already he was nursing his collar bone as well as his arm, bloody hell I didn't remember inflicting that injury also. But on a scale of 1–10 of my retribution, I'd reached 103, and this low life was terrified, much like the poor animal in the shafts.

This owner of horse flesh decided that he could indeed part with his 'beloved' animal, and Tracey soon arrived with her horsebox of rescue. Just one phone call and balls of steel had ensured a better life for the horse my heart broke for.

At this time, the hourly bus pulled up as we were using its parking space, rubbernecking passengers wanted to know why their journey was halted when the driver climbed down from his cab. This animal-lover helped Tracey and I unharness the collapsing horse and with much huffing and puffing, pulling and lifting, we got the soul onto a bed of straw where it collapsed beside the water and fresh carrots.

Tracey drove off, the bus took its passengers to their destination and someone sent for an ambulance, the consequences of my actions that day could have introduced me to a long-term prison cell. I waited with bated breath for weeks, but no policeman arrived. My sister did not have to lose her sibling, all was well.

Of course, the electric shock treatment was hell on the earth, and I would not recommend it. And even with a warning, my brother was so desperate he admitted himself to the hospital to help with his desperate fight with depression. He submitted to its volts, a few months after I had recovered as much as I ever would. Then, he killed himself.

The E.C.T. closed forever many doors in my mind, but it also opened doors I did not even know were there; that had remained locked until then. I became psychic knowing things I could not possibly know, but I did.

Peter Sutcliffe, the Yorkshire Ripper, was on his murderous prowl at that time, and I saw his bearded face in detail long before his latest kill and his apprehension by the police and the ensuing publicity. Now, if only I could sketch, I'd have been able to show the police what I knew for a certainty, but can you imagine the reaction of the boys in blue when a woman recently wired up tells the tale of the killer's face that she has seen and will never forget? I did of course tell my friend and they believed me, for I had proved my newfound gift many times before, to their astonishment.

One day a friend of my young sisters, a man, and quite a few years older than her asked if he could take her to a party in Liverpool. He himself had never actually been to this address, and he was tagging along with his brother and his girlfriend. I told him I'd think about it as this birthday party was not in my neighbourhood.

I did not have to mull it over long as one of my visions came in coloured clarity. Along with my sightings always came a relevant smell, and the pong of oranges was overpowering.

A steeply cobbled street of old terraced houses, a front door painted with flaking grey paint, the bottom screw of the seven was missing, and it hung drunkenly to one side touching the one.

Somebody had painted the steps a garish red (probably with a cabbage leaf) as the paint was daubed onto the wall and also the old natural stone pavement.

Music shattered the silence of the street; strange, there did not seem to be any traffic. A hand belonging to an unseen person knocks at the ratty door, a voluptuous black girl in a red dress, drink in hand, opens it and beckons beyond her to two large black men.

The air was filled with the overpowering smell of oranges and cannabis, and in the harbour some distance away stood, at anchor, the San Francisco unloading its cargo of oranges.

Needless to say, my sister never went to Liverpool that night, but her friend did. He had been most put out by my refusal but got the shock of his life when he arrived at my described seventeen Banbury Street. Over his shoulder, oranges hit the Quay Side, tons of citrus bound for England's greengrocers.

Now, this confirmed that his girlfriend's sister was more than a bit strange, but God help him he could not give a logical explanation for what he had discovered that party night. Now, he was more than a little scared of me.

So, when I told him some weeks later to take a different, longer route back to the holiday camp he occasionally worked at, he mulled my warning over and thought, *"Stuff it, I'd rather have a lie-in."*

I told him of a large roundabout on a country lane, that in the centre of it was what appeared to be a castle turret surrounded by bushes and grass. 'Yes', he knew this place well as it was on the shortest route to his destination.

So, the sleepy git had his lie-in at his lodgings, leaving it to the very last minute to set off, just as young blokes often do and pretty ladies also.

He takes his familiar short route; I don't suppose my warning not to go that way even entered his head, as he listened to his booming music. Then BANG! An almighty collision that nearly ended his life. Changing tapes, he'd gone onto the roundabout, overturned and hit the oncoming red car I'd told him of. Blokes, aren't they stupid? They just won't be told, will they?

Many years later Carlo Sanchez was to listen to this enlightening episode of my life, and he explained it thus. That our minds are like radio receivers, being able to get some far-off stations but not others. A mind still undamaged by trauma or ECT could pick up the more local usual stations, but these will probably be difficult to locate ever again should the mind be damaged. Now should the precious mind become traumatised in any way, new stations never before received now become accessed, and I had them aplenty!

The smell of beer and cigarettes filled the night air, loud music escaped from a roadside pub, and revellers enjoyed the pavements twilight gathering as they drank, smoked joints and joked, their raucous laughter mingled with the heavy beat from within.

A small grey metallic car pulls up adjacent to traffic lights, my grown-up looking sister at the wheel. This large man dressed head to toe in black leather tries without success, to open the passenger door she drives off, frightened but safe.

I tell my younger sister what I have seen in her future and warn her to always lock the doors of the grey car that she would one day own.

Many, many years later whilst reminiscing about my times of visions, I reminded her of my warning. I laughed, but she was oddly silent before telling me that what I told her had indeed already happened. Waiting for the traffic lights to change, the man, with rape on his mind had pulled and tugged at the locked door of the grey car. Dear God, who was to be his victim now that my sister had driven safely off?

There was once a wonderful athlete called Lilian Board, was she a runner? I can't remember all these forty years later.

The sad news was that the lovely, seemingly healthy, young woman had Cancer and was dying. Now, my mind was a receiver of a far more puzzling, painful kind. There is no explanation of how her debilitating symptoms come to replicate themselves in my body. Rather like a twin can feel its siblings' pain and anguish maybe. But I had never met Lilian, I'd only marvelled at her Olympian prowess on TV.

I had no option but to take to my bed, my body became weak and I vomited without control. I was delirious most of the time. My doctor could find no medical reason for my malaise, and I was deteriorating very quickly.

My sister helped me downstairs one Sunday, and I lay covered in blankets on the settee before the coal fire. But no blanket could quell the shivers of my now painfully thin body. I'd not eaten properly for so long and could not be tempted by the lovely food my sister prepared. This in itself was totally out of character as I was known for having a generous appetite. No squash that, I'm a greedy git.

Mid-afternoon, I suddenly felt alive, full of strength and vigour, with no pain, no sickness. I was back to how I'd always felt, but thinner (that was a bonus) I called to my sister in the kitchen for a cup of chocolate and a piece of toast. Her delighted face watched as I struggled to stand unaided, on legs weakened by weeks and weeks of unexplained illness. And in all of that horrific time Lilian filled my thoughts, why would a stranger do that?

I ate the buttered toast tasting of heaven, drank my choccy drink and settled down on the sofa to watch TV. My sister was snuggled under the blanket beside me when the teatime news came on, and the headline was that Lilian Board had lost her brave battle with Cancer at 3.30 pm that Sunday afternoon. That was exactly the time I shook off the shroud of death that had enveloped me.

Thank God that was the only episode of such pain and anguish that my newly activated mind exposed me to.

Never, ever underestimate the complicated power of what our skulls contain, my experiences have left me in awe and still I don't comprehend how I can have lived the illness and death of Lillian Board and survived to tell the tale.

2oz of Corned Beef

I was still trying to come to terms and recover from the E.C.T. that I later found out had stolen years of my happy memories but had left me instead with years of torment that I had regrettably turned to E.C.T. to try to erase. The one advantage of this barbaric so-called treatment was it opened the door in my brain that had never been accessed before.

I became psychic and often saw impending danger, etc. The Technicolor transparency before my eyes would also be accompanied by a relevant strong smell, and I was never, ever proved wrong.

So, on this particular day, I felt well enough to go shopping with a supportive neighbour. This stick-thin lady was anorexic, bless her, long before it became a sick fashion celebrity illness. (Just like my genuine bipolar is today!) And these phoney prats have Chihuahua dogs in their handbags, etc. What have these people got, instead of brains? Rice pudding?

When well enough, it was my habit to help the old man around the corner with shopping, he lived in the house that in much later years would be dear departed Caroline's, my best friend's home.

He gave me his small list of shopping, most of which comprised of cooked meat, which in those days, the butcher would freshly cut the amount you wanted in this case 2 oz. of each. Grace and I were in the Co-Op basement as she was trying to find a new mattress that would treat her protruding bones with more kindness than the solid one her husband needed to support his bad back.

And it was whilst sitting there, waiting for her decision about a bed, that one of my visions came to me. Grace turned to speak to me, only to find me in floods of tears, unable at that point to explain why!

Bless her; she sat holding me tight whilst other shoppers looked on in morbid curiosity. Eventually, between sobs, I was able to tell her that I had just seen something to tear my heart into shreds, and I just had to get out of that store. What I had just seen was my brother lying dead and that he had killed himself. I will not go into details of his demise, as he was a very private man in life, and in death he shall remain so. Grace did not come home with me on the bus but stayed to try to find the night-time comfort her emaciated body craved.

I sat near the window on the bus, tears streaming down my face, oblivious to the stares of other passengers, hating a sniggering wild-looking man opposite, who dared to still be alive when my talented, articulate, mentally tortured brother was dead. I had just been bereaved of someone so very, very, special.

Letting myself into Mr Green's house, he did not hear me as his hearing aids were on the side table. At first, I thought the grunting sounds he made were either a heart attack or he had the incredible squits, brought on by eating food that could easily have found its own way to the rubbish bin.

Standing behind the sofa he was slumped on, I saw that the old git had on his dithering bony knees a porn magazine, and he was beating the hell out of his flaccid wrinkled prune, that I suppose, used to be his knob. This vile bit of useless gristle did not seem inclined to even twitch no matter what the incentive, but that vile old scrote just kept on wanking!

At this point, I coughed as loudly as I could, and at last, the old git realised he was not alone. Did he look embarrassed and shove the mag under a cushion or close his pee-stained flies? Did he hell! Now, this vain old man had a Bobby Charlton comb-over that started above his left ear. For this was far cheaper than his alternative to the crown Topper (toupee) that he used to wear with some pride, daring with a steely gaze the local yobs from taking the piss. This toupee after about five years was becoming more than a little ragged, and its final demise was when his cat used it as a birthing blanket the night she delivered nine kittens.

His ill-fitting pipe tobacco-stained dentures clattered at the sight of me leaning over to place his shopping beside his hearing aids. As I did so, one dithering boney hand reached up and grabbed my booby. This electrified me into action as good as any E.C.T. Tipping the cooked meats out of their bags, I laid them flat on my right hand and with my left hand held his bloody head in a vice-like grip, he sputtered and fought, but I was far too strong, and the cooked meats he had requested were mangled, up his nose, in his ears, throughout his strands of hair, down his neck and any bloody place except between the bread, for which it was intended. At one point, I almost laughed as his glasses were still propped on his startled face, the lenses all clogged up with corned beef.

The money he'd left for his shopping went towards having yet another of my birth-deformed little children operated on (and this is another story) so at least something clean and wholesome came out of that vile encounter – me being groped by a geriatric perv.

When my lodger came home from work, she found me heartbroken in bed. She tried to comfort me when I told her what I'd seen whilst in the co-op basement with Grace. She was telling me that maybe, just maybe this time I was wrong, but in our hearts, we both knew the dreadful truth, because my visions were NEVER, EVER wrong.

The knock on the door came as Sadie was still hugging me – we both knew what the call was about. Strangers stood on my step, and when I invited them in, they confirmed my heart-breaking vision of that afternoon, and they explained that they were relatives of my brother's wife who was now his heartbroken widow.

This poor lady had returned home and called out a greeting to her husband who would never reply. That day her soul died also, even though her body carried on this life, without the man she adored, for many a long lonely year.

The old sod who had dared to grope my titty lived for another couple of years; I was told he finally got rid of his comb-over. Never again did I go near him, and I often wonder who would replace me to do his shopping for 2oz of corned beef? I don't know or care how he managed without my help. I bet he probably wanked himself into oblivion on his filthy couch, that being his choice of demise. Good riddance

Depression Slays Heroes

It was snowing that March day of 1930 when his twenty-year-old mother pushed her firstborn in to what was to become (as then unknown) such a heroic life.

Created as a mistake not of his making, that eternally sad little boy paid the price of his uninterested parents many times over, the mental damage had begun. He turned to his granddad and great Aunty Eliza for the human comfort and love he craved (denied him by his parents), and they lavished him with praise and built up confidence that one day would be his saviour.

When he was twelve, I arrived, and it seemed I was much wanted, thus making his existence even more unhappy; apparently, he was a quiet studious boy, heading for great things, according to his Grammar School reports (that I still have)

He was very mechanically adept, and I'd sit on the steps in our courtyard and watch him take apart and rebuild his Vincent motorbike, aged barely seventeen he knew instinctively just what to do.

He loathed the austere, unloving, cold atmosphere of that hypocritical posh house and left to live with Aunty (still just seventeen) now this was all her dreams come true for she was a spinster lady who lived with her single sister, she always wanted the children that were never to be, and she adored the polite, clever, loving boy who relished her rice puddings and hugs, "yes", he was her beloved child.

At seventeen, amidst a river of tears, Aunty hugged her darling lad farewell as he waved his goodbye from the handlebars of his trusty Vincent and started out on a journey that no one in their wildest dreams could foretell where it would lead.

Now ninety-nine percent of all Cranwell applicants to be pilots had University educations and because of this, there were applicants many years older than the Grammar School Boy of just seventeen who asked to be considered for flying. They did not send him away with a flea in his ear and end his long-held dreams, but instead gave him test after test, which he passed with flying colours, which made them realise just what they had been lucky enough to find.

So, his training began, he went from strength to strength and at the age of nineteen passed out as an officer in charge of his own squadron of Mosquitoes and Spitfires. He'd done it!

One day he must have been on leave at Aunty's, and he came to get me out of class to spend time with his little sister before returning to camp. Never had (or since) have I been so proud as when he asked for me wearing his uniform (my teacher looking as if she could gobble him up) and off we went for a picnic in Bluebell Woods, for once we were both happy, a very rare happening as later life was to show us.

At the tender age of sixteen, I also made the same mistake as my mother had, at least she waited until she was twenty all those years ago, but unlike her, I married a monster and paid the price of my ignorance with eleven years of hell, but Aunty's little house came to the rescue when she was too old and poorly to still live in it. So, I escaped.

Meanwhile, my hero brother's flying skills were becoming legendary, and he had the highest rating possible at twenty-one, A1 Z1. This meant he was of the highest calibre of pilots, in prime Top Gun physical condition, and security cleared to fly in any zone of the world. Many years previously he had signed the Official Secrets Act, this he kept to, never letting me or anyone else know where he was flying from or what part of the world was utilising his amazing razor-sharp mind and death-defying aerobatic skills as he threw jets around the skies whilst audiences gasped with wonder and delight. I'd watch him on TV performing his ariel routine at Farnborough air show, proud does not cover it! He soared with the red Arrows for gasping crowds, he taught American pilots to land jets on ice in Greenland, and I only found this out when he retired at forty-six, his flying hours over and soon also his illustrious life. Even though no longer with the RAF, he was still obliged to keep all of his flying career secrets and, to this day, some fifty-odd years after he decided to leave this life, all of his logs from his heroic flying are unobtainable. Indeed, if you search the internet, you won't find any mention of my big brother; it's as if he had never been. But he had!

Although he did once confide in me that should his secret flying logs become public knowledge, perceptions of life on earth and the universe would never be the same. For what he had encountered whilst night flying around the coast to guard against enemy attack, were not of this world, and fascinated him.

The year was 1976, so hot, and we both loathed it and set about hosing each other off amongst the back garden flowers. He had needed desperately to be with someone who understood his complex brain. Only I would do! So, he'd climbed upon his glorious Honda Goldwing motorbike (the Vincent of his youth long gone) and came to stay with me.

"There is just one solution to our problems my dear, death." I hear his pathetic prophecy many times and know it to be true, but unlike him, I've carried on tolerating the crippling bipolar for all of my seventy-eight years. How I wish he was still in this life? He would be ninety years old now. I like to think back to the laughter we shared that blistering hot August day of 76. Would we still have gone amongst the flowers and drenched each other? Two old codgers having the playful childhood we had been denied.

I managed to get him off the handful of medication he threw dry down his throat, my pleading words had been useless, but chucking the sods down the toilet proved to be very effective.

Then, there was a wonderful turning point (at least that's how I viewed it!), he was tinkering with the Goldwing and suddenly (out in the sunshine) amongst the flowers, this wondrous sound escaped his beautiful lips. He was whistling with the trills of flutes and violins; soulful sounds that tore the heart and made you hope that all would be well after all, but not to be, as time unfurled.

Bless that glorious hero; he had already made unbreakable plans to leave this life that he could tolerate no longer. Depression was slaying him bit by bit. He used to take the bike to the places of his youth in Derbyshire, only to be disappointed by the inevitable changes he found there. Housing estates and trade parks instead of fields and woods. His depression was far more vicious than any Cancer, and I watched him fade, my heart full of dread "there is only one solution to our problems my dear, death"! God help me, he's going to leave this life.

Early September 1976, a still hot day as he climbed up on the Goldwing, but not before he held me by my shoulders with those strong capable hands, and with tears rolling into the beard he had recently grown, his glorious green eyes were haunted by sadness as he said "goodbye little Sister" I knew, I just knew those were the last words he would ever speak to me, I wiped away his tears that had mingled with mine, and said the words he needed to hear, "be happy, do what must be done" my permission for him to leave.

At home alone, just a few days later he lay down and created his own destiny, balls of steel Johnny boy was no more.

The weather had turned, and heavy rain pounded the car roof that followed him towards the huge marble cross on the hilltop, we passed the airbase gates where a lightning jet stood guard, on it proud and shiny was a plaque of its history. There in whatever year he had tested it and taken it to the stars and back and when his metal bird became fatigued, he had gently placed it to rest no more to trawl the skies together, Johnny and his shiny metal friend.

The rain dripped off the cap of the little black airman who saluted the passing remains of the man the whole squadron and pilots everywhere held in awe, balls of steel Johnny. Both at forever rest.

We reached the top of the hill where the cross loomed and cast its shadows. We went inside a small chapel, dingy and so depressing with a vase of dusty plastic daffodils to sully his memory. These I fling outside to be washed clean by the pouring rain. I turned in surprise as I heard the lid of John's casket being removed. Oh God, nothing could have prepared me for the shameful lack of care and skill that was before me. For there he laid, his clasped strong hands not needed anymore, but his beautiful head, his handsome young head was deformed. Whoever had performed his autopsy when they sawed off his cranium to harvest his brain, to pick through it to try to find out and understand just what he had that made him so fearless with split-second reactions, with hands so strong they could bend and break six-inch nails and tear a telephone directory in two was a disgrace! Did they ever find it? Who knows? Yes, he was Top Gun, an air warrior, and held in great esteem; yet he had to be kept a secret. So, the unwanted words of no meaning were spoken by a stranger at the funeral he had forbidden (John would hate that hypocrisy).

I knew, because he was such a perfectionist, that the misaligned bone on his forehead would have sickened and displeased him, so with tender fingers and loving respect I pushed his skull back to its handsome shape, I was crying and cursing the uncaring sod who had deformed my hero, but now my big Brother you are beautiful, forever. My tears had spattered his ivory silk shroud and fell upon the greying beard, but I did not wipe them away, I sent them on his last journey with him a part of me. He would have liked that.

At first, I thought it to be violent thunder as I looked to the darkening sky and there, hovering so low you felt you could almost touch it, its wings dipping in a sad salute of goodbye, was one of his metal birds saying its last farewell. If it could have spoken, I'm sure it would have been happy that John finally had found the peace life denied him, in another dimension. For did the shiny metal bird not know all of his secrets, loneliness and fears that no human (except me) ever heard, and the rain fell, and he slept his eternal sleep.

P.S. I wonder, does Heaven have spraying water to cool down a laughing (at last happy) reunited brother and sister? The heat of the day never fading the scented flowers; and our damaged minds on earth, purified forever, in the heavens I believe we deserve.

His first command – he was just 19 years old when he passed out as an officer.

Funny Overalls

My big brother had been dead some weeks when a friend suggested we went to seek out an old lady medium of honour and repute. We knocked on the door of a tiny bungalow adapted for her disabled husband.

She was a sweet little old soul who showed us into a chintzy parlour whilst her old husband snoozed in his invalid chair.

Pauline had her reading first. Now you must understand that Mrs Dove knew nothing of us, not our names, phone numbers, nothing. And so, she began by going over to the piano in the far corner of the lounge and started to play all the old songs, usually heard in pubs. It turned out that Pauline's departed mother was indeed a pub pianist and had been for thirty-odd years until the Cancer stilled her flying fingers. Much was said that was captured on tape, and the last prophecy would prove itself true, come the spring.

On-going to place birthday flowers on her grave in the springtime, there was the ultimate proof of life after death, just as promised her mum's grave was a carpet of Forget me Nots, the old lasses favourite flower, no other grave was graced by even one pretty blue bloom.

Then, it was my turn, and Mrs Dove clasped my hand and told me how sorry he was for the pain he had caused, she said he had not long passed over and if he knew then what he knows now he would never have put an end to his life.

She mentioned him polishing a long silver metal rod, wearing 'funny overalls' that she just could not place or recognise. She talked of dials that he was wiring up behind a grey glass rounded shield-like thing. Funny overalls still plagued her. I did not know what any of this meant, but when I got home, I phoned his widow and asked if she could solve the puzzle.

"Oh yes"

She knew exactly was Mrs Dove had seen. When one of John's Lightning's was grounded because its warrior days were at an end (as mementos of him flying that particular jet hundreds of times), he was presented with its radar probe from its giant nose cone. Also, to his delight, he received some of its cockpit dials that he modified to replace the ones behind the grey glass fairing on his Goldwing motorbike. "And what did he wear whilst doing his jobs," I asked her.

"Oh, he always wore an old flying suit; I suppose it kept his mind close to his past flying years"

Funny overalls!

In the weeks and months after he had left this dimension, I became increasingly mentally ill. Scared of sleep because time after time I would wake in tears, my fingers still feeling the grating of bone on bone as I once again realigned his once glorious handsome face. In my dreams, he had awakened and tried to make sense of what had happened to him, and then he would remember that being in that box, disfigured, was all of his own doing. And he'd cry whilst I awoke.

And so, I turned to Carlo Sanchez to do a very dangerous hypnotic procedure that before he undertakes it you have to sign a disclaimer, as people have died numerous times of heart attacks whilst under, having soul retrieval.

Usually I had my treatments in a comfy chair in his office, but this time I was ushered into the lounge of his bungalow and asked to lie on the cushions on the floor. Then he started his countdown, the soft music played and suddenly he tapped my forehead and said,

"Nine times deeper"

And so, I fell into a pit of black, no sounds reached me as before, I was afraid, but this was my last chance of mental peace. Carlo placed me on a raft slowly gliding down a jungle river, the likes of which were not of this world. Animals that were combinations of unknown species, birds with reptile bodies or were they reptiles with wings? One could not tell. Slowly of its own doing the raft came alongside a shore of purple stones, and I was instructed to watch out for an animal repeated three times. This turned out to be a strange tall giraffe with an eagle's head. I got off the raft and what I thought were stones turned out to be squidgy and soft and had the most glorious of perfumes. Feathered creatures I could not christen meandered amongst unknown flowers, probably found only in Heaven. I stood in awe. The ten-foot-tall giraffe-eagle sent its thoughts into my mind, said its name was Sally and not to be afraid, but we must go into the cave before us if I was ever to rid myself of the night terrors.

My mind pointed out to Sally that she was far too tall to enter yet, in the next breath, we were stood side by side in a large cavern with passages leading off left and right. In the centre was colour changing light that came from nowhere, and by the side of the left passage was a huge glowing magenta peony type flower. I was transfixed as it slowly revolved in the air and seemed to welcome me by its mind. The perfume from it was unlike any ever smelt by me, wondrous, sublime, and heavenly, I reached out to touch its velvet petals, and it wrapped them around my fingers and stroked my hand, as I did to it. How could this be happening? But I swear to you it did, it really, really did.

Once again, I stood by Sally and a long metal table was before us, water was running in a gully on its far side, yet it came from nowhere and ended up nowhere, it just flowed. Then, a stranger walked from the right-hand passage dressed in a green gown and mask and stood facing us at the table. His hands rested on its edge and broad leather straps shot out of the table's rim and manacled him so he could not escape. He shouted and screamed, the sound echoing and bouncing off the cave walls. No matter how hard he tugged no matter how he struggled, he was clamped tight. Then, from where he had just come from, an amazing thing happened, a shiny machete spun slowly in mid-air as though by an invisible hand, getting closer and closer to the terrified stranger. It hovered above him then, to his horror and mine, it crashed down and cut off his hand at the wrist. It floated in the bloody water, and he held up his spurting stump now released from the manacle, the machete swirled and danced around him, and his begging screams did not stop it from chopping off his other hand. He ran around the cavern splashing everything with his life's blood.

An unseen voice, deep and resonant pierced the screams and said just three words,

"DO YOU FORGIVE?"

I knew then that the gowned man had done John's autopsy, and I thought what a vile punishment my mind had (in grief) conjured up for him,

"I forgive, I forgive," I shouted out.

At once the table with its bloody water and amputated hands was no more. The gowned stranger stared in wonder at his reattached hands, all traces of blood were gone, and once again he was whole. He walked back the way he had come, gone forever. Carlo counted me back to reality, the missing part of my soul had been retrieved and placed back inside me. I never had that horrific dream again.

Together Again

I know for a fact that I have lived many times (as has everyone) this being proved to me, that whilst under deep medical hypnotic regression, I spoke in foreign languages (that in this life I knew nothing of, i.e., Russian, etc..).

It's 1978, and I've been very poorly after having an artery bypass. I'd lost a lot of weight whilst being housebound recovering for three months, I ended up looking like an expensive, (not bloody cheap!) blow up dolly, all boobies and teeth with long titian hair. At long last, I felt well enough to at last go out.

I had two friends who had never met each other before, and I suggested us three all go dancing. Off to Manchester Ritz ballroom we go, they got on famously and started to dance with anything lucky enough to have a pulse. But not me, I plonked my bottom at a table, sipped my lemonade and told any man that approached me to go away. But one particular vile man kept on mithering me, getting more persistent and drunk as the hours passed. To say, I was fed up is like saying bears don't poop in the woods. This stranger shares my table and quietly sips his pint, the moron slithers over once more and when refused for the sodding ninth time says "Why? Don't you think I can fucking afford you?" Was this lippy, ugly drunk insinuating I was a prosy? Enough said!

I excused myself with the stranger with the pint and told him I would replace it. Without missing a beat, I very quietly tipped it over that vile man's head and surely that would cool his drunken ardour, this did not go entirely unnoticed by the security staff / who escorted him out of the dance hall.

Now it's five to one, and my so-called friends disengaged themselves from their latest partners and asked if I wanted to go home. Dear God, I'd been ready since eight-thirty.

So, we walked past the raised dance floor to go downstairs to collect our coats, as I pass a hand touches my arm and just as I was about to remonstrate with who I thought was the letch, I looked up and all my dreams of a man stood there, smiling. My friends could not believe their eyes to see me in a man's arms, as I'm a real picky, fussy mare. So, we danced to Gloria Gaynor's 'Help me make it through the night.' Then, he did something strange, he held me away from him, looked so deeply into my eyes and said, "First you must answer a question and then I will know for sure, where do I come from?" without hesitation, I said "Baghdad." "At last, I've found you, I've travelled thousands of miles to find your face, and I will never leave you." And he didn't, he came home with me that night and we slept in separate rooms. But what makes it more surreal is that he was in Manchester (from Colchester) for only that night. He was helping his friend move to Umist University. He at once told Ali to collect all his things from the University of Colchester, and he transferred there and then to Manchester. In his pocket was a return ticket to Baghdad for the following Wednesday (this he never used). Even though we were of different cultures, different languages, different religions – different ages (I was twelve years older than he was); we knew we just had to be together, as in all our past lives.

And so the years pass, by now he's a professor of Computer Science and we played and loved and laughed and wished it would never end.

Then, the unthinkable, that bastard Saddam Hussain made him go home, back to hell on the earth, with threats of making his mother homeless (she was only two years older than me, her having him at fourteen after being sold by her family to his father of sixty-two), also his brother was to go to the wars front line, him being only seventeen. God help me, I told my beautiful man to go to his family to ensure their safety, my Hamid had been promised he could return to me after nine months of teaching Computer Science at the University of Baghdad. Little did he know that as he left me at the airport, tears rolling down his lovely face, that his baby brother was already long dead. (International phone lines to Baghdad were always down! No contact with home for ages) so the nine terrible months passed, and he is sent to the front line of the war. (I'm broken I'm truly broken) many years pass and I hope and pray, then on New Year's Eve I get a call saying he's coming home, the War is ending. He tells me to watch for the post as a letter will be on its way. So, I wait Oh God I waited so much so, the postman thought I was after his body (stupid git).

In May my mother died, I brought her home, and she lay in state in my front room. I tried once again to phone Baghdad, but this time I get through, only to be told that my lovely soul mate had been blown to bits on January 1st.

The translating operator cried as she told me. Now, I had a bloody corpse in the front room for weeks owing to a legal mix up, and if she stayed any longer every fly in Europe would come to visit, and I was a widow at the same time. Tragic!

When we were together, we went to Jersey on holiday and to reach the beach we had to walk down steps cut into the cliffside, one day he said: "I won't be able to stay with you in this life my darling, but I will wait for you here, in the sunshine until you come to me." It made my blood run cold, but bless him; he knew what was to be for me, loneliness!

So, there he waits for me in the sunshine as promised, young and beautiful. Please God time turns back for this old lady. "Yes", we have found each other in many lives and dimensions, you see we hold each other's souls, and we must return them to each other to be complete.

So, I don't need to love again as I've known the ultimate, you will never know desire, passion, deep, deep gut-wrenching love until you've been loved by a delicious GOOD Arab.

Do I mind dying? What do you think? He's waited long enough! Love and hugs will be ours yet again!

P.S. This I must also tell you about my divine man. It was 8:30pm, the phone rang. I heard the sound of gunfire, I almost hung up! Then the heart-breaking sound of Ray Charles reached out to me from the war-torn deserts of Iraq: "I just called to say 'I love you'," then my darling sang "I just called to say 'I love you'." Both Mr Charles and Hamid sang the whole song! Can there be such a love as ours? But we *have* known it through each dimension of time, and very soon it will be ours yet again. His life ended in the scorching desert. I believe I was in his heart and mind as he left this life. He had lived just 45 years and I miss him still.

Our one and only holiday in Jersey. So happy.

His first birthday cake made as a giraffe as he had eyelashes like one. Loved it.

Castleton at Xmas, first snow of His life, he loved it. So much love.

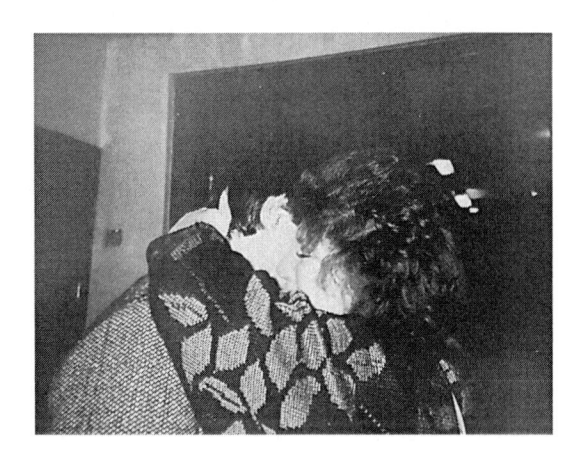

We did not realise this was our last hug and forever goodbye, at the airport where it snowed that heartbreaking morn.

The Dropped Fork

Oh! Bloody Hell, he was delicious that man of mine. Wherever we went, women would squirm with desire as their predatory eyes weighed him up. He had been a pro footballer for Iraq and still kept his body in glorious condition. Injury and conscription into the Army put paid to his time messing with balls (well, that type anyway!). Now, he was using his great mental ability and was taking his PhD in Computer Sciences. We had turned my box room into a study where he could close the door and concentrate. But these bouts of concentration were often short-lived as I'd hear his bare feet running down the stairs, he'd wrap his arms around me, hold me so close to his sweet-smelling strong body and say,

"Close your eyes, my lady."

Then, I would feel his soft kisses find my face and with a butterfly touch he'd kiss away my tears of pure gratitude that a man of such quality and beauty had made me his lady. Yes, I know so well the depth of love and passion that others believe only to be in books. Yet, destiny decreed his life would be cut so very short, but I know he waits for me just a whisper away at the end of life's rainbow.

But whilst he lived and we loved, we shared all that could be. Because he was Muslim birthdays and Christmas were unknown to him, but with me he knew the first of both. He held (unknown before) snowflakes as they melted in his manicured hands, he learnt the words of Pretty Woman and sang them to me as we toured the sunny lanes of Jersey. I taught him the love of animals and smiled when he fed the garden birds. He often got words mixed up and one morning returned from bird feeding looking so sad.

"Oh darling, there's a poor little dead sprout in the garden."

On close inspection, I told him that the feathered creature was indeed a sparrow and that a sprout was green and sat on your plate on Christmas day. Those vile little green buggers! I'm convinced they are the devil's bollocks.

We laughed like hell after we had buried the 'sprout', and bless him he never got angry with me when I took the endless wee-wee.

It was one of our rare nights out, and we were both dressed up to the nines waiting for our meal in the restaurant. Now, he had not complained of a bad back all day, but now he seemed in great discomfort, saying he had probably exercised too strenuously. His fork fell to the floor, and he made a valiant attempt to reach it, but it appeared he could not.

"Would you mind getting it for me, darling?"

"Of course."

And so, I found myself scrabbling under the dark brown tablecloth retrieving the fork. It was then that I noticed the little surprise he had in store for me. There in all its glory was his magnificent erection, strangely looking like the Mona Lisa as he had draped the brown tablecloth over its head to resemble brown long hair but more to the point like the Mona Lisa with Tourette's as he twitched his Phallus at me. Ten out of ten to me in the circumstances. I retrieved his fork and gave it back to him, but not before poking Mona in her eye with it. Ouch!

That man of mine never even missed a beat (of anything), but his lustful eyes said it all. Never was a meal eaten so rapidly, I can't remember for the life of me what it was, I can only remember the dessert and such a generous helping he ensured, enjoyed once we were home.

There were many times when our backgrounds and beliefs brought about misunderstanding, but we always managed to end up with kisses, he'd hold a strawberry between his lips and I'd bite off half of it, its juice running down our faces as our lips devoured each other. Oh, how I miss those kisses and still sometimes I taste them in old lady dreams where I am beautiful, loved and happy once again.

It was raining that afternoon; I heard his key in the lock and knew my day was now beginning, even though it was now twilight. At once, I knew all was not well as he took my hand and asked me to sit. With an embarrassed face, he told me of the young woman who had approached him in the shopping mall to ask the time. He noticed she was wearing a watch, but told her anyway and then much to his concern he noticed she was standing near him in a shop as he chose a dress for me. This situation got much worse when she climbed on the same bus as him and followed him up a long-wet road and was now standing under a tree watching our home.

"Darling, what am I to do? Honestly, I did not encourage her, she is almost still a child!"

And I looked across the road at the wet through young lass who looked about sixteen.

"Please come with me and get her to go home to her mother," he pleaded. And so, we went hand in hand across the busy tea time traffic road to talk to her.

"Why are you here?" I asked.

"I just couldn't help myself, he is just so very beautiful," was her reply.

Hamid wrapped his arms around me and said such gentle words to the young lass who had fallen in love with him in the blink of an eye.

"This is my lady, and I love her very much so please, please go home to your mother where you will be safe."

With running tears, she told me how lucky I was and before she left, I held her slender, young body and wished her also the love I knew. She looked at my man with such longing and a lesser man would have used her obvious desire for their own gratification, and she would have given herself gladly, I knew. But I was blessed with a man of such integrity, an unusual being who also carried beauty within, and I thanked my destiny for the short time that we would share as he sang 'Pretty Woman' to me in Jersey on our one and only holiday, he then took my hand and led me down the steep steps cut into the cliffside. Holding me so tightly, he said what I always knew; time together in this life was coming to an end. "This is where I will wait for you, in the sunshine until we are one again." Not long now my Hamid, not long now! Xx

The Letter That Was Never Sent

Dear Friend,
It's raining and my mind is screaming yet again.

He came to assault my sanity in my dreams. The aftermath is this torture, bits of my soul spread around the house, invisible to those that will not see, but so clear is the pain to those who care enough to open jaded eyes.

I'm on a helter-skelter, I scream to climb off, to be happy, to smile with my heart, but it goes faster and faster, twirling my sanity in its cruel speed, its grasp tears at my essence and leaves me stripped bare.

Just when I think, I, at last, belong to ME; the spectre of the past comes from the shadows, draws me into its chocking embrace and turns my being into desolation. I feel as though my endless tears are my life's blood pouring warm and sticky down my body, never to be replenished, part of me gone forever.

Thank you, my love, for giving me fairyland, for allowing my barbed wire coat to be unworn for such a short time and for allowing my skin to heal from its barbs. But now, I feel the cruelty of them even greater, comfort and peace I know will never be mine. Not while my mind remembers and my soul dreams on, while breath enters my body and sanity is stolen away.

I did not believe it possible to mourn the loss of a human as heartbreakingly cruel as the loss of one of my beloved dogs, but I do, each and every lonely day and night. A million things return him to me in spirit, yet his body is now so, so cold, broken in pieces by the bomb that ended his life in a far-off land.

My ears try to pierce the silence, searching for the once-familiar sound of his key in the door. Then and only then did I know my life for that day really had begun, until then I was just wishing away an empty lonely time, waiting like a faithful old dog for its master's return.

No more hugs, no more loving, no more lying wrapped up together, bodies entwined, listening to the rain assault the windows on magical afternoons. All gone, and with all of those priceless gifts, lost forever, so am I.

I've stroked bottles of pills for many an hour, knowing they held my salvation, but in so doing bring about the downfall of those that truly love me. So, the contents stay intact, mocking me with their promise of eternal peace. I will refuse my sanity's salvation, not because I've become so used to this constant torment (that is now an integral part of me) but because I don't want to have the ones I love and respect so dearly shed the tears that tear me to shreds today.

Thank you for caring sweet friend, for making me smile, for trusting me, for sharing your thoughts and heart, for just being you, and for trying to help me through the agony of my loss.

Have sweeter dreams than mine.

Zara x

Ted 1947-1977

It's well over twenty years that Ted had been my friend, and I can't remember for the life of me just how we had met.

But once met, we had and shared with each other life's joys and tragedies. It was that six-foot three-inch gentle giant of a man, who when my brother killed himself, rushed to my side, giving words of comfort, but most of all offered to be my new big brother, even though he was five years younger than me.

When Hamid died alone in the war-torn desert and with him my dreams of our tomorrows, once again Ted came to my side, and he also wept for his lost Arab friend.

The day came when my sixteen-year-old yellow lab Elsa had to be put to sleep (at home as with all my future dogs) this old lady had cancer in her swollen tummy, and the time for her to leave me was now. I held her still-warm body in my arms, put chocolate in her always hungry mouth told her of my love for her, kissed the eyes now turning hazy blue with the passing of her years and heard the vet tell me that my old companion was no more, her golden wagging tail would be forever still.

I was still hugging her cooling body when Ted my friend called and together we laid the old lass to rest. There can't be enough words of gratitude to the man who dug the hard ground on that November day so long ago. His strong arms held me in comfort whilst I wailed tears of loss against his Arran sweater.

My Elsa had been a comfort throughout all of my marriage to a so-called man, a violent monster who stole eleven years of my young life, now my golden girl was in her deserved peace, hopefully to be reunited with her old mum many years down the line.

Yes, Ted knew full well the therapeutic value the stroking of a pet could have and with this in mind, he took his beloved Bruno, the most regal and dignified of Airedales to visit the sick and dying, like a much-loved Pat Dog. So many of Ted's days off work were spent in this way, just him and his dog, bringing comfort and joy where it was needed most. To hospices and old folk's homes, those two would travel, chat with strangers about bygone times and Bruno would just sit there, so very regal, as the curls on the top of his head were fondled by yet another feeble lonely old hand.

Anyone who does not love animals as Ted and I do will never understand the pain of being parted from a faithful pet. The people those two visited were denied keeping their own animals because of illness or indeed imminent death, and so it was with great joy they awaited the visits of the giant man and his giant dog, bringing with them words of humour and wisdom and kindness and a regal head of curls just waiting to be fondled. I believe the now old Bruno gave his comfort to the dying until the very last days of his own so special life. Now, he lays as peaceful in death as he was in life in his beloved master's garden.

When the pain of losing Bruno had faded a little, it was time for Ted and his family to choose another four-legged friend. For just like me, Ted's life was incomplete without a dog by his side, and eventually he found Bruno's replacement, once again the Airedales he loved, the exuberant Billy.

And now I remember the look of pure joy and wonder on Ted's face as he described the tiny fingernails on his yearned-for new-born son's hands, all he kept saying was "he held my fingers, Zara, he held my fingers" Yes, we shared a lot over our years of friendship Ted and me.

He was a true family man, devoted to his wife and son and the magic of their life was completed by the birth of a little baby girl, yes, he was contented and at peace with the world.

This gentle giant was one hundred percent trustworthy and respected, a rare sort of human in this sickening society. He was the type of man you could leave everything you treasured with, knowing full well that your child, granny, animal, money and home would be perfectly safe in his keeping. Yes, he was so very special.

Now, I would have thought that his deep love and respect for all creatures would have made him the perfect vet, for not only did he have compassion and the necessary brainpower, but also the strong physique needed to handle large injured, frightened animals.

This vocation was not to be, and instead, he chose to be a policeman, spending many of his years in the force, skilfully riding the motorbikes he so loved, as a traffic cop.

Yes, it seems only yesterday he expressed great concern about young lads being allowed to own and drive high powered bikes, without the extensive road safety training he had undergone before being turned loose into the dangerous traffic. He worried about all their young lives in jeopardy and could not see into his own tragic future.

Oh! Teddy bear friend of mine, if only my still embryonic physic powers had for-warned me about your fate, never would I have allowed you to climb up on your pride and joy, a giant motorbike, just last Sunday.

But in the sunshine, you did sit astride that gleaming beast and with your daughter on the pillion; you set out in the sunshine on the last journey of your too-short fifty-year-old life.

Some impatient stranger overtaking on a bend on a left turning was intent on stealing a few seconds of time when he drove on the wrong side of the road. Your side of the road my dear, and with your beloved child clasped behind you, you had nowhere to go except into death, as the stranger's car hit you full on. Another few hundred yards, another minute of time, and the roar of your engine's brakes would have heralded your homecoming to enjoy the meal that awaited the two of you. But instead, your lovely wife heard only the sound of sirens as they rushed to yet another tragedy in the sunshine, little did she know at that moment that the tragedy was hers.

So that stranger, who flouted every rule of the road, stole not only a couple of unneeded seconds, but he also stole your valuable life and put your child in intensive care, her pelvis smashed in two places.

Teddy bear friend you had been dead for four lonely days when just by chance I found out you were no more. I wrote the words of respect and comfort that my heart dictated to your so new widow and held her while she wept for her lost future without you.

I know for sure that the last thought in your mind as you saw eternity beckon you, would be to try to save the life of your beloved child. Well, my brave friend, this you did, and I now know how.

A man walking his dog saw the mayhem unfold in the autumn sunshine, but you dear man shine even brighter than the sun. You knew there was no escape, and so you did the thing that surprises me not at all. Your hands left the handlebars and with the last of your giant strength you threw your precious child onto the pavement, out of harm's way and rode into death alone. You saved your girl Ted; she's still in the hospital, but she will mend in body and in six-weeks time be back home with her lovely mum and brother. In time, she will be able to remember her dad without tears, but the respect, love and pride for you will never fade.

Today I took flowers to the place where your life was stolen from you and placed them with love amongst those already there. Posies from children and pensioners were tucked into the dry stone wall, the wall that bore no sign of its so recent tragic past.

Yet I had to talk to you just once more, for old times' sake you see, so with your widow's permission, I stood and held your icy hand for such a long time, in that respectful Chapel of Rest. There you lay my teddy bear friend, resplendent in check shirt and jeans, for no shroud would ever cover your poor broken body. I thanked you for over twenty years of caring, for being a friend to be proud of and one I will miss until it's my turn to join you. I asked you to forgive me for my mind not being able to foresee your fate, and in so doing, save you from it. *Give me a sign, a sign that all is well* was my repeated request to you. We parted for the last time with me promising that I would try to emulate your years of kindness to me, by always being there to help the family you never wanted to leave.

Was it only four weeks ago that we shared our last cup of coffee? You held my Sophie's old face in those giant gentle hands and looked into the eyes that could no longer see you properly. But Sophie knew it was the old friend who had stroked her since she was just a puppy, all was well, it was only her Ted and the old tail wagged.

Once again you made the gesture of kindness that meant the world to me. That when the time came for me to lose her, once more you would unselfishly come to my aid, yet again. Just as you had for dear old Elsa some fifteen years ago, you would once more dig a grave in my rose garden and place Sophie to rest beside my golden friend. Little did either of us know on the day of our last chat that darling old Sophie would still be here, and it would be you, my precious friend that would lay at rest.

But one thing I'm sure of is that when she does finally leave and break my heart, I will be able to gather the strength you send me from heaven, to dig her grave, for you will be watching and helping, in death as you did in life, for over twenty years.

And so, Billy, you're lovely once so joyful Airedale sits and waits patiently for his master who will never return. How can anyone explain to his doggy mind, that no more will he roam the familiar fields and woods with the master who was his whole life? Poor Billy.

I can't help but feel hatred for the man who drove so dangerously that he stole your precious life on that autumn Sunday. He's a killer as sure as if he had struck a knife in you, it would be only just if he had to stand trial for your murder and also the attempted murder of the child whose life you so bravely saved. And I hope he is haunted for all time, that his dreams are filled with screams and every autumn leaf brings back the memory of what he created, two broken bodies, one already passing through the doors of death, lying on the pavement as the sun continued to shine on that Sunday afternoon.

The sun was still shining as Sophie and I stood outside the house you had visited, the house you had so often brought to life with your laughter. But now it lay silent as we waited for your last visit and this time you would pass by with never a word. Our head bowed in respect, old Sophie sat at my side by the pavement's edge, and the Police outriders escorting your body came into view. It was 3 pm Friday 24 October 1997 and your respectful colleagues were taking you on your last journey, from the home and life you loved to a place none of the living knows. Was it my imagination or did all of you really stop for just a second, for a final goodbye and sweet dreams? And then there she was, the dignified lovely lady who had shared your happy life for so many years, the mother of your children, that she would now have to raise without you, sending me a gentle wave of friendship as she followed your body.

I can't come to terms with the fact I'll never answer the door again to find a uniformed giant teddy on my step, demanding the kettle to be put on, but that's how it will always be for me from now on. Without you!

Standing holding your icy hand in the Chapel of Rest for the first and only time, I asked you to send the sign that all was well; hardly daring to hope and believe I could possibly receive one.

Exactly one week to the day since you left this world, once again Sophie and I walked in the sunshine. Autumn leaves of every hue scattered the ground as we strolled a route never before taken. And there lying distorted and run over was my sign; all was well. I knelt and scooped up the tiny golden bear that smiled at me from its bed of pretty leaves and from the heavens did I hear you laugh once again, or was it the Blackbird calling from the Hawthorn tree? But Ted, the teddy bear is very, very real, he slumps before me now all clean and brushed on the kitchen worktop, beside the coffee I'll alone drink in a minute.

His tiny baby arms are in just the same position as they were when I rescued him from his bed of leaves, a strange position really, for a teddy bear, right arm upright beside a tiny torn ear, his left arm stretched out to the side just like a furry traffic cop, on duty really.

Sceptics will say it's just a teddy bear lost by a crying child, maybe so, but bear and I know Ted sent him, all is well.

And so, devoted husband and father, thoroughly nice man and the best of friends, enjoy your rest. Call the names of the dogs you and I have loved and lost, for surely, they'll abide with you in heaven. Take them once again on the walks they loved, across fields forever green, through woods that never die, alongside streams eternally pure, and in the blink of a tear-filled eye we will all meet up again.

Sweet dreams teddy bear man, all is well!

P.S. So many times over the passing year I have driven along that pretty road of death, each time saying "Hello! my teddy bear" to my long-lost friend. Once again the fallen autumn leaves graced the ground with crimson and gold, the old stone wall still stood strong and proud. And the sun shone, and the birds sang in the trees that are now overgrown. Amongst those branches I *know* what I saw. A vaporous tall dark being — just standing there. I believe it was Ted, still on duty, even in death, controlling the traffic on that pretty road of death where he left this life — forever.

Sweet dreams, Big Ted. xx

Lee – My dearest dear

Many moons ago, I met a gentleman of Irish descent, who I believed to be the right man for me, a possible husband.

We would go dancing, have lovely meals, make wonderful love, and all was well with the world. He obviously knew of my bipolar personality, but bless him, loved me despite it.

I'd met this man at the Ritz in Manchester, he was very elegant and tall with grey eyes and jet-black hair, his tinted glasses added to his air of sophistication. It was in the days of long evening gowns and the white Grecian one I wore that evening obviously drew him into my web. Poor sod!

He was extremely nice to my two children and Elsa my yellow lab and he often bought bags of groceries and even a new rug when Elsa ripped up the ninth one. She continued to tear up rugs until the day she had to leave me; her score at that time being thirteen.

Unbeknown to me Michael decided I might make a half-decent Wife and with this in mind purchased a diamond ring. Along with the ring, came a joke ball and chain with the following ditty.

"Your wandering days are over, you're nair to roam again, to tie you down dear Rover I bring this ball and chain", (how's that for a long-term memory some forty years later?) to be honest it was not the best verse to give to a free spirit like myself, but hey ho!

It's a Friday summer teatime; I'd been to the market with a friend who had introduced me to Simon, a stallholder of curtain material. In conversation, he mentioned he and his German Shepherd needed lodgings, and it just so happened my previous lodger had just legged it because of my resident Poltergeist. (I kid you not!), and poor Simon was to be tormented and frightened crapless by my invisible guest many times whilst he lived in a strange house with a strange woman.

So Michael comes around bearing ring and ball and chain, chocs and flowers in hand, only to be greeted by a poncy man and a snarling bloody great dog. No explanation would placate him; he really believed this chap was a boyfriend — not a lodger — and that he was sharing my bed instead of sleeping in the tiny box room.

Turning on his heel (he'd not even sat down) my future Husband stormed out of the house taking with him all he had brought. Shame really as I could have murdered a Thornton's chocky. We never did marry, each other or him to anyone else, and I believe he's returned to his native Ireland to live out a happy retirement. But Simon stayed as my lodger for over two years but found it nigh on impossible to conform to a few house rules. One, he cleans up after Lee and two, no using my home as a knocking shop. This lad was a great one for the ladies. I could never understand this as I considered him to be effeminate, nice but wet!

Now Simon was no drinker, but he smoked and gambled and shagged his way through life.

After many conquests, he finally decided to settle down; with his track record I never believed it would happen. Then, he met a lovely lady who would eventually become his second wife; together they were to make their home in Brighton and asked if I would keep Lee as he was so happy with me.

It was my delight to have this elderly magnificent Shepherd stay with me, for he and golden Elsa were the best of friends.

Out walking one day, I noticed blood on his right leg; on inspection I found it had dripped from his mouth. The vet confirmed what I had dreaded, CANCER.

I was allowed to pay weekly for the operation to remove that vile bunch of crusty looking adhesions on Lee's gum. He recovered from the op in much pain, for the vet had had to remove part of his jaw and a few teeth also. If I'd known the severity of this procedure and that Lee's life was to end shortly anyway, I would never have had him under the knife.

I went to pick you up from the vet, still groggy from the anaesthetic. When you saw your old mum, you went crazy, howling and jumping up at me. How much of that howling was pain? My brave love, not all of it I hope! I nursed you round the clock, sleeping on the sofa with you resting on me. It wasn't a chore, it was a privilege to share our running out time, for our days and weeks were to be numbered. You seemed to rally around after two weeks, and I thought we had beaten the swine of a disease that had ruined my darling's gentle life. Then, you stopped eating, not even roast chicken or salmon from my fingers. You'd just give a sniff at whatever was offered and turned your gentle majestic head away. It was on the morning that your back legs gave out that I knew I had to help you leave me, and so the vet was called to the home we had shared for many a happy year so you could end your time on this earth where you were happiest, instead of a Vets sterile surgery.

Time has turned your laughing kind hazel eyes to misty blue, the black of your once glossy coat is flecked with grey and you stumble on legs that can run no more.

We have loved for fifteen long years my gorgeous boy and my greatest show of that love is soon to happen. You are wrapped in my arms as you have been all of your life, choccy drops melt on a gasping tongue, the beating of your gentle heart slows, and oh, how I wish it would cease of its own accord. That would save me the heart-breaking decision of ending your now poorly old life.

Lee, my precious old dear, have you heard the ring of the doorbell? For you show no sign. Once you would have run to warn anyone that this was your home and your mum could not be harmed, with you guarding her.

The vet enters, my worst nightmare but your salvation has begun. Sweet, sweet old man. He kneels beside us and lifts your golden leg whilst I whisper my words of love and goodbye. Your majestic head is resting on my chest wet from my tears, slowly the needle delivers your paradise, you raise that lovely face, gaze into my eyes and kiss me one last time and fade away, "thank you, mummy!"

I held you all that tear-soaked night, wiping away the fluids your hardening body expels, I do this with the same love and tenderness as I had when you still wagged your fringed beautiful tail. For you were, and still are, my darling friend, my Lee who I believe waits for me in the paradise I hope we both deserve.

My mind travels back to early morning runs in fields of yellow and white, strong young legs carrying you swiftly to fetch the ball you enjoy chasing so much. Time and again I watch as you retrieve your toy and when you are tired you lay at my feet laughing with exhausted joy. And this was the time when I groomed you, the tumbleweed of your hair blew across the field, later to be collected by waiting nesting birds.

I'm comforted by believing that once again your eyes twinkle with health and happiness, your alert ears miss no sound, your velvet body is strong and vibrant once more, free from the cancer that stole you from me.

In the flower-strewn fields of heaven, you wait for me, where the sun never burns, flowers keep their perfumed beauty and the birdsong melts the hardest heart.

Soon I will pass through this dimension called life and once again stroll the perfumed fields with you my darling dog! No other animal would come so deeply into my heart in the future. I would love each and every one of them, but you were not just an animal, you were my heart and soul, sweet dreams old man.

An Unlikely Friendship

He really was a dirty vile old swine, and I believe if even both his legs had worked, he still would live like a pig. Apparently, whilst still a child he had contracted polio, thus making his legs useless and confining him to a wheelchair and later an invalid carriage for life, but other bits of him definitely worked. His and my lodger Simon's friendship was the most unlikely, Simon with his clean groomed hair and velvet suits (when they were all the rage in the 70s) and driving a Cranberry Red Daimler car, this boy was not short of a bob or two. He showed his unending friendship to the mucky one by providing meat (from one of his numerous butcher shops) plus fruit, lager, treats and also the chewing tobacco that Pong gobbed out wherever he might be. This generosity continued until Pong died in the way of his dreams.

Every year without fail on 7 July, Simon would provide the present that Pong lusted after from the previous year. 'No' not the expensive whisky nor the fish and chip supper at evening's end. 'No', 'no', this had to be flesh living hot-blooded, that was none too picky as to whom it joined with. "Happy Birthday Pong, old boy, your latest slapper is on her way."

Just like last year and many years before, Simon prowled the Longbar in Manchester where ladies of the night sashayed up and down hoping for punters. Of course, when they spied Simon, they thought all their birthdays had come at once. Shame it was only Pong's. Simon told a couple of these painted girlies his requirements for a friend of his whom he would drive them to. The refusals ranged from a straight 'No' to 'Fuck Off' "I might be on the batter, but I've got my bleeding standards." At the far end of the bar was a sorry sight, God alone knows how many punters (in exchange for a five-pound note, a lot of money in those days) it had taken to make her look so used. She had traces of white powder under her snotty nose that Simon did not mistake for Max Factor. He told this lady, now Sukie by name AKA Gladys (who would just love to be 55 again) what he needed and for whom! She did not care a stuff but insisted she was paid upfront (fine) and was brought back to where he found her (fine).

Pong thought 'Fuck it' "just because it's my birthday and I'm in for a jump, it does not mean I have to have a wash" as he scratched himself redraw. The scene was set, God help Sukie. Now to say that the fumes in that two up and two down slum were all from him would be a darn right lie because a fair amount of the stink came from his rotting pet cat that had died some weeks previously. He did his best to contain Tiddles in a plastic bag, but as time passed the post-mortem juices flowed out, (with the persistent attendance of resident rats) and seeped into the tattie rug in front of the one bar electric fire. All he cared about was the 'pretty' lady that was to straddle his withered legs, speared onto his erection brought about by mucky books and a couple of useful little pills, also supplied by Simon at that morning's whisky giving.

Was that Simon's car he just heard? It must be because the dog was barking and so happy as treats were on their way for him too and Pong was really ready to give the 'Pretty' lady a right good sorting. In her worst nightmares, Sukie would never have believed she could get herself into such a stinking mess, but she had a habit, an expensive habit that had to be paid for and with this in mind she slipped off her jacket and skirt to reveal a non-too clean Basque and laddered stockings. (She and the mucky one were made for each other).

His boozed-up mind and cataract eyes told him she was a real beauty and he went at her with relish with his bits that did work "Fuck having no legs I have got some chopper," he rejoiced. She'd only been gyrating for a couple of minutes whilst scratching herself senseless (those fucking fleas) when Pong made a grunt of pure ecstasy, his eyes rolled to the back of his head, and he bloody died! Oh shit, oh shit, oh shit, she tries to get dressed whilst wiping the old blokes' fluids from her stocking tops with her lipstick smeared snotty tissue from the depths of her gold plastic handbag. Oh shit, oh shit and finds she can't stand in her stiletto shoes as she's shaking so much. Sweet Jesus, what time did that fancy posh bloke say he'd pick me up? Bloody hell, what if he's left me in this hell hole, with a fucking smelly corpse? Oh shit, oh shit. Three-quarters of an hour later she hears the car she's been begging for. Simon strolls in to find her in hysterics, and Pong having emptied his bowels also. Now, it's Simon's turn for 'Oh shit', and he runs out to a phone box to call a taxi (this being long before mobiles, I bet he wished they'd been invented then) On its fast arrival, he shoves the truly traumatised slapper in the taxi with directions to the driver to take her to the Longbar, but she said would he mind if she was taken straight home, as her shift was well and truly over?

Simon could hear Pong's sparsely haired, flea-bitten old dog howling from the pavement, as Spot knew his beloved old master was no more, now who knows if Pong would have lived longer had it not been his birthday?

Now, Simon could always think on his feet as he turned them in the direction of the fish and chip shop at the corner of the street. Two cod, chips and mushy peas were bought but never eaten. Well not by humans anyway. He walked into Pong's home as if for the first time that night and immediately dropped two fish suppers on the floor. Next, he ran to the very respectable neighbours, who when they found out Pong had croaked it, were bloody delighted. "Of course, you can use our phone to call the police," they said. This done Simon scampers back to old Pong's hell hole to find the old dog feasting on what should have been their suppers, shared of course by the resident rats delighted that Tiddles (the scourge of their life) was melting in the corner.

A full forty minutes later, the boys in blue arrived and said, "yes he's dead," (duh) and they too started to scratch, Pong the smelly corpse was shifted, the dog and budgie put in Simon's car for safekeeping, Pong's house was locked and police yellow taped up (though God only knows why), because who the hell would go in it? I often wonder how long it took the undertaker to remove the ecstatic grin from Pong's unshaven face? Maybe he left it there for the old boy to take to his next life and boast about how he got that grin. I truly hope that in his next life, his legs finally walked. Sweet dreams, Pong.

PS: I would have done the old boy a great disservice if I did not portray the side of his character that was golden-hearted, generous and with a never-ending adoration of all animals. My conscience would not allow you, dear reader, to hold this strange old boy in bile rising contempt, for his good side far outweighed the needed bar of soap.

In the deprived area of Manchester where Pong spent his life, it was deemed almost normal to see other pathetic creatures like him doing their best just to survive. Nobody gave a stuff about the crotchety dirty old swine with fleas hopping on him, sat in that chair, his withered legs in heavy callipers, and trying without success to use the arm crutches quickly thrown at him years ago in some 'don't give a stuff' hospital.

He had no means of keeping himself clean even if he had wanted to, and so some very unsavoury habits became the norm. He only had an outside privy (toilet) but found it impossible to negotiate his cobbled backyard without yet another fall. So, he found an ingenious way to get rid of his body waste. This being the kitchen sink and an old tin plate, he did his best to catch from his twisted body what needed to be caught but sometimes missed, and the floor held evidence of this, what he did catch the sink received, and it was forced down the plughole with a fork. He seemed to have become immune to the gut retching smell that pervaded his world, and my dear friend Simon could only cope with his regular visits to Pong by tying a silk cravat around his face soaked in Paco Rabanne aftershave, but even so he often brought up his breakfast once in the fresh air. But what really disgusted him were those frigging flesh-eating fleas. Blue Bottle flies lived with Pong in their hundreds if not thousands, the constant humming buzzing and the black moving living curtains at the dirty windows kept out any sunlight that dared to shine on the hovel. He tried his best to combat the fly, maggot and flea infestation by putting up dozens of sticky flypapers as high as he could reach. Most of these fly death monstrosities were completely covered on both sides and looked more like pieces of black carpet hung up. Rats also had a good home with Pong now that Tiddles had croaked it, but he liked them and watched with delight as they polished off the scraps of food he threw to the floor for them, for at least they were non-judgemental and enjoyed the safe mucky haven he had provided for them. Yes, Pong loved all creatures great and small and used a high proportion of his meagre pension to prove the point. Each week he would trundle himself to the local market and get animal supplies in his invalid carriage for all the feral dogs, cats and pigeons on a demolition site near to his home. His mangey lovely old dog would sit between his wasted legs and the budgie Simon bought for him would be on the steering wheel (really true). He was a regular sight in Gee Cross Manchester and sometimes people would have a word with him, but only a very short word because of the stench and fleas from his abode he brought out with him.

 Rain or shine, summer or winter, it did not matter to Pong, his priority in life was helping the creatures he loved with a passion. Twilight came, and he could be seen yet again going to see his animal friends. Oh, so many feral dogs and cats would crowd around Pong's carriage, ever eager for the lifesaving food he never failed to bring them. Pigeons would pass on the word "Pong is here, Pong is here," and the beating of their wings would fill the darkening sky. He'd stay with his animal friends until the last scrap of food was gobbled up and even then they did not want him to leave and would gather around him to be petted and talked to. It's just a pity some kind soul did not do the same for old Pong! Quite the opposite really.

One night a gang of thugs stole his remaining bit of pension money, tipped him out of his carriage like a stranded turtle and gave him a good kicking and peed on him for good measure. The bastards, the cowardly cruel bastards. Not content with the pain and humiliation they had already inflicted on him they went on to steal his NHS specially made boots that metal clamped to his callipers. Without these, his feet and ankles were just floppy useless bits of skin and tissue. These precious boots were his lifeline because without them he was nothing. They were free from the NHS but cost £375 to replace if they went missing (a lot of money in the 70's) which Pong would have to find himself to replace them within the allocated five years life of the boots. Poor Pong had no money, no life, no hope, but he did have Simon who soon came to rescue yet again, with brand new boots. Simon was to say it was the only time he ever saw old Pong cry, this time with gratitude, not the pain and frustration the old boy was used to, I'm surprised really the thieving scum bags didn't also steal his callipers to weigh in for scrap. He was to say later that if he had the means that terrible night he would have ended his tragic existence, as luck would have it he was found at dawn amongst the bricks and rubble by a passing milkman who knew the old boy well. Pong being Pong refused flatly to go to the hospital because he knew for sure they would attempt to wash off years of grime that he used to joke about saying that it was only the muck that held him together. It must have been a rare early morning sight. A milk float clanging along the cobbles with a crippled old bloke's callipered legs stuck out the side wedged into the front alongside the kind driver with his battered invalid carriage amongst the gold tops. Bless that man, he helped Pong inside his home then beat the hastiest retreat from the flies, fleas and rats as the poor sod could not hold his breath any longer. On the slow journey home, Pong had told Billy the milkman of the excitement of his upcoming birthday and had gone into great detail about how it always was and how it would be yet again. Of course he did not know it was to be his very last birthday and 'Yes' Pong did indeed go out with a bang. Rest in peace PONG

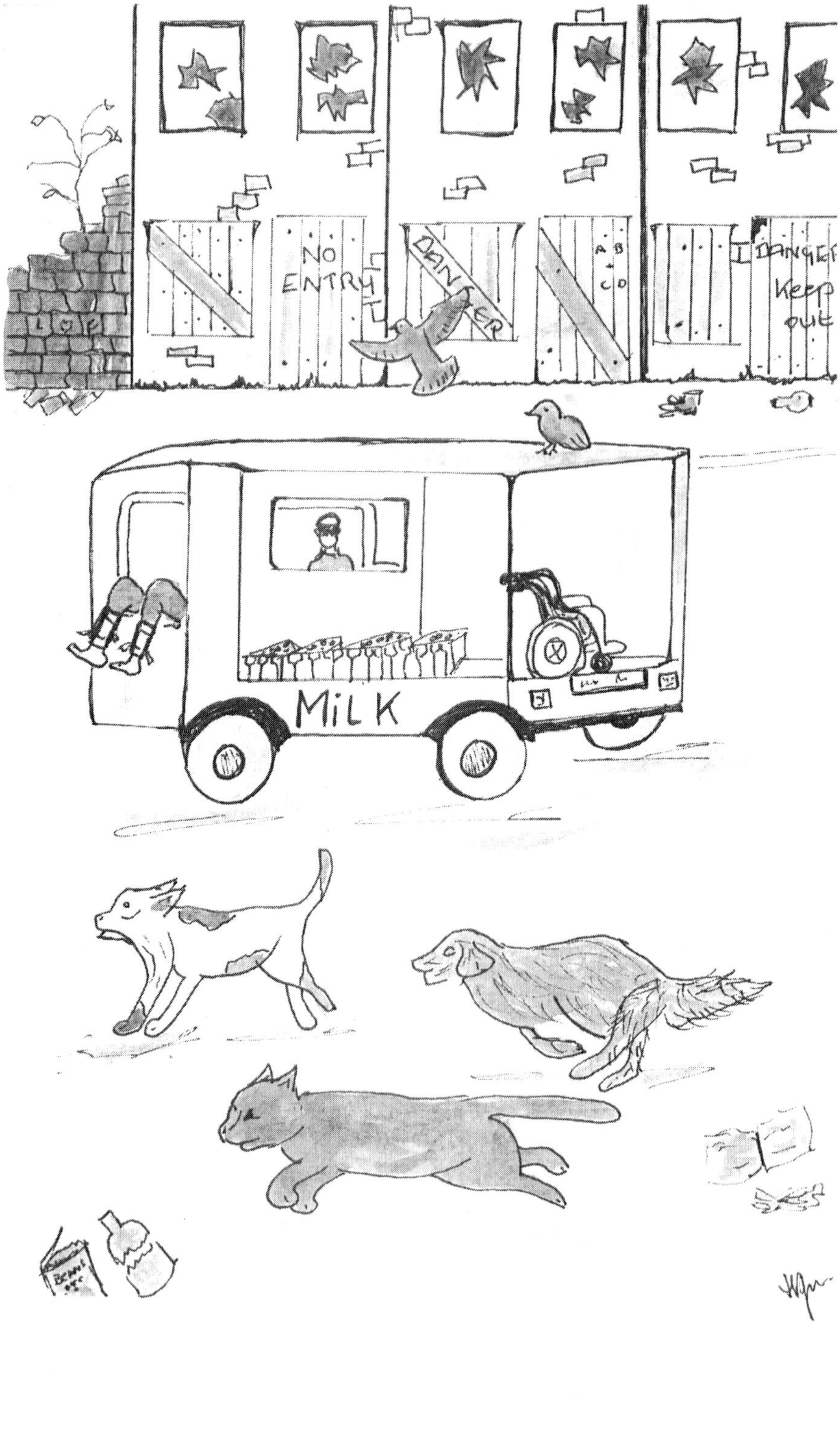
NO ENTRY
DANGER
DANGER
Keep out
MILK

The Missing Link

He was the stuff of nightmares, six-foot-five inches tall, covered in black shaggy hair with a snarling full beard. Many times I'd seen him on TV and marvelled at the courage of any opponent that climbed into the wrestling ring without a whip and chair to fend the big git off. Much like circus lion trainers used to do when I was a child.

Now Simon knew that May Ling (his latest diminutive sexual oriental conquest) was married to this monster, but what he kept in his pants made him throw all caution to the kerb.

I first encountered this little soul when I looked over my banister at 4 am after being woken up, and she smiled her sweet smile from over Simon's shoulder. He knew very well he was breaking my rules by trying to turn my home into a knocking shop! This rampant idiot lodger of mine thought he could fool me into thinking he was alone if I only heard one pair of feet climbing the stairs. So, he'd perched the oriental beauty on his back and his laboured breathing had altered me to the fact he was either ill or up to no good, the latter proved to be true. Needless to say, the pair of them went back out through the same front door they had only just entered. Where did they go? Who cares! Who knows!

Soon his fascination with her wore off (now that's a surprise), and I forgot all about May Ling until her shaking crying little body stood pitifully in the rain on my doorstep, begging for help.

Even though her massive husband looked like he could impregnate a whole continent, much to her dismay, the giant proved to be infertile, this being proved by tests carried out when she failed to become pregnant with the child, she'd craved for almost three years.

She cursed that evening (three and a half years ago) when she waited at tables in a Hong Kong restaurant and caught the eye of what looked like an ape in a suit. He waited until her shift was over and started to woo her with promises of a wonderful life in England, she would live in a fancy house, not in the lodging room shared by the three other workers that she loathed. He sat her on the front row of the arena audience making her feel special like a Queen, whilst he knocked the hell out of the poor bastard who had dared to climb in with him. After each bout he would present her with tiny precious gifts and kiss her fingertips, never once not behaving like a true kind caring future husband. And so, God help her, soon he was. He finished his tour of the Far East and returned home with an Oriental bride to a rented flat in downtown Salford, Manchester. To say that her rose coloured tinted specs were removed is putting it mildly. Bit by traumatising bit they were smashed to pieces as he practised his wrestling moves on her and not in a tender way.

So, is it any wonder when out buying curtain material on a Friday market, this normal, unhairy, gently spoken, kind man more than caught her attention? Soon, she was putty in his hands, and he easily did what the big bugger had failed to do in three years, make her pregnant. Now, if only this story could have a happy ending, but of course it was impossible, she could hardly ask her violent husband for a divorce and marry Simon, who she cared so much for, as 1. Her husband would kill the pair of them in a growling blink of an eye, and 2. Simon had moved on to pastures new.

Dripping wet with rain and tears, she poured out her fear, and I was so bloody infuriated with my lodger's callous treatment of her that I vowed to put right what he had done wrong. She left my home that evening reassured that not only would I fix everything, but it would remain our secret. This I have kept all these years, but I can speak of it now, as little May Ling died of cancer many years ago, never fulfilling her dream of becoming a mummy. And the big git followed not long after. Please God there was no reunion in Heaven.

Now I've told you before that Simon had another addiction, besides women, (gambling,) and this he did with great success at the casinos in Manchester. Not long after May Ling's distressed visit, he rolls home at 5.30 am after a very lucrative night at the gambling tables. He empties his pockets of so much cash I had not got the time to count it before it went into my handbag, for a very good purpose, and Simon slept the sleep of the satisfied.

The little soul was shaking with fear as she was led into the room where she was to lose the one thing she craved, the tiny baby (Simon's child) nestling in her womb. I waited whilst she was ready to leave, and I brought her to stay with me. Simon was forbidden to come back home whilst she recovered, and it was pure luck that the angry giant was throwing people against the ropes in a wrestling ring in France, so never knew she was not at their home.

May Ling and I parted after two weeks, her problem was solved, she was feeling stronger and the extra money thrown on Simon's dresser from his winnings that lucky night that saw her on her way to Ireland. There she had a cousin with a restaurant who gave her a job, a home and sanctuary from four years of constant beatings. Well, bless her; I'm so pleased I could help!

When Simon awoke to his missing winnings, I told him in no uncertain terms they were a memory. Her safety was more important than him. He just shrugged his shoulders and said that was ok, he'd just go out gambling and replace it all.

And Simon continued in his lifelong pattern of gambling and screwing until finally he met a lovely lady to marry and settle down with, and forty years later they are still together. That's almost a bloody miracle! She must be some sort of angel to tolerate his antics for so many years. I wouldn't!!!

Sophie, Our Beginning

It had been quite some time since I'd had to put my Elsa the yellow Labrador to sleep because of her cancer. I'd arranged for the vet to end her happy life with me at home because I did not want her last memory to be of the sterile vet's surgery that she really hated. And so, we lay on the dining room carpet together – she and I enjoying, as best we could, the cuddles and kisses and the chocky drops the fifteen-and-a-half-year-old lady had always loved. She had not heard that the ring of the doorbell was the start of our goodbye. The gentle vet knelt beside us, shaved her golden front leg, gave her quick salvation and my stroking hand felt her sweet kind heart beat its last.

Ted (who was my very best dearest friend) laid my golden girl to rest in my rose garden, and we both stood and cried and hugged in the November rain on my birthday, for the lovely creature that had blessed my life for fifteen-and-a-half years. That man was my friend and helper for many years. Ted was a motorbike police officer who died on his birthday, lying in the autumn leaves, killed by a driver on the wrong side of the road. I grieved his loss. Oh, I was so very lonely without him in my life.

Seeing Molly the German Shepherd playing in her garden with thirteen puppies whose care and feeding turned that poor mum into a skeleton, broke my heart. I was determined that if I should have one of her babies it would never have the pitiful life she had had. Not content with using her as a breeding machine, the lazy owners hired her out as a guard dog to scrap yards and pubs (even when pregnant). This turned a mild happy dog into a growling psycho who had (at one time) greeted me with wags and kisses. No more! She was in her season yet again and of course she was expected to produce enough babies to buy a new car.

Now Ted, my Policeman friend, had told me of this long-haired black German Shepherd giant pup that all of the handlers envied. I suppose its size was a sort of status symbol! It had been born in police breeding kennels and got top marks in training with its lucky new handler. It only had one fault, but a very important one. It always caught the miscreant it was in pursuit of, the problem being that once caught it would never let go of the screaming sod, no matter its handler's commands and not even a few clouts with a nightstick would make it let go of the now shredded burglar who wished he'd never got out of bed that day.

The police wanted very brave big dogs, so it was decided to have him create a litter before his robust bollocks went missing and were made into dangling earrings (not really) Joke!

Anyway, Molly's owner knew the police dog handlers, and he gladly gave his permission for sweet Molly to cop for the attentions of Bear (AKA) Fang, both of these names were totally appropriate and the huge lad answered both to of them, and he only stopped his attentions to Molly when he was good and ready.

So, Molly had his progeny, and he lost his bollocks, but it did not calm him down one bit. Because the police were not about to appear in court themselves for using a dog whose hobby was to shed criminal's bollocks, the decision (though sad) was to dispense with Fang's ferocious services. This reduced radically the reconstruction of burglar's buttocks in A&E. This lightened the workload of night staff for which they were most grateful.

So, the poor brave lad was chucked out of the police and ended up as a guard dog at a scrapyard. I saw him only once through the bars, he never barked. There was this long menacing growl, blazing eyes and pure white teeth exposed below his snarling muzzle. That was bugger off in any language. So, I did!

Anyway, Fang (AKA) Bear was not shooting blanks and poor, poor Molly gave birth yet again to twelve wonderful puppies, I'd watch them from my back bedroom window and decided that now I was without a canine friend since the death of Elsa (my yellow lab) I'd give my love to one of Molly's babies. I'd watch the litter getting smaller and despaired at the sight of some of the human mongrels who strode away with a tiny scrap of black and tan fur tucked under their tattooed arms. Then they decided to keep the last puppy to intensely breed from, just like poor Molly. How uncaring and vile to wear out a poor dog's body by having to produce puppies each season, so the rotten owners can cash in and buy yet more trash. It had got to the stage of just one pup left, (a glorious specimen) the product of its mother's rape by Fang. I never liked the buggers that owned Molly and her last child but I got the £450 purchase price together, knocked on their door, walked right past the vile owner, patted darling Molly, scooped up her remaining baby and stormed out of that house saying just this, "She is mine"! The owner stood there gawping and counting her cash, shrugged her shoulders, shut the door, and it was never mentioned again.

Soon after I got the joy of my Sophie (I did not like the name April, they had given her), they went to work and live in Spain, giving Molly to their daughter who lived on a disgusting drug dealing council estate a few miles away. This woman was a replica of her parents, she did not give a sod about poor, poor Molly, she allowed her to roam the littered streets coming home in hope of food. One day she was extra late back, so instead of going out looking for her, that negligent bitch finished her booze and went to bed. In the morning, she found Molly dead on the torn lino kitchen floor; it was obvious she had died from poison in frothing torment, alone, unloved and only seven years old.

What a terrible end to a once majestic loving, kind, sweet animal, who only asked for love, kindness and din-dins. Shame on them. I hope they rot in hell.

Vincent's Invisible Violin

This six-foot four-inch handsome young man worked the doors of a nearby nightclub, and I was going to make this bonny lad MINE! When I say he needed no coaxing as he was over this older lady like a rash, not too much older you understand, just enough to make, shall we say, his sexual tuition interesting.

Now because these lessons lasted long after his shift at the nightclub, he told his mum, whom he lived with, that he was staying with a friend as taxis he could not afford on a poor wage, and this friend just so happened to be in an orchestra, him being a lead violinist. Of course, Vinny had no interest whatsoever in the violin but this piqued his mother's interest, and she persuaded him to take lessons from the maestro. With this in mind, she purchased a second-hand violin case from a car boot with the ambition of one day finding a violin to fill it and help her young musician son forge his destiny in music. In the meantime, Vinny was to practice on Trevor's stringed instrument after his doorman duties, or so she thought and hoped.

I had at that time a girl lodger whose rent helped me pay off my ex's debts and what was now *my* mortgage. That summer's evening seemed to go on and on and my needs were escalating, if you catch my drift. Sadie and I got a bit giddy and for a laugh pushed a couple of orange fur cushions up our kaftans just so she could see what full-term pregnancy looked like. We staggered out to the pavement in the 9 pm twilight where she got sick of the look and tossed her cushion over the fence whilst mine was still in position. I didn't really know just how the next part happened but a car skidded to a halt, and a worried chap leapt out asking if I was OK. I groaned a bit whilst Sadie giggled against the wrought iron gates. Suddenly, I was hoisted into the front seat of the Merc, Sadie was thrown into the back and off we set to the maternity hospital just up the road. Ringing the entry bell and banging on the door of course brought a nurse pushing a wheelchair to help the soon to be mother. Very shamefacedly I had no alternative but to drag the cushion from up my kaftan and amongst hysterics from Sadie and me saying a million sorrys, the nurse slammed the door and returned to her duties, meanwhile the angry astonished good Samaritan gave me the bollocking I deserved, reversed the Merc, told me to "fuck off and bloody well walk home." This we had to do as neither Sadie nor myself had any money, nor did I have any shoes on. To say my feet were more than sore four days later is an understatement and a fair punishment for a daft innocent meaning prank gone wrong.

When we got back, Vinny was sick with worry as the door had been left unlocked and the dog (he was petrified of) was trying to eat him should he try to enter my home without me there. That night we never even got around to the reason for him being there as he'd got the hump from sitting on a wall for three-quarters of an hour. Now, why that should have affected his neither's I've yet to know.

His mother had bought him the promised violin and with his aunt and uncle sat at the tea table in eager anticipation to hear his impromptu first little concert, she passed him the case and said, "Play us a tune then, our Vinny." Ceremoniously, she opened the case to find it stuffed with empty crisp packets, biscuits, chewing gum and condoms. He had to admit that when he was skint had sold the instrument (that she was still on tick for) to another violinist in the Orchestra. His Mother threw a strop to end all strops. Then, she smacked him around the head with a platter of sausage rolls, stormed off to bed leaving Aunt and Uncle to let themselves out and didn't speak to Vinny for over a week, this he did not mind.

New Year came and he went to a party, alone. We never went out together as it was a purely sexual involvement, which suited us both! There, as the midnight fireworks lit up the sky, he met a young lass — and fell instantly in love. On his last visit to me we just held hands and he told me of his love for the pretty 20-year-old whom he had been lucky enough to meet. Just the right age for this 23-year-old man. Of course I wished him all the happiness in the world. He thanked me for all he had learned in our time together, saying, with a hug goodbye and a cheeky grin, that it would come in very handy as her future husband. I never saw him again. I hope they stayed happy.

Spike

He was a darling little hedgehog who believed me to be his mummy and followed me everywhere. He pattered amongst the autumn leaves in my front garden and most passing people thought he was a clockwork toy, until I held him up for the cuddles he loved.

At night when watching TV, he'd lie on my shoulder gently suckling on my earlobe, never once getting too ambitious with his sharp little teeth. Sophie my serene gentle shepherd loved him as much as he did her, and they would play a game whereupon she would lie with golden legs outstretched, and he would clamber over them to do a roley poley and screech his delighted little his song. My boy never had his spikes up, for he did not need to be defensive anymore, and Sophie would carry him around in her gentle old mouth.

It was so very easy to toilet train him (as I'd had house rabbits in the past) to a cat's litter tray and when nature called he would scurry into the box that held his latrine, be a clean boy and come out to play yet again with waiting Sophie.

I had rescued this (then so poorly) tiny spiked lad from a couple of lout schoolboys who were using him like a football. I'm not afraid to say I clouted both of the young swines with a spare heavy chained dog lead (I always carried a spare lead in case I found yet another stray dog) So sue me!!

Both of my hands were full of dogs on leads, not only my Sophie but a Rottie I had been recovering from a road accident. You know the one, he's the bruiser that accidentally knocked out my front teeth, hey ho! So, I had no alternative but to place the ill hedgehog in my bra, warm and snug his inquisitive little face peeped out as his fleas did their worst on my boobies.

It was destiny working once again, enabling me to help something in dire straits. I'd taken a different route than normal as I was visiting my lovely gay friend. On seeing me on his doorstep with not one but two huge dogs, with my cleavage a squirming and the fleas are a hopping he quickly decided a visit when I was deloused would be preferable.

Mid-morning saw me in the vets with my latest rescue and Jim, my vet, bless him, once again treated my wild friend for free after diagnosing pneumonia, hence the little nocturnal lad was out in daylight to receive his kicking!

BASTARDS!!

So, at home, he got his medication each day and was fed special milk (as he was so tiny) from a dropper and soon was a happy healthy big boy for me. I'd been told of this wonderful lady called Elaine Drewery in Louth, Lincolnshire who had rescued thousands of hedgehogs in the fifty years she'd opened her house and heart to them. I phoned for advice about my Spike and from that first conversation, a friendship lasting over forty years formed.

She said all was sounding well at the moment but to look out for warning signs that herald a death, no matter how you try to save the tiny life, she described the change in poo saying "it will go from pellet form to green slime that would not respond to treatment, also hedgehogs make a quacking sound rather like Donald Duck when death was near. Months passed with my little friend and then I noticed that Spike seemed lethargic. He was fully grown by this time and usually still played like a baby boy with Sophie. Now, he just lay between her golden paws whilst she licked his sweet tiny face. My old dog sensed that all was far from well and on my inspecting his toilet tray the dreaded green poo told me his short life was coming to an end.

The vet confirmed that a parasite was doing its worst, and my spikey friend was not in any pain, there was no cure, he just needed to be kept quiet and happy. Time will tell.

I tore up a pink flannelette sheet and made miniature nappies for his tiny bottom, he let me clean him up without any fuss because our bond of trust could not be broken. I stayed up for two nights caring for him, just willing him to get better. On the second day, I fell asleep with him tucked against my neck. I awoke to feel him pull himself onto my face and with tiny feet on either side of my nose, he talked to his old mummy just like Donald Duck. His dying was exactly as Elaine had described, it was a hedgehog's death call. I rushed my lad to the vet, just in case he was indeed suffering, and I kissed his sweet tiny face as he heaved his last breath when Jim put him to gentle forever sleep.

My little wild friend who loved and trusted me was later laid to rest in a shoebox. Lined out in soft pink material and laid on his back, a tiny pink sheet covering his tummy and a posy of flowers between tiny paws that no longer pattered, believe me he looked like he was just asleep on a tiny bed surrounded by the flowers he loved to play amongst.

This pretty death ritual was not done for my benefit or indeed Spikes, but to show the little boy next door (who also loved that tiny gentle soul) that death could be beautiful, as it's nothing to be afraid of, for it's just a gentle passing into a new dimension.

Sweet dreams my Spike!

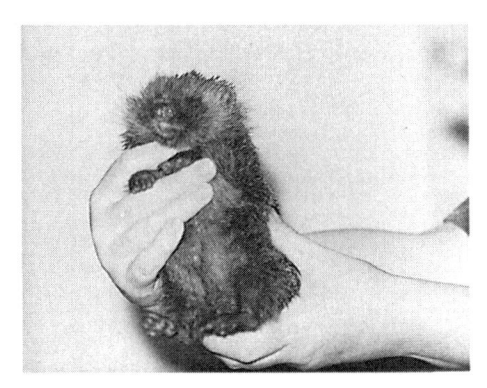

The Poltergeist Part One

Dance, little lady, dance.

I suppose you, reading the following true events of my life, are as sceptical as I used to be, but what I'm going to tell you now beggars all logic and sense.

It's a warm tranquil August evening, birthday presents are being opened and loved. I'd kept what I believed to be the most special present until the last and presented it with love, little was I to know that the pretty Chalet music box would prove to be haunted. On lifting its lid, the ballerina danced her dance to the tinkling sound of Lara's theme from Dr Zhivago. Strange, as when I bought it and saw it wrapped, it played an old song (Roses of Picardy). Jane tried on her new clothes and pretty bracelet and then the music ended. Then, all hell was let loose.

My dogs were howling like wolves, lights went on and off, taps were turned on, windows stuck for years opened, doors slammed, the temperature turned to icy cold and that music box started to play again without being rewound. Dance little lady dance!!

Whilst this was happening, I felt so terribly weak and ill and sat on the dressing table stool. The screams of "What's wrong with you, what's happening?" made me look in the mirror. What I saw made me faint to the floor, for staring back at me was an old, old lady, eyes misted by time, hair thin and white, where had my lovely teeth gone? But it was my skeletal age-spotted hands covered by translucent wrinkled skin that somehow upset me the most. For I'd had such pretty tiny hands with manicured nails, now they were nothing more than aged ravaged, bent, twisted old claws. I believe that by people who study this unworldly phenomenon, what I experienced is called 'trans configuration', it's usually when an evil spirit finds an entry into the living human body, possibly after ECT? God help me, I was now its host and in later years, it would take all the paranormal skill and exorcism of Carlo to release me from its stranglehold.

Can you imagine the terror and confusion of watching me turn from a glamorous woman in her thirties to an old crone, not knowing the final outcome? Now, at 80 years, I've become that reflection.

As I lay unconscious on the lilac carpet, I was told later that I was talked to, sobbed over, water thrown on me, shaken and eventually I returned to me but still feeling so very ill and different in an unknown way.

All through that long night the air was as ice, the dogs howled and even though I found the courage to close windows, and turn off taps and lights, it all just happened again. We were so terrified that we visited the bathroom together, afraid of parting, and the music box tinkled its pretty tune, and the pink lady danced.

As dawn broke, everything just stopped, and calm was restored, but not for long, as this was just a taste of what was to be years of mind-blowing events that became normal in my life. The poltergeist became my friend. Over the many years, it shared my life and home.

Poltergeist Part Two

After that terrifying August night, it seemed like my new invisible lodger liked its abode and decided to bloody stay. It also decided that (for a reason I never fathomed) he hated poor Sadie my teenage lodger, whose rent helped me pay the mortgage. So, help me, the poor lass had to have had nerves of steel to cope with the cruel, dangerous, tormenting pranks Moses (as we named the invisible one) inflicted without mercy upon her.

I suppose it would be about two weeks after Moses made himself very comfortable in my home, that whilst making our tea there was a loud cry as Sadie toppled down the stairs. Not really injured, but seriously bruised. She told me through sobs that a hand had grabbed her ankle on the third stair from the top. She insisted it to be the third stair, as that was where a curtain of icy air had manifested itself at the same as Moses had. I made her sweet tea (the panacea of all ills) bathed her swollen ankle in Witch-hazel, bound it and gave her a very welcome meal on her lap tray to eat. No sooner had she lifted her knife and fork when the invisible force snatched them from her grasp and flung them with such force into the alcove where the wallpaper was torn and stained with gravy. And now the dogs were howling trying to escape, lights and taps did their on and off dance, and the house was like an icebox. Christ almighty, not again! Then to all our terrified eyes, Moses introduced us to his latest phenomenon. In the corner above the TV, a four-foot cone of smoke appeared (and no the TV was not on fire!!) Spiralling round and round and a strange sickly, sweet smell, unlike anything I'd ever smelt, intoxicated the air. This (to say the least) unsettling state of affairs lasted for about two hours, all of us huddled together, afraid to leave each other's side. Then, it just stopped. The dogs at last lay in a peaceful slumber. We all went to the toilet, and then had a brew and a piece of Jamaican Ginger Cake. Lovely!

The next morning the sun shone with its welcome rays, and I decided to check out the third stair carpet from the top in case it was loose, even though Sadie insisted she had been thrown down. The house was lovely and warm on that sunny morn, all except that third stair. (Was that where Moses had taken up camp, one has to wonder?) The carpet was secure on its grip rods, but just to make doubly sure I banged in a few tracks. That carpet was going nowhere!

It was quiet all day; the dogs lay in the sunshine as I tended to the garden I loved. Soon laughter and chatter filled the silence whilst I prepared the evening meal. Sadie asked about having an early bath, as she felt dusty after all the stocktaking at work. Told this was ok she toddled off upstairs with not a care in the world. That was until she reached that third stair, felt the icy air engulf her, then the icy hand grabbed her ankle and hurled her once again down all of the stairs. Poor, poor Sadie, what on earth had this young girl done to deserve such violence? What did Moses know of her that I didn't? What had she done in this life or ones before it to engage such wrath?

Sadie soon got to the stage of climbing over the third stair and in so doing avoided being the brunt of his malice. And of course, I'd asked Moses not to continue, as one day he'd kill the girl and who would believe a certified dingbat (me) when I told them a spook had done it? No one!

Things quietened down for a few weeks, the calm before the storm.

There it goes again, the dogs howled their warning of things to come, taps and lights did their thing, house icy cold and I was pissed off, for Sadie said she was moving in with a mate and I'd not only miss her but also the rent she always paid, on the dot, that helped with my mortgage.

This was to be the last Saturday night together as she was due to move out the following day. We sat on the edge of my bed whilst she applied her make-up, her handbag being on the ottoman in front of us. Now, believe this or not, that is your choice, but I can assure you that what I relate to now, really, really happened.

Our jaws must have been hanging open at what our eyes just could not get a grip off, for before us the unbelievable did happen. Slowly, oh, so slowly, Sadie's handbag (that held all her worldly, important possessions, i.e., passport, money, birth pills .etc.) slowly, oh so slowly, just faded away, just like it evaporated without moving from the velvet ottoman until it had vanished completely. Can you imagine just what that did to us all we reached out and like fools, patted where it had once been, looked on the floor, why I ask, had we not all seen it just fade away? And with it went the money that Sadie had saved for her share of the rent in her new home.

That lass was so shook up (well you would be, wouldn't you?), and we put the fact that she was an avid gymnast down to the reason she knew how to fall, thus saving broken bones. That night she could not manage to eat and sat in shock and through her tears telling me she had to leave the house, she loved living in with me, until Moses came that is. But bless her she had stayed for quite some scary time whilst she tried her best to save yet again a deposit for a flat from her meagre wage. Dance little lady, dance.

Poltergeist Part Three

I had a black wingback leather rocking swirling chair. Unfortunately, some of the bearings had fallen out making its motions noisy and uneven. Many were the nights, after they had all gone to bed, that I'd sit and talk to Moses, asking him to tell me who he was, and where he had come from, but my questions were never answered. So, I left out a pen and paper in the hope the little bugger could write. Do you see I'd become in awe of all the things it? She? He? could achieve and felt rather smug and proud that he had chosen me to live with, when indeed the world was his lobster. (I told you I was strange and Physic)

So, I'd sat there in the dark talking to a poltergeist, not a trace of fear in me for instinct told me he meant me only good. The black chair started to rock its crazy motion, up and down, back and to, back and to, at the same time what sounded like a piece of invisible metal ding dings, dinged up and down the chrome grille of the gas fire. The daft teasing sod was letting me know I had nothing to fear from him. For if I did have fear of him nothing I could do would stop it.

Poor Sadie had still not saved enough to pay her portion of the rent she was to share with her friend. And so, she had no alternative but to stay with me longer and I charged no rent either to help her, but I knew just why she had to leave. She was by now in fear for her life!!

Now, I had been told of this phenomenon whereby a poltergeist has the power to transport objects from one place to another and in part three, I will tell you items, never known to me turn up (unwanted) in my home. I often wonder what some mind blown person felt when a strange handbag (full of got knows what) just appeared, maybe on their kitchen worktop! Who knows?

It was weeks later when I was hoovering around the house, that I went into the back bedroom, and my mind was blown by the sight of Sadie's overflowing handbag, just placed safely in the centre of a single bed. The stories that bag could have told (if it were possible), how in God's name can you rationalize events like that?

Sadie madly saved up again and because it was the fault of my home and Moses that she just had to leave to save, not only her body but her sanity also, I let her off a couple of more weeks much-needed rent.

My mother was now widowed, my father having dropped dead by the bed my mother lay in one Boxing night after his visit to the bathroom. God help me she was moving in with me, in effect taking Sadie's place, but nowhere near bringing with her the fun and laughter that young lass always had. So, whilst Sadie arranged a final night of frivolity with her many mates at work, she realised the dress she was intent on wearing that night was still in my wardrobe at 309. She finished her shift at 10 pm and come home for what was to be the very last time. On opening the front door, she went to put the light on – no light! This did not worry her as she assumed the money in the meter had run out. And anyway, she could see ok as the street light outside shone into my bedroom.

Up the stairs, she goes making sure to avoid number three and went into my bedroom (whose door bears no locks or handles) and proceeds to get the chosen dress from the wardrobe. And then, all hell breaks loose. The dogs, lights, taps do their usual thing, and the bedroom door slams tightly shut. Try as she might Sadie could not wrench it open, remember it had no means of fastening it, well not of this world anyway!

I'd taken my mother to see the film *Elsa the Lioness,* and as we got off the bus and turned the corner for home, I was worried to see police and ambulances outside my home. What could it possibly be? I soon found out. Sadie was covered by a blanket and being led into an ambulance whilst trying to get the local bobby to believe the strangle marks on her neck had been made by a malevolent spirit, and that 309 was very, very haunted. This I confirmed but who the hell would believe me, knowing I had mental health issues? Sadie spent some time in a mental institution and never wavered from the account she gave of her injuries. I don't think anyone believed either of us as it's just beyond belief and comprehension. Two weeks later, she left to take a Nannies job in France (of all places). That passport, on its return (from God knows where) was so much needed after all, and I never saw that sweet brave girl again.

And still to this day, so many years later from that very first, terrifying night (just once in a while), from the depths of a rarely used cupboard, comes the tinkling melody of Lara's theme, that reminds me, yet again, that I don't live alone after all, but all is well.

Dance, little lady, dance.

Just for me, one more time.

Yabba

It's October now, I've lost all of the summer to tears, fear of the future and this soul-destroying loneliness, my only constant companion.

I will try to weave you the threads that have created the tapestry of my life. To give you an insight into the bipolar mind, laughing, joyous, invincible, artistic, funny, accomplished, driven, sensual, then the opposite of all the emotions that kept me living were the dark satanic useless incompetent uncomprehending soulless days, weeks, months that wrapped me in a shroud of black misery, begging to be no more!

9.45 pm, the voice in my head said manically "I'm still with you" and at the same time I could not control the left side of my face and my lips were snarling, my vile face reflected in the night-time lamp-lit window, Sirius was still with me!!

I read my journal myself now and found it hard to believe that the mind can be taken on magical journeys and that on these journeys a soon to be familiar new mystical friend comes to help me time and again. 'Yabba' (the Arabic word for daddy with beautiful eyes) was the name I gave the huge tiger that came out of my shadows and was like a faithful dog. Clearing away the cloying, restricting cobwebs of my childhood, then walking with me along a tropical beach, making me laugh when he got the crab (that I warned him to leave alone) struck on his majestic face.

His huge footprints would indent the sand we walked upon together and much of the time I'd feel his rasping tongue lick my arm or face. Just like a loving trusting dog he'd take my hand into his mouth, huge teeth would nibble so gently, his mind would tell mine "Trust me, I will not hurt you!" He became a friend so dear to my sanity, that in quiet moments my subconscious would trawl the shadows and darling Yabba would come purring from them, always comforting and giving my tortured mind the courage to face another day.

On this rainy afternoon of 6 October 1997, I struggle to put down to paper the wonderful adventures that Carlo enabled me to experience through hypnosis and regression. Small doors in my subconscious open with vivid snippets of what I have seen, places not of this world that I have visited, too confusing to recall, but I know for certainty once they were all mine.

Carlo kept me alive all summer long, the hypnosis sessions holding me up safe in life's stormy seas; Yabba led my subconscious from one terrible event of the past to another even more horrific one. Each time he was able to expel its pain, and I'd return to this dimension feeling refreshed and cleansed, unafraid.

To this day, I can close down all conscious thinking, call my beloved striped giant from the shadows, watch his huge disjointed floppy paws carry him to me, feel his raspy kiss on my face, and his whole body reverberating with purrs of pleasure at finding me once more. He is so very real to me, here in my dining room on this wet October afternoon. Yes, it defies my logical mind (as I'm sure it does yours) I suppose I'll never, ever, *fully* understand just how Yabba comes to be sitting beside me, but he is, believe me, please, he is!

Each hypnosis session would of course be different and dear Carlo had his work cut out trying to expel my long-held torment. But bit by bit, he built up my self-esteem and also made me unafraid of driving to unfamiliar places and calmed down my fiery reactions to things that angered or disgusted me. But the one thing that was the most important to my quality of life, the expelling of pain brought on by the loss of a love I valued so highly, has been unobtainable, for still, I cry daily for what is long gone. Oh yes, for a time after the gentle, soothing semi-conscious hypnotic state I'd be without the pain, my tears would not flow, and I'd find it difficult to even remember the man who I loved dearly had died. But as the reality of life set in, a million memories would come flooding back, the pain dam would burst wide open, and square one would be where I'd find myself yet again. All so very disappointing for a dedicated therapist who had given all he had to save my sanity and in so doing my life. Thank you, Carlo, for bringing me back from the brink so many times, but as you told me after we had known each such a short while "You're a one off my dear, so complex, so filled with pain, I can only do my best, but your mind is far stronger than mine in many ways. And by the way, I know you are also psychic." Strange that Carlo spotted so soon after meeting me that my mental ability was not of the recognised 'norm'!

Many years previously after disastrous ECT treatment, a door, up until then firmly closed, opened with such power that it was frightening for all to behold.

Now my subconscious had yet again been tapped into, not with excruciating ECT as before, but with hypnosis, and I once again knew things logic says are impossible. Here, I recount one such happening but believe me, there have been so, so many.

A morning in August 1997 at 9.15 is, to be precise, and I was deadheading my beautiful front garden flowers. Without warning, a 'knowledge' came into my head. I was to tell a neighbour not to be upset or scared because Aunty Connie was waiting and coming to get her mother, also the number 237. So, I phoned my neighbour, asking about her welfare. She said she was so tired as her old mum was dying, and all the relatives were gathered. I asked her if the name Connie meant anything to her, it did not, but her twenty years older sister had recalled a cousin Connie. The 237 I took to be a time and firmly believed that was the time her old mum was to pass over. This did not happen. A short time later, I was told to get a peach rose from my garden, take it across the road and tell the grieving daughter to lay it beside her dying mother's face on the pillow. Feeling bloody confused and stupid I obeyed, only to have the old lady's daughter burst into tears of joy, remembering how her dead father had lain many of his 'beloved' red roses (his wife's favourite) on her pillow before sleep. Now my neighbour was distraught no more, she knew for an absolute certainty that her mum's lost loved ones were waiting to welcome her to paradise.

Two days later and at a time other than 2:37, the old lady went on her last journey, for me more knowledge was to come. I was going to tell the unusually peaceful lady (after all she had just buried her old mum whom she loved so dearly) "Fred says tippy toes dances once more." What a bloody silly message that held no relevance at all to me. "What was your dad called?" I asked the bereaved daughter.

"Albert," she says.

"Tell me, did your mum and dad go dancing long ago?"

"Well Mum did but Dad had two left feet, so Mum danced with her sister's first husband. Long dead, killed in the War.

"What was his name love?" I asked.

"Oh, his name was Fred I believe, his nickname for my mum was 'tippy toes', he was a wonderfully kind man." I'm sure you are wondering about 237 as indeed I still was at that stage, this being the only part of this physic jigsaw that did not tally up, but soon that last piece was to fall into place. I later learnt that during the old lady's funeral service, the Vicar said, "We will now turn to page 237 and sing Jerusalem (mum's favourite?)." Need I say more! Don't ask me how my mind receives the absolute knowledge that it frequently does. I can't conjure it up at will, it just comes to me, unannounced. Just like when I was deadheading my flowers that sunny August morn.

I feel I need to say at this stage, that during a three-hour hypnotic session called "Soul Retrieval" (where your subconscious travels to a place of wonder and past wrongs are righted) I was told that I was to continue writing this book (started years ago) as it would bring enlightenment and understanding, a river of tears and because of my words, I would live on far beyond my death in a million smiles. I asked if there was anything I must do with my physic powers, thinking I'd become a healer. I must admit that the thoughts of helping a cripple walk from my door, unaided, delighted me. This was not to be. To my great disappointment and fear, I was told I was to help the police find lost children and murder victims. I asked when this would come about, and the answer was that it will come as a gift on the morning of your 56th birthday. That will be 3rd November, 1998. But already I've had a taste of what the spirit world and destiny had in store for me.

A few weeks ago, a young boy went out on his bike in an area far from where he was later found dead, quite a distance from his home. I lay in bed watching the terrible story of his death on breakfast TV at 7.30am. Suddenly, there was the face of his killer, before my eyes, in mid-air, between me and the TV set. So real, etched in my memory forever.

Very shook up I went to tell my friend, I also phoned Carlo with my latest knowledge, which believe me has never been known to fail.

Just phone the police and say you can describe the van to them that carried the child off. This I did, but did they believe this dingbat?

On recounting what I knew to my friend, yet another piece of knowledge came into my vision, a red transit van, the sign on the passenger side crudely painted out in unmatched red smeared paint, the front nearside wing long ago bashed in and now rusty, back doors open and the sight of a man's lower arms throwing in the body of a child. Alive or dead I did not know, but I heard the metallic thud as his young body hit the floor of the empty transit van. No one who has ever experienced events of this nature, as I have, will ever understand just how traumatic it is. One is left drained and helpless. On advice, I phoned the police again with my knowledge, they politely took note of it. I only hope they didn't think I was just some time-wasting menopausal old crank with mental health problems, do you?

To this day the boy's killer is still at large, only time will tell if I'd hit on the absolute truth, but in the meantime, pray with me that the vile beast that stole such a young life does not strike again and send other parents into the bottomless abyss of despair.

PS: many years later a known paedophile was caught by DNA for the kidnapping and murder of that young boy, along with many rapes of children and one other killing. He was given life without parole, how disgusting that hanging such a predator was disallowed. Bring hanging back!

The power of the subconscious mind!

Needing Carlos' Help Yet again

Getting ready to go to my therapist last Wednesday for yet another spirit release everything that could go wrong, did. I firmly believe it was a concerted attempt by the nasty sod living within me to stop me from keeping my appointment – it knew its 'life' with me was in jeopardy once again.

So, keys were lost, bowels played up, and I had to return home after just starting my journey to Carlo to use the bathroom, for the fifth time. I slipped and twisted my ankle, then the car would not start, there were even road works and dilatory prats at twenty miles an hour, enough red lights to grace a Christmas tree, a Combine Harvester for Christ's sake, in the middle of a town! Then a funeral, how I envy the occupant of that nice oak box, and the very last straw was my nearly knocking down a very startled pensioner right in Carlo's driveway. But get there I did, nerves frayed to hell and only four minutes late.

What I'm about to tell you now is difficult for even me to believe, and I unfortunately am the poor sod whom it traumatized.

Just as once before (on the other spirit release), I was taken down very deep and very quickly to a state where only the subconscious mind can be accessed. Communication is by hand signs only, in my case a pointing right forefinger for 'yes' and a clenched left fist for 'no'.

It seems that almost immediately the evil spirit that had come back to torment me through dark dimensions started to mock and threaten Carlo through my genuinely unknowing mouth.

I believe Carlo when he tells me that for forty-five mind-blowing minutes, he struggled with a frightening entity, finally managing to persuade it to go into the light, and in so doing find the peace both it and I deserved. It transpires that through many lifetimes it had been my mind's unwanted twin, crouching darkly within me, always waiting for an opportunity to make its presence known. This it did so many times, and I had to fight with all of my being, not to use to full capacity my killing temper. For that's what it urged me to do, kill,

kill, kill, and I'm adamant that it engineered situations throughout my life that it knew full well would trigger in me its lust for pain and bloodletting.

I will only know the full extent of what happened in those forty-five minutes, (which is completely lost from my conscious mind) when I receive the copy of the tape Carlo made at the time. All I know is that when I returned to this dimension in his suburban consulting room, Carlo's face bore a mixed expression of total fear and incredulity. For the second time with me, he had stepped into grave danger, trawled the cavern of evil darkness and made the child of Satan show its ugly self, not only through my mouth but also God help me, through my face. Once again, the transconfiguration had taken place and Carlo had looked at the face from hell, snarling, spitting, mocking, and threatening. Hands clawing at the green velvet comfy chair where I sat, still entwined through the ages, me and Satan's offspring. Poor Carlo was drenched with the Holy water he had poured over himself, as protection from Beelzebub.

Carlo removed the microphone from me and tested the tape that had hopefully just recorded something utterly beyond rational belief and yet was horrifying reality.

There it was, the voice of a mocking demon. I felt so ill drained of all strength as if I'd been to hell and back on a bike. I suppose I had because what happens to me was something not in this world. Something that defies all logic that makes all sceptics mock and that makes all the hairs stand rigid on the back of your neck.

When the copy of the tape is ready and I, at last, hear the contents, I will do my best to portray them to paper, as up until now all I know are bits Carlo related from notes taken at the time. I find all of this both frightening and fascinating, but one thing I know for sure is that since the spirit release happened I've been at peace; my head has held *my* thoughts only, instead of horrifying ones. I've not been happy, but I'm grateful that the mental torment that constantly made my life a living hell seems for the time being, to be gone.

What I now feel I must point out, is that all of my doctors after one another have put their own interpretations as to my mental state. I have been labelled Schizophrenic, Psychotic, and Manic Depressive. This covers most of the known mental illnesses. But not mine. Every treatment, ranging from Counselling to ECT, to Sleep Therapy and every tablet a throat can swallow; I've endured in my quest to be well. All of the above have failed miserably and as a last resort to try to quell my persistent death wish, my devoted GP funded my treatment with Carlo, this being a first, as this type of treatment is poo-pooed by the medical profession in general.

After reading what I've told you, the last thing I need is for you to relate to what has happened to me. My case is one in a million, mental illness in people is mostly just that, they are ill; they are not also possessed as I was. None of you must, after knowing of my hellish experiences, run to the nearest money extracting so-called quack therapist and allow your mind to be tampered with, for that is the road to true insanity, one which you will be unable to retrace your tortured steps. The credentials of any Doctor or Therapist must be scrutinised at great depths before you undertake their offered help. Needless to say, Carlo was both honourable and impeccable, and in him I have complete trust and faith. He is not only an extraordinary therapist, but one who knows exactly just what he is undertaking and its outcome. He is also a fine human being, and I'm eternally grateful for the mental cleansing he's allowed me to know. At long, long last.

So, if any of you are poorly in your mind, oh how I empathise, only one such as I, who have lived the horror of a different mind plus satanic possession, truly understands. Try your very best with the conventional treatments offered, but from my disastrous experience with ECT, I can only advise you to leave it alone. If all fails to give you the peace of mind that should be yours by right, then and only then, search until you find, as I did, your very own Carlo and from the depths of my heart, I wish you health and happiness.

Ruby Ruby

I stayed working at the Charity Shop as long as I could, but it got to the stage where I dreaded those few hours of time I donated, so I left.

Two things made my continuance there impossible, one of these being that my personality did not exactly meld with some of the other charity workers, them being perhaps forty years older than I was. There was a lot of 'one-upmanship' and I flatly refused to join in with their silly games. The Manageress, a real sweetie, begged me to stay – it seems that she looked forward to the laughter I brought with me, on those Wednesday afternoons. Yes, laughter in small doses I could sometimes muster, but mostly I would be in tears. So many of the donated bags of clothes I would open, and my heart would lurch, as once again my fingers would caress clothes sometimes identical to those of my lost love. My mind would travel back to times of happiness, I'd feel once again the warmth of that lovely strong, but always gentle hand, as it clasped mine, now only in memory. He'd be wearing the replica jacket of the donated one on the table before me. I really just could not take the unprepared for pain that lunged, time and again from the depths of those black bags, to stab me once more. So, with hugs and tears I was gone, with promises of my return to the Charity Shop, should my mind ever heal sufficiently (it didn't).

Now, I had to find something else that would be near enough impossible to make me mourn his loss, something to fill my time and bring me smiles instead of tears.

Night school, that is where I'll go, I'll use up some of the empty hours and learn. My friend was delighted when she heard this latest news. I could see her trying to envisage just what life-enhancing tuition I was about to undertake. Her face was a bloody study when I told her about stained glass and line dancing. Both of these pursuits have turned out to be far more difficult than the experts make them look.

At the age of fifty-four, I am of course in menopause and have been for probably three years. Not having had a 'nasty' for over twelve months, I did not associate the stomach cramps on that Tuesday night with the onset of a very belated 'nasty'. Thank God, I discovered this before I set out and was now suitably protected as I went to line up with a motley crowd.

Picture this, if you will and I defy you not to laugh. We're all in lines, the pensioners and I, some of the old dears being really into the swing of things judging by the array of Stetsons, spurs and miles if swaying fringing.

"Right class let's see if you can remember "Ruby Ruby" called out the instructor whose bloody coordinated feet defied my comprehension. Now Ruby Ruby was a bitch of a routine that only last week I'd failed miserably to master what other dancers got the measure of straight away, and they showed me up for being a plonker. Now, I really must admit that I laughed with them as I stood in the corner, like a naughty schoolgirl, jumping up and down on the spot with sheer frustration.

Once more, I joined the stomping line-up, at last I was getting the measure of dear Ruby, when the thing that all ladies dread started to happen to me.

At first, I thought it was just my imagination that my 'nasties' protection had somehow twisted uncomfortably down the trouser leg of my jade green velvet tracksuit. I felt really strange around the nether regions, but in that stomping, lasso-throwing line-up it was impossible to discover, Why?

With rising panic I felt this wodge from hell, slowly and inexorably wind its merry way down the right leg of my trousers, only to deposit itself smartly between my gold shoed feet. God alone knows the bird's eye view the seasoned ones had on the gyrating line up behind me. At this time, I will point out that I had neither a handbag nor pockets, so what in God's name was I to do with the beastly thing that now lay resplendent between the feet of a total stranger? For by now of course the line of dancers had moved up. With as much dignity as I could muster, I picked up the sod and shoved it up to my sleeve like it was the thickest hankie of all time. The only redeeming factor of this escapade is that nature had only given me a warning in the bathroom back home and the beastly wadding was as pristinely clean as the moment I had tucked it into my black lacy panties.

On getting home, my first port of call was of course the smallest room, there I discovered that the sticky outer casing of my cause of gross embarrassment was still firmly attached to the said frillies. Some manufacturing cock-up failed to seal the wadding firmly inside, but more to the point, I then discovered I had a full packet of the street-cred robbing sods in the cistern cupboard.

Needless to say, the Managing Director of the company that had ruined the dulcet tones of Ruby Ruby, has been given the nod, and how! It's been pointed out that the cost of running the gauntlet of lines of snickering pensioners (their spurs all a jangle) does not come cheap and that I expect un-insulting compensation by the return of post. Failing this I will of course face said Managing director across the Small Claims Court. I await the outcome.

Wednesday will bring my third stained-glass class, this true skill I find difficult but worth pursuing. The fact that my right thumb (broken by a German Shepherd badly injured in a road accident) now has no power in it, does not assist my grasp of the glass cutter. And I suppose it would help if I cut down my half-inch long painted fingernails but this I refuse to do because I like them.

I believe my love of stained glass started as a child (doesn't everything?) when I would try with tiny hands to catch the sunbeams that bounced off the magnificent leaded French windows that secured me in that mausoleum I had no alternative but to call home.

So now I struggle with razor-sharp sheets of glass. A terrarium being the first masterpiece we have all got to knock up. I thought I'd be able to walk in on that first lesson, weigh up what tools I needed and straight away be able to get stuck into a Tiffany lampshade. How wrong I was, only now do I realise the skill, bravery and patience that goes into making one of those glowing beauties. Anyway, I've cut out all the pieces of my boring terrarium and copper foiled the edges, next I believe comes the soldering, but that's for another wet Wednesday evening at night school.

I've not been too well today once again my mind is having thoughts not relevant to my life now, and another hypnotic experience with Carlo tells me that once again a rather dark spirit has come to reside inside this many facetted mind of mine.

At 11 am Wednesday 15 October 1997, once again I will sit in Carlo's consultation room – he will take me into a very deep hypnotic state where only the subconscious can be accessed and hopefully once and for all exorcise the offspring of Satan that I believe still lurks within me.

£2,000 worth of Follicle

I first met this giant of a man when he carved the headstone for my now-dead mother's grave, and from that event forward we became mates, just mates.

I suspect he liked to watch my rump as it leaned over the pool table, a game he tried in vain to teach me. But that was as far as our laughing friendship went. This lovely man obviously saw past the sexy body and found a mind he could connect with.

We spent many an hour laughing in my home when he had finished his monumental masonry work at the Cemetery just up the road.

Now my muscled friend was divorced and, therefore, had no one to accompany him on his visit to a private clinic. (Not that sort of clinic you dirty-minded sods).

He had red curly hair that had thinned to reveal a scalp burnt sore by the sun with his constant work in an exposed graveyard.

He loathed the fact that his hair had buggered off at a rate of knots and bewailed the fact that it spoiled his chances of a leg over, should one ever be on the horizon.

So, with £2,000 of hard-earned readies we toddled off to a building of torture, and there he sat in a chair far too small for his huge frame. A white-coated sadist injected my panicked mate with enough anaesthetic to stun a horse. At this point, all was well. From a drawer came out what can only be described as a miniature pneumatic drill, this instrument of torture bounced off Peter's skull leaving rows of bleeding small holes, and this was only the bloody beginning. Next what looked like a small stainless-steel apple corer retrieved the hair follicles from my sickened friend's hairline at the nape of his neck.

With speedy dexterity, said sadist implanted the living follicle into each of the waiting holes. Three hours later my friend had a bonce like a badly ploughed field, and £2,000 was placed in the sadist's greedy hands.

As stated, he was a big bloke, far too large for the mini he was about to try to fold himself into. In his pain (for now the anaesthetic had mostly worn off), he misjudged the door height of the car and proceeded to scrape off £1,000 worth of follicle on its door frame. With a howl of pain, he retrieved what he could of the mangled bloody mess and tried vainly to smack the sods into his bleeding scalp.

I wanted to roll about in the gutter with hysterics, but this would have been an insult too many for the poor sod, so I gave soothing words of comfort that were of little or no use.

His battle-scarred bonce finally healed and looked like a proper bastard, and he never went back for an expensive remedy or top-up.

After this fiasco, he took to wearing a cap, which he still does, as an old gent, some forty years later.

We still talk, once in a while on the phone, telling each other of our daily aches and pains, the frustrations of an old life and anything else that takes our fancy. He has been retired from his back-breaking work for many a year now and lives in happy contentment with the wife he loves dearly. She quite obviously did not care about his unusual skull and saw the wonderful man inside. A magical marriage of years had begun.

They live amongst the hills and fields of Derbyshire the fields that he's always loved, surrounded by the animals that were always a part of his life. He's happy and contented in a way he never thought possible, but the wasted £2,000 of long ago would come in right handy now, to supplement his pension, as he often tells me.

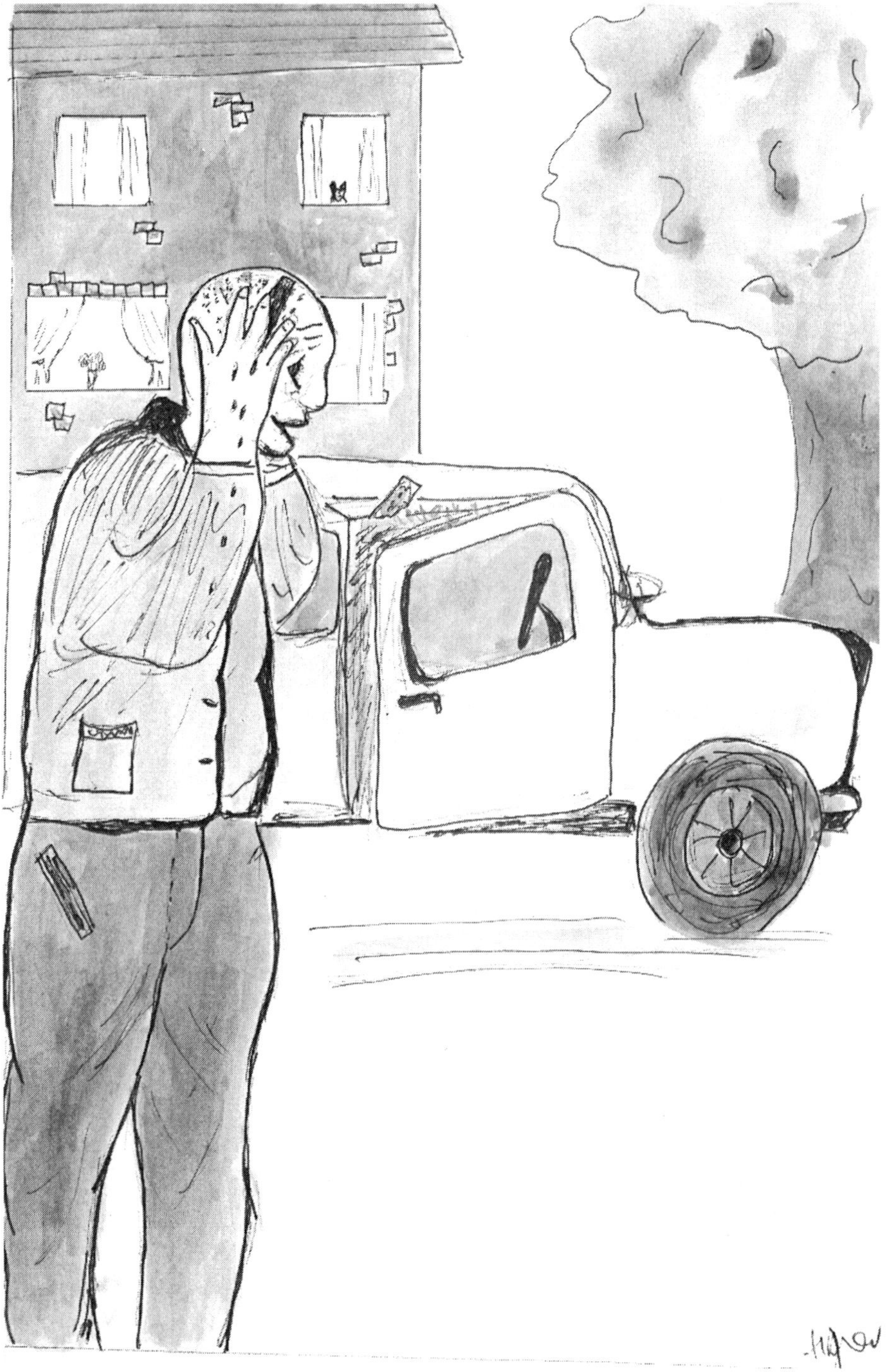

Lost Property

I have a great distaste for the filthy moronic dog owners who leave their dog's poo for all to tread in and in so doing, possibly blind a child or indeed an adult. Because this smelly mess carries the Toxocara worm that once ingested from an unwashed tiny hand leads to a life of darkness, so please, please clean up after your dogs.

It's the day before Christmas Eve; the rain is hitting the window as I'm looking through. I decide it's far, far too wet to take my German Shepherd Sophie for a walk. That's OK with her, as she has known for all her life no dry weather, no walkies! I stroke her regal head as I watch a cagouled man stand and let his dog poo on the grass verge outside my home. He's starting to stroll off, as I shout "Hey, dirty bastard, get it cleaned up!" Deafness is obviously an affliction, as he ignores me completely.

I'm still incandescent the next Christmas Eve morning as I wait at the window like a praying mantis on heat. Around the corner, he comes dog on a lead, poo on grass, rain pouring down. "You dirty git!" Once again I tell him to move it. He does not!

As always, I'm wearing a kaftan, this I drag off and quick as quickly replace it with a purple wet look raincoat, the fashion of the era. No time for shoes, so the black socks on my feet were soon to be sopping wet. I cared not; for now I was on a mission! Whilst running around the corner to my car, the torrential rain disturbed my red hair mousse and as it poured down my face and neck I looked like a victim of the chainsaw massacre.

Catching up with the striding dirty git, I sat and watched where he lived, Temper now had me in its grip, for not only had my Christmas barnet hairdo been ruined, but I'd flashed my nethers to a stranger when the wind blew the front of my mac open.

I drove back to the grass verge containing my displeasure and with bare hands scooped up the stinking mess and threw it into a plastic bag. The fact that my pooed-up hands would contaminate the car keys and the steering wheel did not enter my head as the red and purple mist had descended, and I was going to have the dirty bastard.

Returning to the house I'd seen him enter, I mulled over my options of retribution. (Remember the family motto? An eye for an eye!)

Looking at the pretty wreath on his front door, the fairy lights surrounding the window, the grass that was not contaminated with poo (why would it be? I'd received it all!) I decided I'd do my worst.

I knocked at the front door which he also did not answer, his dog barked at the sound. Then, I pushed my note of disgust through the polished letterbox.

By this time, so help me God, I'd lost it completely, with deft fingers I scrolled his Christmas greeting in shite on his previously spotless front door. Satisfied with my artistic skills, I drove home to disinfect, not only myself, but a large proportion of the car.

Hair in rollers, awaiting my visitors, it occurred to me that I was already bound over for a previous escapade. Now, trouble was on its way.

The policeman who answered me wished me happy Christmas and then silently listened as I told him of my morning, shall we say, adventure. With much laughter, he asked me to repeat what he had incredulously heard whilst he put my voice on speaker, the better for all the Bobbies to enjoy.

I repeated my story of doggy doo's amongst great guffaws of laughter as some bright spark shouted, "At last, we have Bronson on our patch, nice one."

After the hilarity had calmed down, I enquired what would be the outcome of my retribution as I was already bound over to be of good behaviour and I didn't think Christmas greetings in crap fell into the category of good behaviour.

Asked why I'd written the words Happy Xmas, I explained there was not enough crap to write Christmas, as it was only a Spaniel. This response had said copper choking with mirth. He explained that I had indeed done the gent a favour, as in Law the crap was his lost property, and I'd only returned it to its rightful owner.

Later on, the dirty git was to be fully pissed off as he was fined a thousand pounds in court for leaving dog waste on public ground. Of course, he would have known that I'd made the phone call reporting him, do I care? do I hell.

Strangely enough from that time on, he took a different route whilst walking his Springer Spaniel, and I never saw him again, or his lovely dog.

Now my friends reckon that I'm such a sod that one of these days my target will knife me.

I'm deadheading flowers when right outside my wall, on the pavement, a huge pile from a Great Dane had been deposited.

I can't believe that on the other end of the lead, the filthy git on two legs is dragging away the still defecating huge hound, leaving a steaming trail of poo.

In no uncertain terms, I told him to clean it up, his reply being "if you want it cleaned up, do it your fucking self" What a Gent!

So, these were my instructions, were they not? A plastic dustpan and brush quickly contained the huge dollop, and rather like a competitior in a smelly egg and spoon race, I caught up with the hurrying bloke and his hound.

His headphones must have drowned out my footfalls as he did not hear me behind him. Too late my dear, too, too late. Pulling the hood of his parker towards me, I deposited his lost property into it, gave it a slap and wished the startled bugger a safe journey.

He did not of course knife me as my friends had predicted, but I bet he wished he dared.

Like I said I can't be doing with poo left by uncaring dirty gits, clean up your mess or let the dog leave its bloody waste in *your* garden. Cos otherwise I'll come after you and put it through your letterbox.

Approximately 19 Foot of "Mean as Hell" Muscle

So, this is the unjust price you pay for loving all creatures! In the next room to where I am writing, lies the mind-blowing reality of many of my nightmares, but I've learned to cope. Strange how one can adjust and conquer one's lifetime fears.

I was deadheading the roses that summer Sunday lunchtime, alone as usual. I watched with envy those happy couples passing in cars, going on adventures to God knows where. Why not me? Really the face of the man coming towards me should be imprinted deep in my mind's eye forever, for he was about to change a lifetime's dread. Yet, try as I might, 4 years later his worried face escapes my memory. "Are you the lady that rescues all animals?"

"Yes," could be the only reply.

"Thank God for that," says he, and he explained that he'd come to find me all the way from Chester after being given my name and address from his local Rescue Centre.

Bloody Hell; my reputation for being a soft touch where animals were concerned must have spread far and wide.

"You see, I've got a three-year contract in Saudi Arabia, and I can't take Lucy with me. I've tried the zoos and no one will take her. I'm sodding desperate."

Now hang on a minute. It can't be a litter of pups moving in the strange canvas contraption being dragged on a metal frame and silent castors up to my front drive? This point I quickly pointed out to the flustered gent.

"Oh, did I not tell you? I used to be a reptile keeper, and I've had her since she was an egg."

Old fear and panic gripped my stomach as he proceeded to unzip the canvas contraption that held all my nightmares. 'Jesus' it was the biggest, meanest, sod I had ever been unfortunate enough to come across.

Proud as a new dad he stroked the scaled head of a 10-foot Burmese Rock Python! My reaction, it has to be said, was pretty swift for a menopausal, old fart and from across the other side of the front garden, I told him it was only fit for shoes and handbags!

Tears streaming down his face, he sat all dejected on my front step and said the never to be forgotten words: "And you're supposed to love all creatures. I've come miles to find you – you're my last hope."

Now, what else could I possibly do? I had to invite the poor sod in but he'd not leave his treasured, undulating git outside.

There was a barrier of my purple dralon suite between me and it as he demonstrated just how gentle the swine was. "She only eats dead food and she'll tell you when she's hungry she just lets her jaws hang open, bless her."

Bless her, bless, fucking bless her!! This was no cutie pie, and my pants were in danger of being soaked with the wee-wee I was so desperately clinging on to.

By now, the sod had fully unfurled herself from her devoted daddy and was stretched out across the room. Like I said, 10 feet of bloody trauma. "I'll leave you plenty of money in case she needs a Vet, and she only eats every few weeks, and I'll rig up her vivarium for you and leave instructions on her 'keep'."

Oh, God. I had to get to that toilet but how? Dearest Lucy was between me and the door, and I considered leaving by means of the window until I remembered I'd screwed the bugger closed to deter the burglars that roamed our area. But ever considerate Daddy scooped up his girl, and I beat a hasty retreat.

Sitting behind that locked bathroom door, I could not help but wonder what the hell I'd done to deserve this.

Yes, he went to Saudi and like a soft sod; I had the lodger from hell.

True to his word, she lay contented in her glass house but came the day when her jaws hung open, and I had to do the dreaded feeding bit; with closed eyes, I dropped in the dead rats she was to devour; closed the room door and left her to it. To this day, I have never seen her "gorge" a hearty meal Thank God!

Time, as they say, puts all things right, and she and I are living proof. We treat each other with respect and now, when I don't have any rescued animals that would be endangered by her appetite, she is allowed the freedom of this house. Darling Sophie, my glorious German Shepherd gives Lucy a very wide berth.

Forgetting the Lodger from Hell's freedom, I lay relaxing in the warm bubbles, soft music soothed me as I nodded off, I never heard the key in the door that brought to me the man I (believed) loved, but I felt his gentle, lovely hand stroke my soapy tummy, and I needed him to make love to me. Yet again the greeting on my lips turned to a horrified scream, for it was not my beloved's touch I felt that day, but by now a 13-foot Lucy coming full pelt for her best din-dins yet! To say that between us, we wrecked the bathroom, is putting it mildly. Soap dish off and the sink pulled from the wall, broken wall mirror, tiles, carpet sopping wet. Oh, how we fought Lucy and me! At least, I had to be grateful that my wet soapy body made her crush on me less constrictive and with flailing arms. I managed to take hold of the back brush. Holding its bristles I stabbed into her gaping jaws, she knew I meant business and must have thought, "sod this, it's easier to eat rats at least they don't fight back." And with that, she relaxed her grip and slid into the bathwater that was left whilst I had a nervous breakdown.

Hours later my beloved arrived to find me exhausted and bruised and "dear Lucy" surveying him from the last of the bubbles. Soon my bathroom was rebuilt with a shower instead of a bath. This pissed her off as she liked to shed her old skin in a bath. TOUGH!! Now I digress!

Once more, he rang my doorbell as he had done intermittently for over 20 years. "For Christ's sake lock up that bloody big dog" was the greeting I got from the Puff in the Gas Man's uniform. He really was as camp as a row of pink tents but such a lovely chap. We had become friends over the years that he had read my meter. "Had three months passed already?" It did not seem 2 minutes since his last quarterly visit, now it was bill paying time again. Not only the gas but all the other rotten bills seemed to come in at once. This quarter I was extra strapped for cash as Lucy had formed some type of obstruction and had needed a Specialist Vet. These brave lads did not come cheap, and the money left by her dear Daddy for her care had long since run out. Consequently, the waiting bill money had to be spent unblocking Lucy's nether regions. I'd phoned up a recommended Vet who was supposed to know his stuff. "Bring it in and we'll take a look," I explained she was a bit difficult to handle (that being the understatement of the century).

"It's your decision, love. But I have to charge a call-out fee." The monster by this time was approximately 14-feet long and weighed about 12 stone. Now I ask you – could you get the vicious bugger to the Vet? Sod the extra expense, get the Vet in NOW.

He was wearing tweeds and a cravat (quite a dandy really) and was carrying his bag of instruments and potions. Strange how you conjure up a face from the disembodied voice at the end of a phone. From the sound of him, I expected a rugged, big chap someone able to cope with the Lodger from Hell, but before me stood this cheerful little wisp of a man. God help him!

"Let's get at the rascal then," says he as he approaches the room I've pointed to. I heard the bag drop as I was halfway up the stairs. A strangled cry of alarm and a door slamming shut came next; with him on the outside of it. That wisp of a vet was ashen-faced. He tried valiantly to control the violent shivering that the sight of the mighty one had brought on, but failed miserably.

"Why in God's name did you not tell me it was that bloody big? Don't you know you've got a killer in there?"

I thought, *you are telling me? I'm the unfortunate sod that it took a bath with not so long ago.*

He went never to be seen again. Finally, after a lot of searching, I found a Vet man enough to handle the thing that I lived with daily. I've digressed again, haven't I? Sorry!

So, the meter was read. Strange, Mr Meter Reader never mentioned that sign that read "I'm silent, I'm deadly and I live in here" bearing Lucy's picture and displayed in the window as a warning to anyone foolish enough to enter uninvited.

"Cup of tea, love," I said.

"Yes, please pet. Two sugars," was the reply as he leaned against the door that housed the under-the-stairs gas meter. Two sugars he got in his tea that he was never to drink. A strangled "OH SHIT" followed quickly by a thud was my warning that all was not well. Lying in a crumpled heap was that sweet little Puff, a rather suspect damp patch forming on the front of his navy-blue trousers. Yep, the big git had done it yet again! Knowing that someone strange was in her territory, she'd come silently over the banister to investigate. He must have felt her face stroke his and, glancing back, saw another 12 or so feet of muscle about to follow through. No wonder the poor sod was in a dead faint with wet pants!

Not long after, he awoke to find me sitting on the stairs; yard brush in hand; beating back Lucy, yet I couldn't help laughing at someone else's misfortune. Lucy was coiled up in the hall wondering, I'm sure, what all the bloody commotion was about. With an expression never to be forgotten. That tragic little face whispered the words that were to send me into hysterics "Tell me it's a fucking nightmare!" He legged it out the back door; over a spiked fence; never to be seen again.

Not so long after this, I got a letter from the gas company. It read: "Dear Madam, owing to the unusual inhabitants of your home, would you be kind enough to read your own meter from now on. Yours sincerely, S Brown." I wonder why? Was my sweet gas man in a secure unit somewhere?

It was a winter's twilight late afternoon when my Doc, who I had sent for that morning, finally got out to my home. I'd sent for him to verify my own diagnosis of shingles. He placed his shoes on the front door mat and followed me into the dining room. He offered profuse apologies for the lateness of his call, his reason being an outbreak of flu that had thrown his timetable all to cock.

The dining room was lit on that stormy afternoon by just a couple of little table lamps, as was my way because I found the gentle twilight gave me comfort. The settee was pushed into an alcove and therefore was in semi-darkness. Stethoscope out at the ready the Doc threw his medical bag onto the settee on what looked like a pile of cushions. He was soon to find out when his bag was pushed to the floor that cushions don't move but 16-foot pythons do! How was I to know that all reptiles were the phobic, terrifying monsters of all his nightmares awake or asleep? No matter the size of the reptile, he found them abhorrent and Lucy's 16 feet of pure muscle was just too much to bear. Of course, if I had known of his phobia, I would never have let him encounter Lucy cause that's just cruel!! Anyway, he did and this story can be written about a day never to be forgotten by either of us.

For a chunky chap he had an admirable turn of speed (and he was later heard to boast that the revs he reached to leave my property were his personal best!) Poor screeching, gasping, shaking man. At least, he kept his dignity and did not keel over in a dead faint, nor did he wee-wee his pants as poor Sam had done when that big bastard stroked the side of his face with hers.

My doc looked decidedly ill as he grabbed his bag from the carpet and by then his Asian skin had turned a sickly custard colour. He shot up my hallway at a rate of knots, grabbing his shoes from the mat as he passed by. On the other side of my now closed front door he shoved his black socked feet into them and FLED.

The next day I went to his surgery, as I'd not got the nerve to call him out, yet again, to the house of all his horrors. To this day, he has made just that one and only home visit to me, but if I really needed a Doc to visit, he would send one of his locums after regaling them with the story of how, long ago, he was very nearly a python's lunch.

So, I'd returned the abandoned stethoscope and said a million sorrys, and I was not surprised to be told that "yes, I did indeed have shingles". Horrid, aren't they?

How I hate tattoos on sweaty mind-dead men, and here was a prime example of my dislike about to measure up for double glazing. Showing off his suntan with the aid of a cutaway, soiled, T-shirt, he got ready to climb the ladders. "You're obviously not frightened of heights then" was my observation as he footed the bottom rung. "'Fraid of nowt my love," came the common reply.

We'll just wait and see about that, I thought as he climbed up to measure the glass. So intent was he that his measurements were correct, he only looked at the window and not through it but then he did. Never have I seen a ladder descended so quickly. He missed every bloody rung by placing his hands and feet at either side and sliding down the ruddy lot. I have to admit that not only was he quick but most inventive!

Looking up I saw the cause of all that haste, dear old Lucy had decided to warm her tummy and had plastered herself against the sunny window. Anyway, I couldn't afford the new windows what with all those Vets bills. They would have been nice. Though maybe one day!

I've just been in her room to check that she's OK. Her jaws were hanging open. "Oh well, I suppose I'd better throw her a rat or two or three or four! I remember that awful day when Lucy and I fought for supremacy. The consequences could have been far different, for that giant girl was intent on my death when she slithered into the bath with me. My fertile mind can envisage the News of the World headlines we would have made. "Suburban housewife's liaison in the bath with python ends in tragedy." Guess it would have made titillating reading matter. Some would say it is a pity the general public has been denied this, but believe me, it would have been an awful end: crushed and drowned by the now 17-foot of mean as hell Boa Constrictor, not to forget being eaten!

Oh yes, I forget to mention that Lucy's dear devoted daddy, the one who went to Saudi for only 3 years, you do remember him, don't you? The bugger that got me into this mess, well it's now over 4 years since he introduced me to his pride and joy. The money he left for her care is now only a memory as I wish to God she was! Sometimes, she can be nearly kind and sweet. It's been known for her to rise up beside me and stroke my face with hers. Maybe she loves me after all, my 17-foot and still growing, Lodger from Hell.

Because Lucy was not only one of the largest reptiles in this country and was also an endangered species (I'll never understand how or why because who would want to take on such a monster?), she was much sought after. This being so, I decided to re-home her, good fucking riddance!!

There was a water garden that expressed great interest in owning her with the hope that she would then breed with the smaller (11-foot) male python they already had. No monies changed hands; I was just glad to see her go where she would have a more natural environment and have the chance to become a mother. She had only been gone a matter of weeks when I got a distressed call from said water gardens. "Can you have your snake back please?" This was the last thing I wanted or expected to hear as I'd already started to turn her vivarium room into a craft room for myself. "Might I ask why?" I asked with more than a little irritation. "Because she's eaten her bloody husband!!" was the panicked reply.

What can you say to that? I'd warned them of her powers, did they think I'd been joking? And, so, she came back to me much fatter than I'd remembered her. Well, she would be would she not with 11 feet of her husband being slowly digested? I did not need to feed her for God knows how long as her jaws stayed firmly shut.

It was with great joy that I answered a phone call from a reptile enthusiast in Sheffield. Through the grapevine, he'd heard of Lucy's short-lived marriage (that incidentally had been consummated) and later, with her new owner, was to deliver a large clutch of eggs.

The day came for her second departure (and it would be the last) from me. A special heated and kitted out van arrived along with six muscle bound blokes, to handle the giant sod that, up until then, had been my job on my own. Mike, her new owner, was in awe as she was all his dreams of a lifetime come true. He must have been bloody mad! He asked politely if I minded putting the cowl over her head to keep her calm. I did as he had asked but calm she refused to be. Snakes can't be bullied, cajoled, or tempted (even by Gas men or food) to do anything they don't want to. They tried between them to pick her up and get her into the huge strong sack that proved much too small to transport her to the van. We managed to get her into my hallway with the front door open. Her tongue tasted the outside air, and she went into rigor. That is to say, the whole of her body went rock solid and looked like a felled tree. They each took a portion of her and one behind the other tucked her under their right arms. All was well until it was discovered that she was much too long to fit in the van, and the lady was not for bending. The hourly bus stopped; this fiasco was to the delight of his passengers who refused to continue their journey, for this was just too good to miss.

I remember reading once an article about one such circumstance where an old-fashioned dolly-type clothes peg became the problem's solution. I had a few of these left over from when the children turned them into dollies. Giving instructions to these panicked men to lift her to shoulder height (because I had a bad back and could not bend down low), I limboed under her and inserted the dolly peg into her cloaca (genitals) gave it a couple of wriggles and low and behold she gave an ecstatic shudder, went all loose and was then hastily shoved into the van before her only climax was over!

But, dear reader, this was not the end of our time together. My craft room was up and running and one day I got yet another dreaded phone call pleading with me to take back the "Lodger from Hell." NO CHANCE!! Whilst she might have been his all-time desire, Mike found he was scared crapless of her and with good reason. Whilst brooding her eggs she had severely bitten him when he went just a bit too near to inspect how her future offspring were doing. He had to have a couple of fingers amputated because of sepsis, and the friggin' coward thought her mummy would once again come to the rescue. "NO," he asked what he should do with her as the Zoos in this country would not or could not, help. My advice is "have her put to sleep and do not turn her free on swampland" as some morons do when their baby snake becomes unmanageable after a few years. This would be putting a killer into the community, so silent, so deadly, until it was too late, and its victim was its dinner. Nothing human or animal would be safe from those coils.

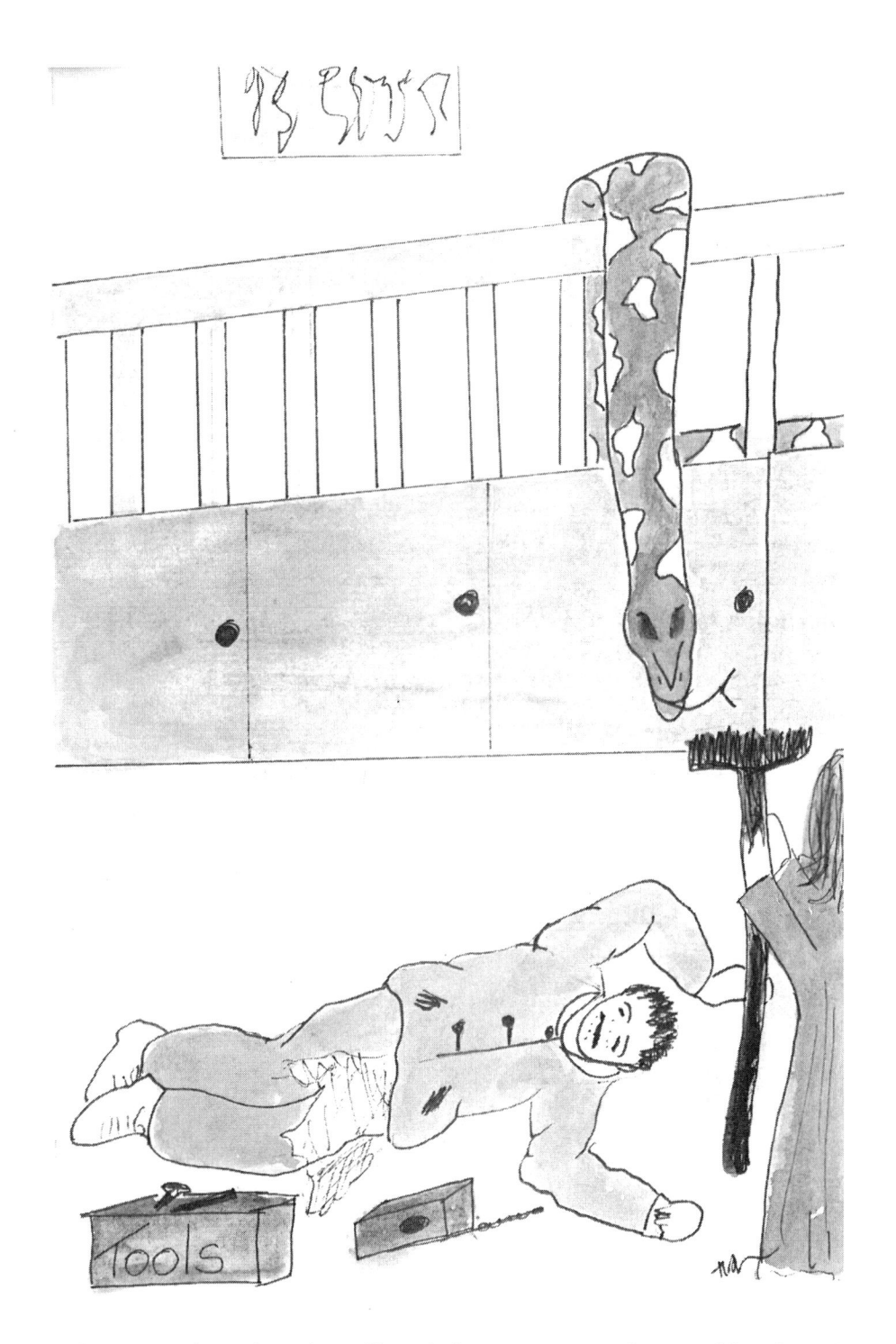

I suggested a rather nice office chair or numerous shoes and handbags be made from her beautiful giant skin, shame to waste her, my magnificent evil Lodger from Hell!!

I never heard from Mike again and decided also not to get in touch with him. This was a lesson to us all. Let wild creatures stay just that – wild in their natural habitats. To remove them is both selfish and cruel, and the only thing I have left of our time together is a 16-foot shed skin! And a new bathroom.

Dear reader, 19-foot is my approximation for my lodger from hell. Over our years together, I tried and failed miserably to measure the writhing swine. I'd wait until she had been fed and was in a placid mood (Or so I hoped) then I'd creep up to her and place the measuring tape on her head with a chunk of blue-tac. Slowly, slowly I'd mark off each three-foot of muscle with said blue-tac then she would repeat what she always did. Coil herself up, thus making measuring a no-no! So, forgive me if she was not 19-foot as I presumed, maybe she was more or less. Who bloody cares? I refused to become a Python's lunch just to satisfy the curiosity of anyone who would never have the balls to go near the giant sod in the first place. I dare you to try to measure something as big and nasty. On second thoughts, don't bother.

The Slowest Chamois in the World

I first met Tony when I was buying bacon in his butcher's shop, he was so busy clocking my boobies that he then cut off his fingertip with the manual slicing machine. To add insult to his injury I refused the back bacon he'd sliced for me, because it was now covered in his blood.

In later years when he was more than just my butcher, we would laugh at this encounter for he bore the permanent reminder in the shape of the scar where his digit had been reattached by a microsurgeon.

Wednesday afternoons were our playtimes as the shop was closed, and I was open!

Came that Wednesday afternoon, he did not arrive as usual (it was in the days before mobile phones) but even if I had been able to reach him, he would have probably lied about his whereabouts, as this boy was liberal with his services, I suppose he took a bag of selected chops .etc. to all of his lady friends as he did me, and it's a wonder he stayed in business for as long as he did.

All gussied up in the finery of seduction, I'd prowled the windows watching for the familiar van that never came. BASTARD! My hormones were raging, and I just had to have satisfaction. Nothing else for it, I had to be the giver of my own pleasures, so toys at the ready I lay on top of my duvet exploring my places of pure delight. It was whilst I was throwing my head about in climax that I noticed something that should not have been there. Standing on my bay window, his mouth hanging open in disbelief, eyes popping, was my window cleaner, his hands barely moving across the glass. How long this lucky muppet had been watching the action I can't say as I'd been lost in erotica for quite some time. Not a word was said, I drew the curtains, and he went down his ladder and went away. I really did not expect to see him again, but the cheeky git turned up on Friday as usual, would you not have thought my impromptu display would have exempted me the two and six (twelve and a half pence) window cleaning payment with the slowest chamois in the world?

You know by now that an 'eye for an eye' was the family motto I lived by.

Loverboy had given me excuses for his absence from my boudoir that Wednesday and believe them I did not. Revenge was on the cards, and it came in the shape of the lady that ran the poodle parlour next to his butchers' shop.

This buxom lass was as liberal with her favours as he was, and with this in mind I agreed to the threesome Tony suggested. It was to be held in the closed poodle parlour, not very sensuous, but needs must. Both shops were closed at 6 pm and at 6.30 pm we were hot to trot, but not in the way that naughty butcher expected.

My pal had stripped to fancy undies and greeted the bulge in his trousers with a frisky fondle, before leading him to the dog clipping table that she had covered with a fur throw (or was it just clipped off dog hair?) I can't really remember.

Dear God, was he excited as his hands and feet were put in restraints (meant for dogs on four legs) surely all his mucky dreams were about to come true? Wrong!

Putting down the vibrator she'd been grasping my laughing friend picked up the shears that had seen better days and set to work on the panicked body of the now cursing butcher.

First, she shaved his body hair in patterns (God that wench was so artistic) before joining them all up leaving the surface skin like a proverbial baby's bottom. In those seventies days, sack and crack were left hirsute, but he was to find himself a petrified trailblazer.

"Hold his knob up for me pet, will ya," was her instruction to me, and whilst I held between finger and thumb his flaccid todger, she ripped out his luxuriant growth with rusty clippers missing many, many teeth, he obviously thought it prudent to stop struggling whilst his bollocks were shawn, no doubt in fear of singing falsetto for the rest of his days. Poor Bastard.

The screams from him were of pain, far from the ecstatic ones he thought would bounce off the walls of the poodle parlour.

The result of this revenge was that his conkers looked like a ploughed field of turnips, and he'd have had one hell of a job selling them off at half price in his own shop window. Now the instrument of torture she applied with much dexterity to his scrotum had been found in the back of a drawer, long forgotten, and had been replaced many times over by clippers that cut instead of dragging out clumps of hair, the excited chap of half an hour ago squirmed in pain whilst we unbuckled all but one of his restraints and the last I saw of him as we slammed the shop door and ran for our lives was him stroking his trashed bollocks whilst shouting threats of what would happen when he finally caught up with us. We made ourselves scarce for a couple of weeks, giving him plenty of time to calm down, and his mutilated body had started to grow hair again.

Isn't revenge sweet, eaten hot or cold? Never again did he let me down on a Wednesday afternoon, but it did take him many months to forgive me and resume our playtime, by then his nuts were furry once again… Happy Wednesday.

Smiles

Before me sat the very type of person that I loathe, my face said it all! He looked so utterly out of place in filthy trainers, torn jeans, ratty bomber jacket, shirt with food clogged on it, unwashed straggly black hair, broken nicotine-stained teeth, cruel dark eyes and a nose falling apart from the abuse of the substance he obviously snorted. Yes, this was the epitome of someone you kept your distance from.

I'd been invited to a physic reading, to make up the numbers, as my new lodger (whose place I had taken) was herself flying that day. So, I sat amongst the nine hosties I knew so well and waited for this, so far unseen, physic to arrive. He'd been booked over the phone after mind-blowing recommendations but what stood before us now was an arrogant, smelly vile excuse of a man.

A couple of the girls went into the luxurious bedroom for a private reading; one came out beaming the other in floods of tears. For this unkind cretin had told her he knew of her previous unsuccessful IVF treatments and that as she sat there, she was, at last, having the twins she craved. To say, she must have been ecstatic is an understatement, but in his next breath he brings her crashing to earth with the words "Don't get too excited coz you're going to miscarry, but two years from today you will give birth to two healthy boys."

Now, this is more than specific and still crying she bought a pregnancy test, the little blue lines in the wand proved that vile sod only to be correct. Two and a half weeks later finds her in hospital. The babies of her dreams are flushed from her body and she is beyond heartbroken. And "yes" exactly two years later as she pushed her healthy twin boys into this world, she remembered the prediction of this joyous event and smiled the smile of motherhood.

I now entered that pretty room, furnished in the French style, after my weeping friend had fled from it.

The first words out of his mouth were "I know you don't like me, and I don't fucking care and by the way, you do know that you are also physic, don't you?"

Then, he tells me of my future, most of which has come about. He sits drawing whilst he talks and finally throws me his artistic efforts, no skill whatsoever, but the accuracy made my blood run cold three weeks later!

The shop near the chemist had been empty for many months, and the local word was that it was to be an undertakers. People got up in arms at this and protested constantly, I thought it a bloody good idea as the area was full to bursting with elderly old folk, and the parlour would have had no end of clients, as I told the other residents at the meeting, aimed at making all corpses a no, no. One, they were quiet; and two, they don't drop litter like the customers would of the other proposed business venture: a takeaway. Both of these propositions were to fail in the following months of negotiations.

He also told me of this younger man by seven years already known to me, who was going to love me as I'd never been loved before. "The only trouble is his wife," I was warned. "Bollocks," I thought. Next, he mentioned that one day I'd have more money than I would ever know what to do with. "Double bollocks," I thought. Then, he said the words that I rehear time and time again in the passing years: "You will always be alone," and for year after lonely year I am always alone, and I hate it.

Shortly after this reading (which we all paid ten pounds each for he clutched the hundred pounds and went on his way, no doubt to buy yet more white powder to snort up damaged nostrils!) his predictions started to come true.

Work started on the empty shop, as at last a decision that pleased most people had been made, it was to be a hairdresser's, I looked with interest when it was about to receive its finishing touches, and my heart pounded with the memory of that reading. Standing before me was a decorator holding high a piece of wallpaper whose pattern was, you've guessed it, red and black lightning type flashes. I'd kept the psychic sorry excuse for a drawing and now held it in my hand, amazed at its accuracy. He might have been callous and vile, but he was all-knowing, depicting traffic lights, crossroads and the style and colours of a hairdresser's shop.

I had known the man who was also to be part of the predictions for a few years.

I'd first said "hello" to his family when they moved into the house previously owned by two charming gay chaps. These flamboyant lads used their creativity in home décor, and their purple ceiling sporting silver stars was going to be a beast to paint out. This opinion I expressed to these new neighbours, and we all laughed in the sunshine.

In conversations with this family (who lived over the crossroads that had been drawn) they were quite frequent as I used to walk past their home on the way to my then friend's home. Because I'd only ever seen this chap working with cars in his front garden, I presumed that Paul was a mechanic or such and our conversations were only ever banter or shared interest in my latest animal rescue.

Come the day when I hobbled past after having an op that involved God knows how many staples in my groin. These buggers really hurt and seeing my pain Paul asked what had happened? I explained that a bloody sadist surgeon had put enough shrapnel near my nethers to knock up three rabbit hutches. Laughing Paul takes my hand and leads me into his garden showing me with pride a clump of ten red tulips. Little did he know that I had an arrangement with a park gardener who saved me the dug up (should have been thrown away tulip bulbs) these were swapped for a couple of bottles of cider. This yearly practice worked just fine, I got a fabulous garden, and he cycled home pissed.

Telling Paul of my lush garden up the road, he asked if he could come and see it. On my hobbled way back from my (now ex) friends, he joined me, and we strolled in the spring sunshine to admire the bulbs I'd given a second chance of blooming again.

Fragrant hyacinths filled the air, the tulips stood tall in all their glory and I uttered the words that were to change my whole life "would you like a cup of coffee?"

his "yes please" reply found us sitting in the lounge on opposite sides, my darling Shepherd Sophie snuggled up to him on the sofa whilst he stroked her lovely head.

This chatting went on for some time. and then a very strange, strained silence befell us. I looked into the garden wondering how to restart our previous early banter and on turning around I saw to my disbelief tears running down his bearded cheeks. I went over to him and when I held his hand, he told me something terrible had just happened. Bloody hell, did this man have an incontinence problem I knew nothing of? Because if I'd known there would have been no chance of him sitting on my new velvet sofa.

The upset Paul went on to explain that he was a pastor for the church (news to me) that he'd been married for many years, he loved his wife and told her this daily, but he loved his God even more and he had just committed a sin against his vows of marriage by falling in love with someone else, he'd fallen head over heels in love with me! (The crazy dog lady) in the beat of a heart.

I know this sounds like Mills and Boon slushy crap, but I swear it to be true.

On arriving home, his wife asked what was wrong with him and much to her dismay, the plonker told of his unexpected love for the crazy dog lady. I wonder which of the three of us was the most shocked?

Long story short: he left his wife of many years, made his daughter cry and disown him, upset his precious God, and moved in with me. For I now realised that I also had feelings for this man and believed him when he said his wife had never loved him as he once did her.

His guilt made him return to the matrimonial home many times, but what he had found with me always lured him back and his mind became tormented by guilt and love.

In the end, he left for the very last time amidst many tears, telling me that if I had not been as I was (bipolar) he would have stayed all of his life with me. My bipolar had once again stolen my happiness, and I cursed once more my parents for creating such a damaged human being, albeit unknowingly.

Him leaving me and in so doing taking my future with him (or so I believed) sent me into a depression so deep that it lasted four whole terrible years, in which time I never went out and a kind neighbour did my shopping. I, my home and garden went to hell, and the only thing I could do was love and tend my beautiful loyal dog Sophie

So, the prophecy of the past had come to be: "Yes." I'd been loved as never before, this being proved by what that man gave up to be with me. But bad deeds reap bad rewards, and my deserved punishment for stealing a husband (a man of God) was to die a slow mental death, alone for four long years. The saying is 'what goes around comes around' etc. applies to me also.

Two correct predictions down, yet more to happen. That vile knowing man had told me that one day I'd have more money than I'd ever know what to do with, one's mind obviously jumps to a lottery win which would have been truly remarkable, as I never played it.

But in a small unexpected way, his words are indeed so true. Because I do all my own jobs, live a life without booze, ciggies, holidays, going out, bingo, all the things so-called normal people empty their wallets for I often have a small amount of spare cash once the bills are paid from my pension.

Along with monetary birthday and Christmas gifts (that I ask for because I'm in the lucky situation of not really needing or wanting anything), this spare money is saved until it reaches one hundred and fifty pounds. This I send away to have another of the little children I grieve for, operated on across the world.

What a terrible existence just because of a natural birth defect and even worse than the never-ending scorn was to come at the age of nine. For then, these deformed mites were put into the sex trade for a succession of vile so-called men to rape them year in and year out.

This situation tore my heart, and I was determined to do all I could to help save them from a life of hell.

And so, with each one hundred and fifty pounds I send to Operation Smile, I know I've not only mended a little face. I've also turned on the light in haunted brown eyes, no longer will their disfigurement push them into being at the mercy of disgusting sodomists, now they can have the deserved education that will enable them to have a better life. The villagers will embrace them hopefully and young precious lives will, at last, be happy and safe. So, if your heart is generous and your purse is overfull think of the little damaged souls across the world that you also could change a life for, just like I have done, 19 times so far over many years, for the little children that I will never know but care about so very much.

At the moment of writing this, thousands of miles away, a tiny girl huddles in fear and pain on the muddy floor of the shanty, but that is her home. Her tummy rumbles with hunger, the only water she has to drink is contaminated by the animals that defecate in it. A tiny, tiny brown hand tries to brush away the flies that torment the open wound on her face, taunts from the school children that she dreams of being one of (should a miracle happen) fill her with fear, and she hopes the darkness of her hut will keep her safe.

But hold on to your dreams of a miracle little girl for the crazy dog lady on the other side of the world has saved up yet another one hundred and fifty pounds, help is on its way, your childish dreams of a perfect smile are about to become true for your whole life long because from across the miles, I send you hugs and kisses and of course a radiant smile. Sweet dreams xx

For years I'd lusted after a Kunzite and diamond ring (Kunzite if you ladies don't already know is a clover pink gem with the brilliance of a diamond) and after two years of saving I eventually had the seven hundred and fifty pounds it would cost. (Not a lot really by today's standards of silly money, of, say, ten thousand pounds being paid for a blasted handbag, how can the skin of a dead animal, sewn in a foreign sweatshop and now bearing a designer label be worth all that cash? The people who think it's clever to have such an item swinging from their twice-weekly manicured nails should be bloody ashamed of themselves. With that sort of cash, I could do so much good for those who need it!) (Once again, I've digressed. I told you, did I not, that I had a grasshopper mind, whose thoughts raced and jostled for supremacy making it almost impossible for me to get the mixed up sods down on the paper?)

Now back to the Kunzite ring of my dreams. Seven hundred and fifty pounds was paid to the jewellery company, and a few days later it arrived. I pushed it onto my finger as far as it would go thinking re-sizing would cost another twenty-five pounds. Standing in my front room window where the sunshine was at its greatest, I marvelled at what the earth can reveal if given the odd million years. This gem was all my expectations and then some flashes of purple escaped the clover pink depths of the stone, pure white small diamonds clasped the kunzite, the contrast between the colours just perfect. At last, after all those years of wanting it, it was finally mine.

And then I looked beyond the ring, at the old hand it was perched on, and I was sickened. For its glowing beauty made my arthritic work-worn hands look even more horrible, surely a thing of such beauty should adorn a hand of equal loveliness? So, I kept my dream ring for just forty-eight hours, returning many times to the sunshine to marvel at its beauty. The company gave me a full refund as, of course it still held its security tag, and had only been admired in the sun's rays.

So, now I had seven hundred and fifty pounds of extra money, all bills were paid and little helpless children across the world needed some help. So five sweet lives were given a smile that would last a lifetime with my ring money. They would sit at school desks with children who now accepted them, and they would eat food that did not take a detour back down their noses because

Operation Smile had mended what a birth defect had inflicted on them. This being a cleft palate and hair shorn lip.

Now, eight tots had received what my heart and purse had sent for their future.

But what I will tell you now really defies all logic and reason.

I'd been so ill for over four years, housebound with the torment of my mind and the pain of someone having to leave me (because of the bipolar) who I loved dearly, but who could not match my Hamid, and missed all of the interminable time.

I must have been getting slightly better because the agoraphobia (that is a part of my bipolar) allowed me past my front gate. My dogs needed vaccinations, bills needed to be paid and whilst I was out, I had to collect my pension from the post office. This had of course built up to a sizeable amount as I'd not cashed any for many, many, weeks. So, six hundred pounds made my red purse bulge, and I set off with my dogs to go to the old farm for duck eggs before a teatime visit to the vets.

I loved this old farm that had hardly altered in the two hundred years it had stood there (according to the sepia picture on the wall). Gentlemen in gaiters stood beside ladies in long black clothes, their mob caps covering tightly coiled buns, in a farmyard that time had left untouched.

The old farm dog came over to be stroked at the same time I was loading three dozen duck eggs into the rear footwell of my old Micra car. Waving goodbye to the old lady (who was a direct descendant of the folks in the picture), I drove the considerable distance to the vets. Up the heavily rutted farm track, my car bounced around a couple of roundabouts, up a steep hill along a couple of miles of fast road and I'd arrived at my destination. On reaching to get my purse (which I believed was on the car floor under the egg boxes) to my horror, I found it was not there, panicking I looked in my bag, no purse, all over the interior of the car, still no purse. Now, remember I told you I'd collected my many weeks' pension hours before. My purse still held that six hundred pounds as I'd managed to pay for the eggs with loose change. I know I was turning round and around the vet's car park in panic, wondering how the hell was I to pay for the injections when out of the corner of my eye I spotted something red. Believe this or believe it not, perched on the rear windscreen wiper was my missing purse. Whilst loving that farm dog, I must have put the purse on the roof of the car and the vibration of its movement had made it slide down the hatchback only to nestle safe and sound on the rear window wiper.

What the hell are the chances of not losing six hundred pounds in that way? What upset me the most was the loss of the little poems of friendship my dead friend Caroline had once given me. They were priceless and never to be replaced.

So dear reader, I now had money that really should have been long gone, falling from a car on a journey of over six miles, how could that be? Was the angel of my childhood caring for me yet again? Bless! Xx

If that money had been gone forever, I would have had no option but to manage without it and I decided that without it I would struggle until the next pension day.

Four little faces that I would never see (except for pictures I cherish, sent by the surgeons) would receive the mended smiles that they dreamed of in the dark huts that were their existence. The soil floors which would soon turn to mud, for the yearly monsoon was on its way. Now, they could escape the mud for a few hours a day by going and getting the education they craved in the newly built school.

Trying to help those much less fortunate than myself makes me hope I'm worthy of the clean water I drink and the safe environment I'm blessed with.

The money from the lucky red purse that destiny decided I could do some good with was at once spent on the charity, Operation Smile, to rectify nature's failure and ensure that four little souls really could smile for the first time in their tragic lives.

Very soon after this donation, I got a wonderful letter from one of the surgeons saying without people like me, their work would be impossible. And there in my hands were the photos, before and after, sad mournful eyes gazed out at me and in the photo beside it, the twisted deformed nose and mouth were no more, and eyes full of hope and happiness smiled as never before.

So far, as the years have passed, I've mended 19 little souls and in so doing, turned their lives around forever. They are not destined for the vile sex trade anymore but hopefully will have an educated happy life, full of the laughter they can now make. Dear God, they deserve it! and in the latest will I've made, I've ensured many tinier sweet lives will know the skill of the Surgeon's scalpel and awaken rebuilt and so, so beautiful.

And one very important part that physic was wrong about, all those years ago. The money he said I would never know what to do with? Oh, I know exactly how it will be spent!

As soon as it reaches one hundred and fifty pounds, I send it across the oceans to switch on another smile.

But apparently, I'm going to have to wait until I'm eighty for his next bit of 'good news'. Then, I will be struck down by the greatest pain I've ever known in my left lower stomach. (Now that's something to look forward to for the next ten years) This dreadful agony will not kill me. Oh bloody *no*. I'll stagger on for another four years and die alone at the ripe old age of eighty-four. Nice one! Only the quickly running out of time will tell! and then I won't be able. Or will I? For I fully intend to come back and scare the crap out of those gits who have made my life a misery. Look over your shoulder honey can you feel me behind you? Has the room I created gone suddenly very cold? Are the hairs on the back of your neck standing on end? Is your dog howling to escape from what you can't see (but it can)? 'Yes,' I decided my home was just too nice to leave so I'm sharing it with you! You don't mind do you pet? Boo!

After a while you learn the subtle difference between holding a hand and claiming a soul, and you learn that love doesn't mean leaning and company doesn't mean security. And you begin to learn that kisses aren't contracts and presents aren't promises. And you begin to accept your defeats with your head held high and your eyes wide open, not with the grief of a child. And you learn to build all your roads on today, because tomorrow's ground is too uncertain for plans.

After a while you learn that sunshine burns if you get too much of it, so plant your own garden and decorate your own soul, instead of waiting for someone to bring you flowers.

And you learn that you really can endure — that you really *are* strong, you really *do* have worth.

And with every new tomorrow comes the dawn.

Do Pigs Graze?

The gentleman who had given up everything to be with me bought me an American sports car, a Chevrolet Camaro Berlinetta, this 4.6 litre, left-hand drive beauty was far beyond my capabilities of driving, or so I believed, as I was used to my present Civic, but I'd thought myself very grown-up when I'd owned a couple of Capris in the past, but these low cars were definitely in the past now, because I needed to have a car that did not require an 18 year-old limbo dancer to climb in, and out, and drive it.

So, a Honda Civic it was, I'd had it sprayed amethyst, which despite its name, was not purple but the clover pink I so loved and this was the colour of the kunzite ring of my past which I had owned for just forty-eight hours. (I'll tell you about that later on!)

The day came when my pink car needed work and as my chap was a dab hand with motors, he drove it back to his garage to fix it, leaving his American job (with its keys) at my home.

Towards lunchtime, I got a call about yet another animal rescue. I'd become quite well known for miles around as the woman who would risk life and limb to save any creature in need of help.

An unknown voice asked, "Do pigs graze?" I told her "No, they truffle." (what an opening question) meaning they stomp and rake up the ground with their trotters to find what tasty morsel lay beneath. They are particularly fond of truffles, but they are not allowed to eat them, well maybe just a small one by their owner as these fungi are worth a fortune to a classy gourmet restaurant.

Someone had abandoned a very fat, friendly pig in the spare land next to her bungalow. Not content with what the scrubby field held in the way of nosh, it crashed its way through her fence and started to demolish her vegetable patch. She was not a happy woman. "Can you come and collect it?" she asked. Of course, I could and would, the problem being the only car available to me was the American monster. Just as well really, as the huge lad would never have fitted into my civic.

Sitting on the Camaro's black leather seat I turned the key, and the roar of its engine nearly made me abandon the rescue, then I thought what's the point of having balls of steel if you let a piece of machinery beat you? So, off I set on the journey of about four miles and by the time I arrived, I was a dab hand at controlling something I believed I never could.

The lady was waiting in her demolished front garden for me and thought Jeremy Beadle (a TV prankster) had set up the scene set before her. I suppose she expected a van, possibly a Range Rover, but what had turned up to collect the porker was just ridiculous, a white Chevrolet Camaro Berlinetta.

With pot belly nearly scraping the ground, this friendly boy allowed my German Shepherds choke chain to be put around his sturdy neck. Munching on a polo mint, he followed me to the car and climbed quite happily onto the passenger seat, even the restraining seat belt did not faze him at all, he just sat comfortably looking through the slightly tinted windscreen, munching and slurping on his mints, Oh Bless this big brown and black lad. He was so laid back; he was almost horizontal. The astounded lady waived us off, no doubt to return to her munched-up garden and tried to salvage whatever she could. It would not be worth saving!

Pulling up at traffic lights, I was beside a yob in a Lada who believed obviously he was a boy racer. Double exhausts devoid of bafflers roared as he kept hitting the accelerator, he was picking his nose and eating the contents when he looked beside him and clocked the 4.6-litre beast awaiting green.

His music blared, and his foot went crazy for he was going to show the flash git in the white car how to drive. At this point, I rolled down the electric window and my porky passenger stuck his snotty snout out for a gasp of fresh air, still chewing casually on yet another mint.

The spotty nerd in the Lada did more than a double-take, what he saw had unbalanced him, gluing him to the traffic lights and as I drove away, I could read his lips in the rear-view mirror: "What the fuck was that?" The lights were now red again!

That simple git had not realised the car beside him was left-hand drive, so to all intents and purposes, as far as he was concerned, a fat pig was driving, and doing it damn well!

At the next lights, he still had not caught up with us, and another mile down the country road my potbellied mate was given a home for life at the sanctuary I often used for my rescues.

Hours later my own car was returned good as new and after many thanks, my chap drove his white sports car home. Later, he was to phone to enquire if I'd had some vegetables or whatever on the passenger seat. I could truthfully deny this as my passenger was no vegetable, but God knows he had plenty of the stolen ones inside his fat tummy.

Never again did I drive that car, and it was not very long before the bipolar that blighted my life drove away the man that I'd loved for four years, but time had proved him to be fickle!

The Grapevine has told me he has since married. I hope she is worthy of such a nice man and has not just latched on to the beneficiary of his dead wealthy father's estate. Call me cynical if you wish, or just damn jealous, but the fact is I loved him for just being himself (even though he was up to his eyes in debt with the Taxman), but does she?

Socks

Now, I've always been a very tactile bundle of trouble who never misses an opportunity for naughtiness.

It's a lovely sunny Friday, market day is in full swing, crowded with people out for a bargain sauntering in the heat. Traders shouted their wares and delicious food smells wafted on the gentle breeze making tummies gurgle with longing.

The atmosphere was very cosmopolitan, with people of many races in glorious, coloured costumes mingling with the sombre English. My fella only tolerated these outings for my sake, him being a bit too posh to embrace market tat.

A very tribal lady stopped abruptly in front of me in the crowd to scoop up her brood of five and tie the trainer of a little lad that was having none of it. And in spite of his screams of protest, she finally secured the shoe; it did not help the situation when she heard me mutter "staple the buggers on next time."

I could feel the warmth of his body behind me and took the opportunity to give his bollocks a quick furtle, as is my way, just a show of pure affection you understand, and he'd been enjoying this grope for a few seconds whilst the harassed lady gathered her wits and her kids when I realised all was not as it should be. Surely, these conkers were of the looser variety and on turning around I stared into the lascivious leer of a total stranger. "I'm so sorry, wrong bollocks" was all that could be muttered. His reply being, "No worries love" as he walked off holding a plastic shopping bag over his nethers, no doubt to conceal the outcome of my prolonged furtle.

That man of mine, who I believed to be the recipient of my amorous dexterity, was two stalls back buying black socks, oblivious as to what he had just been denied. Still, the day was young, was it not?

Tutu

It had to be admitted my friend's tiny girl Daisy, was a most delightful child. Bouncing copper curls, green eyes and a ready cherubic smile, she made me feel quite broody. Kate adored her offspring but was obviously worried about an unusual habit her child fixated on and for no known reason had developed and she could not be distracted from. A visit to the doctor was needed so mother and child sought his considered opinion with haste.

On examining Daisy, he noted that she had a very pronounced clitoral region and this being so was extremely sensitive to any touch. The innocent touch being having a nappy change, or bathing, etc. He advised ignoring when she once again threw herself on the couch with her teddy shoved between her legs and with thumb in mouth, she humped her teddy senseless.

This (to both me and Kate her mother) was most distressing to watch and so we both pretended we had not seen the sensual motions of a three-year-old cherub. When Daisy had completed her sexual mission, she removed teddy from between her chubby little legs – clasped him to her chest and instantly fell into a contented sleep. I often wonder if her tiny fertile mind thought "you can shove your dummy mummy because I have grown a far better comforter".

Like all parents at that time with more than a bob or two to spare it was the done thing to enrol one's beloved spoilt child into the local ballet class. Daisy too took to this new adventure a treat and twirled in her pink tutu and danced in matching ballet pumps to the rapturous applause of her doting parents. Each week Daisy progressed with her dance routines and soon it was time for the much-awaited ballet concert.

It was held in the old village hall and the place was crowded with parents who were each convinced their little darling to be the best dancer ever! There were safety bars at the windows (so no escape for Kate from what was about to shamefully happen) and once everyone was in situ the doors were locked and all cameras were forbidden – this was to deter any paedophile interest. The pensioner / ballet teacher at the ancient piano tinkled a few keys and looked over her shoulder to affirm that the sweet dance troupe was ready. There they all stood Sugar Plum Fairies, tutus held to the side, tiny feet pointing.

And then Daisy did the unthinkable…She hurled herself onto her knees and elbows on the wooden stage and with her tutu'd little bottom stuck up in the air she pushed a fist between her legs and did what came very naturally to her, to say the world in that room at once stopped is no understatement. The staggered old pianist / ballet teacher stopped mid tinkle – there was a deathly silence as parents nudged each other and blissfully unconcerned Daisy did what Daisy just had to do!! She humped her fist until the action was no longer needed. Looking a little dazed she righted herself and with rosy red cheeks and beads of perspiration on her copper curls she sat up, then she stood up and straightened her crushed tutu, put her hands on her hips, pointed her tiny satined foot, looked behind her at the puzzled giggling dancing troupe – then she beat out…a 1 a 2 a 3 on the stage and said to the old pianist "right well then play then please", such a polite child!

After a few faltering notes the music got under way as did the wonderful performance. The dance troupe deserved all the clapping and praise they got but Daisy's horrified mum was hiding behind a set of scenery hoping she could slide out and therefore be unseen, whilst dragging with her what she wished was an invisible child. This of course was not to be so as Daisy screeched for the mother she could not see and Kate had to sheepishly creep from behind the scenery and reveal she owned the child who caused such gob smacking consternation. Thankfully the doors were quickly unlocked and mother and child made a hasty retreat. There was some talk of social services being involved but after an interview with Kate's doctor it was deemed unnecessary. Kate and her family moved away from the village shortly after this rude debacle, supposedly because her husband had got a promotion down South. But before they left once again, darling Daisy appalled the assembled guests.

The Weatherman had promised sunshine on this much anticipated happy Wedding Day. It was to be a very lavish affair in a stately home – no expense had been spared and all the guests dressed accordingly.

Kate's cherub (who was to be one of eight bridesmaids) held her basket of petals with pride. She was pirouetting – to the clapping delight of the waiting guests as Grandad finally descended the stairs.

"Twirl Gwanpar twirl" were her instructions to the besotted old boy. With smiles, kisses and love this he did for his adored mite. What happened next brought on gasps of amazement and held back laughter "Wewl Gwanpar, you look the dog's bowocks in your new suit!" Now, I'll never know just why the disgusted / amused gathering looked at me, as it was not one of my sayings, for I prefer a more generous helping, i.e., 'Kangaroo's Conkers'. Whilst the three-year-old cherub could string together whole conversations, R's escaped her and W's were a thing of her future (but she managed!)

Out the mouths of babes!

We kept in touch for a while but slowly our conversations petered out and to this day I wonder what became of them all.

Now twenty years has passed and Daisy will now be a fully-grown woman with a secret place where ecstasy can be found and utilised whenever needed. Often, I hope the lucky, lucky girl.

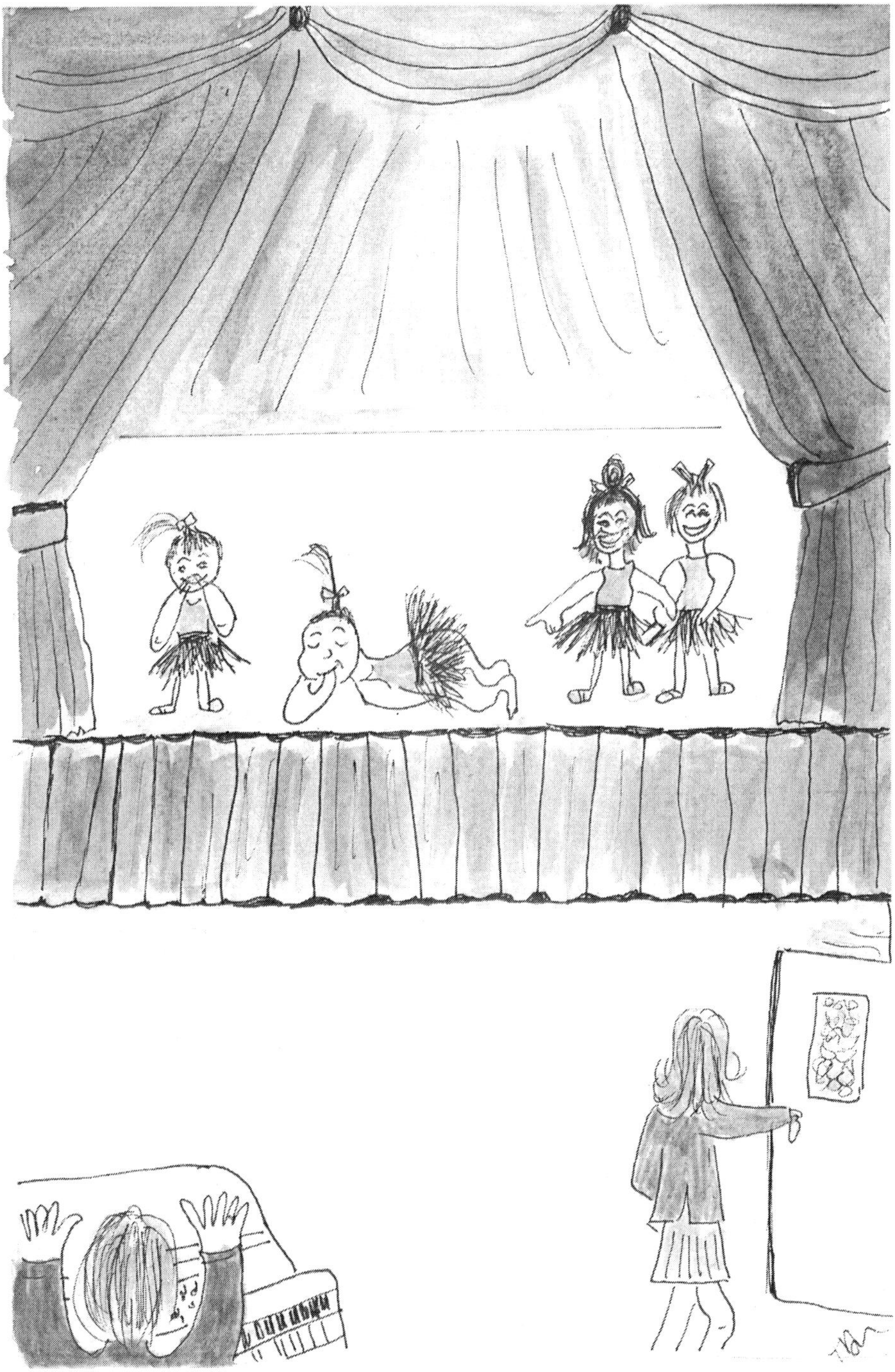

Froth

My life has been blessed with many colourful characters, none more so than Jean and to those that loved her, Jean Jeanie (as the song goes).

We did not meet until out dancing one night (at this point both in our thirties) when a mutual friend introduced us as we boogied in the Ritz dance hall in Manchester. Our years of friendship were from that night on, and she later told me the story of her life.

She started out in the back streets of Bradford in a tiny terraced house that contained her two much older sisters, her drunk letch of a father and her pissed off and frightened mother. Her sisters soon made an escape one night together, sick of their father's pervy embraces. Jeanie, being too young to run, stayed to protect her mum from her father's handy fists and when he went out one night and never returned, they finally believed in a God. Later, it was to be discovered he'd buggered off with the twenty-two-year-old mother from across the street, who had in turn abandoned her three kids. Such is life!

Now, Saj was a gloriously handsome Asian lad, who lived at 43 Gladstone Street, and Jeanie believed he was out of her league. She had been blessed with a figure and legs to die for but was short-changed when faces were handed out. She had a protruding lantern jaw, uneven pure white buck teeth and a nose that should have been kindly reconstructed after a pasting from her drunken daddy, one Saturday night. So, when Saj showed interest, she was beyond delighted. Finally, they married, and she moved into 43, to be a slave to his demanding old sow of a mother and his numerous younger siblings. His old goat of a father soon died, so that was a blessing, one less git to pander to!

Always being surrounded by kids made her loathe them and to make sure her figure was not ruined by pregnancy, she kept her birth pills at Shirley's at number 19, because if Saj had found them, he would now know the reason he had not proved his manhood with his wife's swollen belly. His mother never stopped demanding grandchildren from her eldest son, and he tried his hardest – but the pills kept killing his numerous swimmers. Little did he know!

So, Saj went back to Pakistan on business (or so he claimed) returning six weeks later with a Sari clad fifteen-year-old new bride. Being Muslim, he only had to repeat, "I divorce thee" three times, and he was a single man again, thus making Jeanie a single woman. Not that this mattered, as by Muslim law he was allowed three wives at one time. Greedy bastard! As she pointed out, there is a kind God. Unceremoniously, her meagre belongings were dumped on the street, and with only four pounds two and six in her pocket (saved from her work machining raincoats at the factory on the next street) she was worried for her future. This is all she had managed to save for the rainy day she dared to believe would come for her. For the past three years, that old bitch of a mother-in-law took her wages out of her hand each Friday teatime.

Number 19's door opened, and Shirley gave her a bed for the night, or longer as the case may be. Next morning amongst much laughter, biscuits and strong tea, they trawled the situations vacant column in the free paper, and here her destiny lay waiting. An old gent (recently widowed) wished to employ a decent lady as a housekeeper to live in her own apartment, in his five-bedroom mansion in Mobberley. BINGO! She galloped to the phone box in the next street; grateful it still worked and talked to a Mr Godfrey Harrison.

He sounded nice and told her he would pay her travel expenses to come for an interview.

Two days later (in smart clothes borrowed from Shirley), she stared in wonder at the magnificent home of Mr Harrison. He told her of his days in the army in India and his liking of spicy food. Could she cook it? Could she cook it? Only like a bloody professional! This was the only thing, she had to thank her ex-mother-in-law for. Enforced cooking lessons. She got into the huge stainless-steel streamlined kitchen and presented him with a meal that secured not only employment, but a home to die for.

They became great friends she and Godfrey, as he later asked her to call him. But she had been used to a sex life that she hoped she could enter into with a man old enough to be her father. But he only had an interest in his monthly locomotive mags and any type of puzzle to keep his mind active, he explained, to try and stage off the dreaded dementia.

Her sexual frustration knew no bounds, and she phoned her old mate Shirley, who said she knew of just the thing to get the show on the road. So, she called someone who knew someone, who had a cousin who happened to be a pharmaceutical rep, who happened to have a few pink bead-like pills, known in the trade as 'Thrill a minute'. He sent three with instructions, only take ONE as they really worked their magic FAST, and for hours on end.

By post they were sent, arriving first thing Saturday morning, in return she sent a postal order for three pounds via Shirley (this worked out at one pound per jump) a bargain.

Godfrey's favourite Asian banquet was presented with pride that Saturday night, this he devoured, not realising of course that three extra tiny pink ingredients (there should have only been one) lay hidden in the scorching Vindaloo.

In bed – alone, as usual, reading his locomotive magazine, he did not imagine the stirring of his loins, even from long-ago memory. His old mind was on trains, how could this be? Then, out of his flannel pyjama flies thrusts a phallus that bloody scared him crapless. His shouts of panic brought Jean Jeanie running from her room and on spying all her dreams come true, threw herself onto it! And shagged the poor old sod senseless. This went on for three days and nights, only stopping for a little sleep and nibbles of food. Godfrey begged for it to stop, as his knob was by now was red raw and Jean Jeanie's nethers were not much better. No pain, no gain! It was decided that when he had had a stiffy for so long, being unable to visit the bathroom or get dressed (what did he need clothes for?) anyway, she should ring his GP, who on inspection sent him to A&E where he sat in a chair for four hours with a hard-on. Laughingly, the intern gave him an antidote — but not before most of the nurses and doctors came to inspect his wonderous phallus!,A rather large needle was thrust into his buttocks, adding insult to bloody injury. In the end, she owned up to what she had done, and whilst he laid off the Vindaloo, he eventually forgave her.

But he loved that curry so much that every other Friday night, he took her to a new curry house that had just opened, and that is where she met the owner Syheed, who when hearing she was a dab hand at Indian food offered her a job, should she ever need one.

It was about five months later that Godfrey did not appear dressed and shaved for his prepared breakfast. She called him, to no reply, and after knocking at his bedroom door, without answer, she entered to find her old friend had died in his sleep.

She phoned his estranged daughter Lyne, who had hated her on sight. The feeling was mutual really, as this stuck-up mare had watery, vacuous, very pale, blue, fishy eyes that did not appear to comprehend anything and very florid fat lips that gave her the appearance of a pilchard on acid. When I think about it, she would have fitted in very well with today's bimbos.

Godfrey's love for his daughter had never wavered, and he left her all of his estate, bonds, cash, her mother's gems, his collection of vintage motors and of course his one-million-pound home. Altogether, she copped for over two and a half million. She did not weep one tear of loss for Daddy, but galloped out and bought herself a silver cloud Rolls Royce convertible, and moved into the Mobberley mansion. Once again, Jean Jeanie's belongings were on the step, so to speak.

No home, no job, not much in savings, back to square one. Then, she remembered the offer of a job, not so long ago from Syheed.

A couple of buses later saw her in his restaurant, not only did she get the job that came with the upstairs flat but she also got him.

He lived not far from his business, in a semi his mother insisted he bought in readiness for the upcoming arranged wedding he desperately tried to wriggle out of. No chance, but he still had Jeanie to comfort him. It was on one of these nights of lust (just three weeks before his new missus was about to blight his life) that Jeanie once again used a tried and trusted method to avoid the kids she hated. Rendall's Pessaries were in her bag as usual, along with many other remedies that life made her need.

In the dark, she reached down to her handbag, found what was needed and after expelling them from the foil packaging, shoved two of them up where they were to kill any little swimmers.

She said later, that it was the most exotic, explosive night of torrid sex they had ever enjoyed together, and eventually, they fell asleep in each other's arms as the birds began to sing their morning song.

It was only when the bathroom called, that she threw back the covers to discover a pool of froth, not only down her shapely thighs but also under her buttocks. She let out a squeal of horror, which woke up her paramour, and he shot out of bed in a blind panic, asking what the hell she had used. She assured him it was just the usual Rendall's and to prove it, showed him the opened foil packaging. He then uttered the words that had them not only relieved, but in bloody hysterics: "They're not Rendall's, you silly tart, you've shoved Alka Seltzer up your chuff by mistake."

So, this goes to prove that Alka Seltzer has numerous uses, but for God's sake, don't you rely on them for birth control.

Three weeks later he married his chosen (but not by him) bride. He still visited Jeanie (and as far as I know still does) you see, she had crept into his heart, as well as his bed.

Barbados, Here He Comes

Yet another night of dancing at the Ritz in Manchester. Joyce, my friend, had driven us there in her mini, as at that time I was not fortunate enough to own a car of my own, and would not do for another twenty years.

We danced together most of the evening, her sometimes leaving me to sit alone like a plonker whenever a pair of trousers took her fancy. I'd always been such an aloof bitch and in thinking back to those days I'd probably sent away any possible life partner because he did not live up to my crazy visual expectations. Stupid sod.

Don't they say youth is wasted on the young? How true that is because forty-odd years later I live a lonely life devoid of the laughing gentle company I crave and why? Because I'd probably sent away a lovely man because his bloody shoes were not polished highly enough for my exacting standards. I deserve the empty life I've endured for forty lost years. But still, it hurts each and every day and night, and there's only me to blame and the bipolar. My memory transports me back to the Ritz the huge glitter ball swinging from the ceiling casts stars on which I dance, my young body follows the music's beat, and the red dress on my slim body entices many men to ask me to dance. The answer is always "no thank you," and I continue to dance with the friend who never did understand me.

It's now 1.30 am my feet are sore and so is my spirit. Time to go home from more of the unwelcome pests who had mithered me yet again to dance.

Quite near to the exit stood a bar and as we walked past a handsome man (with titan hair, the same colour as mine) asked if we would like a last drink. Now, I prefer dark men but this soul had a certain charm that could not be ignored. Thanking him for my usual lemonade we chatted and when he asked to dance, it felt so nice to be held close to him on the starry floor.

Joyce, never missing the chance of a free drink, was halfway through a rum and coke when it was time to leave.

This stranger was wearing fashionable garb of the day, a dark brown velvet suit, a nice shirt and tie and the most perfect shoes, now this man certainly held my interest and when he told my friend he would get me home safely, we both believed him.

Holding hands, we walked under the viaduct where a tatty white van and a silver shadow Rolls Royce were parked. "Here we go again", I thought, as it wasn't the first time I would arrive home in a van, sometimes even having a ripped-out bathroom suite in the back. Oh yes, I've lived. But I was taken by the hand right past the van, and the door of the Rolls was held open for me; not only a handsome man but a gent also!

We pulled up at traffic lights and Joyce in her mini was there, bored at waiting for the green light. She looked beside her to see me sitting up high in a Roller. As we pulled away, she mouthed just two words:

"Jammy Bastard."

Tony never asked to come into my home for coffee or any other reason, I found this refreshing, but a little disconcerting, had I lost my Va Va Voom?

Unexpectedly, he turned up a few days later to find me looking like a box of frogs, building a fireplace in my front room.

By sheer chance, I'd managed to get my mitts on loads of Pakistan Onyx and a wall-to-wall fireplace was mid-construction.

Weeks before I was in a very posh furniture shop in Manchester where an obviously gay assistant cursed the fact that some hairy arsed docker had dropped and smashed a cargo of Onyx table tops in so doing leaving empty brass frames that only God knew would be filled again, etc, etc.

"What are you going to do with the smashed marble?" I cheekily asked.

"Drop it in the sea as it's no good to man or beast."

This answer was deep joy to any ears, as I'm never one to miss a chance of making something from nothing. This chap was as camp as a row of pink tents: he drew me a map of the docks, told me which bus to catch to get there, and phoned ahead to tell them that a loss adjuster was on her way and to jemmy open the crate ready for my inspection. Bless that boy!

The hairy arsed docker (cursed so profoundly by the assistant) stood shamefaced with a multitude of lying reasons as to why thousands of pounds of tabletops were in pieces. He could hardly tell the truth, now, could he? That whilst unloading cargo on his forklift truck, pissed, he'd pushed the wrong lever, this truth I was told by his colleague who bloody hated him.

Nailing closed the container the hairy arsed one put a label on stating that it must not be moved without further instruction. This came from my gay new mate who then pocketed the £20 he asked me for, before giving the instruction to the hairy arsed one to deliver said marble to my home, which the now sober docker did without further ado.

So, my paramour surveyed me in overalls, cement clogging my now broken nails, hair in rollers for Christ's sake and my false eyelashes curling around a single knitting needle (I told you I was inventive) Why he did not run a mile? I will never know, instead, he told me to get myself cleaned up, and he would send one of his builders to do the job for me. This kind offer I refused as I liked the challenge of building my first fireplace, and I was on a roll fitting together the broken pieces of Onyx in a crazy paving type pattern.

Up until this conversation, I did not know he owned a construction company that happened to be building houses just up the road from where I lived. I'd seen some of these constructed and voiced the opinion that they were the size of rabbit hutches. Tony took great exception to this and dragged me outside, shut me in the Rolls in all my building finery and on pulling up at the muddy building site dragged me inside the foundations of a house, measured it and proved that it was far bigger than the one I lived in. In stomping through the mud, he had clagged up his lovely new shoes and standing in the rain he opened the boot of the Rolls and selected a shoebox, out of many. Taking off the ruined ones, he hurled them in the mud in a fit of pique and put on yet another brand-new pair, slammed the boot and drove me back home. I was most intrigued at all the shoe boxes in his boot and inquired if there were any ladies' ones? Unfortunately, there were not, and he explained he'd just picked up a dozen assorted pairs of hand lasted ones from a private shoemaker in London. Nice work if you can get it eh!

This man had bided his time and when I'd scrubbed up and looked like the woman he'd pulled a few weeks previously, he decided it was time. We hit the sheets. But, unknown to him at this point was that his money and what it could buy, I found such a turnoff, and I was determined his money could not buy my body. Talk about cutting off one's nose to spite one's face; I must have been bloody mad as I fancied the pants off him.

And so, with throbbing nethers, I always pushed away his advances and many were the times I'd have to sort out my own pleasure once he'd dropped me off back home (I told you I was nuts).

The same applied when he gave me a £100 cheque for my birthday in November, (not much use to me as I'd never had a bank account), on ripping it up and placing it in his breast pocket I told him if he'd have just bought me a block of choccy I would have been more than happy, from his startled reaction I assumed no other woman had been so dismissive of not only his obvious charms but also the contents of his bulging wallet.

Christmas came, and I answered the frantic knocking on my front door, it was late afternoon, and Tony looked like hell. He hurled himself into my hall, cheque book already in hand and demanded to know quickly how much I owed on my mortgage, he explained he was in a bit of bother and had to leg it for an unknown time, but before he went, he wanted to ensure the future of me, my children and my home.

I thanked him kindly for such a generous gesture but told him my mortgage was my debt, not his, and we would all be just fine without his financial intervention.

He was not best pleased to have made a detour that could have cost him his freedom, only to get yet another knockback from me, because waiting at a small airport was his private jet.

A couple of hours later, my children drew my attention to the local TV news, and there was his beaming face on the screen. Apparently, he was wanted for questioning about giving backhanders to a local high up Council employee to ensure his tenders for building land were accepted.

He had told me of many properties he owned abroad, and one of them was his intended destination, which I presumed he safely reached. I never told a soul about what I knew all those years ago, never said anything about the kind man who wanted to pay off my mortgage before he fled. I'd had very strong principles about taking money and even though I did not have 50p for the gas meter when I refused his help, it was the correct decision for me. I must have been bloody mad as it took me another twenty years to pay the sodding mortgage off.

Barbados here he comes!

A couple of months later, I got a card from a far-off land it just said, "all is well." I know he'd been a bit of a bad lad, but he was kind, respectful and decent with me, and I remember our short time together (with no sex you understand) with great affection. It was wonderful for me to be valued, just once, for being me, not a means of fulfilment for randy blokes. Anyway, of course, he had the means to leg it, and fast, his private plane could get him to one of his Villas in far off lands. He would of course have chosen one with no extradition laws, so I hope he had a kind, safe, happy future.

I wonder, does he remember the red-haired lass who made a marble fireplace and was stupid enough to refuse his kind help? The offer of a mortgage-free home. As I said, I'm bloody stupid.

PS: I forgot to tell you, the mechanic who not only looked after his fleet of cars also tended to his beloved jet. The story Darren told me weeks later was that on that never to be forgotten evening when Mr Rolls had to flee to escape years of prison, (that of course would disallow all of the creature comforts he loved to live for) so as not be noticed he chose a Sierra to drive. He'd told me many times that the Rolls was a police magnet; hence: no speeding, no drinking. All the police wanted to do was sit in the luxury that they themselves could never afford. He'd swooped onto the airstrip, got in the pilot's seat he was certified to fly and as it started to roll down the runway, he threw the Rolls key to Darren with just one word, "Enjoy" And a wave goodbye.

For many a year, postcards would fall on my mat from faraway exotic places. Just one word, 'Yes', and a couple of kisses. I presume he had bought himself a new identity that he was making such good use of, judging by the worldwide postmarks.

After say, twenty-odd years the cards never arrived again, was he dead or apprehended for a long-ago misdeed? I'll never find out, will I, but I still wish him well, he was such a lovely man xx.

Blood in the Sand

The merciless sun scorches the barren, arid, land. Sad crops beg for the water that will not come and save them for the rainy season is still far off. The sad child is beaten and broken and starving children surround her in the shanty hut she has to call home. She is waiting for an important visitor who she hopes will view favourably her one-year-old baby girl on this her first birthday. Magdi lies on the hard ground with only a thin colourful blanket to cushion her tiny bones, for she is on the verge of starvation, as are her siblings and mummy, (with yet another huge tummy), and not yet 12 years old. Where the hell is daddy?

The visitor arrives and is made as welcome as possible in a hut with nothing to offer. He looks at what will be his future bride, a little scrap of life on the brink of death, and wonders if he is wasting his money but the mother is desperate for a marriage contract to be made whereupon the 9th birthday of that baby girl, she will become a 'wife' to the huge old man old enough to be her grandfather.

So, the deal is struck and he's not ashamed (as he bloody should be) by the lustful stirrings of his loins at the anticipation of the wedding night eight years hence. Time passes so quickly and he always has village women to satisfy his unsavoury needs. He scratches his scrotum for the umpteenth time that day and wonders how much longer he can live with the syphilis that is eating him alive. He has no care or compassion for his several partners "sod 'em" let them suffer as he is doing – he just hopes he can last 8 years to make a 'woman' out of that baby.

Outside his stinking hovel were small mounds of barren dirt each one the resting place of the brutes previous three child 'brides' (no older than 14 years old at death) and their babies. Peace at last. Stones lay atop of the mounds in a vain attempt to stop starving feral dogs from feasting on the skeletal inhabitants.

So now at last, the monster had saved a pittance to purchase a fourth tiny girl to beat, butcher, rape and without a care – watch her die. It didn't matter as there was room in the dirt to shove her and her bloody kids into it.

EVIL BASTARD.

And so, the years pass, Magdis mother has had two more babies; both born dead (the lucky little souls). They lie side by side along with earlier siblings (five in all) under a stricken tree

covered with a few inches of scrappy earth – their blanket of death.

It's her birthday today, Magdi will be five. It's nothing to celebrate. Little does she know that hell on earth awaits her after an exhausting trudge in the baking sunshine. "Where are we going mamam?", "To see an old lady". Her poor tiny mother is bowed with pain, pregnancy, hard work and the weight of a young weak child who will not live much longer, tied to her back. They walk for hours and finally reach where horror and pain and screams are the norm. An old crone sits on the dirt floor, an array of rusty bits of metal between her filthy feet. Evidence of past brutality is obvious in the dried blood on her instruments and the rags on the ground!

Her mother pushes Magdi on to the dirt floor and forces her skinny little thighs apart "what is happening, what is happening?" Then the pain that no one should ever feel HITS. She tries to struggle free of her mother's vice like grip and can't believe it when her mother (instead of saving her) slaps her and tells her to "stop screaming". She tightly clasped her one and only toy (a straw dolly with a torn red ribbon), for comfort. Her straw only friend couldn't help.

SCREAM INNOCENT LITTLE GIRL, SCREAM for you will until your dying day!

From the secret part of her tiny body, the delicate flower-like genitalia have been sliced and ripped out with a rusty, bloodied knife, the only part of her that would give her love making pleasure, is gone. She was doomed, as thousands before her, (including her own mother) to only know the pain of rape and despair of poverty. No gentle loving, no nice food or clothes. No pretty home, no kind husband to welcome home at the end of his day's work. For men of that culture don't work, they make their downtrodden, beaten, raped, child brides, do it all until endless, torturous child birth and hunger place their used up teenage bodies beneath a withered tree that stands alone in the sand. Sweet dreams at last little lady.

SCREAM LITTLE GIRL SCREAM – and scream she did on that mutilating, scorching hot, day. Her mother showed no compassion as she dragged her bleeding, tortured, 5-year-old child across the sweltering wasteland to what was called home. She was told to lie down. Magdi writhes in agony on the rag covered floor and screamed at to "SHUT UP".

How could this vile mother and all those like her, have torture inflicted upon such a frail tiny body, surely, they could remember how it felt, not so long ago, or was it long ago? For most of these mothers were barely 10 to 14 years old themselves, and this barbaric practice goes on and on, and scores of premature babies die, as do their young mothers.

IT MUST BE STOPPED, WHERE IS A KIND GOD? NOWHERE! If you care, think of your delightful courtship and wedding – a night of kind lust, of kisses and caresses, not beating, torture, knives cut and rape, and ignored screams, screams, screams and yet more. And more years have passed much the same as all the others, Magdi kept getting infections where she had been butchered, the cotton stitches finally broke away and she was left with the tiniest opening to menstruate through. It was a blessing that she had known nothing of the hellish torment about to be inflicted on her malnourished little body, for surely, she would have died of fright, which would have been a blessing.

Her lecherous 'bridegroom' looks at himself in the broken mirror and see's the punishment syphilis has brought about, so with sunken eyes and a doddering step he starts his journey to claim his child 'bride'. Lustful thoughts won't leave his vile mind and he can't wait to penetrate the innocent child victim of his huge erection. At last, after hours of staggering across parched land he sees his destination, the shanty hut he visited 8 years ago. The one-year-old baby was no more, not that one anyway, as she had been replaced by brothers and sisters yearly, all at peace beneath the death tree. In the corner stood a shaking stick-thin little girl in a ragged dress, a patch of blood on the seat of it, so the time had come. As before, a couple of coins exchanged hands- the mother turns away as her little child is dragged screaming out of the only home she has ever known, by this brute of a stranger. A vice like grip is around her struggling skeletal wrist and when she screamed for Mamam to help her he backhands her pretty face and snarled at her through broken nicotine-stained teeth to "SHUT THE FUCK UP". His breath stank! Almost as bad as his huge bent body.

They reach another vile poor hut that was his dwelling, but it was worse than her mothers as it stank of defaecation, urine and marijuana. The smell was so bad it made her eyes water to mix with the tears of fear. "Mamam where are you, what is happening to me? please, please take me away, rescue me" The big nasty, smelly, ugly, cruel man takes yet another swig from a bottle, belches, throws himself on the rag covered so-called bed and begins to snore. That tiny, tiny girl looks down on him with fear and hatred and prays to the God that she knows has betrayed her, "let the bad man die" she prays "let him die" NOW! Of course, like thousands of others as vile as himself, he does not die. Very soon he is awake.

He makes a grab for Magdi and throws her to the bed. She kicks and screams, it does no good at all but makes his erection even bigger and she gets yet another hard slap to the face which makes one of her pretty amber eyes immediately start to swell. He's torn off his stained trousers and she looks upon that huge phallus of his with fear. What is it? Her teeth are chattering, her whole body is in spasm, she tries to keep her legs tight together, but with a rough dirty hand he presses them cruelly apart, "Oh dear God help me' her panicked mind pleads, but God is not listening, does he ever? He's so very heavy; pressing her bony back onto the rough wooden lats of the bed, he keeps on and on thrusting that big thing into her minute sweet body, her screams echo into the night stary sky, yet more slaps that can't quieten her. He stands above her, that giant thing is twitching with lust and dripping slime and fuck her he will and no screams or fighting will stop him, after all she is his 'WIFE' paid for fair and square and he will have his satisfaction no matter how loudly she screams and begs, for this only makes his lust turn to laughter.

The blunt knife he uses on his tobacco will do the trick, she sees the knife and wets herself with fear and panic. Once again, her little legs are prised apart, his nails breaking her fragile flesh and he sets about making sure her body will satisfy his disgusting lust. Once, twice, three times he hacks at her child genitalia, blood splatters the ragged bed. He decided not to make the hole too big as there is no fun in a slack one, is there? Her back arches as he pushes with all his might, the cuts were not big enough and she screams even louder as her flesh tears, his body is moving so fast now, in and out, in and out, in and out, then he lets out a bellow and collapse onto her. His full weight suffocating her. Her life blood now staining the floor. She feels his fluid stream from her mixed with her blood, she prays to die. Sadly, she doesn't. Already she is with child, and syphilis.

SCREAM LITTLE GIRL SCREAM!

Magdi never saw her mother Sagda again for she had died whilst giving birth to her 7th child which lived for just 2 days, whilst being denied of a mother's life-giving milk from withered breasts.

At just 13 years old Magdi joined her own mother and siblings in eternity under yet another half dead tree. All her 5 babies had died of syphilis, barring one named Patam who was rescued after her death, by tireless aid workers and taken to a place of love and teaching and absolutely no girl child circumcision. (Which they are strenuously trying to make illegal). I believe it should carry the death penalty! By cutting off the vile bugger's balls, slowly bit by bit.

If after you have read this, my heart felt words, and you are also moved, well don't just sit there and think "how terrible" **DO SOMETHING ABOUT IT.** From heaven I would like to know that all little girls were safe from the knife, that they had an education, that they could be able to chose LOVE instead of the torture of circumcision and rape, to be healthy enough to have their babies that live long enough to be raised with the love they deserve.

Word has just got through to me from my Aid-Worker friend, Andrea that Magdi's 'husband' is barely alive. The syphilis that he shared with all that he raped has stolen his eyesight. So covered with weeping sores he staggers in the dirt - where he belongs. Good riddance to him and all those evil men who follow in his diseased footsteps, and have done for centuries.

Pray to a 'deaf God' to help the little souls; (who have no reason to want to live), that soon what they have suffered will be **NO MORE.**

PPS when I woke this morning a message had come through whilst I slept. Apparently that bastard had been attacked by a pack of feral, rabid dogs (that had followed his sightless, staggering for 2 days or more). It was decided, (due to the amount of blood in the dirt) that his evil heart was still beating at the time of death. (Oh! Shame). Maybe God is not deaf after all, and those hungry dogs at least got a much-needed meal, all be it decaying still living flesh.

I'm GLAD that child 'brides' years or torment have been avenged in such a painful way. Sweet dreams Magdi, at peace now under your tree of death with all your babies in a forever hug xx

The Cunning Art of Make-Up

I was exceptionally good with the old make-up; I had the gift of turning the plainest or even ugly bride into a goddess on her special day. Because of this, I was employed to beautify brides and maids, thus using up the lonely time that the weekends usually held for me. I worked wonders on myself also, when required. It's marvellous what a bit of make-up in skilled hands can achieve, as all ladies know.

This fact I proved one day as I was sweeping up the autumn leaves. Hair in rollers, eyelashes curling around a knitting needle (I told you I was inventive). My kaftan swinging in the breeze, my face still in the make-up bag. There I was, a blank canvas doing her chores.

Then, to my horror a voice I knew so well spoke from behind me. "Excuse me, is the lady of the house in please?" Jesus, how could I let my latest paramour see me like this? He would be astounded, that the glamour puss he had pursued and finally bedded really looked like a box of frogs. How the hell was I going to get out of this one? I pretended not to hear, hoping he'd bugger off, but he stepped up and tapped me on the shoulder and repeated his question. Bollocks! I spun around and glared at him at the same time shouting, that he'd scared the crap out of me (in a Brummie accent)

"What the hell do you think you're doing creeping up on me like that when I'm doing her cleaning?" I demanded.

I could hardly believe my luck; the daft git did not even recognise his dancing, eating, laughing, amorous girlfriend.

He was informed that her ladyship was having her hair and nails done whilst I did her work, and she would be back later, and 'Yes' I would tell her he'd pick her up at 8 pm.

I galloped in the house, pulled out the rollers and brushed my red hair into gleaming waves over my shoulders. Make-up was done, eyelashes in place, red dress with matching killer heels greeted him at 8 pm.

Bless that daft deluded lad, as we were driving along, he told me how glorious I looked, so unlike the sour, ugly bitch who he disturbed doing my chores. I was most offended by him describing her/me as an old dog and said so in no uncertain terms "How dare you talk about my cleaning lady like that, she's got a heart of gold and works so hard."

Like I said, the cunning power of make-up!

A few dates later, I realised what a shallow git he was. He was handsome, but not caring for me or for that matter, anyone or anything else, just himself. So, I decided to teach him a little lesson he'd never forget, about judging books by their covers.

We were going dancing (or so he believed) after dining at a favourite eatery. He once again started to mock the poor hard-working ugly sod he'd disturbed whilst she shoved a brush, clearing away the autumn leaves. I could not be bothered with verbal retaliation, but very slowly started to wipe away my make-up on a dampened tissue I'd brought with me, for just that purpose. With not a word I watched his astounded face never leave mine, and his tanned face went somehow ashen. Then my masterstroke, I so slowly peeled off my eyelashes and one by one placed them on the edge of his plate. With a remembered Brummie accent, I told him to enjoy his meal, tipped his wine onto his very useful crotch and bade him farewell, never to be seen again. Touché.

Then, damn it, I had to pay for a taxi home, but God it was worth it just to see his gob smacked! Books and covers, my dear. Books and covers!

Avon, or Was It?

During my years of freedom with the chains of mental and physical pain far behind me, I had numerous boyfriends, who were only too eager to share the time and body of what turned out to be a beautiful young woman.

This beauty was a great surprise to me as I'd been told by the man (who went under the heading of husband, and aren't they supposed to be nurturing and kind?) that I was an ugly, fat bastard who no other man would ever want. If this was indeed the case, how come he was intent on keeping this vile caricature of a woman in his life? But a prisoner he kept me, for eleven God forsaken broken years. How I hated that bastard who to this very day walks his dog past the house we shared so long ago. But now he leaves alone the worm that turned, coward that he has always been.

It was the days of miniskirts and once the bruises of continual kicking had long since faded, I decided that my pins were fit for display. Freedom was mine, and boy was I enjoying the attention of the most delicious of men. To my astonishment, I could pick and choose from the best of them and to say I slipped off the rails is putting it mildly. The gargoyle of my youth when I was only sixteen, who had roughly taken my virginity, was replaced with lovers so erotic and tender that I could not get enough of them.

Out dancing yet again, mini barely covering my undimpled thighs, sequin boob tube struggling to contain large and firm breasts, stiletto heels on tiny feet, long, long Titian hair, face made up to perfection and ringed fingers on tiny hands, I was hot to trot (it was the Seventies you know). I knew I looked okay, and this proved true by the numerous men who asked me to dance, most of them I politely refused. Picky even in those days after the self-doubt, I chose the most handsome, best dressed one after clocking his polished shoes, a sure indication of a man's lifestyle.

We melded together; his divine expensive aftershave barely able to smell, its subtlety present on himself, and now the huge glitter ball spun its magic stars onto the dance floor whilst the live orchestra played yet another slow dance I could feel the need of his body, and I was his.

For many months, he came to take me out on a Thursday evening after he drove miles from his home in Crewe and always knocked on my door at precisely 7.30 pm. I took a lot of time and effort getting ready, for I knew he would always look his best, as we headed out to dance and eat. They were happy months, and we never asked questions about where our lives had been when we were apart. Both being excited to share those magical Thursdays, we always ended our night with lovemaking, its erotic beauty never before known to me.

The Thursday before Christmas came, there he stood on my step at 7.30 pm holding gifts of perfume for me and toys for my children, my baby sister waved us goodbye and wished us a lovely night, then sat guarding my sleeping children. At 2.30 am, she went home, leaving us to make love for what was (unknown to me) to be the very last time.

Next Thursday was soon here, 7.30 pm came and went and so did 8.30 pm and 9.30 pm. By now I was very worried, had he had an accident on the snowy roads? I pulled off my finery and went to my empty bed, still so worried and bloody frustrated!

I never heard from him again, but I was determined to find out just why I was no longer featured on his Thursdays.

A friend happened to be an Avon rep, and she kindly drove me to Crewe where we waited outside the butcher's shop he'd told me he owned. There he was, large as life, chatting up a blonde. Far from dead or injured, as I'd suspected.

Closing time came, and we followed his van back to his home, and I waited until 7 pm when I thought he'd be tucking into his evening meal.

The door was opened by a lady, I presumed to be his wife, and over her shoulder I could see his back, sitting at the kitchen table. My timing was perfect. She was very interested in my fake Avon spiel and greedily took the miniature samples given to her. Well, it had to be realistic, did it not?

She told me it soon was to be her husband's birthday, and he might possibly wish to choose a cheaper version of the expensive aftershave he usually used as she was too skint to treat him to it, so Avon would have to do.

As we walked up her hall, my lost lover recognised my voice and his body stiffened in pure panic. Knife and fork held in mid-air above his chop and chips

I could read the thoughts of his frightened mind: *How the fuck did she find me here?* But find the sod I had, and now it was time for my little scary game. With a flourish and much selling spiel, I sprayed not only him, but his uneaten meal with the vilest of vile smells that had been decanted into the Avon bottle, God only knows what it was, but drain solvent comes to mind. He spluttered with distaste at his future aftershave and pleaded (with watering eyes) with me to keep our secret.

And that's how I left them, an unknowing wife waiting for goodies that would never arrive, an adulterous husband who would probably never learn his lesson — not while his todger still stiffened to attention anyway!

As for me, I just needed him to know he was not as invisible as he'd hoped. That ending a relationship without even a goodbye was just not on; he thought he could vanish without a trace. Silly man, did he not know that I could sell Avon?

Beryl's Bordello

I had a dotty friend who just loved it when I pretended to be the French owner of a knocking shop. On more than one occasion, she admitted she had wee'd herself and was so sick of washing panties, she now had the presence of an industrial strength Tena lady placed where it would no doubt test its worthiness.

I'd just started a ridiculous conversation with her that involved punters wishing to have their knobs catapulted at by Jammy Dodgers dipped in vindaloo curry. Strange as it may sound, it's not beyond the realms of possibility as there are some strange sods living out there.

I'm almost in full flow and amid the raucous laughter, she has to excuse herself and hang up as the catalogue bloke has come for his money. "I'll phone you back in five," was her parting shot. Sure enough the phone goes as promised, and I lurched from one lurid/vile incredible sexual antic to another – talk of rag tripe, manacles, nipple clamps and bum plugs and trapezes all get a mention. I told her I was infuriated that she was once again late for her shift, and her punters were gasping with lust six deep from the doorstop, awaiting her attention. Cyril, who expected her to remove her teeth before the action commenced, could wait no longer and proceeded to have a wank behind a convenient patch of multi-coloured lupins.

After testing my mucky verbal skills to the limit and having long since abandoned my French accent, I realised I could not hear Tracy's usual raucous laughter.

On asking why she was so silent, a stranger's voice answered saying it was not Tracy, it was Steve, and did I want to change my gas company? I'd bombarded this poor bugger with utter filth for ten minutes and I suppose it's not at all surprising that I got many more phone calls from the same company, but the feedback from me was never the same. Tracy was most miffed she had missed the latest instalment but still needed her Tena lady, as she imagined Steve playing with his bits in the local call centre.

Now, Tracy heavily relied on a Tena lady which worked a treat (if she only had one cup of coffee and toast for breakfast). But like a greedy git, she had two coffees and liberal milk on her coco pops that morning, this being her favourite cereal of choice as the milk turned into a chocolate drink. The excess fluid made the Tena lady give up all pretence of protection, resulting in a dripping wet gusset. This made the silly sod laugh even more and brought on her usual Migraine, so there my lovely friend lay in a darkened room, head bouncing with lights and pain, a fresh Tena lady in place, just in case memories of her daft friend's antics made her wet herself laughing yet again.

Ebony

Most of the girls had worked well into the early hours and were gratefully getting stuck into a brekkie before hitting the sheets for a totally different reason, SLEEP.

The maid answered the ringing doorbell and ushered in a creature of such presence that all eating and talking stopped, for before them was a rare sight, a magnificent six-foot-tall black woman, who sashayed in swinging her beaded dreadlocks, God help anyone too close or they got a lashing from them.

"Morning ladies, my name's Ebony, when do I start?"

After learning just how Ebony had found her way from Barbados to South Manchester (leaving behind perpetual sunshine for nearly non-stop rain) and the violent reasons that were the final persuader, Za Zar took her under her wing, well she would have if she had had a wing bloody big enough to accommodate six-foot of big, big woman.

She had been doing her 'ting', as she put it, when a client turned nasty and smashed out her wondrous top teeth. As luck would have it, she had another client who was a Cosmetic Technician who recreated Ebony's teeth (in porcelain) from her X-rays so no one; no one could ever guess they were replicas.

She became much in demand, men lusted after her magnificent body and legs to die for, but were scared crapless in case they annoyed or hurt her, because retribution would be hers.

Anyway, Clive used to visit every Tuesday at twelve-thirty on the dot. He would cycle up and park his bike in the lobby and gallop like hell up the stairs behind Ebony, looking up her skirt at this Tuesday's pretty underwear. Ebony always made a little show of dirty dancing with her Rar Rar skirted bum up the stairs and when she reached her landing would do a little dance in time to the always playing raunchy music, then bend over Clive's lust filled head on the stairs below and take off the frillies, wizz them around on her painted fingernail and just drop them on the landing, dash into the bathroom flinging her false teeth into the sink, whilst Clive shoved her fish and chips in the oven and started on his own, straight from the paper.

She would sit before him, and then she would fold up her legs in the Lotus position and set about sorting out his todger. So, this lucky lad had the lot, satisfaction at both ends, utter bliss! Of course, he could also watch from different angles with the help of a strategically placed mirror.

Then, there was a scream; enough to waken the dead from the maid about to clean the bathroom, for there in the sink were Ebony's wonderful gobblers. Of course, she thought our black lass had been knocked about and shot over the landing holding a cricket bat, tripped over a pair of knickers and hurled herself through Ebony's door. I don't know who was the most shocked, Clive eating his fish and chips or Ebony on her hands and knees doing the oral deed. You see Clive insisted she took out her glorious set of teeth in case she had one of her tremors from the Tourette's that was the bane of her life. He was (and rightly so) scared crapless that one of these giant tremors would overtake the willing lass whilst his knob was being attended to, and having to take it to A&E (in a pot of yoghurt) to try to reattach it was not on his agenda, because it would make him late. Hence, teeth in the sink, knickers on landing, as time was of the essence, and he had to cycle back to work within the hour.

Next Tuesday came; no Clive. Hearing a commotion outside on the road, she first spotted many a pigeon swooping for a fish and chip dinner, and then she saw a battered bike, and what turned out to be a very dead Clive. "Oh well," she said. "That's my chippy dinner on a Tuesday fucked," and continued knitting.

Now, Clive was a time and motion man at a local factory who took notice of every second. It was fate that the new assistant at the chippy did not have his Tuesday order ready (at once), and it was those few wasted minutes that brought about Clive's demise. Usually, the 12.08 double-decker bus would not even be in sight, but God help us, there it was, Clive did his right turn and slid under its wheels. His mangled bike told its story, a crowd gathered; the bus passengers alighted to view the gruesome sight. Feral dogs, cats and pigeons aplenty came to feast on what should have been Clive's and Ebony's dinner. She watched from behind her curtains, pretending not to care, hiding the tears she shed for who had become a lovely friend. Hours later, there was no sign of the recent carnage, and it was business as usual in the 'House of Delight!'

PS: How did I know about the teeth and knickers? Easy, I was the maid!

Lilly

Of course, dear reader you could be forgiven for assuming that I also was a lady of the night, yet I was just an ordinary young woman lucky enough to know some extraordinary people, such as darling Lilly. We met whilst delivering our children at the school gates, and she confided in me just how she earned the money she had so much of, many were the times she shared the good fortunes she earned in a way I found impossible to comprehend. Into my home she would carry gifts galore for me and my two children, many of which I treasure to this day. And in return I would make dresses for the twin girls she adored.

She was one of those wonderful women who placed themselves in danger by accommodating the perversions of vile and dangerous men, and in doing so helped to prevent many a rape of innocent women and boys and girls, on the Manchester streets.

On one of our morning chats she also told me the story of her life before the streets and the eventual sanctuary of the massage parlour.

Her very young mother was born to doting parents who had despaired of ever having a family. So, when they discovered a baby was to bless their union, well into their forties, there was much rejoicing in the five-bedroom detached house they lived in, in Hale Barns Cheshire. A nursery was given every attention to expensive detail and with joy, they later brought home their one and only little baby girl.

Private schooling and foreign holidays were the norm for Louise, but she stayed sweet and unpretentious gaining many friends at the Brownie troop she loved attending. It was on returning home from a needlework class, there in the evening twilight, that she was grabbed from behind a tree, thrown to the ground and raped. With a ripped and muddied brown uniform she staggered home to tell her mum and dad. Louise was thirteen years old and unfortunately already with child. Her parents gave her a choice, have it adopted? Or keep it with her family as abortion was illegal in those judgmental hypercritical days, she decided with their gentle guidance to allow a childless couple to know the meaning of a family of their own, just as they did.

Up until the night that would change Louise's life forever, she had been such a happy sweet young soul and was delighted to have been chosen as that year's Rose Bud Queen. Her mum had got their dressmaker to make her a gown of Lavender taffeta, she would carry a bouquet of Ivory roses and lilac freesia and wear a sparkling crown on her long auburn curls. The float she was to travel on would be bedecked with ribbons and flowers, and there Louise was to sit on her velvet throne, waving to the crowds lining the route on what was hoped would be a sunny day, but as her tummy grew and stares and comments from people turned her once magical life into an embarrassed hell, she excused herself from her rosebud duties and another young pretty lass gladly stepped into Louise's empty shoes and also wore her Lavender gown and sparkling crown.

Nine months had passed from her brutal rape, and with tears and clenched fists she pushed her baby girl into the world. Lilly was to be her name. Louise was allowed just one cuddle with her tiny soul as it was rightly thought best that the usual six-week time before adoption would create an enduring bond with her baby that would taint her life forever. She sent Lilly away with a love box she had made whilst her tummy had grown, and this was to be given to the lucky new parents who were to nurture her much loved and missed the baby. She had been shown how to knit by her loving gran and had managed to complete a tiny white matinee coat and matching booties before the time came to whisper goodbye. In the folds of the jacket was a letter sending so much love and an explanation of just why they could not share a life with each other. She expressed a determination that she would in the future look for Lilly and pleaded that Lilly should try, at the right time, to find the mum that had to be torn away from her when Lilly was just a few hours old.

This box of love and tears was to be presented to Lilly by her new mum and dad on her sixteenth birthday. They kept this promise and from that day Lilly sought but never found the once little girl (who was by now a grown woman) who had so bravely sent her to a better life.

Stanley Caine was a doctor; he and his wife Audrey adored the tiny Lilly who had blessed their barren life. They gave her the best education, taught her right from wrong and supported her when she took an apprentice job as a hairdresser. They of course hoped that she would quickly abandon this idea and follow in daddy's footsteps and become a doctor, this was never to be as a tragic turn of events finished forever life as Lilly knew it.

It was a snowy New Year's Eve as police knocked on Lilly's door at 11 pm. She had been told never to answer the door when her parents were out, but on seeing it was the police she felt safe to do so. The news she got from them destroyed Lilly's world, as both her mum and dad had perished as they skidded on ice in their black Mercedes and hit a sturdy hundred-year-old sycamore tree on their way home to celebrate the New Year with her.

After this latest fatal accident involving the sycamore tree (planted in the early reign of Queen Victoria, even though it was protected by order) it just had to be felled. A great shame as it had stood for over a century amongst the hawthorn hedge, planted when all that land was for farming. The spikes on the hawthorn were to deter animals from leaving their boundary and munching on the crops in adjoining fields. Fields that would be turned into roads in the oncoming years with the popular event of cars.

And so, the majestic tree stood on a dangerous bend on a new road, giving warning, much like a lighthouse on a cliff top's edge at sea.

But many over the tree's lifetime were to ignore this warning and whether with the help of ice, snow, fog, drink, drugs or just bad judgment they saw not the danger and became yet more victims. But that wondrous tree stood steadfast, cars lay crumpled at its base their passengers already on their way to heaven, and all it showed for the carnage were even more scars on the silvery bark.

Somehow Lilly acquired the felled tree and had a memorial bench made from it to immortalise the parents she had lost. It was erected in the depths of a majestic gorge, (much loved by ramblers in Derbyshire) for many tired hikers to catch their breath and wonder at the nature surrounding them.

The brass plaque read 'Dr Stanley and his beloved wife Audrey, wish you well'.

At nearly seventeen years of age, she was completely alone, an orphan, but not destitute as her parents had left everything they owned to their beloved girl. It soon became well known that a young lass owned such a beautiful house and car and the local lazy louts made it their business to try and win her over. Loneliness and grief can ensure even the most level headed people make bad decisions. This Lilly did when she became pregnant with the local jack the lad.

Because of the stigma and hypocrisy of those stunted days she married the lazy git, just so that the gold band on her finger made her look respectable, as was the way of those times.

He spent as much of her money as he could get his hands on, reeled home drunk most nights, was not shy of using his fist and feet to injure her and to top it off got a young girl from the local council estate pregnant also.

Enough was bloody enough, and with the help of her dead parents' lawyer divorced the sod without losing one penny of her inheritance. But copped for an exorbitant lawyer's fee.

So now she was a single rich young mum and her twin girls Lucia and Seleena were her joy, she enrolled them in the same ordinary little school as my children and from that day until her untimely death we were the best of friends.

As it turned out, Lilly was very young but also very astute and decided that, once rid of that violent grabbing git, she would create a new life for herself and the twins.

The home her parents left her brought in hundreds of thousands, most of this she put in a trust fund for her beloved girls and with the rest purchased a far smaller more modest abode. The big cars she had been used to driving were to be a thing of the past, as she loved her new red shiny mini.

For almost a year she would arrive daily at the school gates always head to toe in black, never joining in with the inane claptrap of the other mothers. But when once asked if she did not like colours, she replied she was a widow in mourning for her dead dear husband. That shut the nosey sods! up! And it was many months and coffees later, when I was completely trusted, that she confided to me that this was untrue, but it did the trick of ensuring her past (including that dead-beat ex) stayed out of her todays and tomorrows. And this is the one and only time I've shared her secret. From heaven, she will forgive me!

Massage parlours had sprung up in many a huge old once magnificent regency house. These were places where women who used the streets could live and work in cleanliness and safety. Away from the vile pimps who brutalised them and stole their earnings, these sanctuaries brought down dramatically the number of street girls beaten and left for dead in the rain-soaked gutters.

Bless each and every one of them!!

Lilly and the Duck

Lilly would come to my home, after the school run, for a morning coffee and chat and regale me with the dramatic encounters she and her pals had had at work.

Now each room of the parlour was of a different theme to correspond with the wishes and perversions of the punters that just could not get enough, one such room was completely covered in lurid hoseable pink plastic and with very good reason. It was into this wet room that the six-foot-two duck arrived, after being shoved incognito from a van parked outback.

There he stood head to ankle with yellow fake feathers, and with wings flapping he proceed to blow kisses from a huge orange beak at the same time as doing the moonwalk with his massive orange webbed feet. Now, this was a sight the girls just had to see, and they all gathered together in an adjoining room, gawping at the daft bastard through a two-way mirror.

His request of the night was not that unusual. Just dress up in French Maids cosy wear five-inch spiked-heel shoes, get a catapult, plus a dish of red-hot vindaloo curry and a couple of packs of Jammy Dodger bickies.

"Fair enough, your wish is my command", thought Lilly. So, there she perched on heels that were killing her, trying her best not to dissolve into hysterics and wondering at just how the bloke in the yellow feathers had come up with such a desire? Now he was tapping one webbed foot as he fiddled with his wings tips to release the mother and father of all erections. So, picture this, a frigging mountain of fake yellow feathers with a ramrod hard todger stuck out the front, waiting to be assaulted by Jammy Dodgers. Weird!

As if that was not enough, he then lobbed out a set of gonads that a prize bull would be proud of. These immense beauties hung halfway down one yellow feathered leg and had rarely been seen this side of a farm gate. This was one mighty duck!

Pat remarked she would insist on £200 extra to her normal fee of £50 to entertain the duck, the surplus to pay the struck off Doctor who could hopefully stitch her shredded nethers back together again.

Irish Josey was quick to point out that Pat could cope with the monstrosity quite easily as she had a chuff the size of a paper hanger's bucket! Another wag informed the hysterical group that her slack nethers were not unlike throwing a sausage up a windy entry! And that's why punters only asked for Josey once.

Finally she took the hump after they had all called into question what was between her legs, and with a spat of "Fuck off" she flounced off to the client's bar, stole a bottle of gin and got pissed.

Lilly being of a very organised nature had prepared said bickies with blistering hot curry from a delicate China bowl (for this was a posh emporium of sex) and with this done picked up the catapult that never in her life had she used before, steadying herself as best she could on the five-inch heels she took aim at his cock, missed by a mile and scattered the brown mess up one outstretched fluttering wing. This failed first attempt was to herald another twenty-one and by that time his beak, legs, tail and body bore brown evidence of that. But it was his huge orange webbed feet that had the watching girls folding into hysterics, for there lay an array of curry smeared Jammie Dodgers, most of them dripping with the stuff and stood on end between the orange webbed toes.

But Lilly, ever the trooper, scored two direct hits to his knob which did the trick, and they all watched in fascination as his appendage emptied itself and was shoved back inside the sticky feathers with a curry smeared wingtip.

This event was recounted with much laughter long after my darling Lilly was no more. It was snowing when some evil swine choked the life from her body and left her, in all her finery, slumped amongst the litter at the back of the parlour car park.

Her funeral was the most beautiful ever seen, her girl pals (all dressed identically in lavender) carried her Lilly strewn coffin with such pride and dignity, the church where she worshipped with her young twins was also strewn with Lilly's, their perfume sweetening the rafters, and her friends and punters alike were crammed into that church to acknowledge the wondrous women she had always been, and shed more than just one tear for darling, sweet beautiful Lilly. I missed and mourned the loss of my precious friend for many a year, and morning coffee was never the same without the laughter she brought with her every single time.

Lilly's two girls were legally adopted by Sarah, Lilly's best friend, and she gave them a wonderful life up until adulthood and beyond, just as their real mummy would have done if she'd been allowed to live.

They are grown now with families of their own who know and accept with pride the life and times of Nana Lilly, a character never ever to be forgotten. And now, I can't ever see a duck without also seeing Lilly in my mind's eye with that blasted catapult. And, Jammy Dodgers are out of the question, and I hate curry!

Sweet Lilly – Taken Too Soon

And heaven is where I believe my Lilly now lives. Sent there with violence, and a piece of blue rope that could be purchased in a thousand builder's merchants. The police said they tried their very best to catch the evil Bastard who had denied her a life with her twins, denied her a gentle death as an old lady with grandchildren beside her bed. Denied her a gentle end to a life she would have lived to the full, had she been allowed, in a pink bedroom lit by fairy lights. Instead, what did she get? A fight for survival that she could never, win in that dimly lit snowy car park behind a knocking shop! Murdering Bastard!

The daffodils were nodding their pretty yellow heads in the sunshine when the police finally released Lilly's body. Her friends had had months to save up to give Lilly a send-off like no other.

She was to be taken to a tiny Gothic church deep in the Cheshire countryside, where her parents had a private mausoleum. In this, they lay awaiting their precious girl. And yet, still there would be just one place left to enfold the remains of a dear one. Doctor Stanley always knew of Louise's longing to hold and kiss the now grown-up little girl who she had had to give her away so many years ago. His will stated that should Louise ever be found; in death, she was at last to find her baby girl and lay beside her for all eternity. So then that little family of four would be reunited, and life and death would have turned full circle. No more tears.

Four magnificent dapple-grey horses were chosen to pull the engraved carriage that would take Lilly to her mum and dad. Pink feather plumes adorned their plaited shiny manes, exactly the same pink as the casket that embraced Lilly's body. She was to be laid to rest in the Ivory silk gown she had bought to celebrate her birthday, which would have fallen just two days after she had been murdered. Her girls had matching dresses like Mummy, and these they would wear to say their goodbyes to her forever.

Now Sarah, Lilly's best friend, long ago rescued a white dove from a cat trying to kill it. She finally got it well, and the love between them began. It would nestle on her shoulder as she drove her car and would only be confined to its large cage when it was her time to work. Of course, the bird was also called Lilly, and to see it nestled within its flower namesake on that memorable day, on a pretty pink coffin, made the onlookers weep.

To add to this spectacle never before seen on that quiet country road, was the haunting sound of an alto sax played by George.

This handsome black man was a War Veteran who had had his lower left leg blown off by a bomb in a far-off land, which also left his body full of irremovable shrapnel.

He and Lilly were the dearest of friends, and he knew she only looked upon his wounds with compassion, never disgusted. He played his magical music in the clubs of Manchester for a living and just once a month would visit Lilly – they would share laughter, cups of coffee, as well as their bodies.

Even though George's prosthetic leg gave him hell, he insisted on walking with the top-hatted, tail coated, cane swinging leader of the cortege at the very front of Lilly's last journey.

People came out of their houses, traffic stopped, shoppers put down their bags, and everyone, yes everyone, wanted to be a part of the magical procession before them. And so, they followed it up the gentle hill, where the daffodils nodded their heads in welcome. George was dressed in typical New Orleans musical attire, black patent shoes, black trousers and shirt, white silk bow tie and a striped waistcoat, also in black and white. And there he walked in agony in the sunshine, tears streaming down his cheeks for the loss of his dearest friend. It was time for Lilly to be lifted down from her engraved carriage. This was done by six of her girls dressed demurely in lavender suits with black kitten-heeled patent shoes on their feet. Lilly the dove stayed on the casket until it was gently placed inside the church, then it flew into the rafters and settled there whilst the casket lid was removed for people to say their goodbyes and to marvel at the beauty that was Lilly. As eleven of the eulogies were said with love and tears, George stood straight and proud, and no doubt in great pain, as he played his mournful sax, for pain from his leg was nothing by comparison to that of losing Lilly, his dearest friend.

Speakers outside the church informed the throng all that was said, a hushed crowd wept also, for a stranger that they had never known. The church held all types of people and they filed past the pink coffin and said a few words to her, some stroked her head or kissed her fingertips, and George played on.

Lucia and Seleena, Lilly's pride and joy, stood beside their mummy's pink box, holding her cold, cold hands. Their tiny wrists wore garlands of pink rosebuds, exactly the same colour as the ones around their mummy's throat, ones that tried, but failed, to disguise the brutality that had stolen half a lifetime from their precious mummy.

Crystal tears from sad green eyes (just like their mummy's once sparkling ones) fell to the ivory lace party frocks, chosen weeks before in such excitement.

Each mourner who gave their respects lent to the copper-haired girls and wished them well. Only to receive a tremulous little smile in return.

And handsome George played on. Did anyone else but me notice his pained tearful face and the blood-soaked trouser leg where his agonising wounds still tormented him? His sax was raised up as he played Ava Maria, mournful enough to make the angels and us, all weep.

There was a gentleman who looked different from all the other mourners, he looked so wealthy in his grey pinstriped tailored suit, beautifully polished brogue shoes, lilac shirt, with a grey and lilac paisley tie. He carried his very tall frame with elegance. And when he reached Lilly, he gently stroked her titian curls, and I saw him tuck something amongst them, out of sight. Then, he was gone.

George was playing *"Help Me Make It Through the Night"*, Lilly's favourite lovely song, and *"Together Again"*, as the casket lid was about to be replaced, but not before I gave Lilly my last kiss and teased from between her luxuriant curls just one tiny yellow feather. The duck of her past had come to say "thank you and goodbye." The lid was in place and the sun shone upon it through stained glass windows making rainbows on the brass plaque that read, "Lilly, who was allowed just twenty-four summers." In our hands, we held white Lilies and hugged each other in grief. George played his mournful sax as Lilly glided in her pretty pink box through red velvet curtains to be turned to ashes. It was only when their mummy had slid out of sight that her precious little girls finally gave in to the tears, held back so bravely for so long, from haunted green eyes just like Lilly's.

Was the dignity and decorum in ones so young already instilled into them long ago by the private school Lilly insisted upon? To place her babies on a lifetime path of decency, kindness and courage. The same courage she showed each and every night to earn the money to provide for her children, that she had now been forced to leave behind. Two sad weeks passed before Lilly's urn was carried in the sunshine to the graveyard that held just two mausoleums, one of which had open gates and doors, awaiting her. Her parents' caskets had been pulled apart, leaving a space between them for their girl. Just like the space always left between them in their comfy bed, where Lilly as a little one, came in for a morning cuddle.

She now nestled between them as before, and there was a space left for the mummy, that she never found in life, but perhaps might in death.

For a long time, people talked of the grace and spectacle of that day, never before seen and probably never since. Lilies that had strewn the church were handed out to the onlookers and mourners alike, Lilly the dove flew down from the rafters to nestle on Sarah's shoulder where it belonged, and her friends tried to resume life without their wonderful, vibrant friend.

It was a twisted hand of fate that reunited Louise with her treasured baby. She had never had more children as the rape she had suffered as a little girl had damaged her forever. So, she had dedicated her life (just had she had promised in that love letter to her baby so long ago) to finding her. As she lay dying from cancer, in the hospice, a salvation army colonel came with news she had waited to hear from all those years ago. At long last her Lilly had been found dead, just like her mummy was about to be. But Louise died a happy death, knowing doctor Stanley had ensured that one day she would be reunited with her baby, and so she also travelled up that hill, but without the same pomp and splendour of her girl years before. The giant doors creaked open one last time, and she snuggled down against her lost child, yes, destiny had worked its magic at the top of the hill, in the sunshine. And, the daffodils nodded their heads in joy, and the birds sang.

I went back just once more to that sleepy village, it looked just the same as I remembered it. Once again, the daffodils danced their heads in the spring breeze as my old legs trudged up the once gentle hill that now seemed so steep.

As I rested, I could not help but notice a waiting limousine. A white-haired old gentleman sat in the back, and the years just rolled away. For we both knew the reason for him being there. His chauffeur sprinted down the path and steps on young legs, tipped his hat to me and drove the duck away. Memories, so many memories! And finally, before me stood that little family mausoleum. I tried to catch my laboured breath, hanging on to the railings, now even more rusted with time. Lilly would have been seventy years old that day, she had laid there, in eternal sleep, longer than she had lived. Another name had been added to the plaque that remembered those that lay within, the plaque that had adorned the sturdy wooden doors for two hundred years. Little Louise had at long last found her little baby girl and that tiny tragic family had been reunited, in the sunshine amongst the daffodils, and the birds sang. So many flowers of remembrance adorned the railings, a spectacular heart-shaped wreath of lilies perfumed the air, just had they had done in that tiny church, all those years ago. The card read, "To our beloved mummy, we did not share this life for long enough, but in the next life it's forever. Love and kisses Lucia and Seleena.

I recognised some of the long-ago names who had also remembered sweet Lilly. The regency house where they shared so much, had long since been demolished to make way for a trading estate. But Monique got a charmed new life away from all that she hated, a very wealthy client wanted her just for himself, so she was rescued and made to feel loved and respected and was taken to live in luxury in Canada. How lovely!

But everything paled into insignificance when I looked between the daffodils at the edge of the railing. So, there it stood carved in strong, pink marble, beautiful and proud, the most wondrous duck ever to be seen, and tucked under one wing was just one Lily, you see I just knew who that old gentleman was. So many years had passed since the night that Lilly made all his dreams come true, the duck had returned, even though he looked three days older than God. I placed my posy of pink rose buds and lilac freesia against the webbed feet and laughed, and cried, for the past, and for the stolen lost years of friendship.

Twilight was coming, and I had to catch three buses to get me home. I'd never make this epic journey again, for it's such a long, long way from Manchester to the depths of Cheshire. I'm old and weary now, you see! and so, so tired, and my Lilly beckons me to her, so we can share daffodils in eternity and many more cups of coffee as we laugh once again, together at last.

The murdering bastard who stole my Lilly's life, that snowy night, was never brought to justice, and I can't help but wonder how many other lives he's stolen, with such cruel hands. If by any chance you are reading this: You son of Satan, rot in hell, with your maker!

If It Should Be

I can't remember just how long ago it was, I saw a distressing letter in the agony column of a magazine, probably fifty years ago or so.

It was from an old lady who had had to have her beloved companion, an ill, very old Spaniel, put to sleep. People told her to get a grip on her grief. After all, it was ONLY a dog and to go out and get another one (just like choosing a new pair of shoes) Bless her, she needed reassurance that in (as she put it) killing her best friend, Heaven, and he would forgive her.

Her heartfelt anguish really touched my heart, as I knew all too well the loss of a beloved pet, a constant, loyal, loving companion when humans had betrayed me in times of my great needs.

So, I wrote the following little poem that I sent to the magazine to be forwarded on to the grieving old soul, in the hope it would reassure her that she had given her beloved pet the greatest show of care and love in helping him leave her.

If It Should Be

If it should be that I grow weak
And pain should keep me from my sleep
Then you must do what must be done
For this last battle can't be won

You will be sad, I understand
Don't let your grief then stay your hand
For this day more than all the rest
Your love for me must stand the test

We've had so many happy years
What is to come must hold no fears
You'd not want me to suffer so
The time has come, please let me go.

Take me to where my needs they'll tend
And please stay with me till the end
Hold me close and whisper to me
Until my eyes no longer see
I know in time that you will see

The great kindness that you did for me
Although my tail it's last has waved
From pain and suffering, I've been saved

Please do not grieve for it must be you
Who has this painful thing to do
We've been so close we two for many years
Don't let your heart hold back the tears

I later got a letter of thanks via the magazine, along with a wonderful picture of an old lady holding a Spaniel pup. I've seen my poem published many times over the years, and vet's notice boards have featured it often. I hope it's given comfort and the confidence, to put aside the torn heart and to open it again, now nearly mended, to welcome yet another sweet creature for years of love.

Chain of Events

Many years ago, I had the gift of a wonderful young lady in my life, tragically, she no longer is, but I don't miss her anymore.

She worked at the airport, and one of the perks was empty seats on planes going, God knows where. Angie would phone and say, "Pack your case, we're off tomorrow." And so it would be, I'd always accepted that these freebies could be cancelled at the last minute, so it did not upset me when yet another call told me the paperwork for our flights was now locked in an office for the whole weekend – no paperwork, no holiday. Case unpacked; passport returned to the draw. I believe everything is for a reason, and soon I would discover why our air trip was never meant to be!

Sitting in the garden the next morning, thinking of what might have been, I munched on the hard crust of toast, and my front crown came off and was duly swallowed. Angie laughed when I told her of my gappy gum and said that's all she needed, me throwing a strop at five-thousand feet. But this was not the reason for us to miss our hols.

I will not go into too many details about my crown's retrieval, but let's say a sieve and much bleach were involved (Yuk, I hear you say as you imagine this fiasco) but would you not have done the same, knowing how much a new crown would cost? (Course you would!)

Sunday dawn's bright and beautiful, and it's decided a little family picnic would use the day just as nicely as a far-off beach.

We were (and still are) lucky enough to live very near glorious countryside and soon found a desirable spot on sloping fields by a dry-stone wall. A magnificent Copper Beech tree-shaded us from the midday sun.

Now, little Angie had never had the need to grow a pair, as mine were large enough for both of us, so when a huge bay mare came to investigate our goodies, towering above the blanket we sat upon, my friend froze with fear.

Having never been afraid of animals, I stood up, kissed its lovely face and shooed it away.

We were just coming to the end of our picnic when thunder rumbled in the distance – it was time to leave, or get soaked.

On standing up, I looked down the grassy hill and wondered what a group of hikers were so interested in, that lay upon the ground. Then, I realised, it was the magnificent cheeky bay mare, legs thrashing in the air, something terrible was obviously wrong.

In those days, I was fairly slim and then of course far more agile than the arthritic old lady reliving this memory from forty-odd years ago.

Shoes off I raced down to the commotion and saw with horror the wild eyes of a horse choking to death.

I knelt by its lovely head, blew on its nose to calm it a little, and then twitched its nostrils with my belt (twitching is a method of making a horse stay still, it looks awful as the nose has to be held very tight and twisted, it does not hurt the animal, but it releases chemicals that semi anaesthetises it for a purpose such as this)

Almost at once, she became calm and on feeling her neck, I discovered a large mass that should not have been there. Bless that bay beauty, her instinct must have told her how much I respected the creature I was trying so desperately to save. She allowed my hand to enter her mouth, I went in up to my forearm and managed to grasp, and pull out a slippery plastic bag and all its contents. Apple cores, empty cans, cigarette packets, etc. A couple of minutes later, that gorgeous greedy girl rolled onto her chest and rested her head on my lap. I stroked and talked to her, telling her not to gobble down the discarded waste of an idiotic human who should have taken their trash home with them. But she probably didn't understand, did she?

I'd completely forgotten the onlookers whose presence alerted me to the imminent disaster (for it would have been a disaster if that magnificent girl had lost her life because of the negligence of a numbnut!), and I was more than a little startled when much cheering and clapping disturbed our cuddle on the grass.

At this point, my friend arrived at the scene carrying my kicked off shoes and was hardly surprised to see her mate on the grass holding and kissing a now fully-recovered horse's head.

The bay and I stood together for one last hug, the threatened rain started to fall and amidst congratulations and 'Well done' from the hikers, we climbed the hill to our waiting car.

Now, this event is to me destiny using her power to save a life worth saving.

If that paperwork had arrived earlier and not been left in a locked office, and my broken crown had not started its downward journey, via a piece of hard toast, if that picnic had not happened under the Copper Beech tree, if I'd looked in a different direction from down the hill, If I had not had the knowledge I had of how to twitch a horse, if I had not been able to reach the bag of rubbish left to kill a magnificent mare by an uncaring git, there in the sunshine on that Sunday, she would have lost her life in the most horrific way, choking to death. Instead, as I stood for one last look, she was grazing on the sweet grass, her coat now wet with heavy rain, safe and well, as destiny had placed me where I could be used.

Who cares about a missed holiday when a life was able to be saved? I didn't, and in quiet contemplation, I marvelled at the chain of events destiny orchestrated to save a bay mare.

By the way, the crown I swallowed that morning is back where it belongs many years later ('Yuk,' did hear you utter) All is well!

Trust

Even as a young child, I loved and envied birds because they could fly free as I never could. Free from the entrapment of a sensory deprived childhood and sixteen years later from the chains of a brutal marriage that bound me for eleven long years. Jumping from the frying pan into the fire is not to be recommended, so heed my warning as a wise old lady of the future.

I was hanging out the washing on a sunny Saturday morning when a young Starling flew into my kitchen window with such a thud I believed the feathered beauty could only be dead. But after a few moments, it started to awaken, and instead of flying off it spun on its back, legs in the air, a drop of blood leaving its gasping beak.

Scooping up this youngster, whose petrolite feathers gleamed in the sun, I ran to the phone to ask my vet's advice. And that was "Bring it in now as I close in fifteen minutes".

I doubt you have ever seen a woman dress so quickly, except of course, if she comes across a cudgel and that's another story — for another time.

And in my panic to save my newfound feathered friend, I dragged on just a top and jeans, no need for underwear as time was of the essence.

A shoebox containing the still spinning Starling was in the matwell of my old Honda Civic, I raced off still having ten minutes to get to the vets at the top of an adjacent long straight road.

Unbeknown to me, a bobby sat having a crafty read of his newspaper, no doubt page 3 (boobies) held more than a little fascination than the a bat out of hell that shot right past him.

Having no option but to stop at the police car's insistent siren I cursed at his slow saunter towards my car as the seconds ticked by "For Christ's sake, I'm on a deadline here!" My mind shouted at him.

Complying with "Wind down the window madam" instruction he leant tapping on the roof of my car and in so doing getting an eyeful of my large chest not constrained by a bra. Now, these two beauties that I'd gratefully grown, had diverted the outcome of my, shall we say, adventures before, and three points (and a fine I could not pay) were a good enough reason to give them a swift wiggle, which did not go unnoticed by the boy in blue (How does the saying go? If you've got 'em, flaunt 'em, this was another motto I could easily live by).

On telling him I was on my way to the Vet, he inspected what appeared to be an empty car and said the words that would endear him to me for the next twelve months.

"Nice dog, I used to have a St Invisible when I was a kid, I'd be about four at the time," his next comment sealed the deal, and I was smitten by the mirror image of my own personality. "I must congratulate you on being able to shift a vintage grow bag at the speed of light" thus informing me that in my panic to reach a soon to be closed Vet I'd shot past his Panda car at sixty-seven miles an hour, and the law stated thirty. The old joke of "Don't be ridiculous Constable, I've only been out for four minutes" was not spoken by me, but it was indeed appropriate.

Pointing to the shoebox in the matwell, I told of my injured Starling and that I had precisely two minutes to go the hundred or so yards to my waiting Vet.

This handsome, funny officer of the law decided he would escort me to my destination and indeed came in to find the outcome of my poorly bird, or was he more interested in my 'Puppies'?

My lovely Vet (who has helped all my animals in life and death) said my birdy had a concussion. "Keep it dark and warm in the shoebox" was his advice, and yet again there was no charge for the latest wild creature I had brought to him to save. This wonderful dedicated vet is a true animal lover and many times he has saved injured wildlife for me, without payment, for he loved the real puppies .etc. that endlessly came to his surgery to receive his skill or be helped to drift away forever.

So far there had been no mention of the penalty my reckless actions rightly deserved, later, when this constable and I were sitting having a coffee in my lounge, I was told a verbal warning would be given to make me see the error of my ways. So, with a stern face, he delivered my telling off enforcing the danger I could have inflicted, not only on myself but any other poor bugger who had the misfortune to get in front of my speeding tyres. Sorted.

My starling stopped spinning and rested in its cosy home, seemingly content with the chopped-up worms I popped into its hungry beak and I had now gently cleaned off its blood. It seemed in no hurry to leave, and I put it in a large cage until I was certain it was healthy once more and this soon became obvious when it flew around my kitchen, before landing on my shoulder. Surely, there can be no greater compliment than when a wild creature instinctively trusts you, as this young bird did me? I would have kept my feathered friend forever if it had not been cruel to cage the wings meant to fly free.

On the fourth day of our friendship, I took him into the garden and sat with him whilst he remembered the freedom he had come from. I admit I cried as I opened the cage door, and he hopped out. I expected his lust for freedom to be swift. But no! before he left me (but not forever), he one last time sat on my shoulder in the sunshine and allowed me to stroke his pretty feathers. My boy (maybe girl) was healthy again and not at the mercy of flesh tearing cats who waited endlessly for their chance of sport. Feathers gleamed their petrolite colours as he perched on the washing line and then on hearing the call of this flock, he soared into the sky to join them.

I thought this to be the end of our friendship, but the next spring came and with it, a large flock of Starlings came to rest and eat in my garden, one of them stayed apart from the rest and perched on the washing line, allowing me near it – almost within stroking distance, but when I got a little too close, he would hop back a couple of inches and yet still not fly away. Twinkling button eyes looked at me, my feathered baby had returned as an adult to say a final goodbye and with wings so strong he soared into the clouds with his flock, never to be seen again, or at least I don't think so. (I'm crying now as I remember my love for him, in four short days he'd found a place in my heart overflowing with care and compassion, silly old git I am).

Not a week had passed from when I was pulled over for speeding by that delicious funny boy in blue until he stood on my doorstep in civvies asking where I would like to go for a night out. Many nights and their pleasures were to follow; we laughed and loved until we needed each other no more. Another episode of my life had come to an end, brought about by my Bipolar. It had started at the very beginning on that sunny Saturday a year ago when a Starling needed help and two playful puppies got the full attention they so deserved, happy memories.

The Honda Civic of that Vets visit went to the scrapyard after many trips to rescue animals and garden centres (that fed my hunger for all things colourful and green) that in turn would fill the garden I loved (hence the reference to vintage grow bags of yesteryear) for cleaning cars was not high on my agenda.

Yet another car boot on a sunny Sunday morning (the reason everything seems to happen on a Sunday is that I rarely venture out on any other of the six days).

People in their Sunday Tabernacle finery climbed from cars and looked with uncaring eyes at the wounded lady Blackbird stranded on the now quiet road. Her black gleaming partner stood guard beside her on the tarmac, was there ever such brave devotion in humans?

These callous buggers of Tabernacle visits turned their so-called Christian God-fearing backs on the plight of the birds needing help, shame on them, did being a bit late to hear the sermoned lies (meant to keep them all in check) matter more? It's a pity they were not instructed to help all those creatures who could not help themselves i.e., injured birds on the road.

I'd barely missed those two birds as I'd driven past, and I was sure they were either dead by the car behind me or the uninjured one had flown away. But no, there they still were as I pulled up a few feet away. I found it strange that two birds needed help at the same time, but it was proved that indeed only the female was injured. Her beautiful face was matted with blood and even though she looked near to death, she managed to struggle as I picked her up crying at her pain and fear.

Her mate never moved or made a sound as my hand held his little wife, and gently I reached for his body also. Much to my surprise, I found him to be in perfect health and even more to my surprise he just nestled quietly in my hand as I carried them both to the car. Now, both of my hands were full of Blackbird, how was I to get into the car and drive? Was my Angel helping me help them? On that pretty Sunday morning, I believe so!

Clasping the girly bird in one hand, I held her mate against my chest with my forearm as I got into my car, once inside I placed them side by side on my knees (where they stayed without any fuss, honestly) and drove the short distance home. Once there, I repeated the carrying process and was able to unlock the front door with one hand, whilst the other arm cradled the settled quiet birds. (Bloody strange).

I cleaned up her sweet face of the blood and once this was done her injury did not look quite so bad. Laying them side by side in a velvet lined shoebox (only the best for my rescues) I left them to quietly recover from their near-certain death on that road.

Once again chopped up worms (sorry worms, but needs must) mixed with the raisins that the blackbirds love, were hand-fed to the girly bird when she was able to take them from me. Her mate sat and fed at her side, never once making a fuss when my hand entered their new shoebox home. He was allowed to fly around the kitchen that I had stopped decorating to enable me to get my new lodgers well. He'd sit on the wall cupboard and if I did not approach him too swiftly, he eventually allowed me to hold him and stroke his black shiny feathers. I experimented by holding a piece of bread between my lips, never expecting him to respond, but that gorgeous creature pecked at the offered morsel when my hand held him close. (I hope you can believe this unusual event, as I swear it's true!).

By now, his mate was stronger and well-fed and watered, and she also wanted to escape the confines of the shoe box, luxuriant though it was!

I'd closed the window shutters to stop them from trying to find freedom through the glass and in so doing maybe both being injured, every consideration I could think of was theirs.

They would sit side by side on the worktop edge preening and chatting like the old married couple they undoubtedly were.

Came the day freedom from my kitchen would be theirs. Putting them in their velvet-lined box for the last time I drove them to the woods, safe from cars and the dreaded cats, the scourge of all flying and scurrying creatures.

I watched them fly to freedom and settle side by side, as was their way, on a Copper Beech tree branch, glowing in the dying sun's rays.

My Blackbird and his missus had been given a second chance of a long life of shared happiness and who knows, maybe Blackbird chicks?

Another day, another rescue of the creatures I so loved.

The Tragic True Cost of Pate Foie Gras

Today will be my last day of life, my existence, for it's never been a life as nature intended. All I have ever known and the thousands here like me, is darkness, agony and terror. Do Geese go to heaven, I ask?

My feet are ulcerated and rotting, oozing with puss because all I've ever been able to walk on is my own filth and that of my fellow captives. My instincts tell me that the once webbed flesh between our toes was created so we could swim; we have never known water, never seen sunshine, never heard our feathered friends sing joyously in their freedom of the skies.

In their frustration my companions sort out the weakest dying ones and pluck out their feathers, for two days now that has been my fate, my head and neck are torn to bits and one of my eyes has gone. A marvellous opportunity for a fly to lay its eggs, and its now growing offspring are eating into my brain. Oh, how it hurts. God why do you allow our pain?

The clanging of metal heralds the start of today's torture. Doors slide open and the vile cruel humans go about their task. Caring nothing of our plight, callous, filthy, strong hands grab each of the prisoners and force a metal funnel down our necks, the delicate flesh tears, we defecate with pain and terror, it matters not to the cruel monsters whose life's work is to abuse us daily. The grain is pushed deep down, and what is the purpose of this torment? so that gourmets the world over can smack their greedy lips as they devour Pate Foie Gras, the end product of a lifetime of torture.

I gave up trying to preen myself many moons ago, how can I when the only access I have to water is the excrement filled so-called drinking water. So, my sparse feathers should gleam white in the sunshine, reflected in cool running water instead of this near skeleton soiled with filth. I'm dying and I'm so glad, as death is my only escape from this hell hole. There are a few others also that have blue paint sprayed on them, I wonder if they know its meaning, as surely as I do?

Is there goose heaven? Will I be able to swim just one time? Will I see my babies hatch and greet the sunshine and swim behind me in a glorious golden flotilla? That is my prayer.

So, look in the mirror Mr Don't Care, do you like what you see? You allow this barbaric procedure to continue to provide you with the wealth for your fancy cars and homes. Is our pain for years on endless years less important than your fat wallet? Yes, I believe it is you heartless avaricious nonhuman. But reincarnation is your future. Then you will be the feathered innocent, covered in filth, crouching on rotting feet, dreading the rough hands that are your destiny. I beg you to stop this vile practice, NOW!

Retribution Soup

It was one of those fancy restaurants in downtown Hong Kong where rich businessmen with little sense of taste, kindness, compassion or decency gather together to gorge. This they had done yet again and with deals to put even more cash in each other's pockets and shove the vilest of food down their greedy throats, they were happy. Shark fin soup, poor bloody sharks, left to die in agony, minus the fins that could have swum them to safety. Bird's nest soup, tiny nests from the inside of a hundred-foot cave, with men swinging on rope ladders to harvest them, made out of bird spittle and bits of breast feather, the sweetest little bit of bird engineering one could ever see. Why would any right-minded person want to eat that?

Get them in a pan, so some salivating moron can say he can afford such a delicacy! These men have copies made of the restaurant surveillance tapes to prove to their golfing buddies how much they have spent. Morons, cruel, cruel, morons.

In the kitchen the camera picked up the chef, busy as always preparing the dishes requested. Just one thing held him in trepidation, King Cobra soup. And there it stared at him, hood up, fangs already dropped down from their hinged position on the roof of its gaping mouth. This eight-foot critter was ready to strike, who would be the winner, the chef or it? But this act of stupid bravery had been performed many times as he had five kids and a mortgage, it did not faze Lo Chi at all. His forked snake rod expertly grabbed the viper behind its hood and before you knew what had happened it was on the counter, headless, with its eight-foot body thrashing in agony. Then, the chef deftly folded back the body skin, turned it inside out and reverently put it to one side, this was to go to the handbag/shoe trade (a profitable little sideline) for pretty expensive adornments for those who could afford them. Now chop up the body and boil it with vegetables and many different spices.

The businessmen waited and waited, the other courses being already demolished, the restaurant manager went to find out what the delay was, and oh, there was a valid reason. The soup of viper had almost burnt dry, what a waste! But what lay on the floor was what shocked him the most. The chef lay in twisted dead agony, clutching one wrist, the wrist that was the final resting place of the head of a pissed off King Cobra.

Not so long ago, the so-tired chef had been clearing up the gore from the mutilated snake, he had reached for its head, just at the moment it reached for him, with hood in full glory and fangs dropped from inside its skull, it struck for the last time its ten-year-old life.

The chef's agony was immediate; he could not believe what his already dimming eyes told him. He clutched and tugged the Cobra's head, trying in vain to release his hand from its backwards-facing teeth, this could never happen as death had the little man (with five kids and a mortgage) in a grip only death could release him from.

If only he had paid heed to the useful knowledge of a man (also now a dead chef) that had died in the same manner as this.

If you leave six vertebrae still attached to the skull, the brain stem still lives for one whole hour, you have to decapitate just behind the hood to ensure the death of the beast, or you will pay the heaviest of prices, death!

Darling Jacky

She was born on a remote sparsely inhabited Greek Island to a wasteful father and a worried mother. But she and her two sisters had little to worry about as they spent giggling pleasure in the ocean's waves, lapping against the shoreline. This, then nearly unknown get-away, was soon to become a target for tourists to enjoy its magnificent beaches, for years to come.

Jacky had been blessed with a magnificent brain, and learning was easy for her. She decided at an early age she wanted to be a dental surgeon and after many years of a hard slog later, her dream became a reality. Yet still, she had a small island's naive mentality and was the perfect target for my relentless kind teasing in the years to come.

We were destined to find each other, and nothing will convince either of us that we had not lived and loved in our previous lives. And this is why.

I had to change my long-distance NHS dentist because he'd gone private, and the charges I could never pay. I was glad really, because driving on motorways scared the hell out of me and by the time I'd reached his surgery my stomach was in spasm and my buttocks clenched tight as can be. I'd gallop into the toilet and come out glassy-eyed and hollowed cheeked to the laughter of the dental nurse who presumed it was the dentist who set my bum alight 'no' it was the motorway. So, it was such a blessing to find an NHS dentist just up the road from my home, and I arrived for a first check-up.

A tiny lady in whites with long glossy black ponytailed hair had her back to me as I walked in. She turned around and both of us burst into tears, we went into each other's arms and stayed that way for some time, to the astonishment of her dental nurse. For we knew each other from another life and had found each other yet again.

From that day onwards, we became very close.

Jacky was in a marriage she wished she wasn't and had a spoilt brat of a daughter who ran rings around both of her parents, who are now divorced.

So, one of our happy Christmas's came around, and I was invited to share the fabulous meal that Jacky's chef husband had prepared. The time of gift-giving came, and we all took pleasure in each other's grateful smiles, and because Jacky did a lot of entertaining (with many different salads and homemade Greek food), I'd bought for her a magnificent Swedish, huge wooden salad bowl with servers. At first, she did not comprehend its usage, because of its size, I suppose, and they don't have them like that on little islands. I'd had a friend type out a spoof brochure to go with the bowl and asked Jacky to read it out, but she declined as her command of the English language was not as it is today. So, the assembled dinner guests tried to hide their bored faces as I opened the pages. Who the hell wants to listen to some foolish woman spout about a bloody salad bowl? Not them!

And so, I began. They soon clocked this was no ordinary guarantee, but my naïve Jacky just looked bewildered at the uproarious laughter from everyone about just a salad bowl? "Da da" now I present to you the one, the only Saladaire (this spoof must be read out loud in the manner of Victoria Wood when she did the hilarious rendition of a beauty store consultant selling the perfume "Rachel") This is a tribute to that wondrous comedienne who inspired me to continue writing, rest in peace, my dear.

CONGRATULATIONS

You are now the proud owner of our wondrous deluxe Scandinavian multi-functional SALADAIRE with complimentary servers.

SOIREE

Create a jaw-dropping centrepiece by filling your deluxe SALADAIRE with leaves sourced worldwide, at great expense, for your guest's delectation.

Have a soiree of carefully selected professional friends and, if possible, invite the local Hells Angels chapter. The sight of seventy-three hairy arsed bikers moonwalking in one's orangery is a sight to behold and well worth the mayhem caused to the neighbours by the blocking of one's cul-de-sac by numerous Harleys. Now, these leather-clad chaps, they always get a party going, at least until the fuzz arrives in answer to noise level complaints from three miles away.

Should the bikers be double-booked, an invitation to the Ku Klux Klan would boost guest numbers, and they love a bit of pineapple and cheese. At the evenings' end they do a fabulous fire show on your front lawn, but please beware that it will shag up your grass!

Worry not about the ensuing asbo as a descent brief will get you off all charges claiming deafness and dementia. Enjoy!

FOOTSPA

Fill your deluxe SALADAIRE with tepid water and release one hundred and sixty-seven snarling miniature piranhas into it. Clasp your buttocks in fear and panic and place your tootsies in the writhing mass. Allow if you dare the nasty little bastards to trash your bunions, this process usually takes forty-five minutes before you hobble, wailing, into A&E. Once in a haven, you will be given Valium plus anti-tetanus and rabies jabs.

On returning home and (in revenge for said agony) pour out the ferocious little swines and club them senseless with the complementary servers provided (option 1) Sprinkle liberally with eye-watering tabasco(fry, of course in virgin olive oil) serve with hot crusty bread and voila, a dish fit for a king!

We have been assured that this is an extremely tasty, exotic snack by all the jungle bunnies who have partaken. Enjoy!

BIDET

Once again utilise your luxury Scandinavian SALADAIRE with complementary servers. Fill your SALADAIRE with warm bubbly water, lower one's tiny tush into the relaxing splendour of your bidet and feel your troubles just float away. To give this wondrous experience yet more exotic pleasure, try tickling one's nethers with the complementary salad fork provided. This option is guaranteed to reach heights of pleasure never before experienced, at least not in a salad bowl.

Once this three-hour process is up, grudgingly removed one's tush and soothe with Castrol engine oil. At this point, it is prudent to wipe the smirk off your face, as questions will certainly be asked. Enjoy!

Now the dear owner of our wondrous product, should option one need to be used directly after option 3, it is advised, should one of your esteemed guests find an unusual morsel stuck between their gobblers, to explain (with a straight face) that it is only the Greek version of miniature curly kale (and being black the most expensive), rather like caviar. Enjoy!

Of course, many of your guests will be peeved and envious of your deluxe SALADAIRE and wish to keep up with the Jones' i.e., you, so dear purchaser, for every recommendation that results in a sale, it will be our honour to present you with a set of twenty-four of our deluxe mouse traps. Enjoy!

This product was designed and produced by Complete and Utter Bollocks Plc.

Managing director – NB Dingbat

Head Office: - Boom Alley, Gaza Strip, Patent no.666.

Any complaints regarding splinters in one's arse .etc. This company reserve the right to respectfully request you fuck off!

Points of interest – Our latest wonder in the pipeline is the sequined electric chair of 80,000 volts and must be plugged into the national grid. This is for the discerning individual who has lost the will to live, but still loves a bit of bling. This marvel is only useable once with each purchaser who harbours a death wish. It provides not only the most frazzled, hissing, stood on end curls but gives a two-minute break dancing lesson.

Any feedback regarding this product must be channelled through a medium. Further to the above purchase, the buyer most probably would be interested in our expansive range of wooden overcoats with brass fancy handles which one would of course need. This product must be paid for in full before use of the sequined electric chair

THANK YOU FOR YOUR CUSTOM

All copyrights reserved.

PS: Jacky and I are still the best of friends, and unfortunately, I don't see Jacky as often as I'd wish because her work schedule is crippling, bye, bye.

Cudgels and Bacon Butties

I'd met this very well-dressed, polite Christian Arab one Christmas Eve. We danced and chatted but at eleven-thirty he asked to be excused as he was going to midnight mass at Manchester Cathedral. Now, this was so very different from the usual and when he asked me to go with him, I accepted. I was and still am a nonbeliever in God, and that experience did not change my mind at all. After the service, he drove me home, beneath the sky so full of stars the tyres of his Daimler trying to hold the icy road, and he was a rubbish, nervous driver.

He kissed my cheek goodnight and said he would phone me soon. His promise was kept the next day and over the following months, we saw each other when he was not at home, on business in Iraq. We only ever talked, danced or ate, never once hitting the sheets.

Probably two years passed in this way, he would come back to England and we'd go out, he was nice but he bored me rigid. After a night dancing, he told me he had at last bought a penthouse flat at Salford Quays and would I like to see it? At least looking at a beautiful building would not bore me, so I accepted. What a place, ultra-modern furniture of the finest and a panoramic view of all of Manchester's night-time rooftops, lights twinkled in the dark that were reflected in the Quays waters below. So, so pretty, and I was pleased that he had managed to find, after much searching, his dream home.

We stood on the balcony and his arms slipped around me, and it was obvious his needs were great. Now, why did I consent to join him in his king-size bed? I'd known the man for two years and never had a lustful thought that contained him. He took a shower and waited in bed whilst I took mine, and on getting under the duvet with him, I went for a little furtle around. My hand found a huge object that I presumed he'd bought from the local sex shop. "Take it off, you silly thing," I said, whereupon he threw back the duvet to proudly display what can only be described as a bloody *cudgel*. For this monster, he had not bought but, much to my horror, GROWN.

Now, there was no way I was even going to try to accommodate that throbbing sod, as I was sure it would put me in the Chapel of Rest or indeed hospital, for it was the length and thickness of my forearm, and I'd not seen anything like it this side of a farm gate.

To say I was swift to get the hell out of there is an understatement and before he clubbed me into submission with the sod, I was gone. Grabbing my discarded underwear, I stuffed it in my handbag dragging on my long dress and finding just one silver stiletto shoe. I barged through the door, closed it behind me, and legged it on bare feet onto the wet pavement outside. Now, what the hell was I to do? But anything would be better than what I'd gratefully escaped from. I really don't think many women would have been able to take and enjoy such a phallus, I'm told that in the porn business it's referred to as a 'fanny ripper'. Charming! Anyway, what use would shoes have been to me, not being able to stand after an encounter with that bloody monster, so run I did, fast, *fast*, from him.

I started to hobble in the direction of my home, many, many, many miles away, I had no money for a taxi, and mobile phones were a thing of the future. The only phone box I found (and hoping to summon help from a friend) had been vandalized – now that's a surprise!

A huge stone wagon pulled up beside me, and a fatherly type man jumps down and asks what the hell I'm doing risking being attacked, walking alone in the early hours. He tells me if he thought his daughter was in such danger, he'd be crazy with worry. I told him of an even greater danger I'd just escaped from and his laughter filled the chilled wet night air.

Telling me to trust him (did I have many options?), he lifted me into the high cab of the lorry, and off we drove. He explained that he had to be at the stone quarry in Derbyshire at a certain time, so taking a detour to get me home first (and in so doing ensuring a late penalty) was not an option.

Dawn was rising; the rain had now stopped as we reached the quarry, just in time for his next load to be dropped into the lorry's back. The smell of cooking bacon filled the air, making me realise just how hungry I was. Workman's faces were a study as my hero carried me towards a grimy chair that he first wiped down with an equally grimy towel. Bless my Knight in overalls, instead of the shining armour of fairy tales.

Coffee, too strong for me to drink, was refused with many thanks but the butty filled to overflowing with crispy bacon was heaven on earth to me.

We all sat and chatted and laughed at the circumstances that had led me to be sharing their precious rashers on that now sunny happy morning and, but for that lovely man, the outcome could have been terrible.

Dearest Trevor was true to his promise of my safe return back home, and it felt wonderful to have been able to trust a stranger.

Once again, he shoved me into his wagon's cab, not because I could not climb, but because my dress was too tight, and I daren't hitch it up as my kecks were in my handbag.

We drove through the dappled leafy lanes of Derbyshire, he put on Country music, and we sang along together in the sunshine.

I suppose it would have been about 10 am by the time he lifted me out of the wagon's cab, much to the tuts of my fucking neighbours. We held each other in the best of hugs and I thanked my shining knight of the road for restoring my faith in the owner of testicles. Just how lucky was Trevor's daughter to have a dad like him?

What was that on my doorstep? It gleamed in the sunshine, one silver stiletto shoe nestled with a bunch of pink roses, that sweet Arab gentleman had forgiven my hasty retreat from his boudoir, and he phoned me often over the years from Iraq to ask about my well-being. His cudgel was never mentioned.

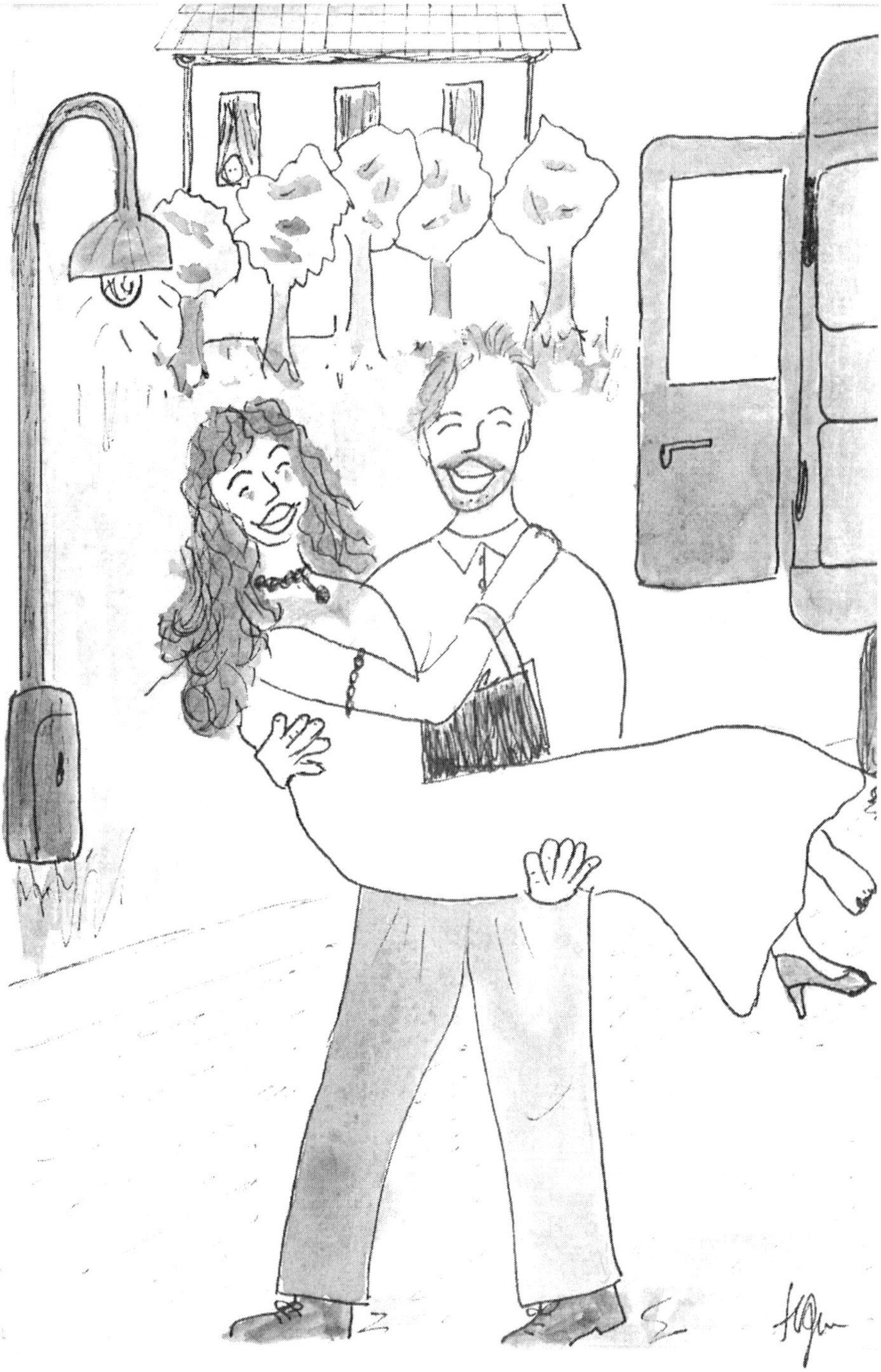

Eyelashes

I think it could possibly have been Spain where we had such a laugh one night, sat in the nightclub the flamenco dancers (yes it must have been Spain) stomped their stuff and bored me to tears. There were quite a few tourists and locals who sat on long benches – quenching their thirst on the never-ending jugs of Sangria.

Sat to my left was a succulent local man out with some lady, and as I say, I was bored rigid. So, I snaked my left hand behind his back and gently started to pull his shirt out of his jeans. Startled, (no doubt he thought I was a pickpocket) he soon settled down to the experience once he'd clocked my chest. Slowly, slowly the shirt came out until I could get my hand inside it and I felt his body quiver as I raked his back with my long-painted fingernails. My friend Samantha did not know whether to laugh or cry at her friend's antics and so just sat there waiting to see how it all panned out. My suppressed laughter on that hot night must have loosened my false eyelashes causing one to droop down my cheek making me look like a stroke victim and after removing my hand from up the stranger's shirt, we scurried off to the ladies to repair the imminent disaster.

But all was far from well, for the eyelash glue I believed to be in my bag was in fact still in my suitcase – so how the hell could I be a sex symbol with one bald eyelid?

"Help is at hand," says my mate as she furiously chews on her gum until a very thin supple strip is pulled out of her mouth. She tries so valiantly to stick it to the lashes, but they were having none of it. I remember we laughed so much trying to do the running repair that we slid down the tiled wall in the ladies' room, in total hysterics. Defeat had to be admitted and we strolled arm in arm back to our hotel under a star-filled sky.

Now, the eyelashes were to be wrapped around a knitting needle getting nicely curled for tomorrow and what it would bring. Make-up cleansed off, foam rollers in hair, time for bo bo's.

"What the hell," looking at the clock it was three forty-five am and that furious knocking at the door persisted, now I loathe being awoken and turn into a Tasmanian devil at once, and, snarling, threw open the door, only to find the Spaniard from hours ago standing there. God alone knows how he had found me, but the look on his face said it all. Gone was the Femme Fatale of his mucky dreams, as stood before him instead was a frigging nightmare in sponge rollers. We were both shocked at what stood before us, but I had the last laugh, I blew him a giant raspberry, slammed the door and went back to bo bo's.

So that was our first night on holiday. My friend had booked the apartment in Madrid as her time as an Au Pair for a Spanish ENT consultant his wife and children had just ended. So, here we were together in the sunshine, due to fly back home in two weeks' time.

The next morning the birds sang their sweet songs in the perfumed bougainvillaea and we decided to go for breakfast in a quaint little taverna we spotted. All done up once again – eyelashes well and truly stuck on, spare glue in my bag (just in case) my long gleaming titian hair dragged out of rollers and I was hot to trot, yes!

We had just started our brekkie when a shadow fell over our pavement table. And there last night's idiot stood in the same clothes as the night before. He was with his two amigos for courage as he started to ramble on in Spanish about how he believed that he had found the love of his life, in me. And how he had asked so many people during the night, did they know of my whereabouts and when he had almost despaired of ever humping me, a drunk said I was staying at the same apartment block as himself. So then the determined daft bugger had to pursue the janitor (with the help of a fist full of pesetas) to reveal which apartment it was. And that was how he came to wake up a bruiser at three forty-five am. Believing there was an unseen (until three forty-five am) third occupant of the apartment he starts to describe the vile old bag that slammed the door in his face. My friend's face was incredulous as to all of this, of course he did not know that she was fluent in Spanish and that she whispered to me the gist of what he said. He finished with, "We will have many babies once you are my bride."

How the hell did I keep my face straight I will never know as he bent to grasp my hands in his and pull me to my feet. Oh Jesus was I going to blow this daft bastard right out of the water. I released my hands from his and put one arm around him grasping his tight bum and with my other hand I gently scraped his cheek and neck with my scarlet nails; his reaction to my sultry attention was a prominent bulge in his trousers. Yep, the lady's still got it! And then, and then, I blew the biggest raspberry ever to leave painted lips. He screeched and jumped back, nearly toppling on the cobbles, whilst his two sidekicks dissolved in hysterics. His Latino charm had only been to get into my pants quite obviously, and once he discovered he had courted for quite some time the vile old bag of the previous night (in doing so making him a laughing stock) the three of them buggered off, never to be seen again, thank God. Now is this not a prime example of the chrysalis and the butterfly?

Hens

In another market, this time in Portugal, my friend and I wandered the cobbled streets, looking at the usual tourist tat and decided against it all. Then, I was abruptly brought to a halt by a situation that I just could not tolerate. Hanging upside down, tied with string around scrawny legs, were three sad, sad hens, barely alive, their clipped wings giving the faintest flutter and parched beaks squeaking.

I heard Samantha say "Oh dear God not again, please no." But it was too late as money had already changed hands, and the near-dead birds were thrust at us. I must have looked a rum sight, me stalking off through the shoppers, muttering obscenities, with a knackered hen under each arm. My friend held the third poor feathered sod and tried to keep up my turn of speed, activated by blinding outrange.

A bus was about to leave with passengers and cargo of all types, and we pushed our way on and stood for all of the journey bearing bravely the sniggers of the sat down gits, one of whom was making neck ringing gestures. I made a rude one of my own in return, using just two fingers!

We stumbled off the bus when we saw a few desiccated trees and sun-dried fields, and I won't tell you the language Sammy used, saying that this would be the last, the very last holiday she would undertake with the likes of her nutty best friend.

Knackered, hungry and thirsty in the mid-day scorching sun we sat under a tree, and she was most miffed when I said the picnic and bottled water were not for us but for the poor hens who needed them more.

Try as we might, we could not undo the tightly knotted string that bound the hen's ankles. "There's nothing for it chuck, you'll have to bite it off, I can't because I'll ruin my crowns." I don't know what she took more exception to, being called 'Chuck' or having to put her gobblers around crap encrusted hen's ankles, but bless that mate of mine, for that is exactly what she did do, she gagged, spat and swore and eventually all three birds were free of their cruel bondage. Prisoners no more they pecked with relish at the sandwiches that we were dying to devour but could not and would not as these pathetic creatures' needs were greater than ours. The plastic sandwich containers made fabulous water troughs and as we left our rescued feathered friends, pecking the earth under the shade of that lovely tree, we knew that all that could be done to help, had been.

Christ, it was hot on that dusty road miles from anywhere, and my friend uttered the words never to be forgotten "All right Mrs Attenborough, what the fuck do we do now?" As luck would have it a clapped-out filthy truck came trundling down the dirt road. And I've never been more grateful for my bounteous knockers. With screeching bald tyres, he skidded to a halt never once looking at my face (did I even have one?). One word was all that was needed to get us back, Albufeira. We rattled along for quite some time and how we stayed on the road, in that shed of a vehicle, is a bloody miracle as he never took his eyes off my tits. And that ogling idiot never missed one pothole or hump in the track as it made my boobs jiggle aplenty, much to his delight.

Back safely in the hotel with the day's adventure over we were starving hungry and thirsty, but all we could face was salad and bread, even though chicken was on the menu.

Rickshaw

I don't know how the poor emaciated bugger had the strength to even stand near the rickshaw, let alone pull the battered sod with its occupants. But this was how he made his living, and I could not deny him the meagre money he requested. His once beautifully crafted raffia hat hung in tatters, held in place by a string under his chin, beneath which was the largest protruding Adam's apple ever to bounce up and down a scrawny neck. His smile was remarkable, thin blue-tinged lips surrounded a few yellow and black teeth, which in turn clasped an evil-smelling cheroot. Those blue lips worried me terribly as I could envisage the poor little bugger dropping dead by the roadside still gripping the rickshaw shafts. It what obvious what he had consumed for lunch as his ragged t-shirt still held strands of dropped noodles. Shorts at knee length, far, far too big for his skeletal frame were held modestly in place with string, but it was what hung out of his shorts that astounded me. Never, ever have I seen such lurid, extravagant varicose veins, they thrusted out like grapes under his papery yellow skin and must have hurt that poor little man every moment of his life. Plastic flip flops on his dirty tired bunioned feet completed the ensemble, and my heart saddened for him. When I tried to leave him for a more robust driver, he was very upset by this, and how very sad was it that he needed our pittance of a fare so desperately!

So, we climbed into his beloved rickshaw and after he seemed to run on the spot for some time, off we set.

In the distance we could see our destination, Rolls Royce's, Ferraris and every wondrous car you could imagine were being valet parked by a fine fellow in pristine top hat and tails, and so we had come to a halt outside Raffles in Singapore for the much-anticipated afternoon tea they are so famous for. We bade farewell to the valiant little man who had weaved in and out of dangerous traffic to get us there safely. Folding money was pressed into his gnarled hand – and when he counted it, his yellow smile lit up the world as it was twenty times more than he had asked for and I hoped with all my heart I'd given him enough to take a well-deserved long rest. But somehow, I doubt it.

I'm a Twat!

They had been childhood sweethearts, and she thought it wonderful she had bagged the school bad boy.

I met them many years down the line from her youthful obsession, and time had proved that he really was just a waste of space. Pity, as by that time he had given her three children, and God alone knows how many other gullible women were raising the screaming outcome of yet another of his nights on the pull.

Even though they had known each other for such a long time and had a family together, they had never actually tied the knot. This they decided to do after he'd been caught with his pants down yet again, but when he swore he was now a changed man, the silly woman believed him.

It was a lovely white wedding, the one of her long-held dreams, but unfortunately he was found in the toilets, about to give the Chief Bridesmaid a right seeing too, that somehow cast a shadow over the day, but in reality, it was only to be expected.

Married life from then on went from bad to worse, with her new husband doing a disappearing act every other weekend. By this time, the cheeky bastard did not even offer up an excuse and with a shrug of his puny shoulders told her to mind her own fucking business. Nice!

Now, it just so happened that this lass was a real firebrand and unbeknown to him revenge was on the cards.

Her opening gambit to him was "If you really love me, prove you've changed by having my name tattooed where every slapper can see it"! This request threw the lover boy into a duck fit, but at last, he relented as long as the message of his undying love was in a foreign language. Very reluctantly he agreed to Chinese.

The internet provided the oriental writing and the tattooist, with intricate care, proceeded to write what he believed to be

'I love Tracey' around her errant husband's neck.

He said it hurt like hell but at least it would shut up his now smirking wife.

Friday was takeaway night and off to the Chinese he went on that summer evening. Waiting for the numerous dishes he'd ordered, he was getting seriously pissed off with the kitchen staff almost sliding down the walls, laughing, when they looked at him. Eventually, his food was ready, and the hilarity had not ceased. Slamming his money on the counter, he was compelled to ask just what was so fucking funny. 'It's your tattoo' he was told. He answered in no uncertain terms that there was nothing comical in a man saying 'I love Tracey' as a tribute to his nagging missus. "It doesn't say I love Tracey, it says "I am a twat". Bang goes his penchant for oriental girls. Loud and very clear they could read exactly what he was. Oh, sweet revenge.

Argyll Socks and Sequined Waistcoats

I awoke that Sunday morning to blazing summer sun, a change from the previous two weeks of rain. The clock told me 6.30 am, time to hit the car boot in a classy part of town, where the sellers arrived in splendid cars, selling splendid bargains.

Almost the first thing I saw was a tall figure of a man leaning against the open boot of a 4 by 4, nothing odd in that you will be thinking, wrong, as this man was blown up rubber, with a drawn-on nest of pubic hair and Poirot moustache and a very dodgy nest-like wig that turned around of its own accord. The fact he was bollock naked got my undivided attention, and a crazy prank stirred in my over fertile imagination. Its owner thought it more than strange, but agreed, when I asked if I could borrow him for a little Sunday stroll in the sunshine and that all would be revealed, much like him!

He was fully inflated, arms stuck out, legs akimbo, head shaking, a sight to behold. I linked arms with my new friend, and together we started our hunt for affordable goodies. Low and behold, hung on the open hatch of a Honda was a sparkling gents sequined waistcoat. Just the job! By this time, a few nudging people were taking more than a little notice, and the air carried the giggles of young girls. Did they think it was yet another prank from that Jeremy Beadle off the TV, who was famous for his crazy goings-on? But no, it was just me, a Bipolar middle-aged lady who had spied an opportunity for a little fun!

The waistcoat seller stood aghast as I questioned my new man (now named Steve) if he thought it suitable for our upcoming nuptials (not quite saying he loved it), as he was made by me to nod his head, which made his vile wig turn somewhat, sending its parting skew-whiff. My face was totally straight as I asked the price in a conjured-up voice that was a cross between Betty Boo and a squirrel. A price was decided (£1), and I asked her help in getting Steve's rigid rubber arms through the appropriate armholes, looking around for what she believed by now to be hidden TV cameras she pasted on a fake smile and set about dressing my intended in the lurid garment. It was a struggle but well worth the combined effort, as both he and I were overjoyed as we had found at least one item of his upcoming nuptial attire. By now, small gatherings of people were dotted about, many of them preening themselves up, as the whispered word was that hidden cameras were recording the prank, and the lady with the rubber man was indeed a well-known actress in disguise. Oh, how I loved all this silliness that brought out the vanity of some of the punters, whilst others did their very best to hide in embarrassment at being clocked at a car boot, as they considered themselves far too posh to attend them, but got ecstatic with a 50p bargain, as we all do!

So, we strolled my Stevie and I in the sunshine, glitters bounced off his sequined waistcoat, and I have to say, that when I whispered that he looked the dog's bollocks in it, the nod of his head made his barnet do another quarter turn, thus bringing his parting horizontal over his rubber head. Deep, deep joy, this was the most fun I'd had vertically for years!

Then, I spotted a very military-looking man. With the usual array of things you don't know you want, or indeed like, until they present themselves for under a pound. Three pairs of new argyle socks lay amongst well used golfing clubs and once again, in squirrel tones, I asked the price. Did I want all three pairs or just one? "One pair would suffice thank you, but would you mind helping one put them on my betrothed, as he has great difficulty doing things because of having no hands of his own?" This moustached (his was ginger) General type chap was a bloody star, he bent down and tugged one sock onto my Steve's left leg stump. Of course it would not stay there as the poor sod had no feet, as well as hands. Not to be beaten, the ingenious gent went in his pocket and produced a selection of elastic bands, on finding one to his satisfaction, he once again went on bended knee and proceeded to anchor the argyle sock to blown up rubber. This he repeated on the second stump of a leg, and there my intended spouse stood, resplendent in sequins and the argyle socks in a rather fetching yellow and red concoction that toned perfectly with the waistcoat. I could tell by the way my dearest kept nodding his mute head that he was delighted that we were managing to get his wedding attire on our, so tight, budget. And so, the wig turned!

At this stage, I thought it a great shame that darling Steve did not have anything between his sturdy legs that would enhance our wedding night. This must have been a great worry to my rubber lad and to hide his shortcomings I purchased a large plastic fig type leaf and with the aid of borrowed Sellotape covered up his missing knob and balls that the poor rubber sod did not sport, with any sort of pride anyway.

All this was of course in the days before phones that took pictures, but some enterprising people had cameras that clicked away and kept a record of what their eyes could not believe.

The car park had filled up with so many people, who I believe hoped to be part of what they believed to be their fifteen minutes of fame on a very popular TV show. Dressed up to the nines, they strolled amongst the cars, yet rarely bought anything, still, my daft prank got them out of their boring little lives, in their boring little semis.

The smell of sizzling bacon was making me hungry; Steve declined a butty as he was worried he'd get grease on his sequins. (You see, I was really into the charade now and decided only to go back to boring normality when my Stevie was returned to his owner). This I did not relish so he and I did one last circuit of the car park, bidding hello to numerous punters who often stretched out their hands to stroke him or hug me. The morning for them had been enhanced by my daft antics, and it was with great regret that I propped him up against the car he came from. A small gathering clapped and cheered, and I pretended to cry as Steve and I parted forever and bless that lady who owned him, she joined in the pretence by getting Steve to wave goodbye to me and the crowd, seeing his wig finally unwind itself and fall between argyle socked feet, was the icing on the cake and brought on the hysterics I'd been holding in for the past one and half hours. I stood and took a bow as people continued to clap, cheer and take photos. I often wonder if they avidly watched Jeremy Beadle in the hope of seeing themselves on TV. Sorry punters it was just a Bipolar prank by a nutty soon to be, old bird.

The clapping continued as I strolled to my car, and I felt a tap on my shoulder. There stood the owner of my Stevie, him resplendent still in all the fancy gear I'd bought him. She asked with panting breath "Well don't you want to buy him"? I'll swear he looked heartbroken at my reply "Don't be ridiculous, he hasn't got a knob."

With that, I climbed into my little Honda and was gone!

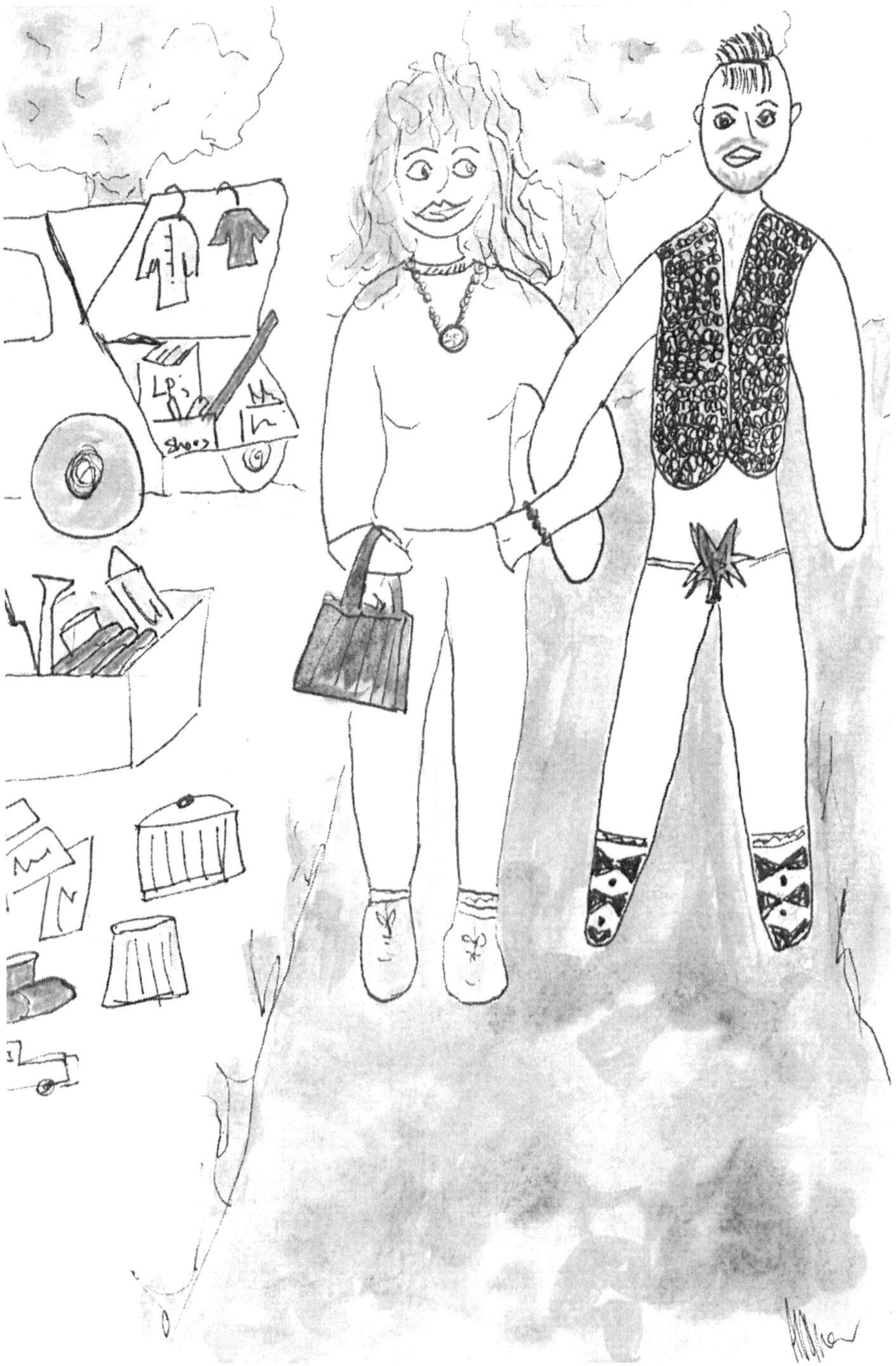
LP's

Trill

We could hardly believe our eyes, yet we should have been used to what staggered before us – on skyscraper red patent heels, it did its best.

Now (it, she) Les, AKA Cindy was a trucker from London whose dress sense veered towards the flamboyant, nay – lady of the night!

Coarse black hair poked through the holes of his fishnets his/her mini skirt barely covering the black stocking tops, bloody tease! The boob tube tried in vain to control knockers to be proud off, leopard bomber jacket and red patent bag (this apparition could coordinate if nothing else) black long wig with heavy make-up, that failed miserably to conceal his five o'clock shadow, and this boy was hot to trot.

We ambled behind her in the park, not failing to notice the numerous birds that followed in her wake pecking the ground with gusto. Picnicking families dropped their butties, for a cartoon had come to life before their bemused eyes.

Feet in purgatory, she parks her minied bum on a bench sitting like any bloke does, knees akimbo, showing everything that had fallen out of the leg of a pair of red French knickers. We had, of course, a bird's eye view from the opposite bench, not pretty, not pretty at all, something you could never unsee.

And yet more birds swoop from the trees and gather at her feet. Peck, peck, pecking, I suppose it was only imagination that a Bald Eagle joined the throng (course it was!).

Then there was this strangled cry of horror and dismay, looking down at her wondrous chest she discovered that one of her titties had deflated.

Now which inventive sod had discovered that if you place birdseed i.e., trill, or any other sort really, in a plastic bag, the weight to size ratio is exactly the size of a woman's breast? The more trills you can afford, the bigger the tits.

The left titty had burst, dropping its contents down the boob tube and onto the ground, hence she became the Pied Piper of all flying and pecking things.

With as much dignity as she could muster and not a few oaths, she fished down her top, tore out the torn bag of bird food and threw the lot at the waiting, pecking crowd. Without missing a beat, she retrieved her remaining breast out of her top, slapped it in her red plastic bag, lit a fag and staggered off.

Flat and hairy-chested once again, she/he now had a dilemma, should he shave off the luxuriant growth that the real girlies loved to stroke at playtimes, or stay au naturel for the next foray to the shop that sold birdseed?

So, all in all, it was a fabulous day out for her, she'd had a body to die for, albeit for a short time (knowing for sure she looked the Kangaroo's conkers!) we laughed till we wet ourselves and birds from a twenty-mile radius had the time of their little feathered lives with full tummies, bless them.

Life's funny, isn't it? Or is it just my slant on it? Love you xx.

Gone with the Wind

I'm laughing as I recall this event; it's so clear in my mind's eye, yet it's forty-five years later.

There is a society called the 'Beaumont', started after a World War II bomber pilot (who had many medals for his bravery in combat) discovered, shall we say, his feminine side. But 'the society' was solely for transvestites, and the people who loved them and wished to understand the torment that these men went through. But now, Dorothy was allowed to be free, no longer trapped in the male body, he now had a glorious selection of ladies' clothes to cover the body that he hated. Yes, Bill was now Dorothy.

It just so happened that I had a crossdressing friend who was so kind and helpful, but who turned into a proper diva if denied his frocks for too long.

Yearly, there was a convention in Bournemouth at a swanky hotel, closed to all except crossdressers and their female loved ones. (These men are not usually gay!). So off we pop, Jesus what a sight, all these Baby Spices, French Maids, twin set and pearls Vicars' wives, and a glorious selection of slappers, etc, etc. It was very disconcerting to the senses to walk into the dining room, for the ears to hear male voices, but the eyes to see only women.

It's a balmy evening, dinner has been eaten and a few of our ladies decide to go for a stroll along the prom. Then, one of them hurtles up the grand staircase outside, screeching that some perv has goosed her arse. Sure, enough said perv is still loitering at the bottom of the steps with a rather battered old terrier, held by a piece of string. Classy!

Now 'Jane' was a six-foot-four ganger on the railway. This lad had overdosed on Vivien Leigh in Gone with the Wind. (He bloody adored her). Now his get-up was a stormer. The biggest peach satin stilettos (sent from America) crippled his feet (he cared not cos he looked the business!). His silk stocking held in place with frilly suspenders, his bra packed with God knows what, (probably trill birdseed) but the dress oh! the dress. Enough peach taffeta (in ruffles) to curtain the hotel we stayed in. This, off the shoulder little number was enhanced by a matching Dorothy bag held between finger and thumb (these would have not been too small for King Kong), fingerless lace gloves up to the elbows and a couple of rings on top of these, bracelets, pearls, necklaces flower in hair, this bonny lad had pulled out all the stops.

Jane did not like her friend (the slapper from hell) being goosed and decided enough was enough.

Imagine this! A selection of trannies stands on every step of this regal hotel, it's a summer evening, and Jane starts her sashay across a busy road, traffic stopped in wonder at the sight of a peach galleon in full sail. With such dignity, she gets to the other side on feet that were in torment, because the dirty old scrote was now leaning against the railings, a satisfied leer on his kisser because he had goosed said slapper.

God, Jane was so refined (big but refined), this lass must have reached over seven-foot (six-foot-four of her, five-inch heels, blonde ringlet wig backcombed to within an inch of its life another four-inches) like I said, seven bloody foot of peach menace.

As she gets closer the little perv had to lean back to get the full effect, (rather like one does to look up at a skyscraper!). With hands like shovels, Jane takes the string holding the dog from the perv's trembling hands, ties it to the iron railings, picks up the perv above her head and daintily drops him into the gorse bushes on the beach below. Traffic stops once again as she prances back to us all standing on the steps, clapping at her audacity.

The next morning, there was some concern as the dog was still tied to the railing, poor little bugger, this worried Jane so she sauntered across with sausages (off everyone's plate)fed the little mite, phoned the local dog charity and had it removed safely.

Now, what happened to the pervy scrote who had goosed the slapper on that lovely evening in Bournemouth? We never found out, as we came home that day.

Maasai

You will probably have gathered by now that I'm not to be messed with, in fact, my friends call me the ultimate warrior!

It's before a long-ago Christmas, and I'd been alone to the last car boot of the season. There I had bought a very large, serrated knife for the purpose of dividing plant roots. This monster weapon lay in the bottom of my shopping bag, and I was careful not to touch it, as it was unwrapped and sharp as hell.

On the way home, I decided to call in at TJ Hughes, a wonderful store (which has since closed down, unfortunately). Strolling amongst the shop's display, I could not help but notice, this six-foot four-inch black man with the distinctive type features of a Maasai Warrior. Now if this tall thin lad was a store detective he could not have been more conspicuous, but why was he always behind me every time when I turned around? For I was no shoplifter, and my days of pulling were a distant memory.

I kept using my mobile to try to find out if the presents I saw would be acceptable for my relatives, but I got no reply. So, I thought, Sod It! I'll buy what I thought to be suitable and if they are not, I'll get a refund.

I'm walking to my car when suddenly I'm pushed between my shoulder blades and stumble forward without hitting the ground, and my Christmas gifts scatter about on the car park tarmac.

Before me now stood the tall Maasai looking chap from inside the store. "Give me your money and phone," he demanded! This prat obviously did not know the geriatric old sod he was menacing was a sight more dangerous than he was. For I'd grown 'balls of steel', what were his made of?

Cool as cool can be, I asked "Are you really sure you want them son?" "Oh, fucking funny" was his reply.

Reaching into the bottom of my nearly empty shopping bag, I must not have been quick enough to comply with his wishes, and his hand followed mine into its depths. Little did this bonny lad know of my lethal purchase from the car boot. By this time, its horn handle was in my hand and with one swipe I cut the thieving sod's knuckles down to the bone. His face was a surprised, screaming study as he surveyed the wounds that would need much repair. Taking off his expensive jacket, he bound his fist, dripping with blood, and told me in no uncertain terms that I was "Fucking old Psycho." On this point I had to agree with him and as he stumbled away to his very trusty Merc, I advised him that's what happens to naughty boys should they mess with a pensioner on a Sunday morning.

Two ladies saw this event and did nothing to help me but when he was gone told me how brave I'd been and one of them said she would call the police. This I had to put a stop to, as in the eyes of the law I was the naughty old lady, that not only carried a very offensive weapon, but had used the sod.

The Maasai had only politely requested my money and phone, how bloody dare he? And I wonder how long it took for his shredded hand to be able to steal again? Forever I hope!

Bipolar, the Ruination of My Life

It was during the night that the thief yet again struck so very silently that my sleep was not disturbed nor did my dogs bark in a warning. Completely unaware of the night's trauma and what it heralded, I reached to remove the earplugs that ensured a sleep unbroken by traffic noise, but they were still in the bedside cabinet. A knotted dread gripped my insides and with my heart beating wildly I forced my eyes to open and then I knew. The pretty colours of my bedroom faded out just as the passing traffic sounds were. Once again, the thief had struck leaving behind all things of monetary value and stealing from me what was really precious. Into his swag bag of pain, he'd stuffed my laughter, concentration, rational thought, ability, just about everything that made me me, and left in its place this shadow of a being that was hardly human, a nothing alone, begging in a tortured mind for the release of death.

Bipolar, the grim reaper of everything that I am, had crept in again leaving me barely alive and wishing myself to be no more.

There is no pattern to its behaviour, it does just at it pleases and comes and goes within the beat of my sad heart, in good times allowing me to create the imaginings of my mind, to be so quick with movement and thought, see the colours bright and intensified that my hungry eyes crave, hear the music that makes me dance in the house, and the most precious of all, my ability to make people laugh, is mine once again. One more heartbeat and all is stolen again, once more I've been poorly, now triggered by loneliness again since my best friend returned home in mid-August 2012. It's now September, and I suppose my torment is lifting as I'm writing again after a month of being nothing. I say nothing because in that time of non-comprehension I've almost killed both of my beloved dogs because rational thought has been impossible.

In all my years of having and rescuing animals, I've never had to deal with fleas on my dogs. Yet now the nipping little bastards were driving my dogs crazy. Poor old Ziggy got flea eczema and chewed his tail until it bled and have you tried to find hoppers in the curly coat of a black poodle? So, I went into cleaning overdrive with sprays and powder not realizing that an overdose will indeed poison not only the fleas but the host animal. In my zeal to stop their discomfort, I damaged my little Lola and her kidneys shut down making her unable to pass urine. I know I was wailing with bipolar torment and anger at myself that I'd inadvertently hurt my girl. I was capable of nothing, yet I managed to make the journey to the vet to get her help, and now after ten days, she is as playful and happy as usual. So please, if fleas come to call don't overdose and should your pet lose its flea collar within days, do not replace it at once as the poison will be a double dose, which results in a dead pet. It frightens me that in our zeal to do what we believe to be the best we are indeed causing more damage than a flea ever could. Here ended the flea lesson!

The structured OCD pattern of my life was very altered by my dogs being unwell, and this led to even more serious consequences and I forgot to medicate myself for eleven days. After getting up, whilst still dark, on Saturday morning to give antibiotics to Lola, I failed to return the back door electronic shutter to its down position, leaving an opening of two-foot after they had been out for a wee-wee. I went back to bed for a couple of hours and felt so disorientated, mithered and downright ill when I awoke. I had to go downstairs one at a time sideways like a geriatric crab. I remember thinking there must be more to life than this crap. The dogs greeted me in the kitchen with such love, they were sleeping there, instead of their room upstairs, until the flea saga was resolved.

The back door was still closed as I pressed the fob (to activate the shutter) before throwing it in the drawer. As soon as I opened the door, Ziggy darted forward, and all hell broke loose. The shutter descended from the two-foot I'd inadvertently left open and was closing quickly down on my old Ziggy. I grabbed the bottom with one hand to try to stop the steel from coming further, the motor screamed in defiance; Ziggy could not hear my command of return, and he wriggled free of my other hand and started to become wedged. I threw myself on the kitchen floor just in time to push my head and shoulders under to take its weight and with all my strength I pushed the heavy steel shutter against a motor intent on complying with its downward instruction.

Ziggy managed to get out unscathed, but now I was trapped half in half out of the kitchen, and the shutter motor screamed. If it were not so serious, it would have been bloody hilarious. Picture this: a rather rotund old bird splayed out on a cold, tiled kitchen floor in a leopard skin kaftan, a solid steel industrial weight shutter intent on reaching its destination (across my shoulders). Oh bollocks, what was I to do? Lola thought it the best game ever and proceeded to slap my bare legs with her teddy, whilst Ziggy licked my face, as it hung over the back doorsteps. With one enormous push on the bottom step and raising my shoulders, I managed to make enough room to pull back and lay panting with relief on the floor, whilst Lola kept up her relentless play.

To this day, I don't know how the motor did not blow, how I managed to get out, where I found the strength to do what I did, how my old dog and myself were not decapitated – how I did not die of a bloody heart attack? So, thank you, my guardian angel, for giving me the strength to save my old dog from a certain vile death, or me from a lifetime of grief and guilt at my own mistakes.

In the weeks I've been unable to function, everything has gone to hell on a handcart, and my garden has not received its daily tending to, the hoover stands waiting to be pushed, my bed stays unmade and the phone is off the hook. I'm unable to tolerate any music or sound, so I watch TV with subtitles in my silent life of hell.

Yesterday (12 September 2012), I had to force myself out as Jim the Vet needed a urine sample to verify Lola's progress. I don't know what made me take a different route home, but I found myself outside number 47, the home of my childhood.

Two removal vans were unloading, and I talked to the new owners, whom I took an instant dislike to.

They immediately started to slate the lady who had sold them my old home. Going into lurid details of her personal life and listing the name of her debtors. I found myself telling them in no uncertain terms that, not only was it not my business, but not theirs either, for this sweet previous lady owner had helped me, a total stranger, when I'd knocked on her door some two years previously, in total despair.

My recurring nightmare was so vivid I'd awaken convinced I was still broken and bloody with my homemade cotton dress stuck to my body with the pouring rain. The sound of the huge door knocker echoing through the house a stern voice saying "and who are you"? Hardly a week would go by when I would not awaken confused and startled by the night-time terrors, only to find myself safe in my comfy pink bed.

I'd gone back to the scene of my nightmares, number 47, the building of my childhood. I'd knocked on the front door, the sound echoed in the hallway, then before me stood a pretty blonde lady, concerned by the crying old lady before her. For I'd endured my nightmare for over forty-five years.

I explained that long before she was even born, I'd lived in the house that was now hers, and of the nightmare that wounded me time and again.

She held her arms out to me and told me she was closing the door, but I was to knock on it again, with sobs choking me I did as she asked, and she then opened it with smiles of greeting, holding out her arms she welcomed me inside closing the door behind us she sat me down with a cup of tea and there my healing process took place. She encouraged me to pour out my grief to cleanse myself of all that was still destroying me, after all those years, and so I told her of that rainy night so long ago when my husband had beaten me yet again, this time breaking my nose by head butting me and kicking me so hard outside into the wet winter night that my back would be forever damaged. In fear of my life (and now I believe it would have been far kinder if he had ended it that terrible night), I started stumbling on bare feet to the house I'd been banished from so many years previously. No one offered to help the young woman, bloody and broken, who staggered past them, alone as always. Finally, I reached number 47 after how long I don't know. I banged at that front door, there was no response, so I went to the side door. This opened, and my father towered above me at the top of three tiled steps. I never got to say a word, I believe I was at the point of collapse when I heard the words "and who are you"? At this point, my mother came scurrying up behind him in the kitchen, she took one look at her daughter and said "what do you think you are doing upsetting your father like this"? And she slammed the door in my face.

Now, if that had been my daughter who needed help so desperately, I'd have told my husband in no uncertain terms that half of that house was mine, and my child was coming into it. But no, she sent me away like a stray, broken little dog to struggle back home to hell. Did she give me a taxi fare? No! Did she put me on a bus? No! Did she hug me and give me comfort? No, no, no! She abandoned me in my time of need and even though in later years (after my father's death) I saw to her every need, my heart stayed cold, for she had damaged me and betrayed me beyond all repair. So that sweet lady listened to my outpouring of old grief, passing me tissues to mop up a torrent of tears.

So, now I was back in the house I'd been banished from, not once, but twice, yet this time I was enfolded in welcome and dare I say love which I deserved and compassion. Taking my hand, the present owner of number 47 gave me a tour of her home, and I marvelled at the joy and beauty she had created. We sat and chatted, and she was enthralled to hear the story of the half-green, half-red-tiled roof. How she laughed when I told her the crazy tale of the Stags head and the screaming gays on the other side of the twilight lit twelve-foot wall. I told her of the secret room (found at last by someone else) that was my refuge from reality (that was now her en-suite bathroom) gone was the outside toilet that stank of rotting horseflesh, where I discovered my transition from child to woman. I told her of the magnificent leaded French door whose magical colours floated in the sunshine on my child's hands, now gone forever, to have been replaced with a window, long before she owned number 47.

She wiped away my last tear and asked me to call again – this I promised I would do. And so, from that soul-cleansing day to this I've never heard the words "and who are you"? Never again awoken in fear and pain, and I'll forever be grateful to the stranger who cared more than the people who had created and broken me.

Two years passed from that day of redemption, and I'd found myself outside number 47 yet again, I'd been hoping to tell the lady that all was well, that she had done me the greatest service and that those banishing words of my father were spoken no more. But the sold board told me only that she was gone, to be replaced with a sour maligning, gossiping pair of sods I took an instant dislike to.

The new owners allowed me to walk barefooted through the once dark house that I grew up in. That now was flooded with light.

Removal men carried on bringing in the possessions of more owners of number 47. I wonder how many there have been in the house's long history?

I stood in the bathroom, now revamped from my little girl days and once more I felt the heartbreak of seeing my beloved music boxes immersed in the bathwater, as my punishment for turning on a tap (an eye for an eye) and ruining a clock.

Standing in my bedroom from long ago I wondered if anyone had ever found the Victorian silver scissors (in the shape of a heron the long beak being the blades) that my frozen tiny six-year-old hands had dropped accidentally between the bare floorboards that winters day. Why did I not ask my daddy to find them for me? I'm sure, now, he would have tried.

Granddad's room brought about the memory of the black writing top box stored beneath his metal frame bed. Inside were embroidered cards from World War One whose beauty gave me such joy. My mother threw them all away when he died. Why could I not have had and treasured them to this very day?

The doorway to the box room leading off the landing was now just a wall, would anyone ever know the secret that half of it held? The little hidden room that was accessed through the sliding door in the back of the giant mahogany wardrobe in my mum and dad's room.

Strange that the story of the Lion the Witch and the Wardrobe is so similar to the reality I found, as a bored, witless seven-year-old and, as I stood in the ensuite it now is, in my mind my mother was calling in frustration to the hidden child she never could find. I wonder what the builder (who after ripping my mother off with a paltry £11,000 purchase price in 1977) thought when he tore apart that wardrobe wall to find my secret sanctuary? I'll never know its original purpose, but dolly and I were content in its womb-like embrace, lying on that old canvas camp bed.

The dining room held memories of a now-seventeen-year-old new mum breastfeeding the little girl whose creation was at that time, a mystery to her. I did not know the act I performed, just twice, could result in a living creature, for sex education was unheard of in those days, to one so young.

Once again, I felt the pain of heavy boots kicking my shins until they bled, yet still I did not cry out and disturb my little child as she filled her hungry tummy from my breast. Her father, yet again, spits his vile curses over the both of us. Oh, terrifying! Fists raised in hate.

Once again, my memory saw my big brother John tinker with his Vincent motorbike, tools strewn around the tiled courtyard as he tuned the bike until it purred (just as they did with all his future bikes). The last of these being a Honda Goldwing which still gleamed long after he took his life in 1976 aged forty-six, that also is now just a sad memory.

The front wrought iron gate still stands there; the one Dad and I drew together when I was eight. The local Blacksmith (who shod all the co-op milk float horses) was a friend of Dad's and created his magnificent work in no time at all. And there, it still stands over half a century later, a good-as-new barrier to those unwelcome.

So many memories, nearly all of them heart-breaking, rushed through my already troubled mind. For it was only yesterday that I finally discovered that because my set routine was altered by caring for poorly dogs, I'd missed many days of my vital medication. These tablets don't make me well, they just make me less ill, so for that, I'm grateful.

So, there I stood, tears of remembrance flowing freely, the removal men had an expression that asked *"what the hell"* but never said a word.

The sour vile new owner walked me past Dad's roses, over the crazy paving I watched him lay as a child, and we stood at the gate made by a true craftsman over sixty years ago.

She asked me if I would return when they had settled in, to tell her of the house's history. I told her this would be my last visit to the home of my childhood. She asked, "why," and I told her truthfully "because I don't like you" she was stunned by my bluntness and stomped back past Dad's roses into the house she had bought cheaply, as a sad repossession.

She would never know of the magnificent Stags head that once adorned the hallway, that is now hers. Never know of the little girl taught to make the sound of clopping horses with coconut shells by a mischievous father. "Yes," years of turmoil and tears are woven into the fabric of that old house. It has stood strong and beautiful through two World wars. Rejoiced in births and grieved in deaths, but rarely laughed in its dark silence. I've paid my last visit to the home of my childhood; I've said my tearful goodbyes to number 47.

The Blue Rinsed Viper

How I hated the continued hospital visits that were an important part of my ongoing treatment.

So, there I sat once again in the bowels of the local hospital, shivering as usual as these places must be kept at a low temperature. I'd not been waiting long when an old lady was pushed in by a porter and just dumped. Bless the old dear, she looked like a typical nana weighing probably no more than six stone – white permed curly hair with a blue rinse, translucent thin skin that showed all her veins, tiny arthritic fingers twisting a wedding ring, no blanket to warm up her wasted little body, for all she wore was a white thin cotton nightgown, with rosebuds embroidered on the yoke. Slippers with pom-poms that were too big for her miniature feet slid off to the floor.

I was really concerned about her, she looked so lost and forlorn her face drooped down to her chest. My heart went out to her.

I crept over to her so as not to startle her if she was indeed asleep. She did not appear to be, so I gently touched her shoulder and said the words I wish I hadn't. "Would a hug help darling?" Well, the old bugger shot me a look that would kill at fifty paces and spat out "No it bloody wouldn't, now fuck off!" Jesus Christ, she was like a blue-rinsed Cobra on full strike and once I got over her venomous refusal of a hug I laughed until I could hardly stand.

At this point, the staff came to take me for the scan, and I thought I'd seen the last of the old sod. The nurse asked why I was laughing and when told, took a very dim view of it. Miserable sod!

But no, when I came out, there she still sat, and being in a cheeky mood, said "I suppose a hug is out of the question then?" To my great honour and surprise, she said, "Well go on then." So, I knelt beside her chair, we hugged, laughed and kissed, and I left her there. I bet she had been abandoned because some poor bugger could take no more of her cantankerous nature. Bless, I thought she was a star!

See Me Bear

For over forty years, the unwashed mongrel of a man had made lewd suggestions of just what he'd like to do to me. As I pointed out many times to him, he had more chance of throwing his short, misshaped leg with a built-up boot over the bloody Pope. Year after year, this inane pestering went on whenever he saw me, which was often, as he timed his daily paper buying trip to whilst I was doing my morning gardening. His suggestive invitations really hotted up! when I got a job as a bunny at the playboy club in Manchester, and he saw me one evening getting in a cab in a bunny costume. He soon spread the word and an endless stream of husbands and boyfriends, or indeed anyone for a taste of bunny rabbit, was saunter past my home at leaving time. The paper shop just loved this as their takings at least tripled, as it was also a 24-hour convenience store.

The years passed and obviously, time took its toll on my desirable looks, and another mode of earning had to be found. This idea of taking numerous courses and finally getting into the very lucrative design business worked.

So, we arrive at the present day, and I have designed many, many gardens for people over the years and turned my own into the local point of interest. People come regularly to inspect the latest designs and take photos of the unusual bulbs, etc. (donated to me by a generous bulb importer to trial run.) I make a report on them before they are mass acquired for the general public's delight. So, I write a very detailed report and in return I get a glorious display for my garden for free, win, win.

The back-garden fences are lined out with numerous mirrors making six-foot-high and twelve wide collages, bought from car boots, charity shops, etc. When the correct adhesive is applied they stick to the wood in all weathers and stay there. This of course at least doubles the size of the garden and when the various coloured blossom LED trees are lit at twilight my garden becomes a fairyland. I just love it! And so, does anyone else who I choose to allow to see it.

There are some wonderful realistic fibreglass animals, made so perfectly life-like and usually about half the size of their living counterparts. The sale at the garden centre boasted half price and loving a bargain I bought Luther a handsome lion, Sheila and her pouched child who is a Wallaby, Gore and his daughter Rilla, guess what they are? And Claudette a full-sized moon bear nestles in her home under the rhododendron amongst fir cones and stones in a natural-looking habitat for the wondrous lifelike girl.

That slavering idiot was once again at my front gate and told me once again in lascivious, certain terms that I was "a fine-looking woman still" and time and again over forty years he has sat in his allotment shed and thought of me…undressed! Whilst playing with his Dirty Vile Bits.

Disgusting, I could be sick at the thought.

I was about to make all of his dreams come true or so he believed. I told him that as long as he kept it our secret, he could at long last see the real thing! The daft bastard believed me as he followed me through the wrought iron gates and up the side of my home. I could hear his club foot dragging on the crazy paving behind me, and hear his laboured, fetid breath coming in gasps that would fell like a skunk at twenty paces. I reached the end of the passageway and like a TV game hostess, showing what a competitor had just won I stood to one side with arms outstretched and said the words that destroyed all his lurid allusions "da da see me bear" at first, he did not clock it, but when he did, he went bloody ballistic. For there sitting in her silent splendour was my Claudette, the most beautiful bear anyone could wish to see.

"You bastard, you lousy prick teasing fucking old witch!" he spat out at me from between brown decayed teeth, I was obviously no longer a fine figure of a woman to him. In my feigned innocence, I said, "Well you always wanted to see me bare, now you have. I suggest you take yourself off to your filthy allotment shed, close the door, read from your stack of sticky porn, wank yourself senseless and cross me off your fucking bucket list." He hobbled off cursing me to hell and back and did I care? "NO" as for almost forty years I'd planned to stitch the vile bastard up, and now I had. He never propositioned me again and oh I'm so very, very disappointed… Not.

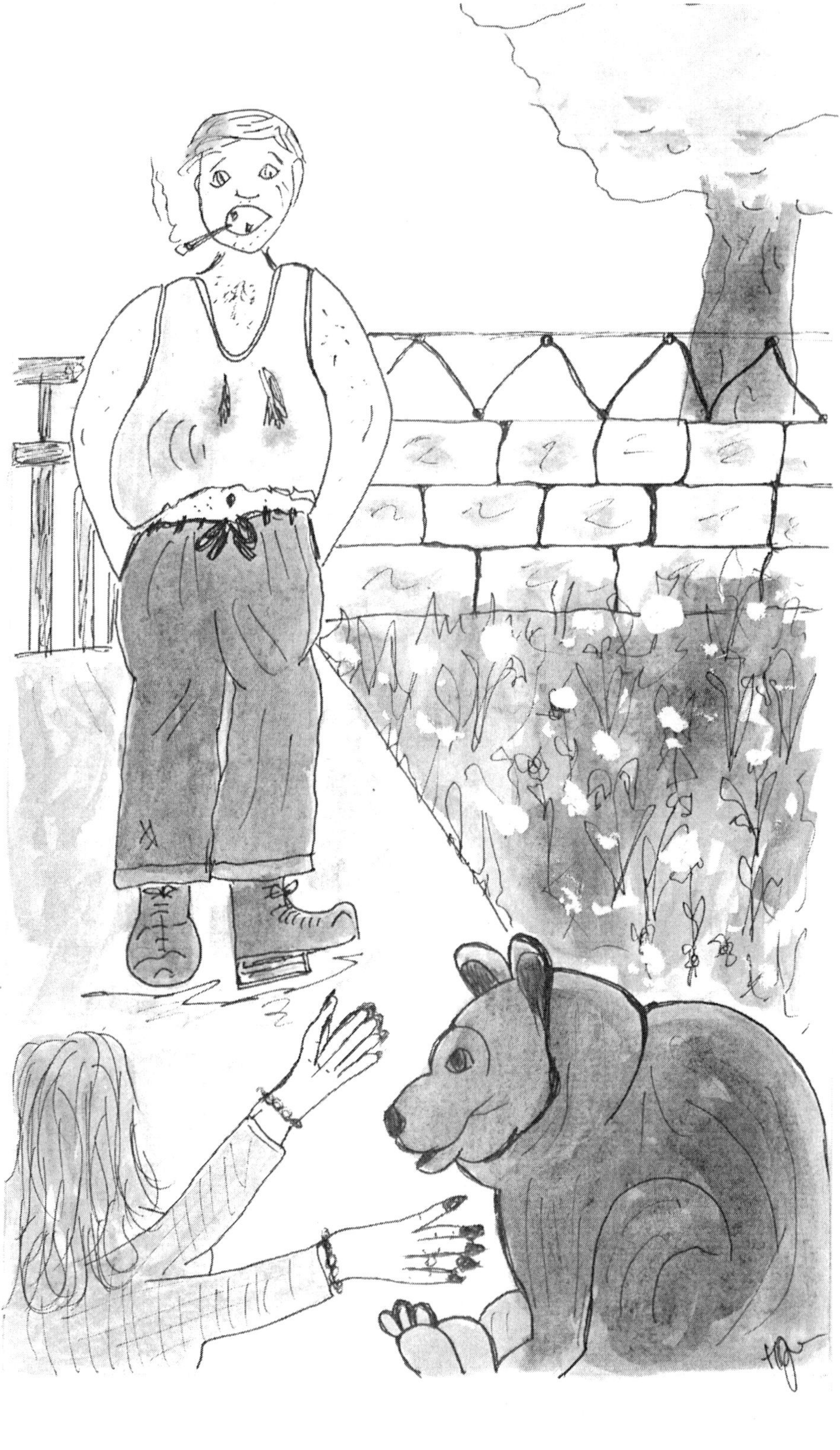

Our Devotion

How soft your fur feels, the gentle brown eyes that have gazed at me with love for over fifteen tenderness filled years, have now blued over and need constant steroid attention. Strange really, no matter how ill I am in mind or body, I never neglect my old friend as I do myself. Your every need is catered for – medication, full tummy, every day runs on your beloved field in the sunshine. "Yes!" you can still run as the hip Dysplasia (the dreaded enemy of German Shepherds) has not blighted your life, yet still, with all my care and love I know our time together is nearing its end. Cancer was the diagnosis, my stomach knots with fear as I envisage the closing of this chapter of complete devotion. Darling girl, you have so enriched my life, I've learned generosity of spirit watching how you always shared your food, toys, home and mummy with the countless lost or injured animals I've rescued and brought home. Never once have you shown aggression; for your beautiful heart only knows kindness surely you are a fine example of how all humans should be. So, slumber on sweet old lady, mummy loves you.

And when, if you are no longer at peace with the life we share together, I will help you leave me, I'll nuzzle the fur around your ears that no longer hear my call, I'll kiss those once glowing velvet brown eyes, now almost sightless with old age, place chocky in your gentle mouth and feel your glorious heart stop its beat, and cry. My old heart be broken.

But for now, through buttercup fields, you still can run delightedly, chasing your yellow ball, my exquisite girl, butterflies with gossamer wings you chase on a summer's breeze, this sunshine morn. Gentle brown eyes, pools of love, your coat gleams with health, warmed by the generous sun. You hear my call and legs strong and vibrant hurry you to my side returning your precious ball. Always by my side, in each other's hearts, you and I. Sweet, sweet memories I will keep until I join you.

But reality lies silent and still and so very cold, pretty 'goodbye' flowers lie between paws that no longer carry you to me, no more will you be warmed by the sun, forever cold, lost to me. Your majestic spent old body now lies in peaceful endless slumber, and I miss you so. For I have had to say 'farewell' to you my dearest dear to send you on the only journey we could not take together. I gave to you my greatest act of love, sweet death when you were ready and with great dignity you let its kindness embrace you.

No more struggles to stand on tired weak old legs, no more trying to see through eyes misted by time, no more straining to hear my words of love and comfort for you are young and healthy once more – so stop and play in heaven's buttercup fields and wait for me. Don't spoil your youthful joy by missing me as I do you, just shake off the fetters of old age and rejoice in your endless youth. For I will find you once again and we will stroll in buttercup fields for eternity.

And so, I had held your old grey face and kissed the misted eyes that gazed with trusting love into mine, you heard so clearly I'm sure my whispered words of love and our tearful 'goodbye'. And your fronded tail wagged for me. Chocolate melted on the tongue that had given me thousands of gentle kisses during our many years together, with a contented sigh your tail stopped its wag, and you were gone from me, forever. Yet still, you live on in my memory, forever gentle devoted and kind – my precious old Sophie, together as always, in buttercup fields.

To the top of a snowy hill we took our last journey on a bitter morn, and you watched your mum lay you to a deserved rest from your secret heaven, where butterflies grace the glens on tireless wings and flowers never fade and sweet creatures like you are made young again, no more the pain of age. And so you lay my dearest dear, safe in death, waiting for the spring buttercups and I miss you so.

And the years will pass and strangers will pause and read the words I carved with love into the stone that celebrated your fifteen years of devotion with me. And the birds will sing their sweet song and we will be reunited at last and our spirits will roam forever through buttercup fields.

And yes, I will take another journey to see the glorious Maple I planted so long ago, that will one day shelter our invisible spirits at the top of a snow-covered hill. That's where you now have laid for over twenty sad lonely years my dearest dear, safe in death, waiting for the spring buttercups and me, nestled by an old dry-stone wall. I miss you!

And did you watch me soon after our goodbye when I brought to you the Maple sapling from our garden that you loved? I planted it with care, a lasting crimson tribute to you, for nesting birds to call home with their babies as the years fly by.

And so, I needed kind understanding hearts and strong arms to help me on my last visit to you, for now I'm an old lady, just as you were. I could see the crimson leaves fluttering in the breeze against a moody sky at the top of the hill. My helpers brushed away the moss that obscured the words of love I'd carved on your memorial stone a lifetime ago. I leaned against the now mature Maple tree, no longer the sapling of years gone by. Lola, the last dog of my life was nestled in my arms as we listened together to nesting birds singing amongst its leaves of crimson glory.

Out wait is nearly over my darling old lady, and the buttercup fields and you are calling to me.

Caroline, My Friend

We first met nine years ago when she rented a house just around the corner from mine. This was the latest in a succession of properties, and her living there was not to last long either.

Her husband (soon to be ex) fancied himself as an entrepreneur, in actual fact; he was a total loser whose financial losses pushed his family ever nearer to the gutter.

Caroline used to teach piano at the weekends to youngsters, but this stopped on the day she walked around the corner only to see her beloved piano being loaded in a van ,sold by her husband for more whisky, she presumed.

At last, she could take no more and left to live in a council house with her daughters, and she loathed it as she was a real lady and the drug dealers on street corners left a lot to be desired. But at least she was free of him and set about trying to get yet another home together for her girls.

At this time, I had many contacts and was able to attain the items she needed at a price she could afford. At last, all seemed to be going well for my friend.

Her old mum and dad lived in Bradford, and she visited most weekends when off work. She was a Medical Secretary, so knew very well that her mother's mithered symptoms signified Dementia. This tiny lady also had a weak heart, had had a mastectomy and was the unwilling owner of a colostomy bag.

Caroline's dad was, at the time, eighty-one years old and found looking after the Wife he'd adored for over sixty years more than he could easily cope with.

So, a very worried Caroline left the council house she hated in the care of her daughters and moved to Bradford to look after the parents she loved.

I really missed her, but once in a while she would collect Ziggy and me, and we would stay in the attic of her mum's Victorian terraced house.

It was lovely up there under the rafters; I could, at last, be the little girl on a sleepover, that I was never allowed when I was really a little girl.

Her mum and dad thrived on the loving care she gave with such a generous heart, and I used to tell her "Every old person in the world should be blessed with a Caroline." She'd laugh and continue putting her mum's delicate make-up on before changing her colostomy bag, never once showing the nausea she felt and in so doing upsetting the mother she worshipped.

Alice was going downhill fast a few months later, and even though Caroline nursed her around the clock, the old lady died at home, safe, clean, happy, and pain-free in her own bed. Just as she'd had prayed to the God she believed in.

The loss of her mother pushed Caroline to take anti-depressants to just get through a day's work at the health centre, that was conveniently placed just across the road from where she still lived with her old dad.

At lunchtime, she would pop home to fix him a drink and his favourite cheese and chutney butties. He now had a struggle with all food as he'd mislaid his dentures.

Now it was his turn to be struck with the dreaded Dementia, and Caroline was worn out making him safe, as he had taken to wandering in the night, sometimes up the street. She had two sisters only a couple of miles away, but just as in many families, the entire care fell on one, exhausted Caroline.

Finally, it became too, too much and with relief and regret she let her old dad go into a home, with 24 h care and chats with people of his own era, he seemed to thrive for a while, playing the piano and singing to the other delighted residents. But before long, then of course he died also.

Caroline had, if you remember, given up her home to care for her parents until their deaths, and relied on the roof her parent's house provided. But this roof was not to keep her safe for long as her two sisters insisted on their share of the house, even though they both had lovely properties of their own, which of course rendered Caroline homeless.

But a solution was very soon found and on the day she closed the door of her childhood home for the very last time, and destiny provided it.

She was so excited at this new start in life. At last, she was not burdened by the debts of an idiot husband; she was not a carer anymore, her girls had got their own homes, and even her old cat died, so she longer had the vet's fees to try to keep it alive. She had now rented her daughter's house as she had now moved in with her boyfriend.

At last, Caroline belonged to herself and with her small inheritance, bought a wonderful piano to replace the one stolen and sold by her ex. She was worried she had wasted money, but I told her it was the finest way to remember her parents, as when she played their favourite tune her parents would dance in heaven to it. This thought seemed to comfort her but the piano stayed wrapped whilst she finished her building and decorating plans.

The 3rd of November was my birthday, and I arrived home from a holiday with my friends to find my card from Caroline waiting on the doormat. Two little bears hugged each other, and the words were 'What would I do without you?' we talked on the phone that Saturday as she was getting ready to drive to bring my present.

"Have you finished your entire jobs darling?" I asked.

"Nearly, I've just got to finish painting one wall then I can put the furniture back and unwrap my piano. I can't wait to play it."

I then made the suggestion that I have cursed myself for, because if I hadn't, maybe my Caroline would still be alive. In trying to be considerate I suggested,

"How about you come up next week instead, wouldn't it be nice to return home to all your jobs already finished?"

This she agreed, and we both looked forward to the next week's visit.

That Saturday night she went out with her daughter and daughter's boyfriend, the story goes they continued drinking when they got back to her daughter's cottage. At around midnight, the daughter went to bed, leaving Caroline and the boyfriend downstairs. At 3 am, Barbara awoke to hear laughter coming from downstairs. Now what happened next, not even the coroner was told the truth about. But it was so traumatic that Caroline stumbled the two streets home, where she took every pill she could get down her, obviously she believed death to be her only option.

The next day (Sunday) her child (who I blame for her mother's death to this day) let herself into Caroline's cottage after being unable to reach her by phone to apologise. Apologise for what? Only she really knows and is still keeping quiet. I hope her guilt makes her life hell. She finds pools of her mother's vomit and then her mother, unconscious, on the laminate floor. Whatever had forced Caroline into this last action was so mind-blowingly severe that it cancelled out all that was now good in her life.

Caroline is put in intensive care in exactly the same bed her niece died in from an overdose only weeks before. How strange is that?

It was such a cold morning when the ringing phone by my bed dragged me from sleep at 5.20 am. Her daughter's voice said,

"Can you get here, my mum has only hours to live?"

At the same time I received this terrible news, I heard an injured dog howling its grief outside. I went out without shoes, stood on the pavement in that freezing rain and listened, then I heard that pitiful howl again, but it was no injured dog, it was my injured soul's primaeval howling of my grief into the darkness.

I've never had the nerve to drive distances as I have the navigational skills of a rice pudding and an uncontrollable fear of being lost, as I once was as a tiny girl.

My son lives only a mile away but hates me, so it was out of the question to ask for his help to reach dying Caroline.

Darling Jackie (who I'd only been reunited with for three weeks) threw herself out of bed when she heard my phoned despair and by 6 am she was driving me to say my "goodbyes" to my best friend. My card from her had said "what would I do without you?' Well, my darling Caroline, you did not have to do without me, for golden-hearted Jackie brought me to your side.

Caroline looked so at peace and but for the assortment of wires she could easily have passed for just taking a nap. I talked to her of the things we held dear and reminded her of how she slipped off the edge of the bed in her silk nighty with laughter when I jived with my dog Ziggy to Jerry Lee Lewis's 'Great Balls of Fire' on the landing. How we had driven to Castleton in Derbyshire where the steep gorge nearly burnt out the brakes on the steep incline. I told her I could not wait to listen to her play the piano (that still stayed wrapped never to be played by her) but in her deep slumber I know she heard my voice, as just one gentle tear ran down her pale cheek.

It took my dearest friend three weeks to die, not from the overdose but from the complications brought on by it. Flying with the Angels.

Her girls told everyone she had been admitted to hospital with a heart attack, so much nicer, don't you agree, than the overdose they would have to answer just one question about WHY? I was never told when or where she was to finally rest, but I believe it to be somewhere in Yorkshire, where her mum and dad rest.

But I'd already said my goodbyes I love you! on that freezing morning four weeks ago. I had howled with grief when told she would never visit me again, but this time I knew it was no injured dog, just me alone in the kitchen wishing I'd never delayed her visit to me, for in not delaying it (the visit) it would never have happened. Yet maybe (just like my brother John) death by her own hand was her destiny.

I remembered the last time we went out; it was to a continental market where the Dutch bulb man displayed wondrous tulips the like of which as I'd never seen before. I bought so many I could hardly carry them, and Caroline chose red ones for the tubs outside her cottage.

Mine came up the following spring, and each one smiled the smile of Caroline in the sunshine. My friend never got to see the lovely faces of her blooms as by then she rested under a tree with her mum and dad.

And now her everlasting memory rests under her favourite blossom tree in my front garden. On it is placed a plaque it reads 'My garden is dedicated to the memory of Caroline my precious, gentle friend who bravely chose her own destiny. Forever flying with the Angels' People stop to admire the tulips I plant every year as a tribute to the friendship that had no end and they ask about you, Caroline. I tell of your untimely death and your laughing happy time with me, and now twelve years have passed taking with them all the adventures we had planned for the future we believed would be ours, that future that was taken by the secret misdeeds of your own child. Shame on her!!

Sweet dreams my Caroline, my friend xx

The friendship that can come to an end, never really began.

Pubilius Syrus, Moral Sayings

Friends bring out the beautiful things in each other that no one else looks hard enough to find.

Friendship is a living thing that lasts only as long as it is nourished with kindness, sympathy, and understanding.

The wonderful things about friends is that they can grow separately and yet not grow apart.

Don't bore your friends with your troubles. Tell them to your enemies, who will be delighted to hear about them.

Friendship has a special meaning when you have someone with whom to share tears and laughter, fears and dreams, and silence when the time for words is past.

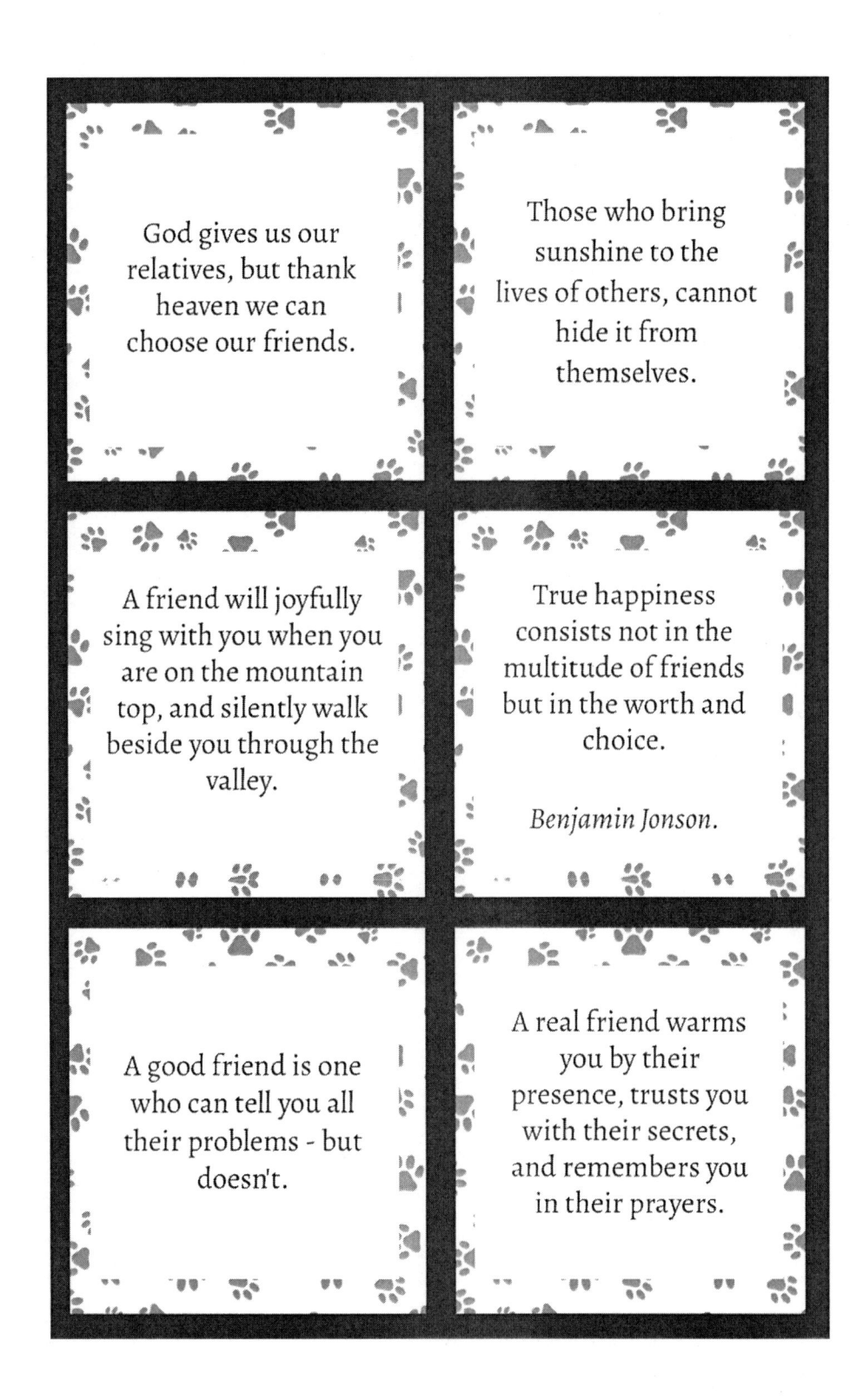

God gives us our relatives, but thank heaven we can choose our friends.

Those who bring sunshine to the lives of others, cannot hide it from themselves.

A friend will joyfully sing with you when you are on the mountain top, and silently walk beside you through the valley.

True happiness consists not in the multitude of friends but in the worth and choice.

Benjamin Jonson.

A good friend is one who can tell you all their problems - but doesn't.

A real friend warms you by their presence, trusts you with their secrets, and remembers you in their prayers.

True friendship is like sound health; the value of it is seldom known until it be lost.

Charles Caleb Colton, Lacon

Because we can't call people without wings angels, we call them friends.

Close your eyes to the faults of others and watch the doors of friendship swing wide.

Before borrowing money from a friend, decide which you need more.

If people knew what each said about the other, there wouldn't be five friends in the whole world.

A friend is someone who knows you as you are, understands where you've been, and accepts who you've become.

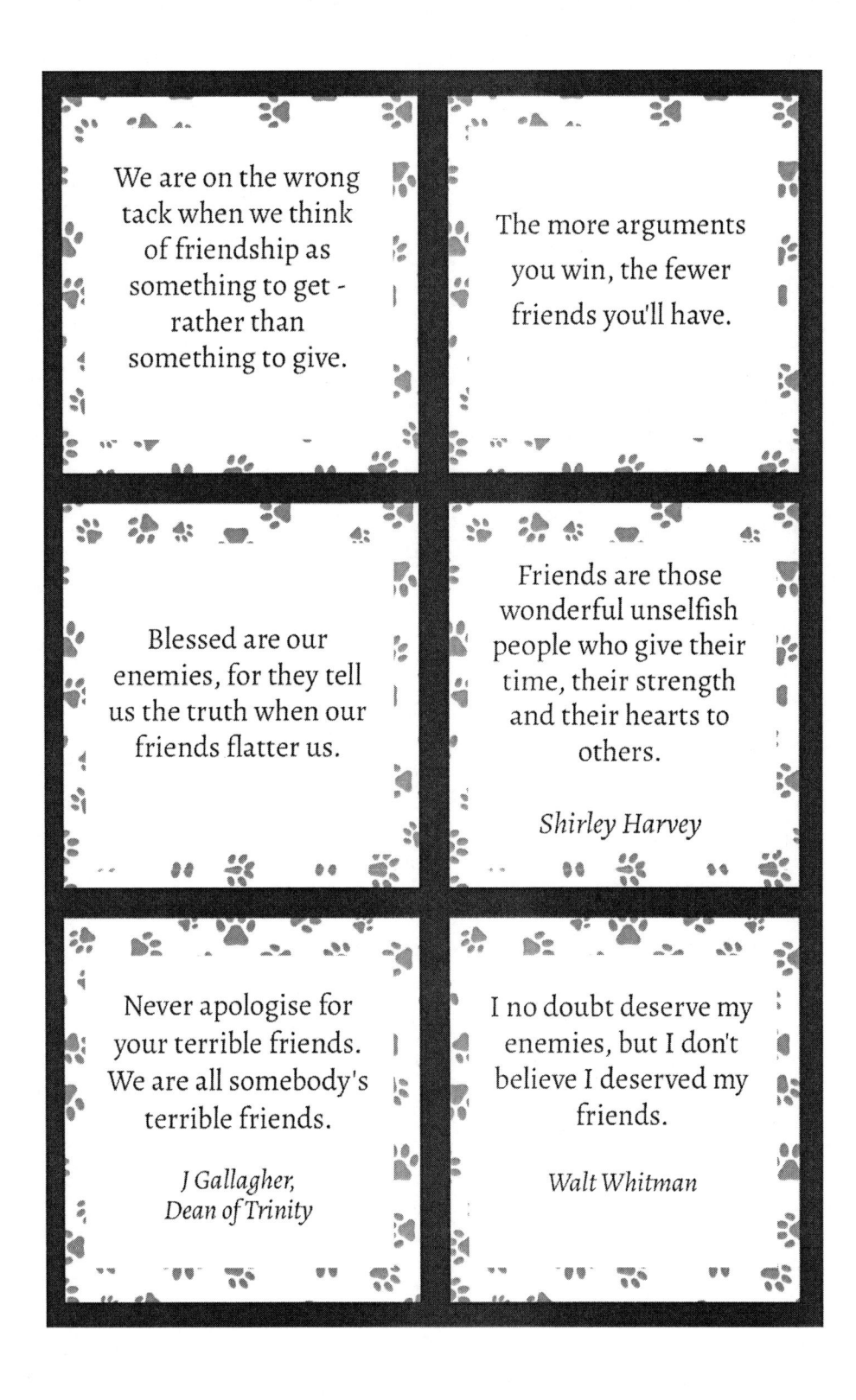

We are on the wrong tack when we think of friendship as something to get - rather than something to give.

The more arguments you win, the fewer friends you'll have.

Blessed are our enemies, for they tell us the truth when our friends flatter us.

Friends are those wonderful unselfish people who give their time, their strength and their hearts to others.

Shirley Harvey

Never apologise for your terrible friends. We are all somebody's terrible friends.

*J Gallagher,
Dean of Trinity*

I no doubt deserve my enemies, but I don't believe I deserved my friends.

Walt Whitman

Eddie

I'd gone to stay with my Caroline and her old Dad in Bradford, and I just loved it there.

They lived on a handsome Victorian terrace made of York stone, and even though they were the only white people living there, the Pakistani residents of the remaining terrace treated them with kindness and respect which was returned in abundance as Caroline's dad, who spoke their native language from his many years in their homeland.

Little were we all to know at that time that we would never share our lives again in that welcoming old house. No more would I sleep in the attic room with my Ziggy, looking at the stars through the skylight, before slumber.

I'm sat here now (in the home I've loved since 1962) – some seven years later, a lonely old lady with nothing to look forward to, what I would give to pack a bag, put on Ziggy's lead and find myself gazing at the stars in that magical old attic room.

For not long after that visit (where we had trawled the local fabric mills looking for upholstery cloth), Caroline's daddy died, and with him, part of my friend died also.

During that visit, Caroline persuaded me to buy a new outfit, and whilst she loved buying clothes, oh God, I loathed it, and I was wearing my new togs on our last search for cloth (which incidentally I never found!) this (up until now) was an unknown place to both of us, and we found ourselves taking a completely different route back to my home, my visit sadly at an end.

The Friday rush hour traffic was in full flow, it was as bad an evening as the day had been, the rain lashed and the wind blew fluttering down the last of the autumn leaves from the trees. We rounded the corner of a steep wooded island with a deep grass banking onto the dual carriageway. Taking care to merge into the heavy traffic, Caroline did not notice what I had, and in that instant, my heart broke. For in the mud at the bottom of banking lay a young foal, trying valiantly to get to its feet in the slippery mire.

Now Caroline was very used to me finding things to help whether they be on four feet or two, whether feet or wings propelled them through life, if they needed help I was the woman to give it. And many is the time I'd taken a route, unwanted or unknown, and right before my eyes is a creature in desperate need and with all the love, time and money I can muster that help is theirs, even if it is death.

So, I stood drenched to the skin, in the once resplendent new outfit of only fifteen minutes ago. It was obvious this little lad had been beaten badly, many, many times, as there were new injuries as well as semi healed ones. His eyes rolled in pain and panic whilst his forelegs thrashed the pool of mud trying to get his back legs to stand. Of course, they never would again, how was he to know, that tiny tortured child horse, that his back was broken?

I cradled his head on my lap as Caroline phoned the rescue charity – now how many sets of headlights lit up the carriageway tragedy before they finally arrived? I'll never really know. But I sat there giving comfort to a terrified baby horse as best I could, it felt like an eternity. The emaciated body shuddered in the freezing rain, and my first request to the man in the blue rescue uniform was for a horse blanket. "Oh, we don't carry those," says he as he picked his way through the mud. "But I suppose I could send for one."

At this point I will tell you, I have no faith whatsoever in that charity, in my opinion, they are all shaking tins, donation seeking charlatans, who use a very big proportion of heart given donations on new vans and pristine uniforms. God forbid they should get muddy, as I had. This episode would turn out to be yet another example of their stinking ineptitude.

A further new white van finally appears, this time it's driven by a red-haired woman who had taken two hours to arrive, and now my disgust knew no bounds when I was informed they only could provide cat blankets, crocheted I suppose by some old dear, them not being enough to cover a Siamese cat, let alone a bloody horse. Further outrage nearly blew all my gaskets, as they informed me that "No," they did not have resident Vets who come out to scenes like this, a private Vet was on call, but he was busy on the other side of the fucking Pennines. God help us, and this was the way old ladies' legacies were spent. Posh vans and uniforms, yet no Vet, no blankets, SHAME ON THE SODS. The mind boggles.

Poor Caroline is at her wit's end as I've turned into a mud-covered, horse cradling vampire, who in one sentence whispered words of love to an injured foal and in the next spat obscenities to the uniformed useless prats who did fuck all!

It was at this point that the male incompetent made the observation to Caroline that he believed her friend (me) to be schizophrenic, the hard-faced useless git, at least I cared.

Then, trolling around the corner came a sight to behold. How this lass even stood (let alone walk) in heels so high is beyond me, but totter she valiantly did. It was obvious by her provocative clothes, she was a member of the oldest profession in the world, and she called out in distress and anger when she saw the foal. Taking no heed of the mud, she took off her skyscrapers and walked barefoot to stroke his sweet face. Then, with language that could put a ship's parrot to shame, she berated that so-called charity for not doing something about the foal after all the concerned complaints she had placed with them. Time and again they had promised to end the cruelty that he endured every day of his short life and yet, here he lay many months later, broken, afraid, starved, and begging for death and Heaven's pastures.

She told of the times she had witnessed him being beaten by this young thug with an iron bar whilst tethered to a tree at the top of the steep banking, the same banking where he now lay, slowly dying at the bottom of it. This information sent me further berserk, so much so the incompetent twat from the so-called animal rescue locked himself in his pristine bloody van and sent for the police. Now, they did not take long to arrive I can tell you, as they believed a madwoman was about to decapitate a so-called Public Servant. They tried to reason with me to let the horse go, but I told them only my arrest would shift me. In the meantime, our lady of the night had returned from God knows where armed with a box of apples and carrots. Her finery of an hour ago was now a sodden memory, but she laughingly said there was probably a blind man somewhere out there who needed a wank. In my heartbroken state, her words lightened the situation and made me laugh like hell at the image.

I demanded a Police Marksman to come and end Eddie's miserable young life and a man with a gun was duly sent for. It was now 10 pm, I'd lay in filth for over five hours and never had I felt more needed and wanted.

Liz, my golden-hearted, now forever friend, told me the foal was called Eddie and like me, she was in tears that mingled with the still pouring rain. The poor little lad knew nothing of lovely treats and showed little interest in the proffered carrot. That is until I chewed up some and placed it in his mouth. Oh boy, this he liked, and in a couple of minutes, he was sampling apple for probably the first time also and there we both lay, with even our bones wet, or so it felt. Me biting off chunks of apple and carrot and feeding it to that darling broken boy. One of the police remarked that apples would not make him well again. He got a viperous reply as well, saying "I was not trying to get the broken boy to live; I was making sure his death is filled with treats, love and kindness, to take to heaven."

The man with the gun stood above us, demanding I move away whilst the merciful job was done. I kissed Eddie's pretty beaten face, placed a final piece of apple in his mouth, and he was still chewing it as the bullet sent him to heaven.

Liz decided her punters could sod off and staggered home alone, and to this day we laugh on the phone and remember the sad broken little foal that started our friendship.

My darling Caroline ended her life not so much later, I wonder, is she now taking the place of me and feeding apples to Eddie, in heaven?

I miss her each and every day these past lonely years without her wonderful friendship, for, in deciding to leave this life, she took with her all the little adventures we had planned to share. I can't face them without her, but still I hope and wonder, can you have adventures in Heaven?

Dear Caroline

Oh, how quickly time passes; it's now nearly five years since we saw one another.

I miss you so very much and hope you're happy in the new home you've chosen. It's such a pity that it's so far away but I know that one day I'll be able to visit and probably stay with you.

Have you got a nice new garden? The one you used to enjoy here at my home is at its best at the moment and people remark on its beauty as they walk past.

Ziggy is an old man now, one hundred and six in doggy years, and I've also got a lovely girly black poodle called Lola. Pity you can't see and play with her, as she's just joyous.

Have you been able to get in touch with your mum and dad as planned? I do hope so as I know it would have made you all so happy.

The weather here has been very rainy, that's ok as the plants thrive on it, but I believe where you have moved to the weather stays perfect all the time.

I miss not being able to put our plans into action, as they are now worthless without you, but possibly when we finally meet up again, we can share yet more adventures.

Until we meet again, sweet dreams love Zara.

PS: Oh how I wish you had not killed yourself five years ago, breaking my old heart, and taking with you all our plans and that your choice of heaven is a happy one, see you soon xxxxx

July 2012

It is now the present day, and the recollections of the past are trying to destroy the euphoric energy of my manic bipolar mind, and I must use this respite from despair to catch up with all the jobs waiting to be done. I can only function in any way whatsoever when the dark side of what possesses me is pushed into the depths of my subconscious, yet always lying-in wait to bring confusion and suicidal despair.

But this morning, a sixty-nine-year-old lady sits on her bed and tries to write in longhand fast enough to keep up with the torrent of words my manic mind spills out. A waterfall of words that I don't know will ever be enough, for this exercise is not to bring fame and fortune, but to try to cleanse my being of all that is locked within, with the help of hypnosis. So much pain, fear, laughter, hope, desire and disappointment, all the past trying to form some kind of order and sense in the written word. My pen flies across the paper, a scribble only I can decipher, my spelling shot to hell, for I must hurry, I believe hungry death beckons me, and I will rush into its welcome arms, home at last. But please death not until I finish my book — my one and only book.

But for now, dear reader, (if there ever should be such a thing as you) are reading this, I apologise for my erratic jumping from past to present, for confusing your (no doubt) healthy minds, for God help me, my written word has made me bring to life tragic situations, long-buried, I've cried and laughed and wished and daydreamed, and at the end of it, all I'm just an old lady sat writing, trying to control a flying pen that seems to have a life of its own.

I've managed, at last, to come to terms with what I am, to allow myself the dark terrifying times when I can't believe I will ever laugh again, but on the wondrous gentle mornings I awake, and the darkness of the night terrors are over and even my mind has been cleansed. Gone now is the half hearing, where every sound is a jumbled mockery, happy eyes gorge themselves on colour so vivid that they light up my soul. I climb out of bed and feel as though my feet don't even touch the carpet, my body is lighter (if only) in tune with my mind. The half-crippled old lady of last night, whose arthritic pain disturbed her sleep, is now reborn.

Facing this wondrous morn, renewed energy gives me the inspiration and strength to conquer whatever my mind inspires. And it's during these blessed episodes that I have created a home and gardens that not only delight me but also the rare people who are ever shown them!

Years ago, I had no idea how to set about and have the innate knowledge of completing any unknown task to perfection. E.C.T. and hypnosis changed all that.

But the instant healing Carlo Sanchez gave my broken mind was long into the future and how I wish I'd been guided to his door thirty years prior. How different my life could have been?

Life now in 2012 is gentle, gone are the lustful cravings of a voluptuous young woman, it's such a release, belonging to oneself and not relying on a man for pleasure. I'm alone, but rarely lonely anymore – my two beloved dogs are my constant loyal companions, and I hear their footfall as they follow me whilst I garden.

With age has come the passion for my garden and many are the persons who stand and gaze at its glory, just like every task I undertake it has to be to its zenith and my garden spills over with the glories of nature. I live around the corner from a hotel, on, what is now, a far busier road than the one I moved to in 1962 as a young woman of nineteen.

This hotel directs its visitors to my front garden on their evening strolls, where they gather at the wrought iron topped Cotswold wall and point out to each other flowers of interest. Cameras and phones take home memories of my garden and as I stand and chat with these unknown visitors, I'm proud that they also love what I have created.

I have a "bugger off" sign on my front gate intended to divert the sods that constantly shove menus, lying political crap, more menus, tarmacking path makers and yet more bloody menus through my letterbox, and in so doing, alert my dogs to the intrusion of their home, this they take great exception to and once again trash the back of the letterbox. All of their barking and damage for a menu that is just bin fodder. So, try a "bugger off" sign if you dare, not only does it stop the unwanted flyers but also gives the camera-wielding garden lovers a giggle on their twilight stroll, to admire my garden.

It's now 9 am, time to release my dogs from their bedroom in readiness for toilet relief, medication, morning picnic and runs on buttercup strewn fields.

I, of course, have been awake many hours, doing the chores of the day, deadheading the flowers and preparing the medicines that keep my pets pain-free. For my rescued terrier Ziggy is now fifteen years old, and his stiff legs need the comforting help of thirty-five quid's worth of medication. Lola is still a little child, a frantic poodle being only four years old, this black bundle of curls was born with a defective bladder and to keep her from unwanted (and unknown to her) wetting, she wears nappies in the house and another £50 per week (I'm not pet insured!) for bladder medication, plus tablets to keep the pituitary tumour on her tiny brain under control. All this readily spent money on my furry children greases the vet's palm week after expensive week and he relishes it! So, be it, a pain-free old boy and little happy dry girl, and a home that does not smell like a zoo, it sounds a fair swap to me for a few pieces of paper, does it not?

Are you bored or laughing? Or intrigued at my ramblings? Do I continue? While my mania lasts, I think I will.

I'm Now 70 and I Bloody Hate It!

In what seems like the blink of an eye I'm there, yet strangely at the same time, I have existed forever. Snippets of who I was, what I became, creep from the corners of my subconscious, perplexing and exhilarating, all aided by my encounter with Carlo Sanchez my Parapsychologist.

Maybe the human crop of 1942 would have been a perfect vintage except for that small damaged seed, ME, who grew into the child a dimension separate from all others? Who then became the beautiful woman whose body men craved and whose mind they fled from? For I looked like every red-blooded man's dream come true, but in fact, I was all his nightmares. And yet, some loved and desired me for many years and tolerated as best they could the outpourings of a mind tortured by Bipolar.

So, as I screamed my dismay seventy years ago at being pushed into a life I should never have lived, the pattern was already set. Bombs broke the night's silence; ack-ack guns traced the searching beams of light amongst the stars. It was 2.45 am 3 November 1942, and I'D ARRIVED!

Seventy years have flown by and yet taken forever. I'm at a place now where I'm no longer ruled by hormones, no longer craving the touch of the latest lover. I'm free of lust, and it's very liberating. I believe it to be Salvador Dali who remarked that the first morning he awoke without an erection, and the need for a woman to sort it, was when he truly belonged to himself and that's how I feel (without the erection of course!) That's how I feel, no longer am I held hostage by bodily desires, and I love it. I know now there is no ulterior motive when a man passing my garden remarks on its beauty, I accept the compliment for what it is, a clean admiration of nature's bounty with no hidden sexual agenda, what a treat!

I awoke alone on my seventieth birthday as I've done for most of the sixty-nine before. I've got partly used to the solitude of my life, but I don't like it; I just tolerate how it is. My dogs gave me their usual rapturous morning welcome, behaving as if we had been apart for longer than a night's sleep.

Even though I was very disappointed by the news that a friend could not share my birthday weekend after all, I held back, as best I could, the black loneliness that waited to embrace me.

Then, the phone rang and rang and my precious sister wished me love and hugs and my lovely Jackie rang from Athens promising she would see me in a few days' time, and she did.

Annette, bless her was not offended when I asked for her company as a more than worthy substitute for Molly Anne, so off we set on my birthday trip out, two friends laughing in the sunshine, who can ask for anything more?

Expensive and flashy places, where you are judged by how much your handbag costs, are not for me, nor have they ever been.

And so therefore we sat, with a steaming platter of the best fish and chips known to man, before us, waiting to be devoured.

Tummies full, a happy saunter arm in arm around that small Macclesfield town and then off to my favourite place of all, within a day's reach that is. Flora is in a place called Henbury in Macclesfield and is owned by a dear little friend of mine called 'Cary'. This wondrous place of themed separate rooms will fill your eyes and heart with delight. To go at Christmas time turns (all who have been lucky enough to experience its wonder) into children once again. This place is a dream come true, filled floor to ceiling with pictures, lamps, mirrors, flowers, baubles, and every pretty thing a childlike heart can desire. At first looking you believe it would be too expensive to even ask the prices, but you would be so excited to realise that Cary's charges enable every one of us to own a little bit of heaven, no matter the contents of our purse.

Twilight, time to get home to yet another rapturous welcome from my darling dogs, they had their food we cuddled and watch TV together. All very simple and understated had been my birthday, but I was content and happy, who needs anything else?

The next day being Sunday, I was invited to share my neighbours, Sandra and John's special place, Willowpool, for a birthday meal. We had the loveliest time and if you ever get the chance to go and find yourself in Knutsford Cheshire, you would have loved it too. Unfortunately, the next time I went to that wonderful place, it had been turned into a housing estate, what a shame!

I'm now seventy and two weeks old and if anyone had predicted I would ever know this day, this time of my life, I'd have called them deluded to say the least. Looking back on the horror of continued mental illness, I don't know how I've found the courage and strength to keep on going, but I have. Never, ever, would I believe that (at this biblical milestone of three score years and ten) I'd have the strength and determination to plant three hundred donated tulips, two hundred daffodils (some of them pink!) plus numerous Hyacinths and Alliums. But I have! Come the spring my garden will once again be wondrous. Will I still be alive to rejoice and admire it? Who knows – who cares?

The garden that stops people in their tracks to smile and take photos of, it sleeps its winter dark slumber. Under the enriched soil, lies a wondrous bounty of nature just waiting for the spring sun to reach its calling point and they will answer, "oh yes" in their hundreds, they will answer its warming excitement and push their beautiful faces up through the darkness of winter, to revel in its glow. All my hard work will be worth it. I'll praise their beauty as I always do and watch with pride as yet another photograph is taken of my magical garden. All is well at last.

Ziggy Doo Dah

As I write this on a July day in 2012, the sun shines after many weeks of rain, Lola sits on my bed interested in life outside my window. Her poodle black curls gleam in the rays of the sun, she is happy and young whilst Ziggy and I are in the late autumn of our days.

Fifteen Christmas days have passed since this decaying, tortured, barely alive scrap of a dog was placed in my hand, so very tiny. A boy neighbour found this tragic mite dying in a gutter alone. Wet through, too far gone to even shiver and just a breath away from merciful death. But death for him was not to be as destiny was averted when his seemingly lifeless body was welcomed into my home. Sophie, my German Shepherd, came to inspect the latest rescue, for this old lady had always shared her life with lost or damaged strays, and this mutilated mess was the latest in a long line.

On inspection, I found to my horror and disgust the vile torture this tiny animal had suffered. Some sub-human maggot had torn off his testicles, resulting in strands of gangrenous flesh hanging from his tiny, malnourished body. Tar had been melted onto his tummy and penis so he could never empty the distended bladder, that I at first took to be a puppy-filled stomach of a very young girly dog. And the vile bastards did not stop there; more torture was yet inflicted and endured with cigarette burns and a much-slashed throat that would need twenty-two stitches to mend.

With lips and tongue of blue, he laid on his back on my hand, legs splayed out, head lolling, no sign of life or heartbeat. I ran a bowl of gentle warm water and mixed a paste of cooking oil and washing up liquid. I immersed the tiny little body in the warming liquid and gently massaged the black hard crust of tar with my concoction. Slowly, slowly, it started to break down (still no sign of life) and when his redraw tiny tummy and penis were exposed, this little lad wee-wee'd and wee-wee'd for a full twenty minutes and in so doing, that huge stomach deflated.

Was that a little movement I felt? Dear God, it was. I dried him and after making a body sling out of a paisley scarf, I placed him against my heart. And there he stayed night and day, only leaving my beating sanctuary to relieve himself. After the decayed flesh was cut from his tiny botty, it healed as did his throat after my vets' ministrations.

Ziggy learnt to trust me and no more wet himself if I picked up a rolled magazine, he expected being hit (as before) and was still very easily afraid. The old lady dog who had helped make him live, now lay silent as he kissed her goodbye. Life had gone full circle, and I needn't have worried about my broken empty, lonely heart after losing Sophie, because that little injured boy climbed right in! and has filled that empty space for fifteen years, so far.

Good Bye Is Closer.

My very being churns with dread as I watch your faltering steps. Your ears no longer hear the words of love spoken as they have been for sixteen and half years now. Your once brown eyes gaze at me through their blue haze, and I know that each day, each moment together is a bonus.

We have loved and played all these years and grown old together.

The damaged baby boy that you once were, grew into a devoted bigger boy, the cruelty of your past hidden from all, except us. Sometimes something unknown to me would transport you back and once again you would cower, making yourself as small as possible, trying to be invisible. Then, I would coax you into my arms to tell you that all was well, stroke your trembling tummy, put a choccy drop in your mouth and see the fear vanish from your eyes yet again.

I pray that I will not have to make the decision to end your life, that nature will take you from me as you sleep in your cosy bed, my Ziggy, my friend, my little broken boy, my little mended old man.

The Last Leaf

A carpet of bronze and gold leaves gentle the crazy paving paths and autumn beckoned winter's icy grip. Bare branches stretched to the heavens; their years' work now done. But in the sunshine of my day of deepest sadness, one lonely leaf danced and played, reluctant to leave the branch that had been its life force. It alone stayed with the mother tree whilst all its siblings had long ago fluttered down, to make my carpet of gold.

By the mauve hydrangea and under the sheltering branches of a magnificent acer, gaped a hole of sorrow, a pile of soil stood at its side soon to be the forever home of my beloved little dog. My darling Ziggy had been my joy and companion for sixteen and a half years, but now he faded before my eyes. I prayed that his strong happy heart would beat no more, that I would find him curled up in his big comfy bed, having left me on a journey that he had to take alone, without his old mum.

Each day he battled to stay with me – still enjoying hugs and kisses, and gobbling up his dinner like never before. The vet's tablets I gave him to make sure he was pain-free, coupled with dementia that blighted my poor old man, changed my Ziggy into a dog so different from the one I loved for sixteen and a half years. He became aggressive towards me, wet and fouled the house times without number and that vile dementia pushed his frail old body to pace back and to, back and to, back and to, endlessly. Yes, he endlessly paced coming to kiss my fingertips as he passed by me yet again. I altered my home and garden to make it safer for my old chap, dreading yet begging, for him to give me his sign that he was ready to leave this life and his old mum.

When he found it difficult to walk, I carried him, when standing to eat his food became a problem; I laid him down to feed him from my fingers. When his feet splayed out like Bambi on the tiled kitchen floor, I got many rubber car mats and covered the floor, so that was another problem solved. I put a barrier of planters across the patio's edge so that he could not pass down the steps into the lower garden and injure himself. The outside light was on all night, and I floodlit the back steps so he could find his way. The back door was open all night for him to relentlessly potter about, and a small table lamp on the kitchen worktop ensured he did not pass from light to darkness.

The progression from being just old to close to death took many months and as each situation affected him, I adjusted my life and home accordingly. I never left him, my neighbour said he was stealing my life and I told her "No I'm giving it freely; there can be no other way between us."

He had two minor strokes, it should have been the end of him, but no, after lying in my arms overnight as I kissed him and told him it was ok to leave me, the morning came, he woke up, and I carried him outside for the toilet, he came in and had such a big breakfast as though nothing had happened to him at all.

It was Thursday the 17th of October the sun was fighting to shine, and my Ziggy had another stroke, it made my old boy stagger in circles and fall down, and I believe it took what little sight cataracts had left alone.

I phoned the vet at once and arranged for my boy to go to sleep the following dinner time, in the home he loved. (That being the soonest the vet could visit) as I did not want my Ziggy to die in a place he'd always hated: the vets.

Those next hours were the most harrowing of my life, and please believe me when I tell you; I've had some terrible events which have very nearly destroyed me.

Ziggy could not be comforted, no matter what, and kept asking to go to the toilet, I don't know how many times I carried him out and supported him whilst he did just a couple of drops of wee-wee. We were both so, so tired my boy and I, but so very long ago I promised him I would love and protect him till the last second of his life and beyond, if only he could manage to live that Christmas Day some sixteen and half years ago, when his mutilated body was put in my hands to try to heal him. In the blink of an eye, all those years have passed and now I was to give him an even bigger show of love than that Xmas day he became my tiny broken treasure.

As I waited for the vet, a set of circumstances, beyond my control, evolved that stole our precious time together, I will not tell you of it now as I don't want the memory of what happened to sully, yet again, his end, even on paper.

"Yes," he died in my arms just as he had lived much of his life. In less than a heartbeat, he was gone from me, free at last from an old body and a tormented mind.

I believe that now his eyes will dance with love and mischief and those old legs, that could not rest, now lie on sweet grass where flowers never fade. I pray he has found Sophie, the mothering Shepherd I loved so much that helped him want to live that fated Christmas day and the months beyond.

It had started to rain by the time I was able to lay him to rest in the garden he loved, the sun was starting to hide, and my soul was torn.

I'd wrapped him in his blanket and gave him a picnic of biscuits for his journey to heaven, leftover from that morning when he turned his old grey face away from me, for the first time ever, that was his sign to me, "mummy help me go."

In his paws a posy of flowers lay, to give to Caroline, my precious dead friend when he reached the heaven he so deserved, and this being his very last journey was the only one he ever took without his old mum.

I told him of my love for him and begged his forgiveness for sending him away from me, and that I could not allow my precious lad to suffer. I really hope he could hear my words and understand.

Just how long had I stayed and talked to him after the last spade of soil became his blanket? I only know I was very wet when I finally went indoors, the rain and tears mingling on my face.

But I remember something so very poignant, the leaf that had not wanted to leave its branch of safety, fluttered and danced down in the last of the sun's rays, a rainbow prettied the sky and that last lonely leaf nestled on Ziggy's grave, both of them could now go back to the earth that awaits us all.

The Ambulance Driver from Hell

Schabyz was the callous, vile jobsworth ambulance man who was sent unneeded to my home the day of my old Ziggy's death; yes, Christyenhoff Schabyz, a vile name for a vile so-called 'man'.

I had made arrangements with my vet to come to my home and gently put my little old boy to sleep. When the time came for this to happen, my vet was operating and could not attend. So, I called a vet I'd never used before – explained how important it was that my darling Ziggy leave this world soon. The next day was the time of the event I so dreaded, and when the vet was late, I phoned in tears to their surgery and was asked if I was ok. "Of course, I'm not ok. I'm having my dog killed, and I'm not well." With this, the dippy receptionist took matters into her own hands and sent for an ambulance to attend to me, and there started one of the worst traumatic days of my life.

Dementia and sixteen and half years of old age had made my boy into a totally different dog than I'd always known and loved. He'd become aggressive – incontinent and a great food thief but with all this, I loved him dearly.

The doorbell rang "Thank God it will soon be over for us my love" I thought. But it was not the vet but an unexpected paramedic. I told him it was a mistake; I wanted a vet, not him, and closed the door. Did he leave it at that? Did he hell! He sent for a backup ambulance that was driven by my worst nightmare. Christyenhoff Schabyz. A vile name that matched the vile man. Both the paramedic and he thumped on my door only to be told they were not needed. The paramedic then went, but Schabyz was to stay parked outside a neighbour's home with his ambulance and sidekick (a scrap of a girl with a smirk and black roots, who seemed to find the distressed old woman with a dying dog slung over her shoulder)-hilarious! Shame on them both.

So, the day that I had planned with great care was shredded by two people who did not give a damn. I'd arranged for a peaceful gentle death at home for my Ziggy, he hated the vets and I did not want his last moments in this dimension spoilt with him being so frightened. A total of £117.50 was the charge for home euthanasia and as we awaited his demise, I thought it the best money I could spend.

I waited and waited, the vet was late and when I phoned the surgery, I was told he had an emergency, it was whilst I was on the phone that Schabyz saw fit to enter into my home through the open front door, <u>UNINVITED</u>. He proceeded to snatch the phone (I was still speaking on) from my hand and started an inane conversation with the vet's nurse. I told him to hang up, he ignored me, so I cut the phone off at the wall of my kitchen. I still had a dying Ziggy over my shoulder. What he did next beggared belief, without a word he snatches it from the wall and walks backwards into the hall holding the phone over his head, far out of my reach, as I tried to take it back from him. Ziggy is distressed. I believed that at any moment the cord would break or the phone itself break from the wall. It did not and then Schabyz did the unthinkable, with my dying old dog still in my arms, he threw the phone with great force against my shin (which hurt like hell), gave me a silent sneer and swaggered up my hall and back to his ambulance, still blocking my neighbour's driveway.

I watched for the vet who was now over one and a half hours late, which seemed a lifetime as my Ziggy really, really needed to be no more. I could not believe what Schabyz then did to further give me mental torture, he waylaid the vet on the pavement and proceeded to have a lengthy conversation with him and his male nurse. Eventually, they both came in and whilst I held my old lad in my arms with strokes and kisses he left this life that we had shared for sixteen and half years.

I paid the vet £117.50 for his gentle skill, and he then leaves but that bastard outside refused to go. By this time, he had wasted the time of a much-needed ambulance for over six hours, that could have (indeed should have) been attending to strokes, heart attacks or whatever came up.

I needed to place my little dead dog in his already dug grave in my garden and when I told Schabyz yet again to bugger off as he was not and never was needed, he told me he would wait until the burial was done, and the Bastard did. More wasted ambulance time. I wrapped up my darling old boy in his blanket and put his teddy and a posy of flowers between his still, cold paws and I wept, oh, how I wept that Autumn Day in the twilight rain. A friend placed him in his resting place and covered him with a mound of wet soil. Years later I still loathe that bastard. He stole Ziggy's gentle death, and got away with it.

Vile swine! I wept as I would do for weeks to come, as the golden leaves of autumn fell onto his final resting place.

And still, the tenacious bastard waited in the rain in the ambulance needed elsewhere, God only knows why? Some baloney about "Duty of Care"; that's a sick joke; a bloody snake would have shown us more care, more respect to me and my dog, that terrible day.

Somehow, Schabyz had found out I was bipolar and he used this knowledge to his advantage. Because I told him I was going to report his disgusting, mithering, callous behaviour to his superiors, he covered his back by sending for help from the police, 'help'! for what? A lady officer attended with the biggest copper I've ever seen who stood guard in my dining room doorway (filling it!) whilst she talked to me, I was still holding my dead dog (this being of course before he was buried). She stated her attendance was a waste of time, as all she found was a grieving old lady holding a dead dog and with this, she and the giant left – but Schabyz did not! Bastard.

When I found out he'd sent for the police (no doubt in the hope of getting me sectioned) I, in a panic, called my mental health nurse, Susan. And, she soon arrived with another nurse as witness of my allegations against that vile man who had stolen, for no reason whatsoever (except that he could), my old dog's gentle goodbye. He spouted his "duty of care" crap to my nurse and stated he was not leaving until he had checked me over and done his paperwork. And so, the bastard came into my home, against my wishes. I had the indignity of having to allow him to touch me and do his paperwork with my two nurses as witnesses.

This man had tormented me for over eight hours, eight hours that his needed ambulance was obviously wanted elsewhere. He just had to be the master of the situation, a situation that would never have happened if that silly wench in the vets had not sent for an unneeded ambulance in the first place.

At last, the torment of my life left and shortly after so did my nurses, I cried myself to sleep, as I felt mentally raped by that vile man, his callous actions dirtied and stole my last hours with my old boy, I only had that one chance for the best ever goodbye, and it was turned by that twat into a cruel farce.

I, of course, put in a complaint to the appropriate authorities which after numerous phone calls and letters, got me absolutely nowhere. The buggers closed lying ranks, and I was told my complaint would go in his work record. I don't believe that either.

Now many years have passed since I said goodbye to my little rescue dog Ziggy, but whilst he was still with me, I bought a little companion for us both, Lola, a gorgeous miniature black Poodle. Whilst I loved her dearly, he bloody hated her and took himself off to his bedroom to receive yet more room service from me, but that's a whole new story. Lola lies by my feet as I write this on Valentine's morning 2020 and a silent tear rolls down my face for the little old boy, in endless sleep, in my garden.

Dear reader if you should have the misfortune to send for an ambulance and that callous, uncaring, arrogant bastard called Schabyz attends, beware as he will make your distressed condition even worse! The ambulance driver from Hell who was/is unfit to be in a caring profession. Shame on him. I will loathe him until the day I die, that stealer of serenity on the day Ziggy, and I needed it most. I have since found out that Schabyz's terrible treatment of the (in pain) old and vulnerable is well known in this area, and yet nothing is done to stop him. Why not? Sack the uncaring vile sod!

You Want a Conservatory Darlin'? No Problem That Will be 50 Times!

He was a real hard man who ruled his family in much the same way as he ruled the poor ship's crew that he was the commander of for much of his military service life. When he took early retirement his ecstatic crew threw a party to end all parties.

Quite frankly his wife and kids used to dread his shore leave and their laughing easy-going way of living was torn to shreds by the bombastic rituals Sir demanded in his home. The time would come for him to return to the sea, (the only thing he could not control) and great rejoicing was had by his bulled wife and two small kids. But the arrogant lump soon retired and he was just about tolerated daily when he returned to eat and bully, even the friggin' Canary tried to salute! He'd taken a job in telecommunications to stave off the boredom of only having three humans, one collie dog and a yellow bird (that gave up singing) to dominate instead of a whole ship full of victims at his disposal.

Now my dear friend Jacob (to those who loved him Josh) was the unfortunate offspring of he who must be obeyed. Along with his (younger by three years) sister Susan, who was sixteen at this particular time of tragic events. She was absolute jailbait with a voluptuous body – long, long legs, such a pretty face – turquoise eyes that always held a promise and a mouth that promised even more. She was an outrageous flirt and dear daddy used to sweat and curse when he came home daily (from the new job he bloody loathed) to find numerous young studs prowling the pavement, taking bets on who would be the lucky bastard to get his leg over said beauty first. And Susan, the precocious flirt would go out in the front garden on the pretence of weeding the bugger, but in reality, it was to display to her lecherous admirers what daddy was determined the dirty sods would never, in their wildest dirty dreams, sample. Poor Jacob (not blessed by his sister's pulling powers) was given the task of keeping an eye on the devious, hormonal minx who was determined to get rid of her unwanted virginity as soon as possible.

Once a year a travelling fair came onto the local reck and after much begging and batting of eyelashes Susan persuaded daddy to let her go, he stipulated that back home by eleven she must be, and her big brother was to keep a watchful eye on his little naughty, randy sister. Daddy did not hold out much hope really (for he considered his nancy son soft) being unable to keep at bay the lecherous advances of teenage hormonal boys and indeed – men.

As soon as they got around the corner the make-up and mirror miraculously appeared from nowhere, and Jacob stood beside her under the street lamp as she preened herself, one last hitch up of her skirt showing a bit of her black lace knickers, one last push up of her thrusting braless pert boobies further to tease any fit lad who fancied a bit (or a lot) and she was hot to trot. Poor Jacob, trying to tame this young madam was out of the question.

Four streets away rock and roll music blared, once there, the lights, rides and bustle of many rides filled her with such excitement but the waltzer was her favourite and that was the start of her life's ruination. I suppose he was handsome in a swarthy, sweaty kind of way and as soon as their eyes met it was lust at first sight. But first, she had to give her boring big brother the slip so she could keep her whispered promise to the fit lad with the bulging zip area.

God it was easy, she just melted into the revellers behind the crowded candy floss stall, and when 11 pm came and the fair closed she was all ripe and ready for the 'plucking'.

So, the virginity she did not treasure was soon disposed of and with wet whispers of undying love, she grudgingly trudged home, making sure the blood on her (now pulled down skirt) would be covered by the jumper tied around her tiny waist.

All bloody hell was let loose as she turned the corner for home, her parents were on the pavement, frantic with worry, and about to call the police as it was now 1am. Daddy dragged her inside and did the unthinkable in this day and age, he threw her over his knee and smacked her tiny arse good and proper. His heart sank as he saw the bloody evidence of just why she was 2 hours late home. And for that one and only time his family witnessed him sobbing, his baby was ruined.

Now the horny dark one was indeed a gypsy who decided that tarmacking drives for trusting homeowners was not for him anymore. Anyway, he was pissed off with having to leg it with their handful of cash before they could inspect his slipshod work, many were the times he'd been chased up the street and once he'd had to leap a privet hedge to get away from an unhappy owner (and his snarling big dog) of yet another fucked-up drive. Washing what he could off his tarmacked hands in his freezing caravan he decided on a different life plan and, with this in mind he took himself to the fair which would be in that location for another week. He was taken on at once because the fairground boss clocked his dirty smirk that the girlies would just love.

He would phone Susan many times only to be told by someone "sorry, wrong number" still they continued their liaison and she grew so hungry for what his loins had to offer. A missed period brought her up really sharp and Jacob pleaded with her to tell their parents. She quaked with fear, as the news seemed to bring on a heart attack on her grey-faced gasping daddy. Her mother sobbed and reached for the gin bottle (usually hidden from her teetotal husband under the sink) two months later dad was out of hospital swearing to kill the filthy bastard who had impregnated his sixteen-year-old goddess. He eventually found the dirty boy and gave him a smacking he would remember all of his life. A wedding (as was the norm in those hypocritical days) was quickly arranged. Not the magnificent over-the-top do that her mother had been saving sixteen years for – but in a dowdy brown, dusty registrar's office where they were pronounced husband and wife. Susan was beyond delighted to have bagged such a stud, whilst he went looking for the proper job she insisted upon.

Soon she was the proud mother of a stunning dark-haired little lad, a mixture of good looks from both his beautiful parents.

In the meantime, Jacob had found the love of his life, a bony girl who loved to not only cook wonderous meals, but eat them too. They had an exciting sex life which entailed dressing up in various costumes. Jacob's favourite was basque and stockings, blindfold and motorbike crash helmet. It was more exciting if hearing and vision were denied to Maggie and she could only 'feel'. So, this day, feeling frisky, she made her famous apple crumble and steak and kidney pie, her beloved husband's favourite nosh. Of course, she could not hear the door open as she had seductively draped herself on the couch (all sixteen stone of her) and it was only when Jacob removed her helmet and blindfold that she clocked she had a guest. Terry, her brother-in-law, stood slavering not only at the fabulous food he was invited to share, but also at the get up on Jacob's missus. Anyway, they had a good laugh and opened a few cans while she put on a dressing gown and served up a meal to not be forgotten. For the rest of his days, Terry lusted over his sister-in-law, but never stood a chance.

I'd paid off the bastard I'd divorced; debts, as decreed by a doddering misogynistic judge. But there were so many things I needed to upgrade in my home and so I had asked Jacob's help and advice. He told his brother-in-law Terry, who had set himself up in the building business, and had got him to give me a quote. So, this stranger leered at my boobs while at the same time getting out a pad for my quotation. I wanted the windows altered, the drive tarmacked, and yes, he did know how to do it! When questioned by me (how the hell was I to know he was a gypsy who lived on his wits with tarmacking as a dodgy sideline)? He seemed very professional yet the glint in his eye spoke volumes (and dare I remark on the bulge in his strides!) were things I could easily control. A few more jobs were added to the list and he noted them down meticulously.

He returned later, as promised, with his interpretation of an estimate. On reading it I thought "what the hell is this all about"? fifteen times for the windows, seven times for the drive and so it went on. Jesus, I finally clocked it, the randy bugger wanted paying, not in cash, but sex. He was told to fuck off in no uncertain terms and with a blown kiss to me he said "Pity, it would have been a blast. Some you win, some you lose" and laughing he sauntered away – forever.

The conservatory I'd desired was out of the question, as paying for it fifty times on my back (or whatever) would leave no time or energy for him to build the sod. Jacob laughed like hell but said he knew I could handle the dirty bugger and see him off. This I had done with no problem.

How a lifetime is so quickly eroded asway, in the blink of a cataracted eye nearly all that meant so much to me – is gone.

I was looking through old photos (faded by time) to place in the book you are now reading and came across ones that opened the wounds I thought had healed years ago. Or so I'd hoped. There the five of us sit smiling around a table laden with Maggie's wonderous fare. This we did one, (much looked forward to), Saturday evening once a month. We laughed into the camera for posterity, never knowing the sadness that would befall each one of us. Jacob and his rotund happy, always laughing Maggie, myself always alone, and

Susan and Terry – still so much in lust. It's a blessing she never discovered just why her housekeeping money was short every so often, even though her 'devoted' husband was 'toiling' all the hours God sent, and was deadbeat and snoring as soon as his head hit the pillow. Oh! naive lady what you don't know can't hurt you, let's hope you forever live in blissful ignorance. Terry would sometimes catch my eye and do a zip-up motion across his mouth. Cheeky sod! One wonderous night out dancing I met my Hamid and a sixth-place was laid for him at Maggie's Saturday night table. He loved being so accepted at once by total strangers, and this divine ritual went on until he was called into the army and forced to fight in the Gulf war that he never believed in. This is where he lost his precious young life, lying mortally wounded, alone, without love, awaiting death in the scorching hot sands of the godforsaken desert one New Year's Day.

His empty place at Maggie's table crucified me and even though I used to look forward to, and love, those Saturdays so much I had to excuse myself from them. I was so very lonely as I imagined the four of them enjoying what Hamid and I once shared. And that loneliness has crucified me for forty long years now. Tomorrow I will be seventy-six years old and still I miss my man all these years later. The people who sat sharing Maggie's fare with me, followed my Hamid to heaven one by sad one over the years. Just me left now, just me and my little dog Lola, reliving memories from photos faded over time. The rain lashes the windows this winter evening, the furious howling wind bends my slender willow tree to its bidding and next door but one's old shed roof has blown into my garden, narrowly missing my Grecian lady statue.

Not long to wait for me now my Hamid, not long.

P.S I never did get my conservatory and it riles me no end to imagine that some floozy (with an eye on her purse strings) with no taste in men and ever-open legs got the bugger instead of me. Morals come at a price! I believe I made the right decision because fifty times for the conservatory plus windows, drive etc would have bloody killed me! Besides I did not fancy the randy, sweaty bugger one little bit.

Maybe, after all, it's just as well I did not get my dream conservatory, as how would I keep the windows gleaming in the sunshine when I'm now too knackered to climb a ladder to clean them? I hate a dirty window!

Bye-bye, take care of each other, by the time you read my book I'll have found my Hamid, yet again! Let's hope heaven is all it's cracked up to be! I wonder does it have conservatories? Also, who cleans the glass? Not me!

Love Zara.

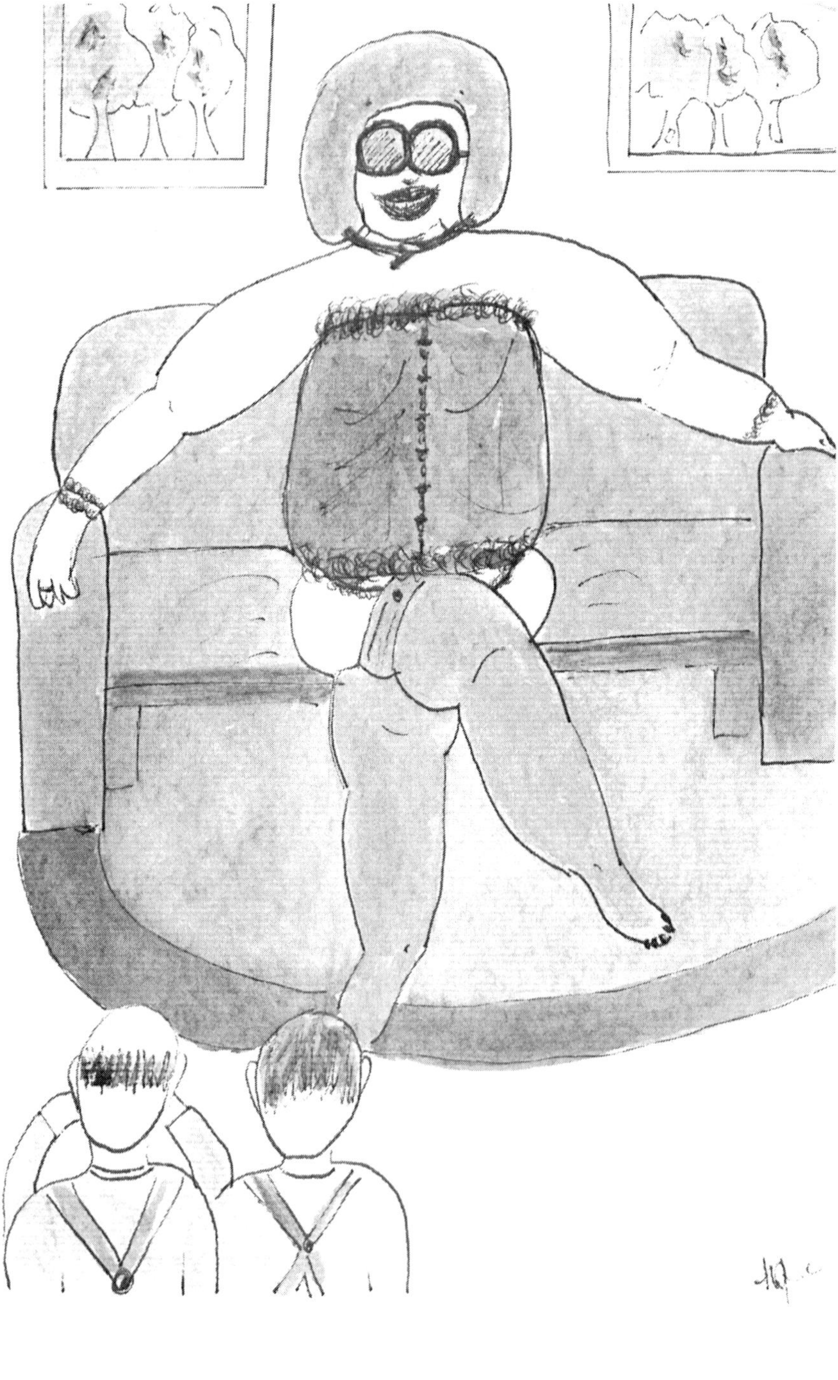

Boom!

I was an extra on the hospital programme George was the star of, such a divine man and so nice with it.

At the end of the shoot, there was a party and at this we became known to each other. Instant chemistry (and after even more champagne and slow dances, where his body told me all I needed to know!) we found ourselves in the luxurious suite afforded all the stars of TV and films. Soulful Blues music lilting low, candles flickering, as we slowly moved to the rhythm, removing each other's clothes as we did so, now our hungry bodies moved as one as he steered me into the bedroom, his luscious lips never leaving mine.

I felt the cold black satin sheets touch my legs as he gently laid me back and started our night of torrid passion. (Please God, let me die right now) We moved as one in a tribal rhythm, faster and deeper, and I was so near to all my dreams, oh God, oh God, just two more kisses, one more thrust, and it would be heaven for me, but instead, Boom! I awoke with such a start, grasped at the sheets that were now pink flannelette, where were the black satin ones? More to the point, where was George?

It was only then that reality struck pushing away my lascivious dream, leaving me gasping and wanting, my body screaming with unrequited lust. It was 6.30 am, raining as usual and as usual the inconsiderate twat next door was throwing his angle grinder, toolbox, etc. into his van and in so doing, waking the whole of the residential road, and beyond.

Not to mention the theft of one hell of a climax next door. I cursed him to hell and back, hoping his conkers fell off and would roll down a grid, never to be seen again.

With my fantasy stolen forever and my body still demanding release, I did what any desperate middle-aged woman would do: a bit of sexual DIY.

PS: an hour later, sorted! But what a waste of a dream, to end all dreams.

Many were the nights (after the disappointment of a lifetime) that I trawled dreamland for a repeat encounter. And once again, I was transported from my pink flannelette bed to the luxurious penthouse master bedroom which held my torrid desires. I'd bought sensuous La Perla underwear, just in case I should find that gorgeous man again. The doorman of the hotel had ushered me into the lobby and there George sat, smiling a welcome. Taking my hand, he ushered me into the mirrored private lift to the penthouse, at once seeking my hungry lips with kisses to die for. We entered a room of total erotic fantasy. The walls and ceiling were mirror covered, all of them etched with torrid depictions of lust, taken from the Karma Sutra. Slowly we undressed each other, kissing and licking the exposed skin left once our clothes were on the hot pink carpet. All through the night I would never forget, we re-enacted the explicit torrid etchings, at the same time being able to watch ourselves do so on the mirrored walls.

Exhausted, satisfied and spent, we at last curled up oh-so tightly between black satin sheets. Soon it would be daylight, and part we would have to, we were kissing and stroking for one last time, telling each other of the pleasure we had given and received. Over George's shoulder, I glanced at the clock it read six-thir... BOOM!

I shot awake in my lonely pink bed, the dream (that I still remember) very vivid in my mind. The thoughtless twat next door was right on time, loading his van on that otherwise silent wet morn. You see, I'd learnt from that first stolen climax (that should I ever find George again in dreamland), I'd make damn sure that our couplings would be over long before 6.30 am and BOOM!

All My Nightmares!

God help me I remember it well, the sight and sound of a huge rusty old wagon. To my horror it parked outside next door and the SOLD sign was thrown down into the garden. That vile eyesore was a blight on our nice residential road for many a year to come. More likely than not, that disrespectful man parked his red truck outside my home, once over Christmas and New Year. It was plain to see the contents, them being a broken iron bath, piping, a poo encrusted loo and assorted rubble. Would you want that muck outside your home? I THINK NOT. When asked to move it, the snarled reply was "I pay my road tax and I can park where I bloody want!" and he did, for YEARS!

Their front 'garden' boasted tall weeds, broken concrete path, builders' rubble and provided this road with its only squat, Oh yes "The Clampetts" had arrived – them getting that name referred to an American TV show of the 1970s about hillbillies finding oil on their land. They up sticks, packed up a rusty wagon; moved to Beverly Hills and turned their mansion in to a scrapyard (notice the similarity?)

She, next door, cottoned on to the fact that I had numerous skills and contacts she could utilize and stupid me allowed her into my life. She would constantly borrow money (always paying it back). The largest amount was £600. This was money saved by her football crazy, monosyllable partner, to follow Manchester United to the USA for a match. She had used it all for God knows what and the time had come to pay all of it for tickets etc. NO MONEY! She came to me begging in a state of hysteria stating "Oh God if he ever finds out I've stolen his football money he'll leave me, you've got to save my life". Foolish me lent her the missing cash. All of my meagre savings and bills and shopping money were handed over to her leaving me with £3.74 till next pay day. She told me I had "saved her life" and she would be forever grateful. UTTER BOLLOCKS, as time has proved just what a lying, conniving bitch she really is.

It must be pointed out that all of that horrid family are racist bigots who loathe all foreigners, even though they are better behaved than themselves. They also hate trees, birds (they are vermin so they say), most wildlife, and curse me for feeding them saying they "shit on my washing" NICE!

The years pass with their decibel level booming music into my once placid home. Their offspring clattered about in high heel adult shoes on wooden floors, shouting, fighting etc, etc, until their mother returned from work at 10.30 pm. It drove me frantic as watching TV or sleep were impossible.

My mother died and was at rest in my front room. At the same time, I got long awaited news from Baghdad. It was the worst possible. My darling soulmate had been killed in the desert of Iraq. Gone were the dreams of our future. The noise bounced through the walls from next door. I phoned to ask it to be turned down as I was heartbroken. That uncaring lout said he knew as I was disturbing his football on TV with my crying. His phone went down and his TV went up. No peace; no peace at all!

The list is endless of the nasty incidents they inflicted upon me. One being I was having my outside wall Tyrolean clad. I asked the thing next door many times, to mark the wall for a dividing line. Yet another grunt and the wall was never marked by him. The workmen came to do the job; measured out the surface and assured me that they were correct. Metal edging was screwed on to the wall and the base coat of cement applied. He came home - at once went to inspect the wall, growled at me that "it was 1.5 inches over his side "GET IT OFF". Next day the workmen were very displeased and said the man was wrong and was a bloody maniac. Of course his actions of spite cost me extra money I could hardly afford!!!

The youngest of next doors' kids was doing a play about the 60s/70s and needed suitable clothing and footwear. God I'm a daft bastard, for I lent her a very, very expensive pair of black patent leather knee high boots with bronze metal high heels. They were returned scuffed to hell and one heel was buckled. When told of this, the mother had the lying, bare face cheek to say "that was how I lent them" door shut. The boots were now bin fodder and I so loved them as they were the only "posh" boots I have ever owned, them having been a present from a loved one. I'm convinced that girl let all and sundry have a go at walking in them. SHAME ON THE LOT OF THEM – NO RESPECT.

They were burgled and the claim was enhanced by a fictitious diamond ring. She of course bought a real one with the pay out.

Also that vile, tree-hating, woman cut one side of my magnificent palm tree that I had nurtured for 30 years. She's a beast!

The above mentioned 13/14-year-old girl was a lad magnet and she would take herself, nightly, to a nearby council estate where the family had come from. There she collected numerous louts on bikes, swearing, spitting and shouting, vile young sods that followed her home and created mayhem outside my home until at least midnight. Once again – no sleep.

I was going on a long awaited, much needed, holiday. All packed, passport at the ready and she tells me that the monosyllable git was going to put up a dividing fence in our front gardens whist I was away. Some of my bushes had migrated over the boundary and because I knew he would just scrap them I re-planted them elsewhere in a panic. Bad start to a holiday.

On my return, no fence. In fact, 3 years later <u>I</u> had one erected. <u>JUST SPITEFUL, UPSETTING, DIRTY TRICKS.</u>

Long ago, so that he could not find out what she was up to, I allowed <u>her</u> post to come to <u>me</u>. This she sorted after collection by her so he'd be none the wiser. A lot of the envelopes were Courthouse franked! WHY?

The years pass and I constantly dread what the inventive buggers next door will do to further persecute my Bipolar brain. SO CRUEL ARE THEY.

The eldest girl gets herself a boyfriend cut from the same cloth. By this time they have created a destructive, lying little sod. Also being dangerous, he decided to hurl over the adjoining fence (God only knows what he stood on to even reach) a 6 foot 2x1" length of timber that he deliberately aimed at <u>my dog in my garden</u> narrowly missing the sweet little soul. So help me, if he had done as intended, with my bare hands, I'd have throttled the evil little sod. When challenged by his grandmother, he swore time and time again "it wasn't me gran" finally admitting it. Not once did I get an apology from his parents. His destruction of my property was vast and expensive. He got a never-ending supply of footballs and these he would repeatedly, viciously, kick at my fence, in so doing, breaking it. His father showed him how to kick the ball high, this he got the hang of at once and proceeded to trash my lovely garden and its lanterns, statues etc. From my window I watched them. His father gave an almighty kick; shouted "oops" which made the kids copy his "oops" with theirs. The ball shot over the 6 foot fence and smashed a huge mirror I had bought only the day before. All went silent and they scurried inside like a plague of rats. I'll point out that to enhance my garden and make it appear much larger, I'd covered the 6 foot fences with a collage of mirrors and it looks divine, but I'm always on edge waiting for the smash. As I have said – no bloody peace.

So the buggers have ruined my fence, broken over £400 of items, tried to kill my dog, and made me suicidal. Enough was more than enough so I took them to Court. You have never heard so many denials, lies and excuses being fed to a gullible Judge from the mouth of a cunning git. There was a Police report concerning how much criminal damage (over a long period of time), numerous pictures of breakages, written statements of people who saw said damage etc and guess what? all of it fell on the Judge's deaf ears and he ruled against me. That bloody woman's face said it all – SMUG – This basically gave them permission to do as they please as there would be no punishment or recompense for all I had lost. That is a bloody disgrace. 40 years of torment and they do as they please. She had previously told me that I would never get the better of her whilst she had a "hole in her arse" – such a lady!

Another vile trick was to inform the DVLA that I was a dangerous driver. After much investigation, they knew it was just malice because I'd never had an accident and held a clean licence. Next door wanted me to be a prisoner in the hell hole they had created for me, never being able to escape with the aid of my old car.

My darling old Ziggy needed the vet, I carried him to my car. Half an hour later I was back and there was a huge unknown van outside my home. So due to yellow lines, I had to park around the corner. Ziggy was so poorly and heavy, I had to drape him over my shoulder. It hurt to carry him and that was because my shoulder had previously been broken and was never attended to. As I rounded the corner, that lout of a boyfriend from next door, was leaning and smoking against the van with the usual sneer across his ugly face. The drive next door was empty (as was the space outside). In fact, all of the road held only his van. Yet again a deliberate act of vile spite by him, he'd seen me get my old doggy in my car and so put his van in the space outside my home knowing I'd have to carry my old boy (in much pain) from around the corner. I struggled to open the gate (whilst he smirked and smoked, throwing the dimp into my lovely garden – the pig). I managed to open the three locks on my front door leaving it open as Ziggy was distressed. Once laid down he settled a bit, and I went to lock the door. That bastard was leaning on my iron gate staring into my hallway. With a nasty chuckle he swaggered off and drove away. I went in, had a cry and a curse, made a coffee, and hugged and kissed my old boy, who I would soon loose.

The latest abortion is a giant shed rearing its ugly head 3 foot above my 6 foot fence. Three sides have been clad in black plastic, the fourth side is unfinished, this being what I can't help but see and be disgusted by. A cheap 2x1 wood frame stretching nearly the length of two 6 foot fence panels. Nailed to this is a grey canvas with blue writing on, very salubrious I must say!

I am not long for this world now – will I be sorry when my clogs have popped? NO!

I'm turned 80 years (but in fact feel three days older than God!) and with so many painful health problems, a hypochondriac would be jealous. Life is a struggle.

Lola, my darling little Lola, also has her problems but they are without pain and I thank God (if there is one) that the decision to help her leave me seems a way off. As I write, her body warmth is beside my knackered, useless, old leg. We are comfy together on the sofa.

I've just been out to feed the birds that next door call vermin (pot calling kettle I believe!). Their wheelie bins are against my fence in the front garden – they will always be CHAVS!

P.S. Should anything untoward or suspicious happen to me, my dog, or my property, my enemies of 40 years should be questioned. After all, they do have a convicted arsonist in their close relations.

This is my beautiful garden that, bit by bit, they are DESTROYING.

It was a boiling hot midday. My dog had just urinated on the paving and that awful 'child' from next door hurled a piece of wood that landed on her wee-wee that was still wet. His intention was to maim or kill, I'm sure. He must have been so disappointed to have failed in his mission.

This was a very big glass URN, so precious to me as it was my very last gift before Caroline ended her life three weeks later. That lying bitch next door told the Court that I'd smashed it myself – bought a ratty football and blamed the brat – and the deluded, biased judge bloody believed her! FOOL. Hundreds of pounds of damage over the years that she got away with. DISGUSTING.

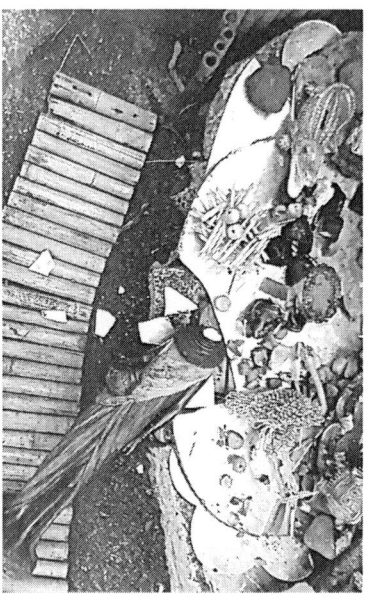

My grandmother owned this set of Maasai ladies – now 100 years old. They had survived two world wars, but not living next door to that destructive brat. (Repairing one in my kitchen) More were to come with other items to repair.

I Died

Yes! You have read that correctly, I did indeed die. And what better place to do it than in an ambulance parked at the roadside? This ambulance was sent to help me for a totally different reason, a D.V.T. in my left leg. No sooner had they manhandled me into their vehicle than I went into Cardiac Arrest and died, (albeit for just two minutes,) but with the aid of an injection of God knows what and a jump start from the defibrillator, a beating heart, the next thing I knew was a relieved voice saying, "She's back."

It was 5 am and the A&E Department was quiet and empty, so I got more than enough attention. I had to keep on repeating to numerous doctors what had brought me in, when all I wanted was to be left alone with the excruciating pain, please just shove me in a corner and let me die. AGAIN, this time forever!

After numerous scans, blood tests, blood pressure, etc. It was discovered that, as the Surgeon put it, I had the 'Mother and Father' of all blood clots. It started in my left foot, all the way up my leg, through my tummy, then my chest and ended like little grapes on the branches of my lungs, and this was the reason I'd been feeling so very ill for a long time and was always breathless, a D.V.T. They wanted to transfer me to a Vascular Surgeon at another hospital, but he would not touch it as it was one continuous one, like a snake, four and a half feet long, and would need breaking up to remove it. This being way too dangerous because of bits of it breaking off and…guess what? Killing me. Not for the first time! So, Warfarin injections in the tummy were shoved in; they did not hurt but sent my tummy a worrying black colour. Ten days later, it's still black, but now I'm on tablets instead of injections.

I was treated very well in the Hospital, even though I found it impossible to adjust to the trauma of leaving my home and therefore being out of my comfort zone, you see, not only am I Bipolar but along with that, I'm agoraphobic.

I live with just my little dog in an isolated existence and the noise, disturbance, hustle and bustle of hospital life, plus the noises of the patients on the dementia ward that I was placed in for many days (without my medication for Bipolar or type 2 Diabetes I might add) drove me to the point of wishing I had died forever in that ambulance. But one thing humbled me greatly. Not since I was a little child had I had anyone wash me, for me I'm very private, but the need to be clean overruled my shyness. A sweet, oh so sweet Nigerian nurse stroked my old body with a soapy flannel, all the time telling me how lovely my old skin was. She treated me with such loving dignity, and I wish I knew her name so I could tell the Ward Sister of her genuine respect and loving gentle kindness. Her sweet action had me crying like the little child I used to be, that being the last time I had felt soapy tenderness.

Over two years ago, I fell down my stairs and heard the loudest crack, at the same time as excruciating pain in my lower back. It was the wooden radiator cover that I'd hit in my fall, but found undamaged, and I was convinced the cracking sound was from my back. The agoraphobia and bipolar made going to the hospital impossible for me, so I just put up with the pain for months on end until after a long time I either got used to it or had it buggered off. In the hospital, they did numerous X-rays and 'yes', I had broken my old back in two places, now fully healed up (but wrongly). We war babies are made of strong stuff.

My Angel

I don't really know at what age I became seriously ill with Scarlet Fever, that in those days was a killing scourge. My fever was running really high and whilst wide awake in my dark little bedroom, in the middle of the night something strange and wondrous occurred. This being, neither man nor woman, stood gently glowing at my side and said the words I wish it hadn't. "You will get better, little girl."

All of my days I've believed in Angels whether they be good or bad, and I think this night-time visit from one was my first, but far from the last one.

I just wish its intervention between life and death had never happened, and that it had allowed me back to my astral home, instead of binding me to this earth for another seventy cold years. Should I ever meet up again with my saviour I'll really have strong words with it. And what will I tell it "Please stop averting destiny because it's not always for the best. In doing so, you instigated seventy-odd broken years I would have preferred to do without."

So many times, I've called in the night for its help and guidance, and it's been sent to me. Just like helping me not lose the lucky red purse, enabling me to help little children. I have to thank you my dearest Angel for two other occasions where you have come to my aid.

It had been many weeks since I had walked my darling Lola on that lush field that was her joy. The last time she ran in the sunshine, it was there I discovered that, on leaving, one of my tinted glasses lenses had fallen out, the chain still secure around my neck. I searched the surrounding grass and my car, of course not knowing where it could be.

On asking the price of a replacement of the lenses at the opticians, I was told I had to have a pair, at the cost of £95, this I could never afford, so I put the lost lens to the back of my mind and did without my favourite specs.

So, here I was six weeks later on that secluded lovely grass, I could see it had been newly mowed, and the scuffed grass was evidence of football matches. It was a warm day, and I was panting, time for a cool drink. As I walked back to my car, a piece of broken glass glinted in the sunshine, amongst the mowed grass, and so that a dog's paws would not be cut by it, I went to pick it up to dispose of it. And you will believe my surprise when I brushed off the bits of cut grass to discover it was my long-lost lens, unharmed and with a little clean was ready to be replaced in my specs. Just how can that be? Thank you, my wonderful Angel.

This second account I tell you is harrowing, and to this day, still brings me out in a cold sweat.

I awake screaming in remembered terror, looking at my missing fingers that were only stumps, in my nightmares.

Because I'm very safety conscious about the home I've built and cherished since 1962, and because of ever-rising burglary rates, I decided to have fitted heavy-duty steel shutters on my back window and side door, to keep the thieving sods out! This door shutter was activated by a remote fob, as was the window. It would slide down on command and come to rest flush against the rise of the top step, settling with a click on the top of the bottom step. I did not give the shutter presence a thought (as it was out of sight in its housing under the porch) when I put a planter on the bottom step to remind me to wash it, before spray painting.

Bedtime came, the fob told the shutter to slowly descend, I closed and locked the back door, and then a terrible noise came from the usually quiet mechanism. On opening the door, I saw to my horror that the shutter was trying to descend, but the planter on the bottom step stopped it. It screamed and objected, and the fob would not stop it. Then, I did the most stupid thing ever, without thinking of the consequences. I bent down and pushed the planter off the step, this released the shutter and it fell like a hundred mile an hour guillotine, coming out of its casing. It slammed onto the bottom step taking with it two of my fingernails. If my fingers had been just a couple of inches further underneath, I would have lost them, a few more inches further in and I would have been cut off at the wrists.

Picture this horrific scenario if you will (as I have a thousand times.) Fingers or whole hands sliced off, lying in a pool of blood on the bottom step. The broken shutter in a heap, screaming as I would have done, had my Angel not saved me. For I am convinced that I was pushed backwards into my kitchen, where I lay on the white tiled floor, shaking and crying with the fear of what nearly was.

I should have died that night from either blood loss or shock, but just as my Angel had many times before saved me when I'd been falling, she kept me safe.

I pray that one day I will meet this wonderful creature who is always by my side and repeat in person the "thank you"s I say to her every night before I go to sleep. For without her intervention, I would not be able to write and tell you of my greatest fright. (Even worse than the snake in my bath). Thanks, Angel.

PS: After that so near disaster, I painted the shutter fob bright red and hung bits of chain onto it, to remind me to never ever put anything in the way of the shutter's descent and to check each and every time I press that red fob.

That unthinkable mistake cost me £150 to have mended, and when I told the engineer how it had happened, he agreed that it was the horrific stuff of nightmares. Please God I've learnt my lesson and never forget safety, ever again.

Thank you, Angel of mine. X

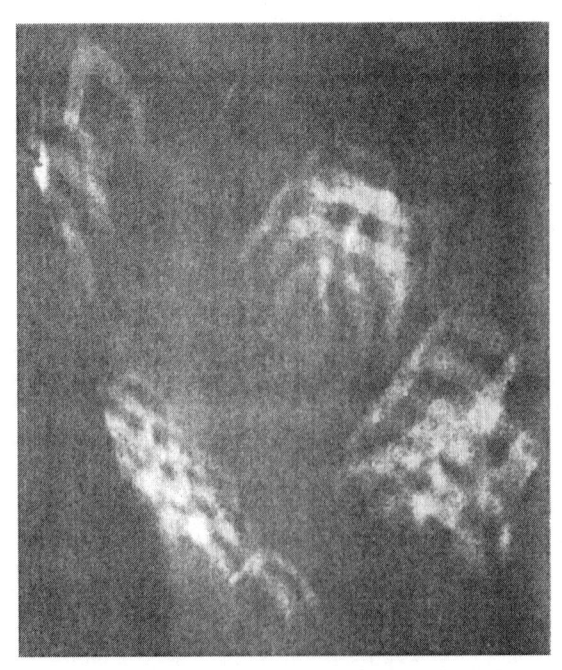

I believe this to be the manifestation of my guardian angel who appears on my nighttime bedroom ceiling.

3 October 2020: The Present Day

It's 6.30 am; I've looked out into my dark wet garden and even my feathered friends are still asleep. I can't continue sleeping as my damaged mind is in even greater turmoil.

The events of the last month have pushed me so near to me ending my life and that of my darling Lola's, but I've managed to push away the dark thoughts and carry on.

It started when I found another three lumps on Lola's tiny body; two came back OK, but the third one, God help me, was all of my nightmares, cancer on her right foreleg.

I wailed with fear and misery, my tortured mind going to the worst of all scenarios. I would lose my little black love. Since finding that vile tumour, I nightly begged my Guardian Angel to save my girl from the Cancer I so dreaded and when it was found, I cursed my Angel for what (in my distress) I saw as betrayal. I wonder if she will not forgive me my terrible curses, even though I have since begged for forgiveness many times.

Then my respectful neighbours put their house up for sale this threw me into a panic for who knows what type of family would replace their quiet decency? So unlike my other neighbours who have given me hell, one way or another, for over thirty years, the damage to my property and sanity culminated with me suing them in the small claims court.

Two days after next door sale board went up another mental blow really, really hurt me, because of my bipolar I'm registered as disabled, along with other mental health problems come, type 2 diabetes, Crohn's disease, Arthritis – untreated broken bones (because the bipolar is accompanied by agoraphobia this making seeking help impossible), the worst was a fall down the stairs which resulted in me lying helpless at the bottom of them, for two days and nights in terrible pain, unable to get up. I would still be there but for the postman alerting my neighbour (who has my spare keys) of my plight. I knew when I fell that it hurt like hell, and I hoped that the loud crack I heard was the smashing of the radiator cover, later inspection proved this not to be the case. Two and a half years later I was admitted to the hospital with acute thrombosis in my left leg. Scans, etc. revealed as what they described as the mother and father of all DVTs running from my left foot (four foot six long) through my tummy, chest and into my lungs hanging like thirty-two small fruits on them this was the cause of my breathlessness. At the same time, they X-rayed my spine only to discover that the pain I felt from the fall that I had suffered two and half years from was indeed two broken vertebrae. No wonder it bloody hurt!

Through many of my year's mental and physical pain, I relied on my psychiatrist Dr Bohen. He was my salvation; pushing away my self-loathing and making me believe that I deserved the air I breathed. He only visited me with his kind wisdom once every three months but after each visit, I felt reborn, able to face whatever life threw at me. He brought with him on his last visit (terrible for me) news that he had no option but to retire, for private reasons that he did not disclose. I sat and cried, for had we not become friends during the four years he had so many times mended my heart and soul? There will never be another Dr Bohen I weep now at the loss of his tender guidance, for I will miss him so much. I have not attempted to replace him with another doctor as I'm convinced no other psychiatrist could compare to him. So I struggle on without help.

A couple of days later, news came via the post that an elderly friend of mine of forty-five years had had enough of this life, and so decided to leave it. I understand their decision completely and pray they have found the peace in the afterlife that was beyond their reach on earth.

So, the time has come to take my Lola to the specialist advised by my vet. Imagine a ratty housing estate, plonked in the middle of this was the most austere, unwelcoming, vile building you would never want to visit. No windows, no trees, no plants, nothing to soothe the nerves that made me hope things were better on the interior that was never shown to me. It was raining, a vet came out into the car park, introduced himself but never had the manners to address me, knelt and touched the tumour on Lola's leg, but never stroked or reassured the worried little lass. He then gave a very abrupt so-called eight-minute consultation, which fell very short of the thirty minutes I had agreed to pay a hundred and eighty pounds for! Not happy at all, and he will not be seeing either of us for any further operation.

The next consultation, this one costing two hundred and seventy-five pounds was wonderful. A clean, tidy, reassuring experience where Lola and I were ushered into a consultation room (out of the rain), and the vet sat on the floor and played with Lola whilst giving me details relevant to the removal of of the tumour on her leg, healing time, and is very positive about the outcome of his work. Because the tumour was of low grade and slow-growing, it was decided to monitor it over the coming weeks and months. If it should start to have a spurt of rapid growth to return to the animal hospital and have it removed, the cost of this thirty-minute operation is one thousand nine hundred pounds. A lot of money for an old lady (or indeed anyone) to find, but it can be borrowed from my stairlift fund. Because without the love and companionship of my beloved little dog, I'll not be needing a stairlift or indeed life.

It starting to become light now, and the first wild bird song sweetens the air; Lola dozes on my pink bed, unaware of her old mum's anguish. Time for coffee and a cuddle.

I hope all goes well, that my book gets published, and that I've made you laugh (a lot), cry (a little), and see life through bipolar eyes.

Mid-October 2020

For hours last night, my mind begged for the sleep that would hopefully give me a rest from my troubled thoughts. I suppose I must have dozed off for a little while, but the clock told me 3 am, as I sobbed into the quiet darkness. Concerned tiny Lola, kissed away her old mum's tears and snuggled close to me to give me the comfort I so needed.

For I have been making a new will, my wishes are now plain and written down ready for my Solicitors pursual. This was due to happen today, but after my night of sobbing hell, I've decided to cancel her visit. I desperately want to take a Valium to help me cope, but sense tells me that if I open that bottle, temptation to take the whole lot will overwhelm me, and Lola will be left alone, wondering why her old mum plays no more.

So, the anguish is mine, to stay with me until I have at last sorted out the dilemma that steals my sanity and sleep.

And it is this, if I should die before my beloved black, curly, little girl how do I ensure that her grieving welfare is paramount? So, this is how I'm trying to arrange that she joins me as soon as possible if no new loving owner can be found. Today, when dawn finally breaks and life outside these solitary quiet walls begins, I will call the vets to enquire if once Lola's life is to end, one of their many vets will come to my home and put her to gently sleep (in the arms of my so sweet, animal-loving friend). So that my beloved dog and I can be reunited. Ashes to ashes!

At first, it was all arranged that my other lovely friend would provide that most important task of all, but life is sending her in different directions, she will be far away and Lola may need to join her old mum quickly!

My dearest friend came yesterday to help me keep my home as I've always liked it, but now, in old age, finds it nigh on impossible to achieve. Lola waited at the door for her and they had their usual play and cuddle, and it was after this that I asked for the ultimate act of help and love from my friend. Bless her, she agreed to hold Lola in her loving arms whilst the vet (in my home) ended Lola's charmed life. She told me through tears that it would distress her greatly, but just like me, she could not bear my little dog to (either be put in kennels until death finally came) or to die in a vet's surgery in the arms of a stranger. Lola must leave this life as she has lived it, happy, secure in the knowledge that she and I will be reunited and stroll once again, young and well, amongst woodland filled with bluebells, will that be so? Let it be for I believe we both deserve it! Please let these tears finally stop.

PS: Since writing this, my wonderful home-help has taken up home on a water barge and is now travelling to God knows where, but I know that she will enjoy the freedom of every day. God Bless!

Yet Another Will That Saddens Me to Make

The existing one is many years old now. It is a very simple, straightforward one, everything was to be left to the two people I treasured. Yet time and circumstances change everything.

It's a terrible existence being old, lonely and poorly, knowing for a fact that you are unwanted, unloved, un-respected, unliked even. But, so be it. I don't think I deserved that, but maybe I do for I have been far from perfect, much to my shame.

This latest will has been such a terrible drain on my emotions, for what do I do with a lifetime's treasure? For I hate the idea of a money-grabbing house clearance company tossing my life's collections into a crowded van, not caring about the damage and dirt that was sure to happen. So, I came up with the best plan I could think of.

The people who have helped me and proved their loyalty and friendship over my empty, sad, lonely years are to be rewarded. I have made a list from one to twenty-two asking them to please come to my home (one at a time) in the company of my executors and slowly wander around, whilst doing so to choose as many items as they can manage to fit into their lives. I'm hoping that in so doing, most of my treasures will have found new homes with people that will appreciate the beauty that once was mine. Maybe two visits will be needed to completely strip my beloved home to just an empty shell. The thought of it now brings tears to my old eyes but I can't see any other decent solution.

I have also given a donation to Vision Aid so that the damaged eyes of children in the Third World can, at last, be pain-free and SEE. Another donation to Operation Smile, a charity I've long supported, so that little sad, deformed, painful faces can be repaired. The same donation goes to Water Aid, pure uncontaminated water that we all deserve, will be theirs.

I have great admiration for all lifeboat crews who risk their lives at sea, saving those in peril, for they do all this (not for the love of money, they don't get paid!), but for the love of humanity.

Donations too numerous to mention I bequeath in the hope that (what are really only pieces of paper with numbers on) will make a difference far and wide. Also, to the dogs and cats rescue centres.

As the future unfolds, without me in it, I hope humanity has learnt lessons from past bad decisions and returns this wonderful world back to peace, beauty and tranquillity. The remaining amount goes to both the Donkey Sanctuary and Brooks Veterinary Services to help working donkeys and horses in terrible conditions, in blazing hot conditions. So, from the sale of the home, I worked on and loved for nearly sixty odd years I hope that help comes to those animals I adore.

And then, the panic sets in. What if just as that long ago spirit, Syrius, stayed in my being over the many lives I have lived (for this has been proven to me whilst under hypnotic regression) I also can't leave this earthy plain? I have this heart-breaking dread of being dead, yet still being here. Of standing invisible in my home, watching people pick through my treasures, not taking off their shoes on the doormat and my lovely clean carpets getting filthy. Am I to stay earthbound trying to guard the home I built? Forever and ever broken-hearted at what I had to leave? I hope destiny will believe I tried my best to help every damaged or lost animal I ever found, and that children in faraway places were helped time and again with my donations. That at Christmas little souls were delighted with the boxes of goodies, I always sent with so much love. Please let me find the peace in death that eluded me in life.

PS: And if in reading this, you are now the owner of what was once mine / I hope you find love and laughter within its walls, I pray you have managed to keep the garden I have created (with back-breaking love) as I would have wished. Enjoy watching the squirrels and birds play and raise their babies in the branches of the Maple tree I planted when I was seventy years old. Just love and care for my old home for me please, just I did.

PPS: I hope you don't mind me visiting once in a while as it's so difficult for me to say goodbye. I promise I won't frighten you! Xx

Pandemic Lockdown

The year is 2020, one that will go down in history as the year life (but not as we have always known it) was decimated, over one million human lives have died excruciating deaths, resulting in rivers of tears from their loved ones, who because of lockdown were forbidden to hold and comfort their beloveds as they passed.

The disgusting tragedy of this virus COVID-19 (or Coronavirus) is that it was not of nature's doing but (allegedly) manufactured by four Chinese scientists in a lab. Or so the story goes; these people can't be made accountable, because all of them have conveniently died. The supposition is rife worldwide as to why they concocted, without compassion, a tasteless, invisible virus that has brought the whole world and its economy to its begging knees, instead of using their wondrous brainpower to at last find a Cancer cure?

The lockdown has meant people had to work from home, if possible, schools closed, all social gatherings were forbidden, you could not get together for a much-anticipated wedding, nor could you gather in grief to send a loved one on their last journey. Nor, God help you, (but is there a God?) could you open your door and run from the violence that tortured your existence to seek sanctuary from a caring neighbour. And so many more black eyes and broken bones happened. The world counselled each day, the mortality rate rises and the news told them of each and every cack-handed restriction imposed by the Government, running like headless chickens in sheer panic.

All people were told (after months of indecision) to stay at home, to only go out for food or medical help, wear face masks and anti-back hands and surfaces, to try and control its spiralling grip on the world. And still, it killed millions more. But of course, there were the inconsiderate idiots who put their pleasures before the safety of their fellow humans. Not a care in the world did they have, as they loaded up cars, found a secluded beauty spot and set about having raves and in so doing turned those places of gentle nature into vile dumping grounds. The police did fuck-all to stop this, as they were overpowered by the sheer number of vile people, thousands intent on causing havoc whilst they partied. Leaving behind countless cig packets, used condoms, plastic cartons, thrown away food, numerous types of drug paraphernalia, sanitary items, you name it, the fields once full of innocent white daisies was trampled and covered with litter and human waste, left for volunteers to clean up after them. Now, I ask: why were water cannons not deployed? Soak the bastards, the force of the water to make them grovel in the mud they were only fit for. I'm ashamed to be called human if I'm genetically connected to trash like them!

This book, after many years (47) of writing it (bit by bit) is finally being typed up by my friend, a new friend who has become very dear to me and has not only proved herself invaluable but is loyal, funny and everything this lonely old lady has prayed for to enhance a lonely life.

I have few friends, but those I do have are all of great worth, each bringing in their personalities, a quality I find endearing and precious. They know who they are and should this virus, or indeed old age carry me off, and should this book ever be published I want them all to know how I respected and loved each and every one of them.

Very soon I will be seventy-eight and eighty beckons, yet in all my unwanted bipolar ill years have I known the world to be in such turmoil, for this is a different type of war as I have known them, whilst all is quiet and buildings stand, humans fall, what a heart-breaking waste of so many wonderful, kind, helpful souls.

It seems like the promised Armageddon as fires rage, taking lives and homes in California (and, before that, Australia) and burning animals trying to escape the flames, breaking my old heart. Typhoons, Earth Quakes, Tsunamis, huge tidal waves perish. Hurricanes, Tornadoes; it's one global catastrophe after another, with the ice caps melting, the seas rising, it goes on and on and the virus? It seems to be unstoppable. Is this nature saying 'enough is enough? I created a wonderful world for you humans and what have you done with it? You have raped, plundered and destroyed my forests and oceans, now I take them back from you, for you don't deserve the gifts I gave with such love? Who knows what is to come?'

Many months have now passed since the virus traumatised the world, separating loving families who had the misfortune to be in separate locations when the lockdown was imposed. I believe most people kept in touch via the technology that my disturbed mind stops me from understanding. But it matters not, for I have no family, now the once-loved ones who do not wish to contact me, nor me contact them. I can honestly say that the lockdown has made no interference in my life at all as I'm always locked down by my mind, only leaving my home to get Lola to the vets or to attend to doctors, dentists, .etc... Very, very rarely do I have a visitor (as was once told me by a medium ("You will always be alone") and so his dreadful prediction has come to pass, but he was not quite correct, I rarely have human company, but I have a being far more trustworthy than any human, loyal and loving, my dog! (And my still resident poltergeist!)

Suspicions about how the virus came to be changed like the wind. Now the word is that the Chinese (who eat just about anything with a pulse) have feasted on bats and pangolins. A gentle, shy, unusual creature with disc-like scales all over its body. The cruel sods capture them, rip off the scales to make yet another medicine (that is proven to be useless) then eat the meat. Apparently, both bats and pangolins carry COVID-19 and when ingested by humans they are now infected (serves them right) and they then pass on COVID-19 to the innocent.

Poor Boris Johnson, (England's) PM looks worn out as he delivers the latest mind-numbing restrictions, thought up by Donald Duck, I'm sure. Now, people are not allowed to visit each other's homes or gardens, to combat loneliness, but it's OK to go down to the pub, mix with strangers and get kicked out at 10pm *en masse*. This of course means that hundreds of drinkers are wanting yet more booze to satisfy their gluttony. To get this they crowd into late-night supermarkets and off licences, spend money they can't really afford, give a two's up to authority, sit on pavement kerbs and get noisily and totally pissed. It's a disgrace!

At the beginning of 2020, all you ever heard about was blasted Brexit and what it would mean to our economy. The TV news (that I never watch), and the newspapers (that I never buy or read), talked of doom and gloom, but this soon stopped, thank God. Sadly, it was to be replaced by something that has turned into a global tragedy. COVID-19 is peaking yet again with the help of morons flouting safety procedures for the sake of their own disgusting, selfish pleasures. I believe we, as humans, will never be rid of this virus until dedicated scientists in labs, finally find a vaccine. But it will self-mutate, just like flu has always done, thus fighting to keep destroying humanity.

The world is still in crisis, COVID-19 has stolen the lives of 2.73 million worldwide (as of today) and 126k in the UK and while I write this the death toll is soaring, a river of tears has been shed, and mourners have been denied showing respect at gravesides because of lockdown, so far this had been proved ineffectual as the death rate is peaking again, due to the selfish refusal of morons to obey the rules stipulated by Government in a vain attempt to control COVID-19.

There is great despondency amongst the people, everything that they enjoy and wish to participate in is now forbidden and closed for the foreseeable future. The suicide rate is exploding, as people can't see a way out of the financial crisis Corona has brought about, thieves are running amok, domestic violence is at an all-time high and so is the disgusting act of paedophilia, nowhere to run and nowhere to hide from the monster that lies waiting within the place they call home.

No one can give a true opinion as to when, or indeed if, the virus can be slain. Already it has mutated, and the vaccine being rolled out is not as useful as first believed.

I'm so glad I'm nearing the end of my existence, for being alive has not been a pleasure, but all of you, please try to laugh, love and be happy, in my memory! Xx

New Year's Eve 2021

I'm sitting alone. Well, never really alone, as I've got my beloved little dog Lola beside me as always, and Moses, my poltergeist, hovers as usual. Will my precious, curly, black friend watch next year's fireworks with me? She without a trace of fear at the thunderous booms that spoils their beauty. I pray so!

After over fifty years, I finally found the courage to open the locked door of my soul and allowed the grief held within to cascade in a torrent of memory and anguish. For I knew that at last my big brother's story must be told, kept until all others were complete. I believed that resurrecting his memory, and the tragedy of his leaving this life would crucify me, and it has!

I can only imagine the life in the clouds that were his sanctuary, where he and the metal bird were as one, where he would listen to each sound it made and understand its meanings, to read all the cockpit instruments so familiar to him, to hear the tower give yet more instructions to go higher, go faster, activate the automatic pilot, then BOOM, the trauma and pain his strong body took as he and the bird crashed through the sound barrier at over one thousand miles per hour, was horrific for him and his comrades.

For these courageous young pilots were at the forefront of aerodynamics as we know them today. Pioneers of the skies.

They took the propellor age into the future; they climbed into the jets (never flown before) and took to the skies with all the pride, skill and courage they could muster. For these boys were all heroes, willing to risk their precious lives in the name of progress. It is to them that we should all owe our gratitude, each and every time we take to the skies ourselves as passengers going on vacations to wonderful lands, safe and worry-free.

The courage and skill of those magnificent young men paid off, as what flies above us (in their thousands daily) is a testament to what they endured, not knowing the outcome. Now, that's courage.

This wondrous young boy of seventeen had been accepted to fly, to attain the dream of all young boys. In the beginning, it was all propeller power

Spitfires, Lancasters, etc. the list went on and on and with skill and joy, he flew them all. Then, the transition of the propeller to jet engine comes into being, and he embraced the chance to take aerodynamics into the future. No one knew at that time just what going at one thousand miles per hour to crash through the sound barrier would do to the human body, would it survive unscathed? Well, he lived to tell the tale hundreds of times before he had to say farewell to the life he lived for. At forty-six, he was retired, his flying hours over. Now, very mentally poorly with a depression that could not be conquered with pills or E.C.T. In fact, E.C.T. made him much worse, the confusion this (so-called) treatment inflicted on the poor souls (like me) that were wired up was unbearable to the genius brain of my brother. God knows how hard I tried, I really tried to give him an interest that appealed. To bestow on him the wanting to live was almost impossible for me as my bipolar made me hate living also.

"Go climb Mount Everest."

"Too bloody cold."

"Go and race cars."

"Too bloody slow."

"Well then go and fly commercial."

Now, this really appalled him, with a look of pure exasperation and disgust he spat out.

"What? Fly with three-hundred twats sat behind me? I don't think so."

Balls of steel Johnny was revered by all that flew with him, for he had become a legend, this loner who had found a perfect way to be alone, him and the metal bird in the clouds, even today, half a century later I'm reduced to tears when jets fly over my home and unknown faces in helmets (in make-believe TV war dramas) re-awaken the grief, I still can't let go of. It took great courage to fulfil his chosen destiny, to lie down and feel his life ebb away. I pray his decision to leave this dimension we call life, finally made him happy. At long last, just happy.

Did any of you ever realise that whilst you slept safe and sound every night in your comfy beds, amongst the stars, in the stratosphere, pilots like my brother flew missile loaded jets circling our shores, keeping us safe from invasion? (From this world and… theirs!) Well, they did and still do I believe.

John was also renowned for his prowess at aerobatic manoeuvres, and I'd watch my TV with bated breath as he threw a lightning jet (at shows worldwide) amongst the clouds.

I'm proud that his skills were recognised by the powers that be, and he was awarded the highest of military ranking A1-Z1 (this meant he was THE finest of pilots, an air warrior, and Z1 meant he was security cleared to fly in any zone of the world) Oh! How he loved those years, just him and whatever metal bird that was his companion on any particular flight. And in the blink of an eye, his flying hours were at an end. From the hopeful seventeen-year-old boy to the renowned pilot of thirty-six years he became, the years had melted away. Now, he had so much time on his hands, unspoken for, this he could not tolerate, and his crucifying depression refused to leave his wondrous mind. So, he switched it off, just like his life in this dimension he died with the courage and dignity one would expect of him. I don't begrudge him his peace at all, for very soon I will find mine, hopefully by his side once again. My big courageous brother.

PS: It must be over fifty years ago that I found the courage to write my brother's story, in all that time it was in a drawer, forgotten.

The years of loss passed in a trice, yet seemed to last forever, then at the end of my book I felt I must tell you about this wondrous man, my big brother, and it hurt me. It was only on proofreading from fifty years ago I found that his story had already been told, but bear with me and please read it once again and dwell on the safety he and his comrades ensured for this little island we love to call home.

And that's another plane tested by my brother John, for all the pilots that come after to be safe.

FLT. LT. JOHN S   (31) attended Stockport School and joined the R.A.F. in April, 1949, before which he was a laboratory assistant. In May, 1951, he was posted to No. 23 Squadron (Mosquitos and Vampires) at Coltishall. In January, 1953, he ferried Sabres from Canada to the United Kingdom and a year later was with No. 25 Squadron (Vampires and Meteors) at West Malling. He was on exchange posting with No. 514 Squadron, U.S.A.F., at Manston in 1957, and visited Wheelus, North Africa, for air-to-air missile firing. In June, 1958, he became staff pilot attack instructor at Sylt and trained German Air Force pilots on Sabres and Thunderstreaks, and German Navy pilots on Seahawks. He also instructed on Hunters, Meteor night-fighters and Swifts. He has been with No. 74 Squadron since October, 1961. His hobbies are colour photography and motoring. He is married and has a son.
Address: 19 Gee Street, Edgeley, Stockport, Cheshire.

John undergoing breathing tests which involved him being in an ejector seat being hurled into a very deep pit of sea water, then having to escape the restraints of the seat, helmet, etc. How terrifying must that have been? My brother was a hero amongst men. Miss him X.

In the coming years he progressed to flying with the Red Arrows and testing numerous types of planes, all over the world. He was A1 Z1 classification; this meant he was the best of pilots and security cleared to fly in any zone of the world. He amazed crowds at air shows worldwide with his aerobatic excellence; in short, he was just bloody amazing. Such a magnificent human being, a loss to the world.

349

The Hero

John and his wife about to go to the Palace for him to be awarded a bravery medal and citation by the Queen. This prestigious award was for staying in his burning aircraft (ignoring the eject instructions!) because he was over heavily built-up areas. His unbelievable courage and care for mankind saved possibly hundreds from injury or death. Roads for miles were barricaded and people had to evacuate their once peaceful homes, you could taste the fear. All you could was sirens as dozens of police cars, fire engines, and ambulances rushed to the isolated RAF runway as far from habitation as possible. The heavens opened, the thunder roared its anger and suddenly there he was. A great roar of joy went up as they saw him come out of the southern sky, very nearly home and just a ball of flames. As he got closer and lower he tipped the wings of his metal bird in a salute of 'goodbye', surely it could be no other way. To this day no one can figure out how he managed to land a burning jet that's interior was melted. Brave men climbed onto the foamed canopy and fuselage to drag out the man they respected and admired the most. He was on fire, God help him, but his so-called fireproof suit helped save his life. The loudest cheer of all time fought the thunder as he was taken to hospital by the waiting Helimed which swiftly delivered him to a nearby burns unit. Balls of steel Johnny had just shown the world his very best.

What a magnificent man XXX.

Eight Weeks of Torment

My book was nearly finished (it has only taken forty-eight years!), and I was glad to see the back of hundreds of pages that I had to proofread.

Then, I became very ill with labyrinthitis (look it up); this created falling, loss of balance, confusion, vomiting, etc.. (try not to get it as you will hate it, just as I did). Six weeks later it had gone and against my better judgment I went for the COVID jab. Hell was to break loose two days later as I was allergic to it. I found myself in hospital unable to use any part of my body properly due to violent shaking, holding cutlery, using the bathroom, walking, everything I had to be assisted with.

Using the toilet (helped by numerous strangers) was the most embarrassing situation that made me weep. Usually, this help came from one of the many Nigerian male nurses who afforded me such dignity and kindness whilst they carried me to the toilet, propped me against them, whilst they pulled down the nappy the hospital insisted every patient wore (incontinent or not) then they rolled up my long kaftan, (so it would not fall in the toilet) and gently lower me onto the lavatory seat. Whilst being so grateful for the help I could not do without – Oh! God, the shame – I'd sit there letting nature do its thing, crying silent tears whilst my helper waited patiently outside the closed door until I knocked to say I'd finished. He'd then lift me off, clean me and gently, oh so gently, rub cream on my bottom as pressure sores were starting. Oh God, the crucifying shame mortified me, as I am a very private woman and no one, I mean no one, has witnessed me using a toilet since I was a child, except during childbirth.

I want you, if you so wish, try to imagine my predicament. They used knickers/sideboards (that I did not need as I was not incontinent) that were the bane of my cuffing life. Because I was near enough crippled throughout my body, changing the sods proved to be a tear-jerking, painful and lengthy affair. After numerous attempts over the days and weeks, I thought I was doing great but could not understand why I had this giant bulge pushing out of the front of my long kaftan, mid-thigh.

After much hilarity by a group of nurses, who stood bemused, whilst what looked like a geriatric kangaroo with three joeys still at home pushed her frame towards them, nappy/sideboard swinging as I shuffled up the endless corridor. On inspection up said kaftan, the staff were propped up the wall in hysterics, now what had brought on so much mirth? For weeks, I had been putting the fucking nappy/sideboard on back to front. All my tears and struggles for yet another cock up, but anyway the nurses loved it!

I found eating and swallowing impossible (even though they hand-fed me) so I lost two stones of unwanted blubber. I'm starting to be its owner again!

Once back in bed, I was subjected to numerous tests, blood pressure, diabetic sugars, physio, etc. They seemed never-ending, and still, I shook and could not talk.

Whilst trying to learn to walk again with the aid of the frame, my legs would turn to jelly and would be useless. This would throw me to the floor which would necessitate the staff bringing the hoist to get me either into my bed or the invalid chair. Yet again, this was great entertainment for the Psychiatric patients who gathered in a clapping circle as I was pushed, shoved and lifted onto the contraption that took no heed of not showing one's nappy the size of a bloody sideboard to the delighted onlookers. The worst fall was when I was being taken for a bath. Once more, I was to be hoisted into four inches of tepid water. But before I even got to the bathroom my legs again gave out, and I crashed to the hard composition floor thus banging my head with such force that it resulted in a lump the size of an egg. Hoisted yet again, (this time into an ambulance for a brain scan) I lay in that other busy noisy hospital for over four hours had the scan and waited to find out the damage. There was no brain damage at all, yet the outside of my skull was a mess and so painful. People joke about seeing stars when the head is abused; well it's true, I did.

But worse was to come, Kristine, my dearest friend and helper phoned to tell me my boiler at home had broken down. So, whilst the nurse held the phone to my ear Kristine explained she had a family member who was a very experienced central heating engineer, reliable, good, clean and honest. So, whilst I lay useless for eight weeks (getting a little better very slowly) the strangers sorted out not only the new boiler, but the zone valve and pump and the solidified pipes (where sediment had settled), stopping the water flow. This entailed carpets and floorboards up, all radiators being carried outside and flushed until empty of sediment and this harrowing fiasco just went on and on, one thing after another with me being given a daily report by phone that filled me with panic and dread. To my logical terrified bipolar brain, I envisaged my home since 1962 being filthy and wrecked. For how could such intensive, intrusive work be carried out without causing mayhem? It couldn't, could it?

Eight weeks passed, and I was able to function better (not good, just a bit of improvement) I had to leave the help and sanctuary of that wonderful hospital, as my bed was needed, and come back to my old life and the reality of what awaited me. I was crying and shaking so much that the nurse that brought me home had to take the keys out of my hand to open my front door. I was afraid of what I would find, all my years of hard work and money ruined. The nurse leaves me crying with trepidation on the front steps whilst she goes to inspect the damage and filth there was bound to be. Guess what? When I eventually plucked up the courage to follow her, I was totally astounded. Instead of soul-destroying chaos, I found everything just as I'd left it eight weeks ago. No dirt, no damage, lovely and warm, as at last the heating chap had fixed every expensive, annoying, plumbing situation that blasted old heating system had thrown at him. He is the most ingenious, careful, honourable, experienced, wonderful workman you could ever leave (on his own) to get on with such a difficult job, also inexpensive compared to others.

And now about my darling Christine, who worked so hard following in his wake, hoovering, cleaning, etc. until everything was back to normal. No easy task when you think of floors being taken up, etc. No drops of radiator sediment on furniture or carpets, no breakages. I could not believe it and wept tears of pure gratitude to the friend who loved me so much she gave me my clean home back.

I really felt that this last story (Please God) should be told, the conclusion of my life's experiences are worth a mention in this day and age where it's not unusual for your so-called tradesman to rip off old people such as myself (and tell the vulnerable old souls that all sorts need doing at an extortionate expense), but they need the money upfront and the vile robbing swine's have the nerve to drive the old person to their bank to draw out probably a life time's savings, the work did not need to be done (and was not) and with cash in hand the bastards legged it leaving tears, poverty, debts and fear, shame on them! But for my Christine this could have happened to me, for how could I have sorted out such a monumental mess from my hospital bed without speech and the means of the internet? (Which my bipolar mind excludes me from understanding) so at the present time, all is well. Lola, my black curly doggy is fourteen now, yet she's still like a puppy despite her ongoing ailments that cost the earth to keep in remission. This will be, I pray, the last episode of my life that patient Ruth is going to type for me. Is she pleased? You bet!

The Old Bamboo Chair Rocks No More

Well, just as promised, Ebony's kind neighbour brought her to stay with me for the foreseeable future, before she herself left for home.

It was Christmas Eve 2021, the sun shone, birds sang in the sparkling frosty trees, and my spring tulips were beginning to push their bright green happy leaves from within their blanket of winter's earth.

Ebony and I had known each other for over half a century, in that time of laughter, shared worries, and so many tears (most of them about Clive), we had formed a bond never to be broken. We so terribly missed our darling Lily, whose young life was stolen so brutally in that snow-covered car park, behind the bordello where she was found, still beautiful, but icy cold, lying with a length of blue rope tight around her neck; one manicured dainty hand trying in vain to release her from its murderous grip. I talked about her to my Ebony whilst she stayed silent to reminisce, for that was her way, just to listen, always just listen, rarely interrupting or saying a word.

I had told her many moons ago how proud I was that she was about to achieve her long-held ambition, that in the not-too-distant future she would leave the life she hated and find peace. This she eventually did, her dream come true! A chocolate box cottage in Cornwall, just a few steps from the seashore, where she could walk barefooted in the golden clean sand and collect seashells to decorate her cottage garden. These morning strolls along the beach, I'm sure, must have evoked memories of her birth home, where the Caribbean sun scorched the land and thirsty plants eternally pleaded for water. Long gone were her days of youth, and she never mourned them, she had despised being the object of man's perverted desires and for the rest of her life remained celibate, just her and her beloved ragdoll cat that she named after me – Zara.

This glorious creature (with habits more dog-like than cat) followed her everywhere whilst she tended her allotment that was once her flower-filled garden. She needed so badly to just, 'give back'. So, she had an open house policy, meaning that anyone in need of garden produces, or a wonderful meal of Caribbean food from the huge pot on the stove (constantly simmering) or sanctuary for a stricken young pregnant girl, banished from her home for so-called misdeeds. To be taken by the hand of Mama (as the locals all called her now) and led inside the clean pretty dwelling, fed with wondrous food, then be laid down in a pink bed to be alone and frightened no more.

Over the years, we kept in touch by letter and phone and once we were due to meet up at a train station, halfway between the two of us. Sadly, this never happened because one of us cancelled due to being poorly, but I can't remember just who? So, our friendship just jogged along, photos of Zara playing with a butterfly, of her kind neighbour bringing Mama afternoon tea, all the carrots, onions and potatoes that were happy to cram into her little piece of long-awaited heaven.

When she got very tired working so hard in the mid-day sun (work that started at dawn and only stopped at last when the sun went over the hill), she sat and rested.

So, over time, that tall magnificent lady became stooped with her back-breaking tasks, her once manicured coffee-coloured hands were caked with God's earth as she uprooted her crops, her nails now broken and full of soil. Time for a rest, so she sat under her Bramley apple tree (the fruit of which she made scores of delicious pies) in the bamboo rocking chair, at once Zara jumped to lie upon her lap and just as a thousand times before, she gently ruffled Zara's fur and sang to her the little songs of her long-gone childhood.

On a day not so long ago Muriel (Mama's neighbour) thought it rather late for the shared afternoon tea (a habit that was borne out of respect, kindness and laughter) so Muriel went to urge Mama to put down her trowel and just rest.

But my Ebony was already resting, Zara was on her lap, but strangely the chair was motionless. Muriel told me she was afraid to go close, but she must find out if help was needed for her friend. Too late, my dear, too late. My Ebony had floated away to the heaven she believed in, her beloved cat friend totally unaware she was so still in the chair that would rock no more, amongst the bundles of newly dug carrots with soil on her calloused old hands.

In the sunshine that Christmas Eve, Muriel carried into my home an ebony wood carved box, one that my friend had treasured since childhood, at one time it held makeup and shells from her faraway beach, now a long distant memory. For Ebony never did return to the place of her birth. Yet its purpose of being was not at an end. The shells were still there amongst my best friend, it looked like they were still on a tropical beach, nestling in the sand that is now my Ebony.

She never let me know she was stricken by the dreaded cancer because, I suppose, she knew it would break my old heart at not being well enough to tend to her needs. So, she had taken the scissors to her wondrous dreadlocks (that for many a year she had coiled up inside a tribal turban that matched her kaftans, (strange we both wore them for working in the garden). Her pride and joy – her hair, she could not wait for her dreadlocks to fall out with the Chemo so she chopped them off herself and sent them to a wig maker who specialised in Caribbean wigs, for those also blighted by cancer. But just one she saved for me. I wear it now around my neck, four-foot-long, shading from jet black at its tip, through shades of grey, to snowy silvery white. And that's how she was that last sunny day, unencumbered by hair or turbans, her new pure white curls gleaming against her weathered old face. So peaceful, no struggle to hang onto the life that she was so ready to leave, she just floated away my lucky, lovely old friend.

I let Lucia know of Ebony's loss of life, she and her sister Seleena (Lilies twins) also thought so well of our departed old friend and offered something so special, that it brought tears to these cataracted old eyes of mine. She offered that when I've also gone, they will go to visit their lovely mum in that Gothic mausoleum in deepest Cheshire, and they will place Ebony and me to rest for eternity with our beautiful friend Lilly, how far into the future is that I wonder? Ebony and I always promised each other that whoever died first would go to be looked after by the surviving friend. That's me. As neither of us has any family to love and respect our remains, it's very fitting that we rest with our dearest friend Lilly. So, thank you Lucia and Seleena.

So, Ebony's will states that her property is to be left as a 'safe house' for all those in need, it will have a caretaker who will carry on her kind devotion and tenderness to those bereft of the milk of human kindness. So, the wonderful spirit that was my Ebony will live on, her door always open. The huge pot of glorious Caribbean food permanently simmering, awaiting the poor and hungry.

As for me, my will states that apart from special bequests to those who have chosen to help, love and respect me, this tired old soul, all the money from my property and indeed the book you are now reading goes to the welfare of two donkey sanctuaries in the hope that the buggers that cruelly treat them rot in Hell, and the donkeys I adore get help, medication and the respect they so deserve.

So, I sit at twilight, this New Year's Eve 2021 fireworks light up the sky. My Lola, as always, cuddled up beside me on the black and silver-grey velvet sofa. I feel at peace, my Christmas was solitary but so gentle, no more fearing the key in the door of cruel yesteryears. (Ebony, forever sleeping in her casket beside me, her dreadlock around my neck, so soft and warm, me between my two favourite black girls, how I wish they were both still warm.)

Darling Ruth (to whom I give praise and thanks for keeping her promise to type my words of forty-eight years) brought me a delicious dinner on Christmas day, stayed for a hug and an exchange of gifts and with a wave was gone, back to her waiting guests at her home.

I just wish I had had more cards, the really important ones, from Caroline, who chose to leave this life, likewise my brother John who chose his destiny also, just pieces of paper on a doormat, you might say, but oh, how I wish they were still arriving.

Goodbye, my dears, be kind to those who deserve it, and tear the balls off those who hurt the vulnerable, whether it be an innocent little child, a defenceless animal or a worn-out old soul. On my behalf, give the sods Hell.

Sweet dreams.

Zara. Xxx Oh! By the way – old age is a twat!

PS: it seems only fitting that this, my one and only book, that was inspired by my Ebony, even though she is now at eternal rest, she concludes my work. She would have been so delighted to read of her trials and achievements. You see, we were so proud of each other. Black is white, white is black. Our blood was, just red. Teeth in sink, knickers on landing.

PPS: I've just tested positive for COVID, will it see me off, I wonder? Do I care? No!

PPPS: The COVID has buggered off! Why am I still alive?

PPPPS: Just what the hell is destiny playing at? It's time I was no longer here. Bye bye. Zara xxx.

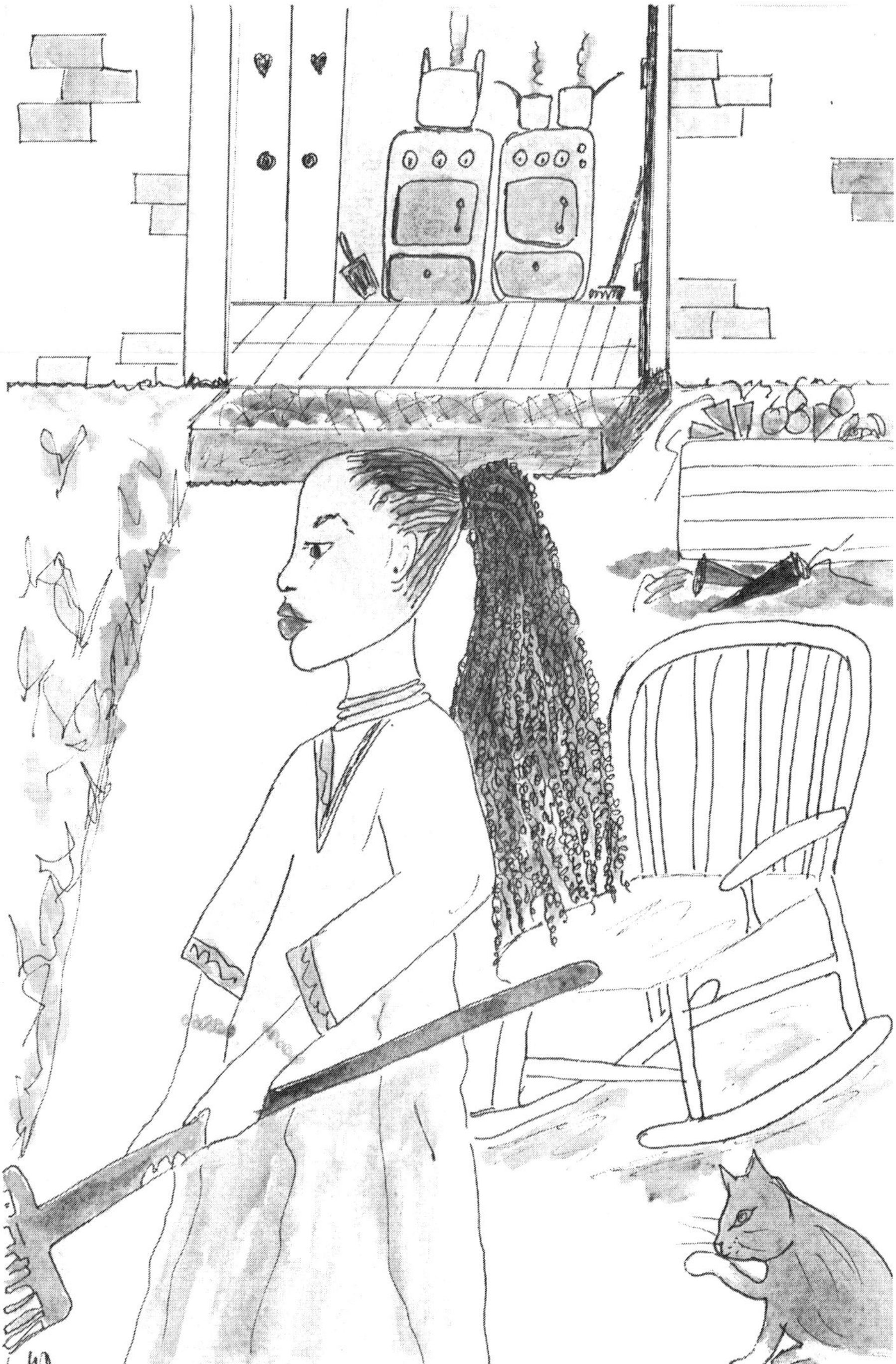

Zara Duvall was born in Cheshire as the bombs of World War Two fell all around. Unbeknown then, she was already blighted by bipolar, which she has suffered from all of her 80 years of life. She describes it as both a curse and a gift. When not in its strangling mental grip she is very funny, articulate and extremely creative. Because change confuses her she has lived in the same house since 1962 and has brought it to a remarkably high standard. Her vocation in life is to rescue all types of animals in pain or distress – rehabilitate, heal and re-home them with people who deserve a wonderful pet. Her hobbies include jewellery design and the creation of one-ff bespoke exotic items of delight, DIY and gardening. She lives in solitude with Lola, her latest dog, as her constant loved companion.

Elsa

Lola

Author with rescued fox

Lee

Sophie

Ziggy Doo Dah

"I think my mum's teeth look better in me, but I can't chew my biscuits with the buggers!"

"I need a nappy, so what? It does not stop me being bloody gorgeous."

Lola XXX